THE CONTENTS AND ORIGIN

OF

THE ACTS OF THE APOSTLES,

CRITICALLY INVESTIGATED.

BY

DR. EDWARD ZELLER.

TO WHICH IS PREFIXED,

DR. F. OVERBECK'S INTRODUCTION TO THE ACTS,

FROM DE WETTE'S HANDBOOK.

TRANSLATED BY JOSEPH DARE, B.A.,
FORMERLY HIBBERT SCHOLAR.

VOL. II.

Wipf & Stock
PUBLISHERS
Eugene, Oregon

Wipf and Stock Publishers
199 W 8th Ave, Suite 3
Eugene, OR 97401

The Contents and Orgin of the Acts of the Apostles
Critically Investigated, 2 Volumes
By Zeller, Edward
ISBN 13: 978-1-55635-505-9
ISBN 10: 1-55635-505-X
Publication date 7/2/2007
Previously published by Williams and Norgate, 1875

INTRODUCTION TO THE 2007 EDITION

THE WORK you are now holding has been very difficult to obtain for a very long time. That is, I am convinced, because the viewpoint its author adopts has been considered virtually heretical by the unofficial magisterium of New Testament scholarship, which has only been growing more and more conservative, like the people of Moses, as the advanced scouts such as F. C. Baur, D. F. Strauss, Julius Wellhausen, and Eduard Zeller passed through the uncharted territory of the new biblical criticism and returned to report their findings. The wonders and dangers they saw there only terrified the greater number of the people who decided it would be better to linger aimlessly in their desert Sargasso rather than press on beyond Kadesh Barnea to conquer new vistas.

But that is not the sole biblical parallel that comes unbidden to mind. Soon we begin to recognize a strange fact: the Baur/Zeller reading of Acts has become a kind of allegory of reading of the reception history of the Tübingen project. It is no exaggeration to call Baur the great Apostle of the Higher Criticism and of the Tübingen School. And then one must nominate Zeller as his Timothy. Eduard Zeller (1814–1908) was Baur's student and son-in-law. The younger man supplemented and carried on his master's great work. (Zeller's Acts book fits in neatly between Baur's masterpiece *Paul the Apostle of Jesus Christ* and his *Church History of the First Three Centuries*, almost as if the three works shared a common authorship.) Baur's Paul is understood as a maverick whom his enemies perceived as corrupting the purity of Torah-Christianity by the importation of alien influences, what Harnack would call "the Hellenization of Christianity." Paul and his colleagues, by contrast, admitted a significant element of discontinuity with what came before but appealed to the revelation of Jesus Christ as justifying the changes they sought. At length, Baur and Zeller taught, the two parties reached agreement, compromising at several points till the result was a Catholicizing mélange betraying the genius of both original parties to the dispute. And history repeated itself (or at least lent itself to the same paradigm) in their own day.

Traditionalist scholars greeted Tübingenism with righteous horror and fielded champions, as the Roman Church would send the Jesuits against Protestantism, to control the damage. J. B. Lightfoot and his congeners set out to refute Baur, retiring from the field once they were confident they had done so. It was the reassurance of their champions' success, rather than any cogent demonstration of it, that quelled the doubts of the faithful, and Baur took his place in a museum of critical fossils. Typical is W. Ward Gasque's ultra-tendentious *History of the Criticism of the Acts of the Apostles* (1975) which grudgingly called Baur "brilliant," even while sneering at him as delusional and dishonest. So much for the modern analogue to Torah-Christianity. No real compromise there, on the part of the apologists; only polite honorifics—just as Acts robs Paul of the dignity of apostleship while politely allowing him that of "most active missionary—in Peter's footsteps." What of the other side, that of real critics who could not utterly abandon Baur's legacy?

Just as Bultmann, ostensibly the arch-skeptic, recoiled from Baur's discovery that only the four *Hauptbriefe* were genuinely Pauline, so have students of Acts distanced themselves from Baur's view of church history. As Bultmann picked up 1 Thessalonians, Philippians, and Philemon from Baur's cutting room floor, virtually all subsequent Acts critics and historians of early Christianity (with rare and welcome exceptions like John C. O'Neill, *The Theology of Acts in its Historical Setting*, 1961, 1970, and Richard I. Pervo) have clung to a "second naiveté" concerning Acts. Many, even like Gerd Lüdemann, having renounced any belief in Acts's historical accuracy, continue blithely to use it as the basis for their "re-"constructions. The resulting consensus position of scholars has been to speak with reverence of Baur and then to ignore him, much as one feels obliged to choose one's words carefully when eulogizing a departed eccentric.

At the very least, these parallels ought to demonstrate that the kind of evolution Baur and Zeller traced between Paulinism and Petrinism and on to Catholicism need be no mere deductive function of an alien Hegelianism. That ludicrous claim survives even in so masterful a treatment as Horton Harris's *The Tübingen School* (1975). So desperate do apologists remain that they persist in their own theological deduction, dismissing Baur's results out of hand on the basis of an *ad hominem* fallacy. It is possible that a preference for the Hegelian perspective allowed Baur to see what others had missed, but do the texts utterly fail to fit his interpretation? Many scholars of even a moderate frame of reference, e.g., Oscar Cullmann and Jacob Jervell, thought not. Does anyone doubt that new sectarian movements (like Paulinism) tend eventually to "calm down" and reassimilate to the parent body from which they broke away? Or how about the debate between Pelagius (thesis) and Augustine (antithesis)? Was it Hegelianism when the Catholic Church chose to settle the issue with the "Semi-Pelagian" synthesis? Sometimes things just happen that way. One of those times seems to have been the first century, in the debate between Paulinism and Petrinism. Another can be located in the aftermath of Baur and Zeller versus Lightfoot and Harnack.

Shortly before her untimely passing, Winsome Munroe noted the similarity of her own criticism of the Epistles (and that of myself and Darrell J. Doughty) with that of the nineteenth century, and she suggested to me that we seemed to be reinventing the wheel. On so many of these biblical subjects several of us have labored mightily to explore new regions, only to find ourselves tracing the footprints of earlier pioneers, such as the great Tübingen critics. In the same way, as I have been privileged to participate in the early sessions of the Westar Institute Acts Seminar, I have mused on how long it has taken to reach square one: the operating assumption, constantly reconfirmed by close analysis, that Acts is essentially fictive in character. The repressed is returning. The tragedy is that of wasted time.

How many of today's New Testament scholars have read the classics in their field? Most of us do not think we need to. We have been fed oversimplified summaries in which the work of the old critics often appears de-clawed and caricatured, with assurances that their work represented an evolutionary dead end. Again, Gasque's book (surely as tendentious as Acts was in Baur's estimation) comes to mind. But if one takes the trouble, and sometimes it takes considerable trouble, to hunt down crumbling copies of the old books, one discovers that the old criticism is far from a museum of freak-births, far even from a collection of revered relics. One is caught up short, startled, to hear the challenge of living voices that will not be stilled. In the present case, no reader will fail to recognize that we stand to learn in these pages not only about Eduard Zeller but about the Book of Acts, things we had not considered before.

Indeed, though I will not pretend to speak as an authority on the subject, I venture the opinion that Zeller's *Contents and Origin of the Acts of the Apostles Critically Investigated* ranks up there beside Baur's *Paul*, Martin Dibelius's *Studies in the Acts of the Apostles* (1956), and Ernst Haenchen's commentary *The Acts of the Apostles* (1971). (To that list we must now add Pervo's massive 2006 monograph *Dating Acts: Between the Evangelists and the Apologists*.) Zeller's book is something of a commentary, though neither as detailed nor as systematic as Haenchen's; it is more of an extensive introduction to the book. But it is so detailed, it often functions as a close commentary on important passages. And Zeller's eye is sharp when it comes to the difference between history and fiction, just as sharp as Baur's and Haenchen's. I have always been struck, e.g., with Zeller's observation of what should have been obvious to me in Acts 9:36–43, the resurrection of Tabitha: the congregation reacts to the death of their mother superior by calling in Peter, as if he is a superhero who can be summoned to rescue his favorites from the inconvenience of death. How had it not occurred to me that such a detail spoke more loudly of the story's fictive character than the miracles it narrated?

We are now, I say, catching up to Baur, Zeller, and Tübingen. We may soon be ready to follow the path farther. Perhaps we will see our way down the way marked by the Dutch Radical Critics (whose works, never welcomed, even by Baur, who shooed away the Dutch School's progenitor Bruno Bauer like Luther dismissing the pesky

Schwenkfeld, have never even been translated into English!). Scholars like Joseph B. Tyson (*Marcion and Luke-Acts: A Defining Struggle*, 2006) and Hermann Detering (*The Falsified Paul: Early Christianity in the Twilight*, 2003) are beginning to reckon with the possibility that Acts was written not to mediate between Gentile and Jewish Christians in the first century but rather between Marcionites and Catholics in the second! What if the "freedom from the Law" championed by the one side was none other than the Marcionite rejection of the Old Testament, and the "Torah legalism" of the other was the Catholic insistence on keeping the Old Testament in the Christian canon? After all, the earliest actual "Paulinists" we know of (as opposed to the possibly fictive "narratees" of the Epistles) were the Marcionites and Gnostics of the second century. Oh, it is a daunting, sometimes frightening, prospect to press onward into the unknown Promised Land of criticism pioneered by our Joshua and Caleb, Baur and Zeller. Let us go on in their company.

Robert M. Price
May 10, 2007

CONTENTS OF VOL. II.

PART II.

THE HISTORICAL SUBJECT-MATTER OF THE ACTS.

PART III.

THE ORIGIN OF THE ACTS OF THE APOSTLES.

THE ACTS OF THE APOSTLES.

Second Part.

THE HISTORICAL SUBJECT-MATTER OF THE ACTS.

THIRD DIVISION.

PAUL.

2. THE COMMUNITY AT ANTIOCH. PAUL'S FIRST MISSIONARY JOURNEY.

WITH ch. ix. 30, Paul disappears for some time from the narrative of the Acts, but in xi. 25 he is introduced by Barnabas to the first scene of his independent apostolic ministry. To judge by the preceding accounts, this must have occurred very soon after his return from Jerusalem to his native city, and not very long after the execution of Stephen. For our author relates, in connection with this occurrence, that some of those who fled from Jerusalem on that occasion preached the gospel at Antioch with effect, not to the Jews only, but also to the Gentiles; on the arrival of which tidings Barnabas was despatched from Jerusalem to that city, and brought Paul from Tarsus to Antioch. As the foundation of the community at Antioch followed immediately, according to this account, on the persecution of Stephen, and that important result could not possibly have long remained unknown to the Jerusalemites, if only on account of the sensation which the reception of uncircumcised persons would have caused among the Jewish Christians,—and as, for the same reason, the mission of Barnabas, as verse 22 also indicates, could not have been long delayed,—we are justified in supposing that our author did not intend to place it later than, at the most, about one year after the death of Stephen. And as in ix. 27, Barnabas is still at Jerusalem, and there introduces Paul to the Apostles, while between this period and his departure to Antioch Paul's sojourn in Jerusalem seems to be interposed, no space remains for the three years of the Epistle to the Galatians, i. 18, which is another confirmation of what we have already said respecting the relation between our account and the Apostle's.

The question here obtrudes itself, whether the establishment of the first Gentile Christian communities actually took place in the manner related by our book. This indeed contains nothing improbable; it would rather correspond perfectly with historical analogy, that the first conversions of the Gentiles should have resulted less from distinct purpose and preconceived principles than from undesigned arrangement of circumstances; and it is equally credible that they should have been connected with the persecution of Stephen, as by it men inclined to a more liberal view of Christianity were for the first time driven into countries in which heathen populations predominated. So far, nothing stands in the way of the assertion in the 19th and 20th verses. But it is another question whether Paul pursued the course with respect to preaching to the heathen which is attributed to him by our book. Although it does not explicitly say that prior to his ministry at Antioch he preached to no Gentiles, no other impression is left upon us; and we can scarcely consider this to be unintentional. It is silent as to the Apostle's journey to Arabia; the three years intervening between his conversion and his first visit to Jerusalem it contracts into a far shorter period, and within this period it makes him appear only before Jews, in the synagogues of Damascus and at Jerusalem; and at the close of it, he retires to his native city till he is introduced into his own field of labour by Barnabas. So much the more opportunely does it make it perceptible how, previously, by the baptism of the Ethiopian, by the conversion of Cornelius, by the establishment of the community at Antioch, the mission to the heathen was promoted in increasing urgency; and acknowledged as authorized and necessary by the primitive community itself, as well as by its chiefs, nay, even by explicit and repeated divine revelations. Here, therefore, Paul does not enter upon this sphere of labour until by precedents and declarations of all kinds, by the utterances of all divine and human authorities, every stumbling-block that could be offered by the call of the heathen had been removed. How entirely different in the Epistle to the Galatians! There Paul, immediately after his conversion, feels himself called to be the Apostle of the Gentiles; there he does not wait for the ratification of his calling by the party in Palestine, and does not confine himself in his ministry, to Jerusalem and the synagogues of Damascus; but even before he has seen any of the original Apostles hé goes to Arabia—by the context, it seems for the promulgation of the gospel,[1]—and after a short visit to Jerusalem, again to heathen countries, to Syria and Cilicia, while to the communities of Judæa he remains personally unknown. If these two accounts are compared, it is scarcely possible to think otherwise than that, according to the one, he avoids the domain of the mission to the Gentiles just as intentionally as, according to the other, he seeks it: that, according to one, he makes his appearance among the Gentiles dependent on the example and authority of the original Apostles; according to the other, purposely avoids every appearance of any such dependence.

To the mention of the community at Antioch, the Acts, xi. 26, appends the notice that the name of Christians first originated there. Baur's doubts of this statement (pp. 90 f.) do not admit

[1] This can certainly not be confidently stated, and, accordingly, the opinions of the learned differ widely.

of being raised to certainty, and their author propounded them only conditionally; but by the whole character of our book, as we have learnt to know it, we are not justified in maintaining that the question respecting the origin of the name of Christian is set at rest by its mere statement.

From Antioch, Paul, in company with Barnabas—to pass over the journey to Jerusalem, xi. 27 ff., which will be discussed later—made his first great missionary journey to Cyprus, Pamphylia, Pisidia and Lycaonia. This journey opens in a significant manner with the conflict with a Jewish magician, which is decided in favour of Paul by the blinding of the former (xiii. 4—12). Of this miracle every one will believe what he believes of miracles in general; but the partizans of a natural interpretation here occupy a favourable position in attributing to natural causes the blindness which took place at once at the word of the Apostle. If, on the other side, the reality of the miracle cannot be admitted from a historical standpoint, it naturally follows that our narrative, as it exists, is unhistorical; and the only question is, whether it is founded on a special fact, or whether it originated purely from dogmatical motives without any historical basis. Although in this case, as in most others of the same nature, nothing can be decided with complete certainty, the latter hypothesis is recommended by the circumstance[1] that in parts the conduct of Peter towards Simon Magus, in parts the judicial punishment inflicted by the same Apostle upon Ananias and Sapphira, seem to contain a prefiguration of the penal miracle wrought by Paul on Bar-Jesus the sorcerer. Paul's speech to Elymas, verse 10, bears great resemblance to that of Peter to Simon, viii. 20. The blindness of Elymas recalls the blindness of Paul, ix. 8;[2] and thus what we have said above concerning the symbolical nature of this blindness has here a parallel application. The bodily blindness of the sorcerer

[1] *Schneckenburger*, p. 53. *Baur*, p. 91.

[2] Comp. with xiii. 11, *περιάγων ἐζήτει χειραγωγούς*, ix. 8, *χειραγωγοῦντες δὲ αὐτὸν ἤγαγον εἰς Δαμασκόν.*

is the immediate punishment and image of his spiritual darkness.

With the encounter against Elymas, the Acts connects the change of the name of Saul for Paul. From the moment at which the Apostle utters his wonder-working verdict against the sorcerer, the author calls him Paul, whereas he has hitherto, evidently on purpose, avoided the name. As the name Saul never occurs hereafter, while the other, on the contrary, had never occurred before, it is undoubtedly intended to signify by this that the Apostle received his later name on this occasion; and as mention was made immediately before of the proconsul Sergius Paulus, there is much to recommend the hypothesis of Jerome, that, according to the representation of our book, this name was conferred upon him by this firstling of his ministry. That it was really so is indeed scarcely credible, for the conversion of a Roman proconsul, especially if it was so rapidly and outwardly accomplished, does not seem to constitute such an epoch as to induce Paul to make an alteration in his name. It is incomparably more likely that for his intercourse with the Gentiles he transmuted it, after the manner of that age, into a form more general among the Grecians, or that, as the son of a Roman citizen, he had from the first borne the Latin name of Paul, in addition to the specially Jewish appellation, Saul.

We must here pass by the remainder of the 13th chapter, with the account of the incidents at Antioch in Pisidia, as we shall be obliged hereafter to enter more minutely upon the speech attributed to Paul on this occasion; the events at Lystra, however, xiv. 8—20, still require our attention. By the healing of a cripple, Paul makes such a sensation here that the inhabitants regard him and Barnabas as Mercury and Jupiter, and can with difficulty be restrained from offering them sacrifices. Subsequently, however, Jewish emissaries from Antioch and Iconium succeed in instigating the people against them; Paul is stoned, and his life preserved only as by miracle. Of these incidents, the former, the healing of the cripple, is suspicious in more ways than one. In the first place, because such a thing as the sudden healing of a cripple lame from his birth, resulting from a mere word, mocks every natural interpretation and every historical view; secondly, because the source of this narrative so obviously appears in the earlier record of a perfectly similar miracle of Peter, that it is almost impossible to mistake it. The first requires no further discussion; and for the second Schneckenburger (p. 52) and Baur (95) have collected all the proofs. The affinity of the two narratives is really startling; not only is the main result alike in both cases, but the adjuncts harmonize completely, and even the expressions are mostly identical.[1] This harmony would rouse suspicion even if it related to an incident credible in itself; but as we have here an incredible one, it proves that in all probability our narrative was not derived from any definite thing, but merely from an imitation of the early miraculous story of Peter.[2] With the miracle, the cause of the attempted adoration of the two is also withdrawn, and that also cannot pass as historical, the less so, indeed, as it is exposed to the suspicion of being derived from an exaggerated repetition of an episode in the history of Peter. If the older Apostles, according to v. 11, are venerated by the people as a species of superior beings, if Cornelius falls down at the feet of Peter, the Lystrians wish to proceed even to the actual worship of Paul and Barnabas; and as Peter bids the Roman centurion rise, *ἀνάστηθι, κἀγὼ αὐτὸς ἄνθρωπός εἰμι*, so the

[1] xiv. 8: *Καί τις ἀνὴρ ἐν Λύστροις ἀδύνατος τοῖς ποσὶν ἐκάθητο, χωλὸς ἐκ κοιλίας μητρὸς αὐτοῦ . . .*
(9): *Οὗτος ἤκουε τοῦ Παύλου λαλοῦντος· ὃς ἀτενίσας αὐτῷ . . .* (10): *εἶπε μεγάλῃ τῇ φωνῇ· ἀνάστηθι ἐπὶ τοὺς πόδας σου ὀρθός· καὶ ἥλατο καὶ περιεπάτει.*

iii. 2: *Καί τις ἀνὴρ χωλὸς ἐκ κοιλίας μητρὸς αὐτοῦ ὑπάρχων ἐβαστάζετο . . .*
(3): *Ὃς ἰδὼν Πέτρον καὶ Ἰωάννην . . . ἠρώτα ἐλεημοσύνην.* (4): *Ἀτενίσας δὲ Πέτρος εἰς αὐτὸν . . . εἶπε*, and so on.
(8): *Καὶ ἐξαλλόμενος ἔστη καὶ περιεπάτει· καὶ εἰσῆλθε σὺν αὐτοῖς εἰς τὸ ἱερὸν περιπατῶν καὶ ἀλλόμενος καὶ αἰνῶν τὸν θεόν.*

[2] We cannot argue with critics like Baumgarten, who accounts, by means of a special providential dispensation, for the entire similarity of the Pauline and Petrine miracles in the Acts, as indicative of the similarity of their apostolic vocation.

two Apostles say to the Gentiles at Lystra, ἄνδρες, τί ταῦτα ποιεῖτε; καὶ ἡμεῖς ὁμοιοπαθεῖς ἐσμεν ὑμῖν ἄνθρωποι.[1] Taken historically, this veneration, even on the assumption of the miracle, has been justly deemed surprising. If it had actually occurred, the workers of miracles, as Baur acutely remarks (pp. 99 f.) would at that time have been far more readily considered as sorcerers, or at the most demons, than as deities of the highest rank; the Homeric belief in the appearance of the gods was long extinct. This representation, on the other hand, must have been naturally suggested to our author, as Lycaonia was also in legend held to be the scene of a divine apparition (Theophany), and as the very deities who were to be worshipped in the persons of Paul and Barnabas had already degenerated into Philemon and Baucis. He may have had another special reason for his story if our conjecture should be correct respecting the original reference of the legend of Simon to Paul (see above). The calumny that Paul gave himself out to be the manifestation of the Supreme God, would then be opposed by the zeal with which he rejects the worship of those who regarded him as a deity. How little this narrative stands on an historical basis is likewise exhibited in several small features. Granting that the miraculous cure had actually given rise to the belief that the two Apostles were superior beings, they must at once have resisted such a dangerous misunderstanding. Our author is, however, evidently anxious to allow the destined homage to proceed as far as possible towards execution; although they cannot of course accept the worship, it must be demonstrated beyond doubt how seriously it was intended. Hence the characteristic trait, that the people express their opinion respecting Paul and Barnabas in the Lycaonian language, which was incomprehensible to the latter (verse 11); hence also the observation in verse 13, that the temple of Jupiter, the priest of which was about to sacrifice to him, was situated outside the city; the preparations for their worship must be made unknown to them,

[1] *Baur*, Paul. 100, after Schneckenburger.

but yet, at the same time, must be quite completed. The less we are able to consider as historical[1] the first of these features especially, even according to the further account of our book itself, the more prominent does the drift of the whole narrative appear.

Better authenticated is the statement respecting the stoning of Paul. That the Apostle was really stoned once, which probably means that he was once felled to the ground by the blows of stones in a popular tumult, he says himself, 1 Cor. xi. 25. But whether this occurred exactly at Lystra, we cannot trust ourselves to decide; for after the supposed occasion of this ill usage has shown itself to be improbable, we have not the slightest guarantee for the correctness of the statement respecting the scene of it; it is, on the contrary, quite as possible that nothing more was known to the author concerning it, and that he merely inserted here the incident known to him from 2 Cor. for the sake of the contrast, or perhaps because he knew of no other place where it could be more suitably introduced.

3. The Apostolic Council.

While Paul and Barnabas were staying at Antioch after their first missionary journey, there arose, as is related in verse 15, in consequence of Jewish Christian claims, a dispute respecting the obligation of the Gentile Christians to accept circumcision and the Law of Moses. To settle this affair, Paul and Barnabas, with a few others, were despatched to Jerusalem. Here, again, indignant Pharisees repeated the claims of the Judaists; but, on

[1] As Paul and Barnabas, in verses 15 ff., are perfectly able to come to an understanding with the people without knowing Lystrian, and as, according to verses 7 and 9, they have also for some time preached the gospel, although perhaps in the Greek language, it must be assumed that the knowledge of Greek was tolerably common at Lystra; and even if the old dialect was also in use, the two must have been spoken together, somewhat as German and French are in Alsace. Even then it is, however, very unlikely that the admiration of the multitude (verses 11 ff.) should have vented itself only in the language of Lystra, which was incomprehensible to the subjects of the admiration.

the suggestion of Peter and James, the assembled church decided that Jewish Christians alone were bound by the Law; Gentile Christians, on the contrary, with the exception of a few points given in detail, were to be released from it. This decision was forthwith communicated to the Gentile Christian communities, and was also delivered to them by Paul, on his next missionary journey.

A previous journey of Paul and Barnabas to Jerusalem is recorded in xi. 27—30, xii. 25; a later one in xviii. 18—23, in which mention is made of Paul only. Besides this, we hear from Paul himself, Gal. ii. 1 ff., of a journey to Jerusalem, which he undertook in company with Barnabas and Titus, fourteen, or more probably seventeen, years after his conversion, in consequence of a revelation made to him; and during this visit he came to an understanding with the Jerusalemites, and especially with their leaders, respecting his doctrine and ministry. The first question is, how this journey in the Epistle to the Galatians is related to those in the Acts? The ancients mostly identified it with the first of these, that of the 11th chapter; recently it has, on the contrary, been almost unanimously agreed that it must be looked for only in the narrative of our 15th chapter, while no one thought of the later journey in ch. xviii. until Wieseler,[1] pressed by the differences between the Epistle to the Galatians and our 15th chapter, took refuge here. We must commence by testing these three possible combinations.

Concerning the journey in our 11th chapter, its identity with that in the Epistle to the Galatians is now justly abandoned by all. Even the object and occasion of the two journeys are quite different. In ch. xi., Paul and Barnabas are sent to convey a small subsidy to Jerusalem; in Gal. ii., Paul goes of his own accord to confer with the Christians of the place. Of such a conference our 11th chapter knows not a word; and it can scarcely be imagined that it could have taken place at that time, as Peter was just then either in prison or flying. Moreover, at the time of

[1] Chronology of Acts, pp. 179 ff.

our 11th chapter, before his first missionary journey, how could Paul, as is said in the account of the Epistle to the Galatians, be acknowledged as the promulgator of the gospel to the Gentiles in a sense which places him on a level with Peter, the chief of the Apostles of the Jews, and in comparison with which, Barnabas, palpably at first the most esteemed of the two, retires completely into the background? In the transactions of the apostolic council, how is it possible that not the slightest reference is made to the earlier conferences, Gal. ii.? How could the whole question in dispute, concerning which so much had been said and done, and a formal compact effected between the leaders of the two parties,—how could this be treated as an entirely new and untouched subject? Many more questions of this sort might be asked, but it is not requisite, for the chronology alone is decisive. The journey of the Epistle to the Galatians was probably seventeen, at all events fourteen, years later than the conversion of the Apostle (for in Gal. ii. 1, to omit the *δέκα*, contrary to the evidence of every manuscript,[1] will occur to none again); while that of our 11th chapter coincides in time with the death of Herod Agrippa, which took place[2] in 44 A.D., therefore at the most eight to ten years after that event.

As, according to this, the journey of the Epistle to the Galatians cannot be earlier than the so-called apostolic council, Acts xv., it cannot be later, and identical with the journey of our 18th chapter.[3] If the account in Acts xv. excludes an antecedent negociation, such as that in the Epistle to the Galatians, in like manner the account of the latter no less distinctly excludes a negociation antecedent to itself, such as that

[1] *Neander*, p. 183, questions this, because the words *κατ' ἐκεῖνον τὸν καιρὸν*, xii. 1, contain no accurate definition of time. But that the author intends to put the presence of Paul and Barnabas in Jerusalem at the same time with the events of the 12th chapter, he shows unequivocally enough when he makes mention of their journey to Jerusalem *before*, of their return journey *after*, the capture of Peter.

[2] Compare, against the assumption above announced, which is still defended by *Fritzsche*, Opusc. 224 ff., *De Wette*, on Gal. ii.

[3] As has been exhaustively proved against Wieseler by *Baur*, Tübingen Theol. Journal, 1849, pp. 458—480.

of the Acts. However the object of the discussion in Gal. i. 15 ff. may be regarded, it necessarily demands a mention of every visit which the Apostle had made to Jerusalem in the interval between his conversion and the writing of the Epistle to the Galatians, or at least of all that he made between that event and the journey of the 2nd chapter. If Paul wished by this discussion to prove (according to i. 11, 19) that his doctrine was independent of every human authority, and especially of the authority of the twelve primitive Apostles, the enumeration of his journeys to Jerusalem can have no other object than to refute the supposition that he was in any way dependent on them, by the history of the intercourse which he had had with them. But for this purpose the enumeration naturally required to be complete; and a transaction of such importance as that of our 15th chapter could in no case be omitted. Even if he only desired to offer striking testimonies of the self-reliance and independence of his apostolic ministry and authority[1] among these, one would think, the transactions at the apostolic council ought not to be lacking, as it was precisely on that occasion that his ministrations obtained the formal recognition of the primitive Church and its representatives. But that it was actually his intention to cite all his journeys to Jerusalem up to the one in Gal. ii., is clearly shown by i. 22 ff., ii. 1. For if he here says that he had remained unknown to the Christian communities of Palestine even after his first journey, and then fourteen years later went again to Jerusalem, it can hardly be understood otherwise than that this non-acquaintance continued to exist for fourteen years. If he wished to convey any other impression, the date, διὰ δεκατεσσάρων ἐτῶν, is not merely superfluous, but misleading. But the manner in which it is to be understood is also made apparent by the similar designation, i. 18. As here the words ἔπειτα μετὰ ἔτη τρία should be rendered *only after three years*, so the parallel words, ii. 1, ἔπειτα διὰ δεκατεσσάρων

[1] So *Baur*, Paulus, p. 113. Similarly *Wieseler*, pp. 180 f.

ἐτῶν, can be rendered *only after the lapse of fourteen years*.[1] To this must be added that, in Gal. ii. 1, Paul goes to Jerusalem with Barnabas, as in Acts xv. 2; whereas in Acts xviii. he goes with Aquila and Priscilla, after having parted from Barnabas, xv. 39. But what is still more important, the whole transaction here described by Paul renders an earlier one like that of the Acts impossible. Ἀνέβην κατὰ ἀποκάλυψιν, καὶ ἀνεθέμην αὐτοῖς τὸ εὐαγγέλιον, ὃ κηρύσσω ἐν τοῖς ἔθνεσι, κατ᾽ ἰδίαν δὲ τοῖς δοκοῦσι, μήπως εἰς κενὸν τρέχω ἢ ἔδραμον. Why was it necessary for Paul now for the first time to report to the δοκοῦντες privately concerning his doctrine, if he had done the very same some years before in the public assembly of the church? How could he fear that the objections of the Jerusalemites might deprive him of the results of his labour (μήπως εἰς κενὸν, and so on), if they had long ago made terms with him and borne testimony to him, as in xv. 26, if he had himself heard his own principles respecting the admissibility of Gentile conversion and the impossibility of justification by Law, with the admission of freedom from the Law for the Gentiles, enunciated by the mouths of the leaders, a Peter and a James? Moreover, how could the circumcision of the Gentile Christian, Titus, be required at Jerusalem? how could it cost Paul such a violent struggle to repel this demand, if for years past a formal resolution of the church had existed, sanctioned by apostolic authority, prohibiting such exactions; and if, as according to the Acts we must suppose, this resolution tallied with the practice of the community at Jerusalem? How can Paul say (Gal. ii. 7) that James, Peter and John, were convinced, during his stay at Jerusalem on that occasion, that the mission to the Gentiles was entrusted to him, and that in consequence they united with him and Barnabas in reciprocal recog-

[1] Only a complete misapprehension of this context could betray *Lange* (Apost. Age, i. 99 f.) into the interpretation in Gal. ii. 1, that πάλιν referred to the adjunct μετὰ Βαρνάβα, as if Paul on his first visit had *travelled to Jerusalem with* Barnabas! The Epistle to the Galatians, moreover, had not yet mentioned Barnabas at all, and therefore could not have referred to him with πάλιν.

nition, if they had long possessed this conviction, and years before had pronounced this acknowledgment in due form? As Paul represents the affair, an earlier settlement, such as is recorded in Acts, cannot possibly have taken place. Finally, if the journey in the Epistle to the Galatians is transferred to a later period, because the impossibility of reconciling its account with that of our 15th chapter endangers the credibility of the Acts, it is very doubtful whether much can be gained by that. For what light does it cast on the historic art or faith of the author if he is completely silent upon such a supremely important transaction, and if of the whole journey during which it took place he can only report, κατελθὼν εἰς Καισάρειαν, ἀναβὰς καὶ ἀσπασάμενος τὴν ἐκκλησίαν κατέβη εἰς 'Αντιόχειαν (xviii. 22)? Is not such an omission of the most important thing just as bad as a false report; and does it not lead directly to a perfectly incorrect idea of the affair? If the understanding in the Epistle to the Galatians was later than that in Acts xv., the latter was *altered* by the former in several essential points; the qualified recognition of Gentile Christianity was changed to an unqualified one (οὐδὲν προσανέθεντο); the demand of refraining from meat offered to idols, &c., was (as Wieseler also supposes, pp. 201 f.) *repealed*. But the reader of the Acts, on whom the prescriptions of the apostolic council are impressed, while their subsequent alteration is not mentioned, cannot but believe them to have preserved their validity. And, indeed, this is just what our book expressly assumes. How could James, xxi. 20 ff., appeal to the resolutions of the 15th chapter and assume their continued maintenance by Paul, if he himself had in the interval repealed those resolutions by a new compact with Paul?

What, after the above disquisition, cannot any longer be subject to doubt, viz. that the author of the Acts had nothing in view in his 15th chapter but the incidents recorded in Gal. ii., will be directly confirmed by the relative position of the two accounts. For, important as we shall find their variations in detail, they are, nevertheless, much too nearly related to be referred to different events. In both cases a journey by Paul and Barnabas to Jerusalem to confer with the Jerusalemites concerning the position of the Gentile Christians and their relation to Judaism; in both, a lengthy discussion, in which Peter and James (in the Epistle to the Galatians, John also) are especially prominent; in both, a final understanding; in both, the transaction related so that it is readily seen no earlier one can have taken place on the same subject between the same people; can it then still be doubted whether it is really one and the same event which is recorded in both; and can minor deviations, important as they may otherwise be, prove anything against this coincidence in the main?

It certainly follows from this,[1] that the journey in the 11th chapter can never have taken place at all, so far at least as our observations are correct as to the object of the account in the Epistle to the Galatians. What is related of this journey is of such a nature that it could be told without historical foundation. The possibility that such an unhistorical statement should occur in the book can scarcely be disputed, after all that has been educed hitherto respecting its unhistorical character. Even the deviations from the authentic account of the Apostle himself, which we found in ix. 19 ff., would suffice to prove this. That our author, moreover, had an interest in making Paul visit Jerusalem in the interval between his conversion and the so-called apostolic council, we shall show later on; the more offensive his many years' absence from the centre of theocracy must have been to the Jewish Christians, the more natural was it for a writer anxious to justify him from the Jewish Christian standpoint to meet this stumbling-block with stories like the one before us. Finally, if we examine the details of the journey in question, it must strike us that they scarcely occur anywhere else in the historically accredited journeys of the Apostle. We know from the Epistle to the Galatians, and from ch. xv., of a journey made to Jerusalem by Barnabas and Paul; the object of

[1] As *Baur* also assumes, Paul, 114. Tübingen Theol. Journal, 1849, 479.

the journey, the conveyance of a contribution to the Jerusalemites, belongs to the Apostle's last visit to Jerusalem, but is also very remarkably passed over in silence by our book. On the same occasion we make acquaintance, in xxi. 10, with the prophet Agabus, acting a similar part as in xi. 28; the further contents of our narrative are the two obvious features that the contribution for the Jerusalemites was in consequence of the noted famine under the Emperor Claudius, and that it proceeded from Antioch, the only community of Gentile Christians by which at that time Paul could have been sent. When a record is thus related to other accounts, it justifies the suspicion that it arose by doubling the same event; and if this same record, by its inconsistency with a better accredited one (that of the Epistle to the Galatians), bears the negative mark of inaccuracy on its front, the suspicion is raised by such coincidence to a high degree of probability.

Even Neander, in the last edition of his work (p. 188), after Bleek's example,[1] considers the silence of the Epistle to the Galatians concerning the journey of our 11th chapter (which in the third he had declared trivial) of such weight, that he admits that, holding to the words of Paul, we can only think that he was never in Jerusalem between the two journeys mentioned in the Epistle to the Galatians; and as it would be more permissible to suppose an oversight on the part of Luke than to do violence to the statement of Paul, we must assume that Barnabas alone, and not Paul, went to Jerusalem in the year 44. Only if it must once be acknowledged that Paul, notwithstanding the distinct statement of our author, was not at Jerusalem, who guarantees that Barnabas went there, and that the narrative in question has any historical foundation at all? and if, taking our record by itself, we do not think this hypothesis utterly incredible, it nevertheless loses all probability if we take into consideration, on the one hand, the historical character of the Acts, on the other, the relation of our narrative to the other, of which

[1] Beitr. z. Evangelienkritik, p. 55.

it appears to be a copy. For the main point, the delineation of Paul, the result would have been the same whether Barnabas was at Jerusalem or not; and even in the former case we could deem the unhistorical statement respecting the journey of Paul as a mere traditional error. This, however, cannot be shown till later.

Hereby a refutation is given to Schleiermacher's[1] hypothesis, that the journey of the 11th chapter is identical with that of the 15th, and that it was only mentioned in anticipation of a future one, xi. 30; that the compiler of the Acts, however, in an incomprehensible manner, took it for a separate journey, and in xii. 25 represented it as such. For the credibility of our narrative and of our whole book, nothing would be gained by this assumption; but how hasty it is, is shown above all by the fact, that to assign the famine under Claudius (44 A.D.), known through Josephus (Ant. xx. 2, 6) as the cause of the journey, would not at all suit that of the 15th chapter; and that the journey, according to our book as well as the Epistle to the Galatians, had a very different object and character.

After these preliminary investigations, we may apply ourselves to the import of the 15th chapter, in testing which we may now unreservedly make use of the Epistle to the Galatians as our safest mainstay. If we compare its representation with that of the Acts, such irreconcilable contradictions appear between the two, that we cannot consider the latter to be historically true in its essential features.

Even the formal character of the transactions at Jerusalem are represented in the two accounts as unmistakably different. The Epistle to the Galatians makes it appear a private negociation of Paul with the most esteemed of the primitive Apostles; the Acts gives it an entirely official stamp. Similarly, the resolve to make the journey is of different origin; according to the Acts, it is undertaken by Paul, Barnabas and their companions, as a commission from the church at Antioch; according

[1] Introduction to the New Testament, pp. 369 f.

to Gal. ii., by Paul who takes Barnabas and Titus with him, κατὰ ἀποκάλυψιν, hence spontaneously; there Paul and his companions have to act in the name of the community which despatched them; here he acts in his own name. "I went there," he says, "and communicated unto them the gospel that I had preached, lest haply I should have run in vain." It is not the pacification of a dispute which had arisen in the community, but the establishment of personal relations between Paul and the Jerusalemites with respect to his apostolic ministry, which is the *object;* it is not the commission of the community, but the spontaneous resolution of the Apostle, which is the *cause* of the journey. I should be reluctant either, with Schneckenburger,[1] to declare this difference "utterly irrelevant," as it is closely connected with the whole character of the respective accounts; or, with Neander (p. 205), to harmonize it by the hypothesis that, although Paul and Barnabas were sent by the community, Paul would even without this public embassy have made the journey in consequence of the ἀποκάλυψις; for the Epistle to the Galatians does not say that he *would* have made it on that account, though he should have had none other cause for it, but quite simply that he did make it. It would be preferable to assume, with the same scholar, that the suggestion of the embassy proceeded from Paul himself, on the ground of the ἀποκάλυψις. Even thus, however, the difference would remain that, according to his own account, Paul negociates only in his own name; according to that of the Acts, in the name of the community: that, according to the former, the resolution to make the journey was taken originally by him, and only subsequently assented to by the community; according to the latter, the same resolution was taken by the community and carried into execution by Paul and Barnabas at their desire: that in the Acts, the negociation principally concerns the community, and Paul only as a consequence; in the Epistle to the Galatians, it chiefly concerns Paul,

[1] Zweck der Apg. p. 73.

and only secondarily the community. Moreover, it would be striking, even on this assumption, that in the Epistle to the Galatians the Apostle makes mention neither of the Jewish Christians (who, according to Acts xv. 1, occasioned the appeal to Jerusalem) nor the commission of the community; for both these circumstances were by no means unimportant in judging of the step he took, and put in a proper light could only serve as a confirmation of the account given in his first chapter, namely, the assertion that he had not originally received his gospel from the older Apostles, and that his few visits to them had not the object of seeking dogmatic instruction from them (Gal. i. 11, 16 f., 18 f.); whereas the very official character of his mission might, on the other hand, easily give rise to the misinterpretation that by undertaking it Paul had acknowledged a position of dependence on the Apostles of Palestine, and, if only as a precaution against such misapprehension, it ought not to have been passed over in silence. The same contrast appears even more unmistakably in the respective accounts of the transactions at Jerusalem. "According to the Acts, a formal public transaction took place, of such a kind that this deliberation and decision has been considered, since the earliest times, not unjustly as the first Christian council" (Baur, 115). According to verse 13, a formal assembly of the community is held, under the presidency of James, the head of the church; a regular debate is opened, a legal resolution is taken, and promulgated to the Gentiles by special delegates, in the name of the community, as the decision of the church and of the Holy Ghost. According to the account in the Epistle to the Galatians, on the contrary, Paul privately expounds his principles, first, only to the heads of the community at Jerusalem; James, Peter and John come to an understanding with him; but of an assembly and a decision of the whole community not a syllable is said. If the two records do not exactly contradict one another, they must treat of different occurrences; we must suppose, with Neander (pp. 206 ff.) and others,[1] that the general assembly was preceded by conferences between Paul and the chiefs of the community at Jerusalem, and to these, as well as to what was decided therein, the Epistle to the Galatians refers. But even in this case, how is it that Paul never alludes to the general assembly?[2] How can he represent the whole affair as if it had been settled by the consent of the three chief Apostles, if, after all, the actual negociation and decision did not take place till later? Why does he not bestow a word on the synodical decision, in the promulgation of which, according to the Acts, he was nevertheless zealously busied? He dwells, Neander (p. 207, note) considers, on what was to him the chief point, the thing which, above all, he was obliged to insist upon in opposition to his adversaries, who wanted to make the authority of James and the Apostles of Palestine to be alone valid. Similarly Lechler; if the opponents appealed not to majorities, but to the importance of predominant individuals, it would not have been at all appropriate if Paul had appealed against them to the great majority in favour of the decision at Jerusalem, or in any way to the public transaction; he had much more hope of producing an effect if he had the Apostles themselves, and especially the most venerated Apostle, on his side, and was able to prove their acquiescence in his principles. But this very proof was given him more completely by the public negociation, than by a private conference of which no authentic record was to be had. For in the transactions of our 15th chapter, those very heads of the Jewish Chris-

[1] *Lechler*, the Apost. and Post-Apost. Age, 246 f. *Ebrard*, Crit. of Gospel History, 2, A. 698 f. *Baumgarten*, ii. 165 f. *Thiersch*, The Church in the Apost. Age, 128.

[2] He says indeed, *ἀνεθέμην αὐτοῖς τὸ εὐαγγέλιον . . . κατ' ἰδίαν δὲ τοῖς δοκοῦσι*, but no one who does not read these words with the determination of finding them in accordance with the Acts will be able in the *αὐτοῖς* to discover any trace of a transaction such as that described in our 15th chapter. Verbally, the words might mean either, "I set it forth to them (the Jerusalemites), but particularly to the most considerable," or, "I set it forth to them, but only to the most considerable in particular." Even if we accept the former explanation, there still remains nothing in the vague statement of a conference with the Jerusalemites that could most remotely lead the reader to suppose that this conference took place in a general assembly of the community, or that they occasioned a formal deliberation and decision respecting the disputed points.

tian party, a Peter and a James, come forward with detailed speeches. Why does not Paul point to these, their well-known public declarations; why does he not hold up to his opponents the formal charter of freedom which the primitive community had set forth in favour of the Gentile Christians at the suggestion of the Apostles above named, instead of relying on verbal assurances, the authenticity of which might at any moment be disputed by the opposite party? Perchance because "he might assume those public transactions and their results as known" (Neander). As if this very circumstance would not have been a recommendation to the argument; for the more public was the recognition of his principles in Jerusalem, so much the more complete was the refutation of his adversaries. Or must we assume, with Schneckenburger (p. 73), that didactic considerations induced the Apostle to renounce the advantage offered him by the decree of Jerusalem, that he did not mention it, because he desired to appear before the Galatians, not with authority, but merely with the development of the truth? Paul does not in reality by any means follow this point of view; he appeals to the recognition of the δοκοῦντες, even while disclaiming any faith in their authority, and he had every reason for so doing to his Galatian readers. How strange that he did not add to this recognition that of the primitive community; that, instead of their public and authentic statement, he encounters his opponents only with private utterances of a far more equivocal character! If those authentic declarations were actually extant, it will be difficult to find a plausible reason for such a course. What the most recent apologists of the Acts have contributed to the explanation of the matter is far from sufficient. The two transactions, Thiersch maintains, are so different, that they could scarcely be more so; in the Acts, it is an affair singly and solely of the rights and duties of the Gentile Christians; in the Epistle to the Galatians, of the apostolic dignity of Paul; the obligations of the Gentile Christians are here no more discussed than is the question of the recognition of the Apostle there. To the same view Baumgarten[1] appends the observation that Paul had every reason to appeal, not to the decisions of the community, but to his private conference with the Apostles, as those decisions do not contain nearly such an explicit recognition of his apostolic labours as the private declarations of the Apostles; and, moreover, the prescriptions of the apostolic decree would have conduced more to disturb than to benefit the misguided Galatians. The whole of this version of the affair is incorrect. In the conferences reported in the Epistle to the Galatians, the chief subject debated is not the apostolic dignity of Paul, but the εὐαγγέλιον τῆς ἀκροβυστίας, the fundamental principle of the Gentile mission, i.e. the same as in the general assembly of the community at Jerusalem. To submit his gospel to his brother Apostles, Paul goes to Jerusalem: on the uncircumcision of Titus, on the admissibilty of Gentile Christianity, the conflict arises; their recognition is the fruit of the negociation; only a sequence of this result is the personal recognition of the Apostle of the Gentiles; only one of the causes which produce it, the recognition of his apostolic services. Besides, the whole discussion in the Epistle to the Galatians does not centre in the personal question of the apostolic dignity of Paul, but in the important one of the Christian's relation to the Law, as is clearly shown in the further exposition in ii. 10 ff. Therefore, why should Paul have passed over in complete silence the conclusive decisions of the primitive Church and of the Holy Ghost (Acts xv. 28) upon this subject, if these decisions really took place, as is stated in the Acts? Or were they, as Baumgarten mysteriously hints, too little decisive and too Judaistic for his purpose? Did he fear, as Ebrard[2] insists, that the adoption of the apostolic letter might injure *his* apostolic authority? For this he had every reason, only we must not conclude thence that he diplomatically

[1] 165 f., 168. The scurrilities with which Ebrard (p. 699) raises himself above the scientific examination of this affair, as of so many others, would be too much honoured by the briefest quotation.

[2] Krit. d. ev. Gesch. 713.

left the apostolic decisions untouched, but that they did not take place as they appear in the Acts.

If we look, moreover, how the relation between Paul and the original Apostles to each other and to the subject in dispute is represented in our book, here again its incompatibility with the authentic statements of Paul is not to be mistaken. According to the narrative of the Acts, Paul and Barnabas are despatched to Jerusalem to procure the decision of the community of that place and of the Twelve upon the disputed question which disturbed the community of Antioch. To secure such a supreme judicial decision, the community is assembled (xv. 6, *συνήχθησαν ἰδεῖν περὶ τοῦ λόγου τούτου*); and, after having listened to the speakers for and against, it decides as the instrument of the Holy Ghost (*ἔδοξε τῷ ἁγίῳ πνεύματι καὶ ἡμῖν*, v. 28), and this decision is transmitted for observance by Paul himself to the churches converted by him (xvi. 4, *παρεδίδουν αὐτοῖς φυλάσσειν τὰ δόγματα τὰ κεκριμένα ὑπὸ τῶν ἀποστόλων καὶ τῶν πρεσβυτέρων τῶν ἐν Ἱερουσαλήμ*). In a word, the community of Jerusalem, with the original Apostles, here appears as the chief ecclesiastical court, before whose judgment-seat important disputes are brought by the Gentile Christian communities, whose decisions are recognized even by Paul as universal ecclesiastical laws. This position, judging from the Epistle to the Galatians, Paul did not allow the primitive community and its chiefs; and according to his principles he could not possibly have allowed it. In his opinion, the right of the Gentiles to the Messianic salvation, the repeal of the Mosaic Law and circumcision, this fundamental axiom of his whole system, was much too firmly established to admit of his still treating it as a disputed point, and consenting to submit it to the decision of others. "If an angel from heaven," he exclaims in Gal. i. 8, "preach any other gospel than that which we have preached, let him be accursed." How could he then admit even the possibility that any other preaching should be required of him? "If ye be circumcised," he declares in Gal. v. 2, "Christ profiteth you nothing;" and we may believe that he did not first arrive at this conviction fourteen or fifteen years after his conversion. How could he then accept the commission to inquire at Jerusalem whether circumcision was, or was not, necessary to salvation (Acts xv. 1)? In reality, his position in this affair, if we listen to himself, was quite a different one. Not to procure a decision in Jerusalem did he go there, but to expound his principles to his colleagues; and with regard to these principles, he is so far from depending on their verdict, that he distinctly declares *ὁποῖοί ποτε ἦσαν, οὐδέν μοι διαφέρει*; and the unqualified acknowledgment of his procedure, not the supreme decision on their side, is all that he has to report as the result of his negociation with them. And as to the presumption of reverencing the decisions of the Jerusalemites as the decrees of the Holy Ghost, Paul, if it had encountered him, would probably have rejected it even more vehemently than he does similar claims, 2 Cor. x. 7, xi. 5, &c. In the account of the Acts, Paul indeed appears, respecting his whole view of Christianity, so subordinate to a Peter and a James, that he has almost changed sides with them. If the speeches of our 15th chapter were authentic, a Peter and even a James would on this occasion have enunciated the principles of Pauline universalism with more distinctness than the great Apostle of the Gentiles. Here it is Peter who declares the Mosaic Law a yoke which neither they who were present, nor yet their fathers, were able to bear; Peter who pronounces that Jews and Gentiles may equally be saved by the grace of Christ; Peter who is able in his own person to adduce the first example of a Gentile conversion. Less decidedly, but still in the same direction, does James express himself. By him also the principle of Gentile conversion is acknowledged and confirmed by passages from the prophets; he too is willing that the Law, although not repealed, should be limited to the Jews;[1] and if Peter has opened the door

[1] This is implied in the words, v. 21, *Μωϋσῆς γὰρ ἐκ γενεῶν ἀρχαίων κατὰ πόλιν τοὺς κηρύσσοντας αὐτὸν ἔχει, ἐν ταῖς συναγωγαῖς κατὰ πᾶν σάββατον ἀναγινωσκόμενος.* Some commentators, such as Meyer and De Wette, interpret these words as accounting for the restrictions imposed on the Gentile Christians: "We must require so much from them, as the Law is too well known, in consequence of the sab-

to Gentile conversion by his example, it is he who proposes the expedient, the acceptance of which renders it possible to receive Gentiles with Jews into one Messianic church. Of Paul and Barnabas, on the contrary, it is merely recorded that they related *ὅσα ἐποίησεν ὁ θεὸς σημεῖα καὶ τέρατα ἐν τοῖς ἔθνεσι δι' αὐτῶν.* That these stories of miracles should have constituted the sole or even the chief import of the Pauline addresses is not likely; even if Paul were convinced of having performed miracles, and if, in 2 Cor. xii. 12, he also appeals to his miracles, he does this only by the way, as if compelled to it; otherwise he wishes to distinguish himself from the Jews by this very thing, that he produces faith, not by miracles, but by his doctrine.[1] At the conference at Jerusalem also, it was, according to Gal. ii. 2, 7 ff., the exposition of his doctrine and the result gained by it in the heathen world by which he won over the older Apostles; of miracles he says not a word. But if it is unlikely that Paul should have spoken as is reported in our record, it is much more unlikely with respect to Peter and James. If a James really entertained the principles which he here enunciates; if he was

batical readings, to release them completely from it without scandal." But (comp. *Neander*, p. 217) on these grounds the observation of the *whole* law, and especially of circumcision, ought to have been required of the Gentile Christians; our account, however, according to verse 28, regards the demands of verse 20 as so indispensable that they require no special grounds, and the limitation to these demands appears simply as a μὴ παρενοχλεῖν, verse 19. Neander himself paraphrases, "As to the Jews, we need say nothing new to them, for they may hear every sabbath-day in the synagogue what Moses requires of them." But of the Jews there was nothing previously said to which the γὰρ could be referred. *Gieseler*, whom *Baur* (p. 119) also supports, sees in our speech the expression of the idea, "the Mosaic Law has been preached so long, and yet there are few who adapt themselves to its reception." Now that the service of the true God is preached without the shackles of the Law, so many turn to Him, and it is undeniable that the ceremonial Law is the only impediment to the general spread of true religion. Thus the leading idea, that the Law stands in the way of the spread of monotheism, would nevertheless remain unexpressed. It therefore seems to me the simplest, with *Schneckenburger* (p. 23) and *Baumgarten* (p. 150), to take the words in question thus: "We will not trouble the Gentile Christians with the requirements of the Law; the claims which Moses or the Mosaic Law may make will be satisfied by their recognition on the part of the Jews. *Schneckenburger* refers justly for this to xxi. 24 f.

[1] 1 Cor. i. 22: Ἰουδαῖοι σημεῖα αἰτοῦσι . . . ἡμεῖς δὲ κηρύσσομεν Χριστὸν ἐσταυρωμένον.

not merely yielding to the force of an accomplished fact (ἰδόντες ὅτι πεπίστευμαι τὸ εὐαγγέλιον τῆς ἀκροβυστίας, Gal. ii. 7), when granting Paul the peaceful possession of his field of labour, but was also himself convinced that the Mosaic Law was not binding on the Gentiles, and openly and decidedly acted on this conviction; if, as Neander believes (p. 211), he even acquiesced in the principle of justification by faith alone,[1]—it is quite inconceivable how this particular man, so accordant with Paul, so tolerant respecting the freedom of the Gentile Christians, could have been the highest authority of a party which everywhere most zealously opposed this freedom, and assailed the Apostle of the Gentiles more malignantly and vehemently, for no other reason than because he had admitted the uncircumcised into the Messianic kingdom,—inconceivable how even a Peter, who must after all have known the real state of the case, should have allowed himself to be so terrified by the disciples of James (Gal. ii. 12) that he became faithless to the principles which he had already acknowledged by his actions. These party-men might indeed have exaggerated the tendency of a James; but that, *on the very point on which the whole party-struggle of that period hinged*, they should have been in direct opposition to their highly revered chief, that they could make the circumcision of the Gentiles their watchword, while James from personal conviction pronounces the word of their freedom, and the whole community of Jerusalem acquiesces in this principle,—that even Peter, even Barnabas, to whom next to Paul the decisions of the apostolic council were most beneficial, instead of referring them to the authority of their own James, and the solemn declarations of the primitive community, yield to their demands without resistance,—this is utterly incredible. If James really entertained and asserted the opinion ascribed to him in our book, for that very reason he must likewise have been spurned, rejected, or at least set aside, by those Judaistic zealots;

[1] Ἐξ ἔργων δικαιοῦται ἄνθρωπος καὶ οὐκ ἐκ πίστεως μόνον, Jas. iii. 24. Neander, it is known, considers the Epistle of James to be genuine.

for what else could have induced them to acknowledge him as their chief but the essential similarity of his principles with theirs? And if these people were really as much feared as, according to Gal. ii. 12, they must have been, they cannot have been merely individual fanatics who had against them, besides the mass of Pauline Christians, the whole primitive community, with its chief (Acts xv. 22); but they must have had extensive support among this community, and could not have appealed entirely without reason to a James.[1] But Peter too cannot have stood so far from them as is generally supposed. He may have opposed the freedom of the Gentile Christians with less harshness than James; but that he declared himself so decidedly in its favour as he does here is incredible, even on account of the incident at Antioch.[2] Here all the observations[3] occasioned by

[1] Comp. on this, the appropriate remarks of *Schwegler*, Nachap. Zeitalter, 118 f.

[2] For that we must not, with *Schneckenburger* (Object of the Acts, 108 ff.), place this occurrence prior to the apostolic council is obvious. How can it be supposed that Paul, after recounting his meetings with the original Apostles, beginning at i. 15, in chronological order, should now suddenly spring aside from the order of time in a manner which his readers could possibly perceive; and how could he speak of the transaction at Jerusalem as he speaks of it in ii. 1, if it had been preceded by such a sharp dispute with Peter? His whole account obviously assumes that the question concerning the Gentile mission was discussed between him and the party of Palestine at Jerusalem. Compare especially verses 2, 7.

[3] *Wieseler*, p. 197, maintains that a contradiction between the behaviour of Peter and the decisions of the apostolic council could not exist, because these decisions do not refer to the position of the Jewish Christians with regard to the Law, but only to that of the Gentile Christians. Peter's first freedom of intercourse with the Gentiles at Antioch was in *excess* of the decisions of Jerusalem; and if Paul afterwards reproaches him with πῶς τὰ ἔθνη ἀναγκάζεις ἰουδαΐζειν, this only means that Peter, although perceiving their merely provisional purport, had attempted to reinforce them. But the account in the Epistle to the Galatians makes any evasion of this kind impossible. If, according to this, the Gentile Christians were received by the Jerusalemites without further conditions as fellow-Christians (verses 6, 9), the limits between the two divisions were herewith removed, the Gentile Christians were declared recipients of the Messianic kingdom as well as the Jewish Christians, and the latter could no longer scruple to eat with them. In no other way does the Acts regard this relation; see xi. 3 and our previous remarks on this passage. Therefore, if Peter at Antioch withdrew from fellowship at table with the baptized Gentiles from fear of the Jewish Christians, this implies that he refused to acknowledge them as fellow-religionists; but he would scarcely have done this if his personal convictions and the apostolic decisions had been what they must be believed to be from our book.

the story of the conversion of Cornelius are again applicable. Not to mention that the appeal to this particular fact, xv. 7 f., is of course as doubtful as the fact itself. Nay, even in Paul it is striking that he does not say a word to remind either Peter or the disciples of James of the solemn compact at Jerusalem, the fundamental ecclesiastical law there established, the "Bill of Rights" of the Gentile Christians. "If the τινὲς ἀπὸ 'Ιακώβου were despotic zealots," Schwegler justly remarks (the work already quoted), "why does not Peter emphatically refute them by appealing to all that had previously taken place? Why does he not make use of his apostolic authority, the decisions of the apostolic college and the primitive church, the acquiescence of James, that series of acknowledged facts? And Paul himself—in the reprimand which he gives to his brother Apostle in consequence of that occurrence—has he no word with which to remind him of the transactions of the apostolic council, the decisions then so unanimously, so peaceably taken, the speech made by Peter on that occasion? No. Peter has forgotten that council, the emissaries of James have forgotten it, Paul has forgotten it. This is hard to believe. If others were not forthcoming, the contradictions quoted would alone suffice to make us look upon the apostolic council of the Acts as a fiction traceable to the pragmatism of the work, a fiction which indeed harmonized with the pacific objects of our author, but which can have no place in history."[1]

Further reasons are found in sufficient number in the contents of the decrees at Jerusalem, as Baur and Schwegler have demonstrated. These decrees are intended to establish the conditions to which the admission of the Gentiles into the Messianic salvation, and the fellowship of the Jewish and Gentile Chris-

[1] A characteristic proof of the decisions of the apostolic council is to be found in *Wieseler*, p. 190. The authenticity of the apostolic decree is guaranteed, according to him, by xxi. 25, as this passage belongs to a paragraph written by an eye-witness and companion of Paul, xx. 5—xxviii. 31. It is obvious that he who disputes the authenticity of the Acts on other grounds does not admit the absolute authenticity of xx. ff. More details on this later.

tians in the Messianic kingdom, are attached. These conditions are three; the continued validity of circumcision and of the Law as respects the Jewish Christians and their successors is admitted; the Gentile Christians, on the contrary, are released from it, yet they too must submit to the restrictions named in verses 20 and 29. In a word, the compact between the conflicting parties consists in this—that each with its own claims is limited to itself, and an observance of the Jewish custom is imposed upon the Gentile Christians only in some subordinate points. Such a compact, even disregarding its official form, cannot then have been made. In Gal. ii. 6 ff. Paul explicitly declares: ἐμοὶ γὰρ οἱ δοκοῦντες οὐδὲν προσανέθεντο, ἀλλὰ τοὐναντίον . . . δεξιὰς ἔδωκαν ἐμοὶ καὶ Βαρνάβᾳ κοινωνίας, ἵνα ἡμεῖς μὲν εἰς τὰ ἔθνη, αὐτοὶ δὲ εἰς τὴν περιτομήν· μόνον τῶν πτωχῶν ἵνα μνημονεύωμεν. From this explanation three things follow. In the first place, no demands were made upon Paul at Jerusalem which conflicted with the principles which he there laid down.[1] Secondly, the agreement between Paul and the leaders at Jerusalem is confined to their reciprocal toleration of each other in their own spheres of labour. Paul was not to interfere with them in their treatment of the common cause within the sphere of Jewish Christianity; and as little were they to meddle with his ministry to the Gentiles; no union in principle took place between the two parties. Thirdly, no further conditions were attached to that compact except that Paul should remember the poor of Jerusalem. On all these points the Pauline account is not to be reconciled with that of the Acts. Or with respect to *the first*, would it have been no unbearable addition to his doctrine, no

[1] The disputed προσανέθεντο means either, they *im*posed nothing further upon me, or they *pro*posed nothing further to me. The latter interpretation, sanctioned by *Wieseler* (Chronol. of Apost. Age, p. 195), *De Wette* and *Hilgenfeld* on the passage, also by *Baur* (Tübingen Journal, 1849, 463), is scarcely established by the ἀνεθέμην, verse 2, and the προσανεθέμην, i. 16, for it is by no means rare with Paul that in the same context the meaning of an expression alters. With reference to the fact, it is not very important which way we translate; for even in Wieseler's interpretation the meaning can only be that no further demand was made on Paul by the party of Palestine.

προσανατίθεσθαι, if he were required to acknowledge the lasting obligation on Jewish Christians of law and circumcision, the unqualified abolition of which he enforced in every part of his Epistles, and if he were even obliged to allow restrictions to be imposed on the Gentiles from which he had pronounced them free? For that both were the case, according to our account, will forthwith be shown in greater detail. Further, as concerns *the third* of the decisions quoted, how could Paul declare the small subsidies to be the sole condition laid upon him, if, in addition to this,—which is, strange to say, not mentioned in the Acts,—all the conditions enumerated in the apostolic decree were likewise established? Perchance because nothing else, save some attention to the poor, was imposed *on himself* as a duty, because the statutes quoted in the Acts did not concern the Apostle himself, but only the Gentile Christian communities (Lechler, p. 258). The duty of upholding these statutes in his missionary work was, however, imposed upon the Apostle; and, according to xvi. 4, he fulfilled this duty; but that he could pass them by unnoticed in the passage in the Epistle to the Galatians is incomprehensible; and Lechler's assertion that "Paul is here proving that it was just the older Apostles who recognized his apostolic ministry, exactly as it was, and that with this object he mentions only what concerns his personal rights and duties," this assertion, applied as it is here, is entirely beyond the mark. Precisely if the acknowledgment of Paul's apostolic ministry was in question, was it least of all possible to omit the guiding principles of this ministry which had been preconcerted with the party at Jerusalem, i.e. the decisions of the apostolic decrees.[1] Finally, if we examine

[1] For similar reasons, *Lange's* expedient (Apost. Age, i. 104) is also untenable: the decisions of the apostolic council are not intended to establish any conditions of salvation; in Galatia, on the contrary, it was exactly these which were in question; Paul was hence unable to quote the apostolic decisions without rousing the misconception that salvation was connected with their observance. Granting that this was the real position of the apostolic decisions, he must all the more have explained them in order to prevent their misinterpretation; in no case could he positively pronounce his οὐδὲν προσανέθεντο; but how little the apostolic decree is unmeaning in a dogmatic point of view has already been demonstrated.

the principles involved in the negociations between Paul and the original Apostles—the second of the points which we have noticed—we can only agree with the remark of Baur (pp. 125 ff.) and Schwegler (pp. 120 f.), that, according to the representation of the Epistle to the Galatians, a merely external concordat was effected between Paul and the original Apostles; that they, indeed, consented not to disturb him in his work, in fact to ignore it; but that an avowal of Pauline principles, such as the Acts puts in the mouth of Peter and even of James, could not have taken place. As Paul in the passage employs himself in explaining the concessions made to him by the party at Jerusalem, he could not tacitly omit the most important of them, the appropriation of his whole principle, if anything of the kind had really been enunciated by that party. If he is silent as to this, and in its place mentions only the mutual promise of leaving each other in peace, he cannot have gained any more important concession. These obvious conclusions can scarcely be evaded by the hypothesis that the private conference spoken of in the Epistle to the Galatians produced the results stated in that writing, but that this could not be used as an argument with regard to the public transaction; for such a difference between that which the chief Apostles conceded in private and that which they conceded in presence of the church would be in every way incredible, even if the whole distinction between a public and a private negociation had not already proved to be untenable.

Quite as distinctly as the narrative in the Epistle to the Galatians, all other historical traces testify against the statements of the Acts respecting the decisions which were supposed to have been made at the so-called apostolic council.

The chief question in dispute regarding law and circumcision is here solved by emancipating the Gentiles from both, while the Jewish Christians remain lastingly bound to them. The latter point is, indeed, not explicitly mentioned in the document of the Jerusalemite community, verses 23 ff., just because this document is addressed to the Gentile Christians only. Although this last circumstance proves that the emancipation from the Law applied to them alone, it is still more apparent from the speech of James; and, finally, a perfectly authentic testimony is given in xxi. 20 ff., if Paul is here advised by the Jerusalemites to take part in the performance of a vow in order to show by this act that he too adheres to the Law, and to refute the accusation that he ἀποστασίαν διδάσκει ἀπὸ Μωϋσέως τοὺς κατὰ τὰ ἔθνη πάντας Ἰουδαίους, λέγων, μὴ περιτέμνειν αὐτοὺς τὰ τέκνα, μηδὲ τοῖς ἔθεσι περιπατεῖν; and to leave no doubt that this speech refers to our account, it continues, περὶ δὲ τῶν πεπιστευκότων ἐθνῶν ἡμεῖς ἐπεστείλαμεν, κρίναντες μηδὲν τοιοῦτον τηρεῖν αὐτούς, &c. After an explanation so definite, it is beyond question that our book does not wish it to be supposed that the decisions of its 15th chapter were made in any other sense. But could Paul have acquiesced in decisions which had this meaning,—could he have acknowledged them as a rule for his apostolic work, and have delivered them to be observed by the communities which he had founded,—he who is never weary of urging the absolute discord between Judaism and Christianity, between the Law and the Gospel, between circumcision and faith in Christ?[1] This is utterly impossible: a compact such as the Acts describes can never have been concluded between Paul and Jewish Christendom.

According to our account, Paul did not even rest here. When, in his second missionary journey, he took Timothy to Lystra, according to xvi. 1 ff., he caused him to be circumcised previously, because he was known to the Jews in his home as the son of a Gentile. Even from the standpoint of the decisions of the council of Jerusalem, this step is extremely remarkable; for as only the mother of Timothy was a Jewess, while his father was a Gentile, he belonged of right,[2] if the extreme claims re-

[1] On this, compare what is said below respecting xxi. 14 ff.

[2] As *Thiersch*, 137, who, with *Lange's* assent (Apost. Age, i. 102), appeals to this, that according to Talmudical principles the son of a Jewess was to be circumcised, according to Catholic claims the son of a Catholic woman is to be educated a Catholic,—which, however, he ought not to call the "claim of Mosaic Law."

specting mixed marriages are not applied to him, to the Gentile Christians whom these decisions emancipated from circumcision. That Paul circumcised him, nevertheless, is attributable to the maternal parentage of Timothy and consideration for the Jews. Timothy, observes Meyer on this passage, was by maternal descent and education a Jewish Christian; he was to be one in ritual also, in order to win over Jews by his means, and to obviate the scandal that might be caused them by an uncircumcised preacher of the Messiah. Similarly Neander (p. 290): By the circumcision of Timothy, Paul resigned none of the privileges of the Gentile Christians, for the Jews had good right to appropriate him as the son of a Jewess educated in Judaism. But Schneckenburger justly rejoins (pp. 69 f.) that, according to the account in the Acts, Timothy is not circumcised for the sake of those among whom he was to labour as a preacher of the gospel, but, when already destined as a fellow-traveller, out of consideration for the Jews remaining behind; and not because his mother was known as a Jewess, but because his father was a Greek; consequently it was only to avoid giving offence to the Jews that Paul took a circumcised person for a fellow-traveller. In reality he must have been already circumcised, that he might pass as a Jew or Jewish Christian; that he was not so, was the best proof of his Gentile descent and education. But how can it be supposed that Paul should here have quite needlessly disowned the principles he had just defended so vigorously in the dispute about Titus; how could this have been supposed even if Timothy could really have been considered a Jewish Christian, which, however, he was not? "Behold," says Paul, in Gal. v. 2, "I say unto you, that if ye be circumcised, Christ shall profit you nothing. I testify again to every man that is circumcised, that he is a debtor to do the whole law. Christ is become of no effect unto you, whosoever of you are justified by the law; ye are fallen from grace;" and this very Paul is supposed to have induced Timothy to take upon himself the whole yoke of the Law by circumcision, and to have lost his participation of Christ and his grace. In a case like this, in which the entire principle of the Apostle, the complete salvation of his disciple, was at stake, is it possible to satisfy oneself with the hypothesis of a "condescension" which may have been recommended to Paul by his experience with Titus?[1] Paul was not such a reed at other times, and certainly not one shaken by such a slight puff of wind. 1 Cor. ix. 20, to which Neander appeals, obviously refers only to an accommodation which does not involve the denial of essential principles. Or if we say, with Neander,[2] "that *as* in the case of Timothy the motive of his circumcision was his parentage, *so* this accommodation can be no foundation for dogmatical deductions as to the circumcision of a Gentile;" that the *as* is incorrect has been shown already; how it fares with the *so* will appear from the passage of the Epistle to the Galatians, which makes no distinction between Jewish and Gentile birth, but pronounces judgment on *παντὶ ἀνθρώπῳ περιτεμνομένῳ*. But to attempt to elude this judgment by the evasion[3] "that the Apostle does not here speak of outward circumcision in and by itself, but of it in connection with the religious conviction of which it was the expression," of a conviction to attain to justification by circumcision and the fulfilment of the Law. What other significance had circumcision in general

[1] *Schneckenburger.* Also *Neander*, p. 291.

[2] P. 290; against *Baur*, p. 129.

[3] *Neander*, p. 372. In the 4th edition, indeed, the circumcision of Timothy is no more mentioned; but that Neander's observation refers to this very thing is shown by its express quotation, 3rd edition, p. 308. *Lechler* (p. 263) likewise helps himself by saying that the circumcision of Timothy was not a question of its necessity for salvation, but of convenience and human considerations. As if for human considerations Paul could have deemed useful the very thing which he pronounces a positive hindrance to salvation! *Wieseler* (p. 194) also endeavours to prove from Gal. ii. 3 ff. that Paul, without injury to his principles, might have consented not only to the circumcision of Timothy, but of Titus also. With others, he supplements the words, *διὰ] δὲ τοὺς παρεισάκτους ψευδαδέλφους*, with, "but because of the *ψευδ.* I would not yield;" and then argues, "If Paul did not allow the circumcision on account of the *ψευδ.*, he would have done it otherwise." But the natural completion of the fragmentary sentence is much rather, "he was not compelled, but on account of the *ψευδ.* it came to a dispute." Only thus arises a suitable contrast with the *οὐκ ἠναγκάσθη*. For the rest, compare against Wieseler, *Baur*, Tübingen Journal, 1849, 465 ff.

except this, that it was a pledge of obedience to the Mosaic Law?[1] and how was it possible to give this pledge if salvation was not expected by obedience to the Law? or at least how was it possible, without committing an act of the most culpable hypocrisy? Sooner than credit the Apostle with enticing his disciples to the commission of this act, we must credit our book with having misinformed us in this as in so many other cases.

Among the restrictions imposed on the Gentile Christians by the apostolic decree, there is one which is likewise alluded to in the Pauline Epistles, i. e. abstinence from meat offered to idols, which is copiously discussed in 1 Cor. viii.—x. But how different here is the Apostle's declaration from that of the assembly at Jerusalem, according to our book! In the latter, this abstinence is unconditionally required of the Gentiles; Paul indeed requires it also if the individual is either not convinced in his own mind of the lawfulness of eating meat offered to idols, or if he might thereby offend the weaker brethren; but otherwise he pronounces it permissible, and the contrary view a prejudice, above which the Christian ought to be raised by the γνῶσις or true perception of the essence of Christianity. This is obviously quite a different standpoint from that announced in the decision at Jerusalem; and the Apostle's concession to the weaker in faith cannot be employed as a vindication of his assent to those decisions, for this concession says merely that the Christian is to refrain from the questionable food *for the sake of others;* whereas he explicitly rejects the demand to proclaim it unlawful

[1] As Paul says, in Gal. v. 2 f., as distinctly as possible. That the same Paul says again, in 1 Cor. x. 23, πάντα ἔξεστιν, and 1 Cor. ix. 20, ἐγενόμην τοῖς Ἰουδαίοις ὡς Ἰουδαῖος, is true; but if these sayings cannot by any means be construed to signify that everything was permitted Christians—idolatry, fornification, for instance—or that Paul had become a Jew in all respects—in justification by works, for example—it can only be deduced from the other sayings of the Apostle what he considered admissible or inadmissible from the Christian standpoint. Among the latter, judging by his unequivocal declaration, must be reckoned circumcision, and, with *Baumgarten* (ii. a, 187 f.), to encounter these, his plain words, with a home-made theory of Christian freedom, would be an unpermissible perversity, even if the theory were not so confused as it is in the present case. It is not here a question of how *we* should regard the claims of circumcision, but of how *Paul did* regard them.

in and by itself, thereby to burden his own conscience; and he requires his readers, wherever consideration for others did not press itself upon them, to act according to their more unprejudiced view.[1] Here, on the contrary, abstinence from εἰδωλόθυτα is absolutely commanded (comp. also xxi. 25); it is designated as an ἐπάναγκες, one of the indispensable ordinances, on the observance of which depended the salvation of the Gentile Christians, their εὖ πράττειν.[2] It is but an empty evasion to pretend this obligation to be only qualified,—qualified, namely, by the conditions of the period, with the cessation of which its validity would naturally expire (Meyer, on verse 20). Of such a qualification there is not a word in the text of the Acts; the restrictions in question are designated positively as τὰ ἐπάναγκες, which thus, without further comment, can but mean unconditionally necessary. And what change of circumstances had taken place in the later years of the apostolic age to make the ordinance respecting meat offered to idols appear superfluous at the time of the 1st Epistle to the Corinthians, if it was needful at the time of the apostolic council? Was Judaism, perchance, so far supplanted in the Church during those seven or eight years that the Jewish Christians were only a sect over against the Catholic Church of the Gentile Christians?[3] Every line of primitive Christian history testifies to the con-

[1] 1 Cor. x. 25 ff.: Πᾶν τὸ ἐν μακέλλῳ πωλούμενον ἐσθίετε μηδὲν ἀνακρίνοντες διὰ τὴν συνείδησιν. . . . Εἰ δέ τις ὑμᾶς καλεῖ τῶν ἀπίστων· καὶ θέλετε πορεύεσθαι, πᾶν τὸ παρατιθέμενον ὑμῖν ἐσθίετε μηδὲν ἀνακρίνοντες διὰ τὴν συνείδησιν. Ἐὰν δέ τις ὑμῖν εἴπῃ· τοῦτο εἰδωλόθυτόν ἐστι, μὴ ἐσθίετε δι' ἐκεῖνον τὸν μηνύσαντα καὶ τὴν συνείδησιν. Συνείδησιν δὲ λέγω οὐχὶ τὴν ἑαυτοῦ ἀλλὰ τὴν τοῦ ἑτέρου· ἱνατί γὰρ ἡ ἐμὴ ἐλευθερία κρίνεται ὑπὸ ἄλλης συνειδήσεως. Just the chief point in this Pauline discussion, its notice of principles, is disregarded by *Ritschl*, when he asserts (Rise of the Old Catholic Church, 114 ff.) that Paul agreed in effect with the apostolic decree; for this requires abstinence from meat offered to idols *unconditionally*, Paul only in case it offended others; in other circumstances, he expressly pronounced it permissible.

[2] De Wette, Meyer and many others, explain the εὖ πράξετε contrary to the language, "you will do well, viz., for the preservation of unity and peace in the Christian Church." In that case there must necessarily have been εὖ ποιεῖν, as the very passages to which De Wette appeals show, Acts x. 33; 3 John vi.

[3] *Baumgarten*, 153.

trary. Or had the Jewish Christians meanwhile become accustomed to the consumption of the sacrificial flesh? Do we not learn from Paul himself how offensive to them was the liberty which in this respect followed from the Pauline principles? Does not the Apocalypse, ii. 3, regard the *φαγεῖν εἰδωλόθυτα* as one of the characteristic tokens of the most abominable heresy? Was not, far into the second, nay, even to the third century, the prevailing opinion of the Church, or at least of a very large party, so decidedly against that freedom, that Justin, for example, to name one among many, plainly calls the Pauline doctrine, though without naming the Apostle, a doctrine of devils.[1] Does not our book itself, a still longer time after the composition of the Epistles to the Corinthians, expressly declare by the mouth of James, xxi. 25, the enduring validity of the apostolic arrangements? But if this is the meaning of our ordinance respecting the *εἰδωλόθυτα*, Paul could not possibly accede to it without denying his most positive principles. He could neither tolerate nor promulgate a decree which prohibited exactly what he permitted; he could do this the less, as, according to what has been already said, it was not by any means a merely subordinate concession which was concerned, but what was at that time an important question of principle; for though the consumption of sacrificial flesh was considered by Paul a matter of indifference, and compliant as he shows himself for this reason when it is merely an affair of refraining from this meat in an individual case, he was unable to allow this point to serve as an opportunity for rejecting the *principle* of Christian liberty which he had enunciated, and an abstinence which he had

[1] Tr. 25: Καὶ ὁ Τρύφων. *Καὶ μὴν πολλοὺς τῶν τὸν Ἰησοῦν λεγόντων ὁμολογεῖν καὶ λεγομένων Χριστιανῶν πυνθάνομαι ἐσθίειν τὰ εἰδωλόθυτα καὶ μηδὲν ἐκ τούτου βλάπτεσθαι λέγειν.* (Exactly what Paul says, 1 Cor. x.) *Κἀγὼ ἀπεκρινάμην· καὶ ἐκ τοῦ τοιούτους εἶναι ἄνδρας, ὁμολογοῦντας ἑαυτοὺς εἶναι Χριστιανοὺς καὶ τὸν σταυρωθέντα Ἰησοῦν ὁμολογεῖν καὶ κύριον καὶ Χριστὸν καὶ μὴ τὰ ἐκείνου διδάγματα διδάσκοντας, ἀλλὰ τὰ ἀπὸ τῶν τῆς πλάνης πνευμάτων,* &c. That Justin has the Gnostics in particular in his eye makes no difference in the question before us, as the principles here disputed do not differ from those of Paul in the point under discussion.

required out of consideration for others, to be unconditionally and absolutely prescribed. Had he once allowed it, it must be supposed that he would not then have acted in opposition to the solemn compact concluded at Jerusalem, and have even led his Corinthians to disobey the same decisions which but few years previously he had promulgated for observance among the communities of Syria, Cilicia and Lycaonia. Neander endeavours to justify his conduct by the observation that, "as these decisions rested on mutual concession, if the Jewish Christians did not fulfil the conditions and refused to acknowledge the uncircumcised as their brethren, the obligation on the part of the Gentile Christians would lapse also" (p. 423). But who were they who did not fulfil the compact? The Apostles with whom Paul had concluded it? Neander not only secures himself against this on every side, but he also admits, on account of xxi. 25, that respect for the apostolic decree was always maintained by the Apostles in Palestine. In that case, however, Paul was not justified in annulling the compact one-sidedly; and if we nevertheless see him behaving in a manner antagonistic to this assumed compact, we can only conclude, not that he broke it, but that he never made it.

If in the ordinance of the apostolic council respecting eating the sacrificial flesh, its incompatibility with the conduct approved by Paul was suspicious, so is there apparently too great harmony with regard to another of the apostolic edicts; abstinence from πορνεία is so completely a matter of course for all Christians, that it is surprising to see it imposed on the Gentile Christians in an edict which does not otherwise refer to general moral duties, but to external demeanour and customs indifferent in themselves. For the explanation of this phenomenon, Neander's observation (p. 219) can scarcely suffice, that impurity was here prohibited only on account of the close connection with idolatry in which it was wont to be placed by the Old Testament. To this Baur justly objects, p. 141, that if impurity in general was considered to be disallowed, much more would this be understood of impurity combined with idolatry, and a special prohibition on this subject was not at all requisite. In our passage, πορνεία is evidently considered, not as a general moral transgression, but as a disregard of positive divine injunctions involved in the complete renunciation of Judaism, as an abandonment of that observance of the Law which it seemed might at least be required from the Gentile Christians; in this sense it is put on the same level with eating sacrificial meat, blood, and things strangled. Now if the Jerusalemites were of opinion that impurity was as much a natural consequence of the Gentile Christian freedom from the Law as the unscrupulous use of sacrificial meat, they would have done flagrant injustice to the standpoint of the opposite party, and it would have been the duty of Paul to enlighten them on the subject, and to prevent the acceptance of a definition resting on an assumption so insulting to his view of Christianity. But this hypothesis is all the more improbable, as the Apocalypse likewise puts πορνεύειν in the closest combination with the φαγεῖν εἰδωλόθυτα with reference to the Nicolaitanes, who in all probability were Pauline Christians.[1] The fact that in these two books, partly the accusation, partly the suspicion of πορνεία, is expressed against the more liberal Gentile Christians, seems to prove that there was something in the mode of life of the latter which to the opposite party appeared like πορνεία. This can scarcely have consisted in actual licentious impurity; for, in the first place, one can hardly believe that the Gentile Christians as a whole would have become so utterly untrue to the claims of Christianity; and also this juxtaposition of πορνεία with the eating of sacrificial meat seems to indicate that it referred to some deviation from Jewish custom of that time, no doubt equally inoffensive to morality; whether it may be looked for, as by Schwegler,[2] in deuterogamy, or more likely, by Baur (pp. 142 ff.), Ritschl,[3] in the contraction of marriages which

[1] See my remarks in Tübingen Journal, i. 713 ff., which are modified by the details given in the text on the subject of πορνεία.

[2] Post.-Apost. Age, i. 127.

[3] Rise of the Old Catholic Church, 119 f.

appeared unlawful from a Jewish Christian standpoint. We cannot be surprised that for such a special point the general word of πορνεία should be used; generalizations like this lie in the spirit of party polemics;[1] but it is another question whether Paul would have sanctioned this view and representation of a custom to all appearance inoffensive in itself and offensive only from the Jewish standpoint.

Besides the contents of the apostolic decree, we must also briefly touch upon the representation given in the document in verses 23 ff. It is usual to praise this writing for its simplicity and primitive character, and to consider these qualities a guarantee of its authenticity.[2] This conclusion is, however, very uncertain; why could not a later person have imitated the tone of an apostolic writing? Meanwhile, independently of its main contents, there are some things which cast suspicion on its verbal authenticity. In a perfectly simple document, entirely void of design or calculation, such as we have here professedly, verse 26 could scarcely have found a place. What object was to be gained by the recommendation of Paul and Barnabas, which so strikingly contrasts with the meagre tenor of the remaining portion? Those to whom it was addressed did not require such recommendation, because the authors of their Christianity stood much nearer than did the Jerusalemites, and because nothing is previously said of any personal attacks upon them. Even in one case in which this had occurred (2 Cor. iii. 1), Paul explicitly says that he should have scorned such letters of commendation. Our author must have thought otherwise, for his whole work, as we shall see in course of time, is nothing but an ἐπιστολὴ συστατικὴ in favour of the Apostle; and he must have intended it for readers to whom a recommendation proceeding from the original Apostles might be neither superfluous nor

[1] Thus, for instance, in the mediæval transactions respecting celibacy, *fornicatio*, without further comment, is the standing designation of the marriage of priests among the opposite party.

[2] So *Neander*, p. 223, Remark 1. *Meyer* on xv. 23.

ineffectual. When we further look at the verbal peculiarities of the document,[1] Bleek imagines that he has discovered a small sign of its authenticity in the fact that, in verse 25, Barnabas is named before Paul, while in other parts of this paragraph, and almost from the commencement of the 13th chapter, the reverse order prevails; and another of its composition by James in the greeting with *χαίρειν*, which, among the New Testament Epistles, is to be found only in James i. 1. But the precedence of Barnabas, in addition to other passages, occurs also in xiv. 14, xv. 12, and is doubtless entirely accidental;[2] the good Greek *χαίρειν* can here, as little as in the Epistle of James, serve to render probable the authenticity of documents the authors of which are supposed to be natives of Palestine, and all other signs bear witness against the genuineness of the Epistle of James; that it is not foreign to our author is shown by xxiii. 26. Similar good Greek expressions are to be found in verses 25 and 28, *ἔδοξε*; verse 28, *τὰ ἐπάναγκες*; verse 29, *εὖ πράττειν* and *ἔῤῥωσθε*; a word peculiar to the author of the Acts is, verse 25, *ὁμοθυμαδόν*. Finally, Schwegler[3] justly draws attention to the resemblance in construction between our epistle and the prologue of the third Gospel.[4] If these indications stood alone, we should attribute no great weight to them; combined with all the other proofs, they aid in making the want of authenticity in our record palpable.

It results from the above discussions that the story of the apostolic council can by no means pass for pure history. It is

[1] Studien und Krit. 1836, 4, 1037. Similarly also earlier, *Riehm*, De Font. Act. Ap. 146 ff., and others mentioned by Riehm.

[2] What *Baumgarten* remarks against this, 174 f., seems to me too far-fetched to require discussion.

[3] Post.-Apost. Age, i. 127. Comp.:

Luke i.	Acts xv.
1. *ἐπειδήπερ πολλοὶ ἐπεχείρησαν.*	24. *ἐπειδήπερ ἠκούσαμεν ὅτι.*
2. *ἔδοξε κἀμοὶ παρηκολουθηκότι πᾶσιν ἀκριβῶς καθεξῆς σοι γράψαι.*	25. *ἔδοξεν ἡμῖν γενομένοις ὁμοθυμαδόν πέμψαι πρὸς ὑμᾶς.*

[4] *Schwanbeck*, on the Die Quellen d. Apg. p. 262, thinks indeed that the prologue originated in imitation of the apostolic missive.

certainly based on some foundation in fact, but those facts are merely the occurrences narrated in the Epistle to the Galatians; what goes beyond this is incompatible either with the authentic statements of Paul, or with other events of accredited history. The official mission of Paul by the community of Antioch; the position which he assumes in the Acts with regard to the original Apostles; the discussion of his affairs in the formal assembly of the church; the speeches which are attributed on this occasion to Peter and to James, to Paul and to Barnabas; the resolutions of the assembly and their promulgation by an apostolic missive; the course which Paul is said to have pursued in consequence concerning Timothy,—all these features can only be pronounced unhistorical. Not even is Ritschl's[1] hypothesis admissible, that although the transactions of the 15th chapter, and especially the speeches of Peter and James, are unhistorical, the apostolic decree, on the contrary, or at least its nucleus, verses 28 f., is genuine. Ritschl rests this hypothesis on the remark that the author founds this decree on Pauline principles (verses 7 ff. and 14 ff.); which would in reality have led far beyond its limits, and to the complete emancipation of the Gentile Christians even from the laws for proselytes enunciated in the apostolic decree. Hence, if he composed the speeches of Peter and James, he must have found the decree already in existence. But our author makes the concessions to Judaism which are certainly contained in the apostolic decree, only as a means of warding off the more extensive demand of the circumcision of Gentile Christians; for him the nucleus of the apostolic decree does not consist in the rules for proselytes in the 29th verse, but in the μηδὲν πλέον of the 28th. If from the principle which he puts in the mouth of Peter he does not draw all the deductions which are, strictly speaking, involved in it, this cannot prove more than that he was either considerate or illogical in their application, not that the conclusions which he draws from them proceed from another. Moreover, any one

[1] Entsteh. d. altkath. Kirche, 120 f.

who, like Ritschl (p. 132), supposes that Paul himself was completely in accord with the apostolic decree, deprives the above argument of every appearance of justice.[1] But that this assertion is incorrect, that the historical character of the apostolic decree, as well as of that of the other narratives, is refuted by Paul's account of the incidents at Jerusalem, by his principles and his conduct, we have already seen. Criticism must altogether renounce the attempt to select single portions of the well-rounded description of our 15th chapter; one stands or falls with the other; and if the whole is not an authentic record, we may regard it as a free composition carried out by the author on the basis of the Pauline narrative in the Epistle to the Galatians.

4. Paul's Second Missionary Journey.

Some time (*τινὲς ἡμέραι*) after the transactions of the so-called apostolic council, Paul entered on the journey which brought him to his chief field of labour in Asia Minor and Greece. Having separated himself from Barnabas on account of Mark, he passed with Silas through Syria and Cilicia, Lycaonia, Phrygia and Galatia, and went by Mysia to Troas. The whole of this extensive journey is most briefly treated in our book. Only from Lycaonia comes the record of what we have discussed above, the circumcision of Timothy and the promulgation of the decisions of Jerusalem; the journey through Phrygia and Galatia is registered with a mere *διελθόντες τὴν Φρυγίαν καὶ τὴν Γαλατικὴν χώραν* (xvi. 6); and concerning anterior Asia Minor it is observed

[1] Besides the reasons discussed, Ritschl supports his hypothesis by the fact that the demands of the apostolic decree coincide with those of the Clementine writings, and also that the four points required of the Gentiles are enumerated in the same order as in Lev. xvii. f., while they are inverted in the speech of James. But the first circumstance, so far as it is true, proves nothing; for why should a later person not have known and considered the demands of the Jewish Christians of his own time? and the second is not correct: of the things strangled of the apostolic decree there is no question in Lev. xvii., but only of the *θνησιμαῖον* and *θηριάλωτον*, verse 15, the consumption of which is, however, not entirely forbidden; but sacrificial meat is not mentioned there. And if it were otherwise, what would it prove?

that the Holy Spirit prevented Paul and Silas from preaching the gospel in those parts.[1] There is nothing incredible in the last statement; bent on reaching the centre of heathenism in Europe, Paul might be reluctant to linger in Asia Minor, and what his inward judgment told him on this subject he may have felt as the voice of the Spirit. More we cannot say, for the Apostle's own Epistles afford us no data for comparison. On the other hand, from these same Epistles and from Acts xviii. 23, it seems quite probable that it was on this journey, here so cursorily mentioned, that Paul founded the churches of Galatia, inasmuch as neither there nor here do we meet any trace of any other journey on which that could have occurred, nor on which we could find time for it.[2] But then it is very striking that this certainly not unimportant institution of churches should be so entirely ignored, when, from xviii. 23, it cannot possibly have been unknown to the author. We shall be obliged later to inquire into the cause of this phenomenon; here we have only to state it.

From Troas, Paul passed over to Macedonia. We are not entitled positively to declare the vision which induced him to do so (xvi. 9) to be unhistorical, but neither can the possibility be denied that it may be so, and that in the man of Macedonia the

[1] xvi. 6: *Διελθόντες δὲ τὴν Φρυγίαν καὶ τὴν Γαλατικὴν χώραν, κωλυθέντες ὑπὸ τοῦ ἁγίου πνεύματος λαλῆσαι τὸν λόγον ἐν τῇ Ἀσίᾳ ἐλθόντες κατὰ τὴν Μυσίαν ἐπείραζον κατὰ τὴν Βιθυνίαν πορεύεσθαι.* Meyer here construes: "After they had passed through Phrygia and Galatia, being prevented by the Holy Ghost, . . . they endeavoured," &c.; so that Phrygia and Galatia are reckoned with Asia, and the prohibition to preach would have applied to them. But the Acts (according to *Wieseler's* demonstration, Chronology of the Acts, 31 ff.) by Asia understands only the regions of Mysia, Lydia and Caria; and, moreover, the construction adopted by Meyer seems less simple than that which refers the *κωλυθέντες*, &c., to the following *ἐπείραζον*.

[2] For the hypothesis of Mynster, Paulus and others, which *Thiersch* has also repeated (On the Church in the Apostolic Age, 124), that the communities of Galatia were no other than the churches founded by Paul at Iconium, Lystra and Derbe, in his first missionary journey, is incompatible with Acts xvi. 1, 6, xiv. 6. Although these towns may have belonged to the province of Galatia after the death of Amyntas of Galatia, the Acts in the passages referred to does not follow the political but the usual ethnographic division. See *Wieseler's* Chronol. of the Apost. Age, 281 f. *Hilgenfeld* on Gal. xx.

author of the Acts symbolized the craving for salvation with which the population of Macedonia and European humanity in general called for the Apostle to come over to them (Baur, Paul. 146). In Macedonia, the first place in which Paul and Silas appeared was Philippi[1] (xvi. 13). This first appearance is at once signalized by an occurrence which by its entire character must awaken sundry suspicions, namely, the arrest and liberation of the two Apostles. Even the cause of this arrest, the incident with the soothsaying slave, xvi. 16—18, contains much that is remarkable. Baur has justly shown (pp. 146 ff.) that the author wishes this girl to be regarded as one actually possessed by an evil spirit, and her cure as a miracle; and that supranaturalistic theologians, strictly scriptural theologians, have no right to hint at any other view, and from "their standpoint to distinguish between the objective and subjective elements of the record;"[2] in other words, to explain the miracle by natural means.[3] This would not, however, entirely exclude an explanation of the kind: any one who does not share these supranaturalistic preconceptions might still assume that the slave-girl was of diseased mind, and her condition turned to profit by her master or masters (the plural in verse 19 is certainly remarkable); that her utterances recorded in the 17th verse were occa-

[1] Where, be it observed in passing, the river in verse 13 cannot be the Strymon, as the commentators generally, and even Baumgarten, suppose, for the Strymon was more than a day's journey distant from Philippi. Comp. *Rilliet*, Comment sur l'épître aux Philippiens, p. 12. Probably the small river Gangas or Gangites was intended, which flowed past Philippi. Comp. *Forbiger*, Handbook of Ancient Geography, iii. 1069 f.

[2] *Neander*, p. 299, ed. 1.

[3] It is so far praiseworthy that *Baumgarten* renounces any diminution or evasion of the miracle, and when he (p. 208) further supposes that the soothsaying spirit was really connected with the Pythian Apollo, i. e. with the demon who was worshipped as Apollo (1 Cor. x. 20), and for this reason he spoke the truth about Paul and his companions, for the Pythian Apollo was the most moral of the Olympian gods. When Baumgarten amplifies our record in this manner, at any rate all respect is due to the courage with which he endures everything for the sake of his faith in Scripture, even to the appearance of absurdity. In the present case he goes beyond what the text requires, for that the πνεῦμα πύθωνος designates Apollo, or a demon of Apollo, cannot be proved; neither does the well-known passage in *Plutarch*, Def. Orac. 414 E, say so even remotely.

sioned by what she had heard respecting the strangers; that Paul, believing in her possession, commanded the evil spirit to come out of her; and that the impression produced by his word and appearance worked a momentary or more lasting abatement of her malady by natural psychological means—according to the notions of the period, by the exit of a demon. That similar effects occurred in connection with Paul's ministry, we must believe on account of 2 Cor. xii. 12. This view of the affair cannot, however, be regarded as established; for if the narrative is once for all incredible in its present miraculous form, it is just as possible that it is founded on no fact at all as on one capable of natural explanation; and the general character of our author as a writer is not adapted to add weight to the balance in favour of the latter hypothesis.

We shall, however, be obliged much more decidedly to question the historical truth of the further account. The masters of the slave, it is here related, enraged at the diminution of their profits, brought Paul and Silas before the prætors (the duumvirs); and as the people also rose up against them, they commanded them to be beaten and cast into prison; but at midnight the loud prayer of the two captives was followed by an earthquake, all the doors of the prison flew open, and all the prisoners were loosed. This event, combined with the demeanour and words of the Apostles, made such an impression on the jailer, that he not only took them to his house and entertained them, but was baptized, with all his household; on the following morning the prætors also wished to let them go, but Paul, relying on his privileges as a Roman citizen, refused to accept this until they had themselves fetched them out of the prison, and had thereby made them a solemn apology. For an event such as this to appear incredible, it is not requisite to stand upon a platform from which there can be no mention not only of a miracle effected through prayer, but of prayer itself.[1] Every one who has not sold his thinking to the most crass faith in miracles,

[1] *Neander's* insinuation against Baur, Hist. of the Planting and Training, &c., 303.

must stumble at the miracle of our narrative. Even if it be attempted to re-arrange it in one way or another, to say that the earthquake followed immediately on the prayer of Paul and Silas—although this result, regarded as miraculous, is as incredible as are miracles in general—to contemplete a natural coincidence of the prayer and the result is altogether impossible, especially on account of verse 25, where the words ἐπηκροῶντο δὲ αὐτῶν οἱ δέσμιοι are obviously intended to establish the cause and connection of the earthquake: if an endeavour be made to overcome this stumbling-block, there would still remain the yet more offensive statement of the 16th verse, that the fetters fell from all the prisoners in consequence of the earthquake. That chains hanging loose could not be unfastened in any natural way by means of an earthquake,—that, on the other hand, irons or pegs (ξύλον, verse 24) fastened into the wall could not have been thrust out in this way without breaking the limbs of those who were confined in them,—every one who has an idea of mechanics must perforce admit, with Gförer;[1] and that, moreover, according to Gförer's further remark, the whole miracle is entirely superfluous, as the liberation of the two prisoners was effected, not by the miracle, but by the command of the duumvirs, is equally indisputable. But if this must be granted, neither can the earthquake and the springing open of the doors be allowed to stand as historical: the more evident it is that the earthquake is merely a means of liberating the captives from everything that can impede their flight, hence of their fetters above all, the more certainly must we, with the falling off of the fetters, abandon the whole event, which would be objectless without this result.

Not less puzzling are the remaining incidents in our narrative. At the very commencement, the procedure against Paul and Silas is highly striking. The magistrates allow them, it seems, without a hearing, to be beaten and cast into prison. Even if such a brutal proceeding might occasionally occur

[1] Die heilige Sage, i. 446 f.

against aliens, it would scarcely be possible for any authority to indulge in it against Roman citizens such as Paul and Silas; and, at any rate, the duumvirs of Philippi, according to verse 30, would not have ventured to do so had they known the accused to be Romans. And why did they not know them to be so? Would they have neglected to appeal to their Roman citizenship? This would either have been a helplessness such as cannot be imputed to Paul and Silas, or an intentional seeking of suffering, which belongs as little to the character of the Apostle.[1] Or was the proceeding against them, according to the usual supposition, so tumultuous that even the simple Ῥωμαῖός εἰμι was not heard by the authorities? As, according to verse 20, a formal judicial procedure was opened, and as nothing is said of a popular judgment against the accused, this can scarcely be assumed. And when Neander appeals, p. 305, to the τρὶς ἐῤῥαβδίσθην, 2 Cor. xi. 25, it may be rejoined that we do not know the details of this three-fold scourging. In connection with our narrative, the corporal chastisement remains inexplicable, even without disputing the Roman citizenship of Paul and Silas, a possibility to which we must indeed return later on. Moreover, under the given circumstances, of what use was the order (verse 23) to guard Paul and Silas with peculiar strictness? For the object of our narrative, this order certainly has its favourable significance: the more strict the vigilance, the greater is the miracle of deliverance. If Peter, according to xii. 6 ff., was led away by the angel from between two soldiers to whom he was chained, and past two warders, the flight of Paul must be rendered possible from bonds equally difficult to unloose (verse 24), and from an ἐσωτέρα φυλακὴ; but the motive of the duumvirs cannot be surmised. As specially dangerous criminals, they cannot have regarded the two Jews, who were accused of no other transgression than proselytizing, otherwise they would not have released them of their own free will on the following morning;

[1] *Baumgarten*, it is true, contrives (p. 225) to recommend such conduct with great unction.

for that this took place on the report of the jailer (Neander, p. 303), is (1) not stated in our text, and (2) is in itself improbable, as such a report would have sounded much too incredible in Roman ears not to have produced a fresh inquiry instead of a dismissal. There is no more to recommend the hypothesis (in the same) that the duumvirs were more favourably disposed by what they had heard of the prisoners in the interval; for after the brutal treatment they inflicted upon them on the previous evening, they can scarcely have been the people to have made further inquiries concerning them, or to have been won over by the tidings of their preaching. The release of the prisoners, like their maltreatment, therefore, seems, according to Baumgarten's correct view (p. 225), to be an affair of caprice, such as a brutal official perhaps allows himself against vagabonds; while the assumption that they were here dealing with dangerous individuals requiring care and vigilance, cannot be attributed to the duumvirs. As, on this side, the causeless severity of the prætors' conduct appears strange, so, on the other, does the humiliation to which they submit on hearing of the Roman citizenship of the prisoners (verses 38 f.); for as it was unknown to them on the previous day, the disregard of it could not bring on them a responsibility sufficient to induce them to stake their whole official honour on a compensation, the demand for which might indeed here, after the miracle of our narrative, be natural in Paul, but does not quite harmonize in other respects with the character of the Apostle as he describes it himself, 1 Cor. iv. 11 f. Certainly, if the accused had invoked their civic privileges, and had been scourged notwithstanding, the judges might subsequently have been terrified at the consequences of their conduct; but if such an appeal had been omitted, it is utterly inconceivable how they could be charged with the violation of the laws respecting the procedure against Roman citizens. It is indeed a question how matters stood with respect to the Roman citizenship of Paul and Silvanus. With regard to Paul, the statement of our book, it is true, receives an important corroboration in the circumstance that after his arrest at Jerusalem he was sentenced in Judæa but was taken to Rome, as we cannot imagine any sufficient cause for it, except the appeal conceded to Roman citizens alone; and if the binding of the Apostle, even after he made himself known as a Roman citizen (Acts xxii. 30, xxvi. 29), as well as the statement in the Second Epistle to the Corinthians respecting a three-fold corporal chastisement inflicted apparently by the Roman authorities, seems to stand in the way,[1] we must in the end, as long as the reason adduced is not removed, remain satisfied with the assumption, as to the first of an inaccuracy in the representation of the Acts; as to the second, of our ignorance of the details of this three-fold violation of the rights of Roman citizenship. But now, according to verse 37, not only Paul, but Silvanus also, is supposed to be a Roman citizen. This is very remarkable. "Josephus and Philo," observes Schneckenburger,[2] "who carefully enumerate all the favours bestowed on their nation and on individuals of their nation, cite no other instances of Jews enjoying Roman citizenship save Antipater, the progenitor of the family of Herodias (Jos. Ant. xiv. 15), Josephus himself (vita, p. 1031), and the Jews resident at Rome descended from prisoners of war (Philo, Leg. ad Caj. ed. Francf. 1014). If Josephus obviously represents his reception as a remarkable token of honour, it conveys an indirect indication of the rarity of the case that a Jew should attain this honour, which was, moreover, likely enough, considering the known prejudice against the Jews." Now there is certainly to be found in Josephus, Ant. xiv. 13—19, a decree of the Consul L. Lentulus, whereby the Jews who are Roman citizens are released from military service out of consideration for their religion; and a second of L. Antonius, by which permission is given to Roman citizens of Jewish nationality to erect a synagogue; and in B. J. ii. 14, 9, we even find Jews

[1] See the Commentaries on 2 Cor. xi. 25.

[2] Zweck d. Apg. 243.

who are Roman knights.[1] But although this seems to prove that (probably in consequence of the above-mentioned release of several thousand prisoners of war) there were not so very few Jews in possession of Roman civic rights, it is certainly remarkable that the Apostles of the Gentiles should both have been Roman citizens; and although such a coincidence could not be doubted if the evidence were more reliable, the case is otherwise after we have seen in what an uncertain context the statement respecting the civic rights of Silvanus occurs here.

If we take the scene about the jailer into consideration, we shall not be able to avoid sharing the scruples which Baur, p. 151 f., has raised. When the jailer sees the doors open he wants to destroy himself, thinking that the prisoners are fled; that in spite of his own innocence, and even before he has examined, he should contemplate this desperate step, is very strange, even if the blindness of excitement might perhaps explain it. Paul consoles him by announcing that all the prisoners are there; but how can Paul know this in the darkness (verse 29) and in the ἐσωτέρα φυλακὴ in which he is? and how unlikely it is in itself that of all the prisoners not one has made use of the opportunity of flying! For the supposition [2] that the example of Paul and Silas miraculously restrained the others, gives them a tenderness of feeling for which, at least, one might look in vain in our prisons; and it also overlooks the fact that the fellow-prisoners could have been no more aware, in the darkness of the night, that Paul and Silas remained, than could Paul and Silas that they did so. Finally, how does the keeper of the prison know that the earthquake was a vindication of the two Apostles especially, and how could he venture, of his own independent authority, suddenly to liberate these his prisoners, when he had just been on the point of destroying himself on account of the release effected by a higher power? Even if it be possible to discover an answer to one or other of these questions, the in-

[1] See *Wieseler's* Chronol. of the Apost. Age, 62.

[2] *Meyer* and *Baumgarten* on the passage.

credibility of which cannot be strictly proved, it is nevertheless very suspicious that the veracity of an account can only be rescued by the assumption of the most extraordinary events being accumulated here.

As a whole, our narrative contains a chain of improbabilities, out of which it seems scarcely possible, even by conjecture, to extract an historical foundation. That Paul was exposed to ill usage at Philippi is also said in the First Epistle to the Thessalonians, ii. 2. Herein, however, we learn no details respecting the history of this ill usage, and it becomes a question whence the author of our narrative derived his statements,—whether he did not, after all, spin his account from the passage in the Epistle to the Thessalonians, by analogy with other histories of persecution, especially from the history of Peter above mentioned (Acts xii).[1] Further data for the discovery of the historical foundation of fact might be sought in our narrative itself; since in it, as in the case of Pet. v. 17 ff., two reasons for the liberation are commingled,—a supernatural one, which is, however, not essential to his actual liberation (the earthquake), and a natural one (the command of the duumvirs),—it might be conjectured that the latter alone is historical, the former being merely interpolated in order not to leave Paul without miraculous divine assistance on the occasion. But, as in ch. v., we are obliged to regard not only the supernatural assistance of the angel as suspicious, but also the human aid of Gamaliel; so in the case before us the conduct of the duumvirs is not much more explicable than the previous miracle; and if we remove the latter, the former only becomes the more inexplicable. This means of evolving a foundation of fact is therefore cut off from us; and, as in many other cases, we must leave it undecided whether there be any foundation for our narrative, or how much.

[1] *Baur* thinks the reverse (Paulus, p. 483), that 1 Thess. ii. 2 is taken from the Acts. Other reasons, however, induce me to think it probable that the Epistles to the Thessalonians are older than the Acts.

After the events at Philippi, our attention is next drawn to the appearance of the Apostle at Athens; what is related of his previous experiences in Thessalonica and Berea affords no definite marks by which to estimate its historical character, and we can only admit, with Baur (p. 482), that the accusation of the Thessalonian Jews, xvii. 6, *οἱ τὴν οἰκουμένην ἀναστατώσαντες οὗτοι καὶ ἐνθάδε πάρεισιν*, bears the colouring of a later period; for at that time, on their first appearance in Europe, such a reproach could hardly be made against the preachers of the gospel, which till then had scarcely spread beyond the confines of Syria; and although we may remember, with Neander (p. 311), that passion is wont to speak the language of exaggeration, we shall not be able to conceal from ourselves how much more natural this representation would be at a later period which really saw the *οἰκουμένη* agitated by Christianity, than at an earlier one in which the world-wide commotion was only just beginning.

Formerly, no offence was taken at the remarkable narrative about Athens. Baur has only recently pointed out that this account is also full of design and premeditation; that everything is arranged to make the contrast of Christianity with Paganism and pagan civilization appear as strongly marked as possible; that one scarcely sees how Paul comes before the Areopagus; that the Apostle's speech (verse 31) falls too rapidly and abruptly on the resurrection, the mention of which must have made the worst impression on his hearers; that the assertion in verse 23, respecting an altar to an unknown God, contains a confusion of which Paul would scarcely have been guilty on the spot. Something might be objected to the last point; for although Baur has, p. 175, exhaustively proved that in all probability there was no altar in Athens with the inscription of *ἀγνώστῳ θεῷ*, but only with the inscription *ἀγνώστοις θεοῖς*; and even if the former referred, not to *the* unknown God, but to *an* unknown God, it might nevertheless be possible that Paul misread and misinterpreted the inscription. On the other hand, we must admit the correctness of his remaining observations. It is indeed usually supposed that the Apostle was not brought before the assembly of the Areopagus, but that it was only the site of this court, which was held in the open air,[1] which was used by the inquisitive multitude for listening to Paul. But the circumstance that among his few converts an Areopagite is to be found, indicates, according to Baur's accurate remark, an actual assembly of the Areopagus; and every one will, in the first instance, be led to understand this by the words in verse 19, *ἐπιλαβόμενοι αὐτοῦ ἐπὶ τὸν Ἄρειον πάγον ἤγαγον*, in combination with verse 22, *σταθεὶς δὲ ὁ Παῦλος ἐν μέσῳ τοῦ Ἀρείου πάγου.* Paul is seized as *ξένων δαιμονίων καταγγελεύς*, verse 18, led to the Areopagus, and, in the midst of the Areopagus, he holds forth—how can this be understood by the reader otherwise than that he was obliged to defend himself before the Areopagus as the authority which guarded the existing laws, and especially the laws of religion, against innovations? Does not the *καταγγελεὺς ξένων δαιμονίων* recall the accusation against Socrates, even in expression: *ἀδικεῖ . . . ἕτερα καινὰ δαιμόνια εἰσφέρων* (Xen. Mem. i. 1); and the bringing of Paul before the Areopagus, of Stephen being brought before the Sanhedrim?[2] The only difference is, that everything proceeds more harmlessly, that Paul is not accused but merely examined. This particular cannot have been historical according to the whole character of the transaction here related, for a judicial sitting cannot proceed as does the one before us, verse 32; whether it be assumed, with Baur, that the legend of the conversion of an Areopagite, Dionysius, induced our author to transfer the scene to the Areopagus, or whether this occurred merely to procure for Paul the most solemn opportunity possible for the exposition of his doctrine, and also to parallel the discourse before the Jewish Sanhedrim by one before the most venerable judicial

[1] *Hermann*, Greek Antiquities, i. 232 f.

[2] Comp. with verse 18 f., *τινὲς δὲ τῶν Ἐπικουρείων*, &c., *συνέβαλλον αὐτῷ . . . ἐπιλαβόμενοί τε αὐτοῦ ἐπὶ τὸν Ἄρειον πάγον ἤγαγον*; vi. 9, 12, *ἀνέστησαν δέ τινες τῶν ἐκ τῆς συναγωγῆς τῆς λεγομένης Λιβερτίνων*, &c., *καὶ ἐπιστάντες συνήρπασαν αὐτὸν καὶ ἤγαγον εἰς τὸ συνέδριον.*

court of Greece; or, finally, whether yet another motive comes into play here, which may perhaps reveal itself to us later.

As to the speech of the Apostle, the first question is, what guarantee have we of its authenticity? Now if the only answer that can be made to this query is, that on other occasions our author not unfrequently puts words into the mouths of his heroes which they certainly never spoke, — such as Peter's speeches in the first and eleventh chapters, Gamaliel's speech and the discourses at the apostolic council, the two accounts by Paul of his conversion and of what occurred after it,—the overwhelming probability is that he does so in the present case; that in the recognized fashion of the ancients he treats freely composed speeches as if they had been actually made. And if historical probability is not seldom violated by this proceeding, we are fully entitled to conjecture that it is only our author who, in verse 31, makes the Apostle, entirely without provocation, come forward with doctrines which must have been most offensive to his auditors, and which, when put before such an unprepared assembly, could only have the result recorded in the 32nd verse.[1] The didactic wisdom of a Paul does not appear to correspond with such conduct; so much the better does it harmonize with the manner in which in our book a sudden and highly offensive turn produces a concluding scene and a general stormy rising of the auditors against the speaker. (Comp. vii. 51 ff., xxviii. 25.) This is not the only point on which we may rest the hypothesis that the speech at Athens is derived from the narrator himself. Paul does not merely stand before the highest religious tribunal in a position analogous to that of Stephen before the highest Jewish authority, but his address is as nearly related to that of his predecessor as it could be under the altered circumstances. As Stephen is brought before the Sanhedrim by the members of some Jewish schools

[1] For Neander's hypothesis, p. 325, that verse 31 only intends to give an extract of the Apostle's words, is contradicted by the exegetical evidence; the author gives this verse, just as much as the earlier ones, as the Apostle's own words.

in consequence of a dispute; so the adherents of the widest spread school of Greece at that period bring Paul before the Areopagus; as Stephen is accused of upsetting the religion of his fathers and endeavouring to introduce a new one, so is Paul questioned whether it is true that he preaches new deities—the same, in fact, only translated into Greek; as Stephen explains to the Jews that the service of the Temple must certainly cease, for God does not dwell in temples built by hands, so does Paul say the same to the Athenians,[1] naturally adding the further application to idolatry; as, from Old Testament history, Stephen describes to his Jewish auditors the benefits which God has conferred on the people of Israel, so Paul, referring to the ideas and maxims of Grecian philosophers, depicts the benefits which He bestows and has bestowed on all nations, while at the same time he palliates the previous misapprehension of these benefits, as he does in the speech at Lystra, xiv. 16, and as Peter does in another case, iii. 17, by the ignorance permitted by God; finally, as Stephen, by the unexpected vehemence of his concluding words, calls forth an uproar against himself, so does Paul's discourse, verse 31, suddenly take a turn which at once occasions its interruption.[2] Such being the mutual relation of the two accounts, it is impossible to avoid the conjecture that the two speeches and the events within which they are framed issued from one and the same mind—that of our author; that the scene at Athens is merely a counterpart to the scene of Stephen at Jerusalem; and that the differences between the two, which certainly obtrude themselves on every one, are merely owing to the scene at Athens being enacted on Grecian instead of Jewish soil, and being adapted to a harmless result instead of a tragic conclusion. On these grounds we are certainly not justified in declaring the

[1] vii. 48, 50: *ἀλλ' οὐχ ὁ ὕψιστος ἐν χειροποιήτοις κατοικεῖ . . . οὐχὶ ἡ χείρ μου ἐποίησε ταῦτα πάντα;* xvii. 24: *ὁ Θεὸς ὁ ποιήσας τὸν κόσμον καὶ πάντα τὰ ἐν αὐτῷ . . . οὐκ ἐν χειροποιήτοις ναοῖς κατοικεῖ.*

[2] In verse 31, the words recall in expression those put into the mouth of Peter, x. 42, also a slight symptom of the Lukan origin of the speech. See, further, in the last section of our third Part.

whole statement of the Apostle's appearance at Athens to be unhistorical; but we are entitled to question it by the general character of our book, which is of a nature that does not allow criticism to rest satisfied with having no distinct proofs of incorrectness in individual cases, but compels it also to require positive pledges of the veracity of its statements, at least in all cases in which are mingled elements of a doubtfully historical character.[1]

We shall return afterwards to the report of our book respecting Paul's ministry at Corinth (xviii. 1—18), so far as it gives occasion to critical remarks, and we therefore pass it by at present. For the same reason we shall not enter minutely on the Apostle's journey to Palestine, xviii. 18—23, but will turn at once to what is related of his sojourn at Ephesus.

The first thing which here strikes us is the problematical appearance of John's disciples, xix. 1—7. This appearance is problematical because the details of the description do not blend into any connected view. On one side, these disciples of John are *μαθηταὶ*, i. e., according to the unvarying idiom of our book, Christians; they have accepted the faith in Christ (*πιστεύσαντες*, verse 24); on the other, they are still so far removed from Christianity that they have neither been baptized in the name of Jesus, nor have they heard anything of a Holy Ghost. If this by itself appears contradictory, the difficulty increases when we hear in xviii. 24 f. of another disciple of John, Apollos, who is instructed in Christianity (*κατηχημένος τὴν ὁδὸν τοῦ κυρίου*), and appears with distinction as a teacher (*ἐδίδασκεν ἀκριβῶς τὰ περὶ*

[1] I write this, apprehending that apologists such as *Lechler* (on the Apost. and Post.-Apost. Period) may again see in it one of the strangest evidences of the boundless caprice of our criticism. For my part, I can only regard such opinions as a further proof of how little the majority of our theologians comprehend the nature and task of historical evidence. Instead of first inquiring whether a statement is sufficiently corroborated, and judging that to which the requisite evidence is wanting by other grounds of historical probability, the trustworthiness of the witnesses is assumed on the most superficial evidence, and hence the correctness of their statements is taken for granted, so far as they do not contain anything absolutely incredible. But what can be incredible to theologians whose first postulate is miracle?

τοῦ κυρίου), yet nevertheless knows nothing of the baptism of Christ, but only of the baptism of John. How, we musk ask with Baur (p. 183), can these two be thought of together, and combined into a clear idea? Neander is of opinion, like Olshausen before him, that these disciples of John had not advanced beyond a very deficient knowledge of the person and doctrine of Christ (p. 362); and he applies the same view to Apollos (p. 378), regardless of the κατηχημένος τὴν ὁδὸν τοῦ κυρίου and the ἐδίδασκεν ἀκριβῶς τὰ περὶ τοῦ κυρίου. Similarly, Baumgarten (ii. a, 336) thinks that Apollos considered Jesus, like John, merely a forerunner of the Messiah, as if any one still unacquainted with the fundamental article of the Messiahship of Jesus could be called a proficient in the doctrine of Jesus! But should we still entertain any doubt, Neander removes it by the assertion (p. 361) "that by an intrinsically hazy and indefinite phenomenon no image can be produced in clear and distinct outlines." This observation, only partially true in itself, cannot in any case justify the combination of such incompatible features as the accurate knowledge of the Christian doctrine and the non-acquaintance with Christian baptism which nevertheless formed one of the first elements of Christianity; comp. Heb. vi. 2. These features are in truth absolutely irreconcilable; hence they can only form a part of our author's delineation, and not of objective fact; and the question cannot be, how we are to explain the historical phenomenon which they record, but merely, how we are to explain the record itself.[1] The further narrative of John's disciples must be judged by the standard of our earlier discussions with regard to the γλώσσαις λαλεῖν, which cannot here of course be understood in any other way than as the Acts, according to its unequivocal declarations, ii. comp. with x. 47, xi. 15, wishes it to be understood. It is, moreover, remarkable that the disciples of John, in xix., are baptized afresh; while nothing is said of such a ceremony with regard to Apollos.

[1] More of this below.

The account of the disciples of John is followed, in xix. 11 f., by a description of the Apostle's miraculous ministry at Ephesus, which, from its marvellous character, is among the most incredible things of the sort transmitted in the New Testament. So many and such great miracles are supposed to have occurred by means of Paul, that even the handkerchiefs and aprons which he had worn healed the sick and the possessed on whom they were laid. It is impossible to think of any natural explanation of this result; for the faith of those who were healed, to which even De Wette refers us, must in truth have been able to remove mountains, not in a figurative sense merely, if it produced such an effect not only in one or two cases under specially favourable circumstances, but *methodically*, as was the case according to the representation of our book. But even from the standpoint of the miraculous faith presented in our book, such an utterly crass and magical representation of the healing power of the Apostle has too much that is offensive; and it requires something to assert, with Meyer, on this point, in the name of historical criticism, that "the healing power of Paul, being analogous to the miraculous power of Jesus, was capable at his desire of being conducted to the suffering subjects by means of the clothes which were begged from him." We at least should be at a loss to know what relic-legends "historical criticism" would be ashamed of, if it could accept such hypotheses.[1] Paul's apostolic power of miracles appears in a light all the more brilliant, the more completely it throws into the shade both Jewish and heathen magic. It is probably in this sense that we must regard the circumstance that our author immediately appends to the description of Paul's miracles the two episodes of the Jewish exorcists, xix. 13—17, and the burning of the books of magic at

[1] Whoever may wish for another confirmation of this opinion, can now find it in *Baumgarten's* vindication of the narrative (Comm. ii. b. 15 ff.), which, with comparatively small alteration, might be transferred to the holy coat of Treves or any other relic of the kind. It actually seems that if the genuineness of the holy coat were to be proved, Baumgarten would consider the miracle quite in order.

Ephesus, xix. 18 f. Both incidents are credible in themselves; it is quite possible that a band of exorcists, giving themselves out for sons or disciples of a Jewish high-priest,[1] may have made an experience of the futility of their arts in the person of a lunatic who had heard something of Paul and of Christ. There is nothing intrinsically improbable in the fact that at Ephesus, that abode of Greco-Oriental magic, some were found among the newly-converted who had formerly plied forbidden arts, and who now burnt their books of magic; even if the value of these books, 50,000 drachmae, appears somewhat high, according to the price of books at that period. But the context in which these things are recorded casts suspicion on them also; for the narrative of the Jewish exorcists partly presupposes the miracles of Paul, and partly serves them as a foil, and so far it seems to be designed to strengthen the impression of the preceding obviously unhistorical statements; but with this incident our record, verse 18, also connects the burning of the books of magic by representing it as an effect of the fear to which it had given rise. We have no right to substract from this context; and although we cannot assert that the narratives in question owe their origin to the context alone, and must therefore be unhistorical, we are nevertheless equally incapable of deciding how much is historical.

From the same point of view, Baur (Paul. 191) also regards the narrative of the insurrection of Demetrius, xix. 23 ff. He considers it as an ideal representation of the fertile ministry of the Apostle, which threatened to depopulate even the temple of the Ephesian Artemis, of world-wide celebrity. And we cannot deny the possibility of this view when we take into consideration the general character of our book. In this case, however, besides the circumstance that the narrative does not suffer from any internal improbability, several small features, for the fabrication of which no inducement can be found (such

[1] As the word is interpreted by *Baur*, in Paulus, 189.

as verses 29—31, 33), speak in its favour;[1] and although the vivid colouring of the scene may partially belong to the author, the fact nevertheless appears correct that, shortly before Paul's departure from Ephesus, disturbances broke out against him.

5. Paul's last Journey to Jerusalem; his Imprisonment in Palestine.

Before the insurrection of Demetrius, Paul had already intended to go to Jerusalem, but previously to visit Macedonia and Achaia (xix. 21). After this occurrence he carried out his purpose (xx. 1). He passed by Macedonia into Greece, remained there three months, and then, being prevented by an ambush on the part of the Jews from taking the shorter sea passage, he returned through Macedonia to Asia Minor, took ship at Assos, and passing by Miletus Tyre and Ptolemais to Cæsarea, went thence to Jerusalem.

Our author imparts no details respecting the motive and occasion of this journey. In xix. 21 he only states: ὡς δὲ ἐπληρώθη ταῦτα, ἔθετο ὁ Παῦλος ἐν τῷ πνεύματι, διελθὼν τὴν Μακεδονίαν καὶ Ἀχαΐαν πορεύεσθαι εἰς Ἱερουσαλὴμ, εἰπών· ὅτι μετὰ τὸ γενέσθαι με ἐκεῖ δεῖ με καὶ Ῥώμην ἰδεῖν. It must be owned that Schneckenburger[2] is right in saying that this wish to go to Jerusalem, for which no further reason is given, proceeding out of the affairs and results of the ministry at Ephesus, can only be understood by the rule of xviii. 21, where the Apostle, equally without inducement, travels there merely because he is absolutely determined on passing the next feast at Jerusalem, especially as it is one of the national festivals of the Jews to which he is so

[1] The statement, 2 Cor. i. 8, which *Wieseler*, Chronol. of the Post.-Apost. Age, 54 f., refers to our narrative, can as little be cited in its favour as the θηριομαχεῖν, 1 Cor. xv. 32, since, according to the Acts, Paul incurred no personal danger; and if, as is certainly not impossible, we endeavour to find in the events here indicated the historical occasion of our record, we must not only, like Wieseler, abandon accuracy and completeness in the latter, but historical truth as well.

[2] Zweck der Apg. p. 67.

urgently hastening that he even passes by Ephesus in order not to miss it: ἔσπευδε γάρ, εἰ δυνατὸν ἦν αὐτῷ, τὴν ἡμέραν τῆς πεντηκοστῆς γενέσθαι εἰς Ἱεροσόλυμα (xx. 16). In favour of this view, Schneckenburger, not without reason, refers to xxiv. 11, 17, where Paul explicitly defines the object of his journey to be, that he may worship and sacrifice in Jerusalem, and to the complete silence of our author respecting the journey of several months' duration to Achaia, which falls entirely into the background compared to Jerusalem; whereas the regulation of the Corinthian affairs must alone render it an important act in the ministry of the Apostle. We see from the Pauline Epistles [1] that Paul had a very definite motive for that journey in the collection, the produce of which he no doubt wished to convey himself, in order to make use of the favourable impression of that large assistance to reconcile the party in Palestine to his ministry among the Gentiles. That this motive should have remained unknown to our author is absolutely incredible, at least if he was really a companion of the Apostle; but even a later one must have been informed of the state of the affair, both by Paul's Epistles, which can scarcely have been unknown to him, and by the account of the journey by an eye-witness in the latter part of the Acts. That our author was also aware of it is very probable from xxiv. 17. If he nevertheless preserves silence respecting the real motive of the journey,[2] he must have had his special reasons for doing so. What these were can only be investigated later; but we may even now assert that we have to do here not with a mere *gap* in the narrative, but with an actual *alteration* in the fact. Not merely is the real cause of the journey omitted, but another is stated in its place, which

[1] 1 Cor. xvi. 1 ff.; 2 Cor. viii. f.; Rom. xv. 25 ff.; and also *Schneckenburger*, 117 f.

[2] For xxiv. 17, taken literally, can be understood only as referring to an act of personal piety towards the people of Israel, as the gift of a sacrificial offering in the service of the Temple, or such like, not to the conveyance of the alms of a community to needy Christians; and to discover, with *Baumgarten*, ii. b. 48, the collection in xxiv. 4, because the companions of Paul could only be thought of as the bearers of such a donation, requires as much courage as ingenuity.

from the Apostle's own declarations cannot possibly have been his own decision. This appears still more distinctly from the circumstance that our book makes Paul, even before his departure from Ephesus,—nay, even before the insurrection of Demetrius,—express his fixed determination to go to Jerusalem; while Paul himself, in an Epistle, 1 Cor. xvi. 4, which was undoubtedly written[1] at this very time, still makes the journey to Jerusalem dependent on the result of the collection, which he could not ascertain before his visit to Macedonia and Achaia. According to this authentic statement, it is highly improbable that he was so resolutely determined, as our book maintains, even before the insurrection of Demetrius; and if the assertion is unmistakably connected with the whole representation of the journey to Jerusalem, the latter becomes not a little suspicious.

In the account of the journey in xx. ff., the incident about Eutychus next attracts our attention. The recent expositors, indeed, mostly deny that an actual raising of the dead is here intended; but that it is so, has been exhaustively proved by Schneckenburger (p. 54). How little verse 10 proves the reverse is shown by comparison with Matt. ix. 24; besides which, it is only after contact with Paul, with which we must imagine the communication of renewed vital power to be connected, that it is said of the deceased, his life is in him. On the contrary, the whole proceeding accords so completely with instances of raising from the dead both in the Old and New Testament,[2] that we must assume the same here (what other meaning can it have, than that Paul throws himself on the apparently dead youth

[1] On this see *Rückert's* Commentary, pp. 9 f.; *Wieseler's* Chronology of the Acts, pp. 318 ff.

[2] Verse 10, *ὁ Παῦλος ἐπέπεσεν αὐτῷ καὶ συμπεριλαβὼν εἶπε·*; comp. 2 Kings iv. 34, *καὶ ἐκοιμήθη ἐπὶ τὸ παιδάριον*, &c.; and the whole narrative, 1 Kings xvii. 17 ff.; Acts ix. 36 ff.; Matt. ix. 23 ff. As Paul here says, verse 10, *μὴ θορυβεῖσθε· ἡ γὰρ ψυχὴ αὐτοῦ ἐν αὐτῷ ἐστιν*, so Jesus, in Luke viii. 52, *μὴ κλαίετε, οὐκ ἀπέθανεν*; Matt. ix. 24, (*ἰδὼν τὸν ὄχλον θορυβούμενον*) *ἀναχωρεῖτε, οὐ γὰρ ἀπέθανε τὸ κοράσιον*; and, still more closely, Mark v. 39, *τί θορυβεῖσθε καὶ κλαίετε*, &c.

and embraces him? for these are not the movements of a person medically examining a case of apparent death). Similarly Schneckenburger justly maintains that ἤρθη νεκρὸς, verse 9, is not synonymous with ἤρθη ὡς νεκρὸς, that the former does not assert the death of Eutychus merely in the name of the people present, but in the name of the writer himself. This certainly does not exclude the possibility that the person supposed to be dead was not actually dead, nor that our author, in the source whence he derived his narrative, may have found the record of a merely natural though extraordinary incident; only in the latter case he would have changed the colouring of the original record and introduced into the simple narration of what happened the conception of it as a miracle.

From Miletus, Paul summoned (xx. 17) the elders of the Ephesian community, in order to take leave of them once more. The authenticity of the speech which the Acts puts into his mouth on this occasion is indeed warmly defended against the doubts of modern critics[1] by the opposite party,[2] but the actual refutation of these doubts has scarcely been successful. The first question here again is, whether, independently of the nature of the speech itself, we have sufficient grounds for asserting it to be genuine. As nothing is told us of the manner in which it was transmitted to the author, the assertion can only rest on our general reliance on his trustworthiness. But are his other records of a kind to justify such reliance? Do the speeches in our book especially bear the general impress of authenticity? After the results of previous investigations, we can only answer the question in the negative. There remains therefore nothing but internal evidence derived from the speech itself as it lies before us. And Neander really imagines that he has discovered indications that it did not originate in the same mind with the rest of the Acts. The three years' sojourn of the

[1] *Baur*, Pastoral Epistles, pp. 92 ff.; Paul. 177 ff. *Schneckenburger*, Zweck der Apg. 133 ff.

[2] *Neander* elsewhere, 473 ff. *Baumgarten* on the passage.

Apostle at Ephesus, xx. 31, does not quite accord with our author's own calculation, xix. 10. Yet this accordance exists not merely if we refer the τριετία to Paul's total sojourn in Ephesus and its neighbourhood, but even if we refer it to his stay in Ephesus alone; for if to the two years, xix. 10, the three months, xix. 8, are added, besides the indefinite period, xix. 22, we obtain for the sojourn at Ephesus about two years and a half, a space of time which might well be designated in round numbers as τριετία, with more justice than, for instance, the day and two nights during which Christ laid in the tomb are usually reckoned three days. Further traces of authenticity Neander discerns in the mention of the teaching from house to house, verse 20, which is certainly not mentioned in Luke's previous narrative, but is excluded by it; and in the warnings of prophetic voices, verse 23, which however, regarded as unhistorical, would point rather to Luke than to Paul; regarded as historical, to the one as much as to the other; finally, in the 22nd verse, where an importance is ascribed to Paul's journey to Jerusalem that does not appear in other parts of the Acts. But the last is not correct; a higher necessity for the journey to Jerusalem is asserted by the Acts also in xxi. 12 ff., and even in xix. 21; moreover, it may also be asked if the words, δεδεμένος τῷ πνεύματι, verse 22, are not to be interpreted by analogy with verse 23, "bound (imprisoned) in the spirit." The Apostle's sayings respecting his approaching end are also supposed to prove the authenticity of the speech; for as the result did not correspond to these expectations, they must have appertained to Paul himself, and not to the author writing subsequently.[1] But of the Apostle's *immediately* impending death, verses 22 ff. say nothing,[2] but only that Paul should not again be liberated from his captivity; and according to the Acts this

[1] *Baumgarten*, Comm. ii. b. 60 f.

[2] And equally little do the three critics whom Baumgarten unaccountably opposes with the question, how they can here assume a *vaticinium post eventum*, when they all say at the same moment that the prediction was not realized.

did not take place. Such traces of authenticity, therefore, cannot prove much. In our estimation, several opposite features have far more weight. In the first place, the language of the speech is unmistakably that of Luke, not of Paul (see below); and if we do not possess the Apostle's words, it is impossible to know how far we have his thoughts. Then the sayings respecting the impending fate of the Apostle (verses 22 f., 25) and the false teachers who should arise in Ephesus (verse 29), include predictions which look incomparably more like a *vaticinium post eventum* than a conjecture uttered under the circumstances of the time. Although Paul may have had a "presentiment" of his impending death (Neander), he could not possibly by natural means *assert* (ἰδοὺ ἐγὼ οἶδα) that none of those assembled would see him again;[1] and if the distinct prediction of false teachers may in itself be more easily explained from the Apostle's standpoint, the more minute description of them suggests the standpoint of a later period; instead of opponents present before him, who were not lacking (1 Cor. xvi. 9), he speaks only of those who were to come after his departure (or his decease),[2] and that, too, not only in the community in which he was already able to perceive the germs of these heresies, but also extraneously (verses 29 f.). These heresiarchs themselves are portrayed without any definite and distinct outline, such as we usually find in the Apostle's polemics, but only in the general expressions which were habitually employed in the second century with regard to the heretics of that age;[3] they are ἄνδρες λαλοῦντες διεστραμμένα, λύκοι βαρεῖς, μὴ φειδόμενοι τοῦ ποιμνίου. This vagueness of expression was natural if a later person wished here to indicate appearances of which a more minute portrayal could not be given without a glaring anachronism; the same cause will also account for the

[1] See *Baur's* Paulus, 179.

[2] Similarly, 1 Tim. iv. 1; 2 Tim. iii. 1, iv. 3, &c.

[3] So, for instance, *Justin* says, i. Apol. 58, with reference to Marcion: ᾧ πολλοὶ πεισθέντες . . . ἀλόγως ὡς ὑπὸ λύκου ἄρνες συνηρπασμένοι βορὰ τῶν ἀθέων δογμάτων καὶ δαιμόνων γίνονται; and with the same metaphor, *Ign.* Smyrn. 4, terms the heretics, θηρία ἀνθρωπόμορφα.

indistinct description of the heretics in the Pastoral Epistles; in the mouth of Paul it must surprise us. Thus we have here an historical prolepsis, not the Apostle's, but his historian's. Verse 23, comp. xxi. 10 ff., seems to contain a similar anticipation of the future. To this must be added, that the whole tendency of the speech seems to betray the interests and standpoint of a later period. For whereas, under the circumstances given, we ought to expect that the admonition and instruction of the elders of the Church would constitute the chief import of the discourse, it takes instead, according to Schneckenburger and Baur's just observation, an entirely apologetic direction. It opens with the description of the fidelity and self-sacrifice shown by Paul at Ephesus; the mention of menaced dangers which immediately follows is likewise employed to illustrate the Apostle's contempt for life in the service of the Lord (verse 24); hereupon follows a renewed assurance of the conscientious fulfilment of his office (verses 26 f.); then, after a short admonition and caution against false teachers,[1] verse 31, again a reminiscence of Paul's apostolic zeal; and until the end (verses 33—35) a further elaboration of the same theme. Did Paul require such self-justification, not to say self-laudation, before the elders of a church in which he had laboured for three years: and can we expect that a man so devoted to his cause, in taking leave of disciples and coadjutors whom he never expected to see again, instead of all that might be useful to them and to the church they managed, should have nothing more important to do than to call to mind his own services with ever fresh reiteration? Is this not incomparably more suitable to a later admirer of the Apostle, who had already learnt by experience that these services were misunderstood by many? The greater number of commentators, indeed, refuse to acknowledge this tendency of our discourse, obvious as it is. Although nearly the whole speech treats only of the merits and faithful

[1] This may also have an apologetic object, whether it be to distinguish Paul from the heretics who appealed to him, or as a caution against the adversaries who vituperated him.

service of the Apostle, he is not supposed to speak actually of himself, but of others, i.e. of the elders present, to whom he offers himself as an example. This view is certainly founded on a true feeling of what ought to be expected of an apostolic address under such circumstances; but in the address itself the admonitory object is observable in but few passages (verses 28, 31, 32), whereas the vindication and laudation of the Apostle occupy a space entirely disproportionate. At the conclusion of the address especially, in which the chief importance centres, this apologetic design distinctly obtrudes itself; for while we know from the Pauline Epistles what stress the Apostle laid upon the fact, in opposition to his adversaries, that he did not allow himself to be supported by the churches (1 Cor. iv. 12, ix. 12 ff.; 2 Cor. xi. 8, 12), we see on the same testimony (1 Cor. ix. 6 ff.; Gal. vi. 6) that he was nevertheless far from requiring from others a sacrifice which he himself made for special reasons; and Neander's distinction (pp. 480 f.), that the elders of the church were differently situated in this respect from the perambulating missionaries, finds no support in his own sayings; in verses 33—35, therefore, the Apostle could not hold up his own example for unqualified imitation, but he could merely mention his conduct in order to offer himself as a pattern of the disposition which gave rise to his mode of action as a model of self-sacrificing love. But is it consistent with the character of the Apostle, in lieu of the example of Christ, to place his own so much in the foreground, not with reference to the special treatment of given circumstances and practical questions conditioned by his position, as in 1 Cor. vi. 6—16, x. 32 f., xi. 1, but for moral purposes in general?

On these grounds we can only consider the speech as the work of our narrator, without admitting even the *partial* authenticity which Schneckenburger[1] wishes to preserve for it; for, in

[1] If our speech is a composition of Luke's, it may easily be conceived that, without impugning its essentially historic character, many features *ex eventu* may be mingled with it.

the first place, we have not the slightest positive reason for this hypothesis; secondly, the whole tendency of the speech proves itself to be historically improbable. But with the speech the entire situation becomes improbable, being, indeed, recounted solely for the sake of the speech. Beautiful and affecting as is the concluding scene, and credible as it is that such scenes not seldom occurred, we must feel scruples about this one, if only because in verse 38 it hinges on the unhistorical saying of verse 25. What the narrative really gives us is much less a record of this particular incident than a retrospect of the whole apostolic ministry of Paul, which the author clothes in a farewell address from the latter in the same manner as the author of Deuteronomy clothes his new legislation in a farewell address from Moses; and our concluding verses represent, not so much the impression which the Ephesian elders received from Paul's discourse, as the impression which the reader of the Acts is to receive from the previous narrative.

The further journey of the Apostle, until his arrival at Jerusalem, offers no stumbling-block to historical criticism; even the single unusual occurrence recorded of it, the prophecy of Agabus, xxi. 10 ff., is not of the sort that might not actually have occurred; any one who knew the disposition of the Jews of Jerusalem against Paul might well foresee that he would scarcely leave the capital without injury.

So much the more suspicious is the very first thing related of the Apostle in Jerusalem (xxi. 17 ff.), his meeting with the elders and the step which they induce him to take. By their advice, he resolves on defraying the costs involved in the fulfilment of a vow in behalf of four Nazarites, and in undertaking the sacred rites appertaining to it (*ἁγνίσθητι σὺν αὐτοῖς*, v. 24). We need not here inquire whether this expression implies an actual adoption of Nazaritism, i.e. an abbreviated Nazaritism of which we know nothing more; or whether, as Wieseler has recently rendered probable,[1]

[1] Chronol. of Apost. Age, 105 ff. Yet compare, on the other hand, *Baur*, Tübingen Journal, 1849, 480 ff.

it merely signifies a share in the concluding sacrifices and purifications connected with it. We need not even inquire more minutely whether, consistently with his principles, the Apostle was able to partake in either of these rites. With respect to Nazaritism, it is scarcely credible; for what meaning could there be in such a vow if not that of a meritorious work, a light in which Paul could scarcely regard it; hence, how could he submit to it without hypocrisy? That participation in Jewish sacrifices, or even the defrayal of the costs of such sacrifices, would have been impossible to him, we cannot quite so positively assert. Although he was individually able to dispense with these external sacrifices, still we do not know with certainty whether they appeared to him absolutely irreconcilable with faith in redemption by the sacrifice of Christ, and whether this may not have constituted an occasion for that compliance with Jewish customs which, according to 1 Cor. ix. 20, he made a point of duty wherever it might be advantageous to the cause of the gospel. But, even admitting this, it is nevertheless quite incredible that Paul should have consented to the course here ascribed to him in the sense and manner recorded by our book. According to it, James tells him that it has come to the ears of the believing Jews that he induces the Jews who are among the Gentiles (the Hellenistic Christians), to circumcise their children no more, and to forsake the Mosaic Law. Now, to prove that this accusation is untrue (ὅτι ὧν κατήχηνται περὶ σοῦ οὐδέν ἐστιν), and that he also faithfully adheres to the Law (στοιχεῖς καὶ αὐτὸς τὸν νόμον φυλάσσων), Paul is advised to undertake the Nazarite sacrifices. On this representation he actually does so. In our book, the proceeding cannot certainly surprise us, as was already intimated in treating of the fifteenth chapter; neither James nor Peter does anything that is not required or taken for granted by the decisions of the apostolic council. James assumes that, in loyal obedience to these decisions, Paul not only observes the Law himself, but also induces the converted Grecians to follow it, and to circumcise their children, as, according to these very decisions, both he and they, born Jews, were bound to do; on the other hand, he admits the Gentile Christians to be differently situated, and that Paul was justified in demanding from them no more than the observance of the so-called precepts of Noah: Paul on his part recognizes this assumption, and to confirm it in practice he submits himself to the proof of subservience to the Law recommended to him by James. This Nazarite sacrifice is merely the declaration in act of his continued acknowledgment of the fundamental law by which, at the apostolic council, the relation of Gentile and Jewish Christians to Mosaism had been established,—an acknowledgment which is not recorded here at the conclusion of his public ministry without significance; it guarantees that he had firmly adhered during the whole of his official labours to the principles which he here repeatedly acknowledges; that it is really a mere calumny when it is reported of him that he has seduced the Jews to desert the Law. Hence, far from seeing in this transaction, like Neander (p. 187), only a compliance on the part of the Apostle with the weaknesses of others, it much rather appears, from the standpoint of our book, as the simplest and most natural application of his principles; as a born Jew, Paul the individual is as much bound as all other Jewish Christians to observe the Law, and he does not think of evading this duty. Neander's advice, "not to lay too much stress on James's words in verse 24," i.e. not to heed what our book enunciates with incontrovertible distinctness, to close our ears to the unwelcome explanation—this advice we cannot follow, for the very reason that it is not at all required by the context; in this Paul is really a *νόμον φυλάσσων*; why should he scruple to acknowledge himself as such?

The case is certainly different if we turn from the Paul of the Acts to the historical Paul and his principles. The former could do without hesitation what is related of him in the Acts, but would it have been possible for the latter? Could he publicly and explicitly declare that he had always adhered to the decisions of the apostolic council; that as a Jew he deemed himself bound to observe the Law, and actually fulfilled the obligation; that it was mere calumny if it was reported that he seduced the Jewish Christians no longer to circumcise their children, and not to observe the Law? If we listen to Neander alone, in place of all the rest, one might almost believe that he could have done this without scruple. "Without deviating from principles of the strictest veracity, Paul might repudiate these accusations, for he was far from wishing to anticipate historical development in such an arbitrary manner; it was, in fact, the principle enunciated by himself, that every one was to remain in the position in which the call to Christianity had reached him, in no case voluntarily to abandon it," &c. (p. 486); "he only opposed (p. 485) the external observance of Judaism in so far as the justification and sanctification of mankind were made dependent upon it. It was his principle that no one was to abandon the earthly, national or civic position which he occupied at the time of his conversion to Christianity, unless some important reason impelled him to do so; and in accordance with this principle he allowed the Jews to persist in their Jewish peculiarities, of which the observance of the Mosaic Law formed a part." What light work has Neander made of the proof of this pregnant assertion! His only evidence is 1 Cor. vii. 18 ff.: *Περιτετμημένος τις ἐκλήθη, μὴ ἐπισπάσθω· ἐν ἀκροβυστίᾳ τις ἐκλήθη, μὴ περιτεμνέσθω . . . . . Ἕκαστος ἐν τῇ κλήσει ᾗ ἐκλήθη ἐν ταύτῃ μενέτω. Δοῦλος ἐκλήθης, μή σοι μελέτω· ἀλλ' εἰ καὶ δύνασαι ἐλεύθερος γενέσθαι, μᾶλλον χρῆσαι.* Hence, because the Apostle dissuades his followers from making any violent alteration in their external relations and circumstances, the religious confession of Christians was indifferent to him also! Because the Christian as such was not to abandon his earthly, national (how equivocal! the national religion was a part of the nationality of the Jews), civic positions, could he likewise as a Christian continue to be a

Jew? (and why not a heathen also?) Because the Christian might feel that he was free in Christ even when a slave, he could do so also as a slave of the Law. Because Paul disapproves of converted Jews putting on an artificial foreskin,[1] and hereby displaying the same over-appreciation of externals as the Gentile Christian who was circumcised, he would probably have disapproved equally of Jewish Christians neglecting the circumcision of their children, as if this had not been prohibited by the principles laid down in the very passage quoted; for the children of Christians are called ἐν ἀκροβυστίᾳ (compare also 1 Cor. vii. 14); hence to them also applies the μὴ περιτεμνέσθω. On such negative testimony, principles are attributed to the Apostle against which every line of his Epistles is a protest. The remarks occasioned by the fifteenth chapter are applicable here also. Paul says without reservation, in Gal. v. 2, that him who is circumcised Christ profiteth nothing; he is a debtor to fulfil the whole Law, and has forfeited grace; and of him could it be calumniously reported that he restrains the Jews from circumcising their children? Paul everywhere declares even when expressly dealing with Jewish Christians, that for Christians the Law is repealed, and there is no other assertion that so profoundly permeates his innermost thoughts; but nevertheless it is, forsooth, mere calumny that he no longer observed the Law himself, and restrained others from its observance![2] It is scarcely necessary to linger any longer over the contradictions in which Neander's evasions are involved;[3] and as to the assurance that the Apostle disapproved of the Law and circumcision only in so far as justification was made dependent on them,[4] we may simply refer to what has been already observed on the occasion of the supposed circumcision of Timothy. Finally,

[1] Compare the commentators on ἐπισπᾶσθαι.

[2] See the whole Epistle to the Romans, but especially vii. 1 ff.

[3] Still less are we disposed to enter minutely on *Baumgarten's* historical Metaphysics, Comm. ii. b. 147 ff.

[4] Besides *Neander*, *Meyer*, *De Wette*, and others.

after the above, we need scarcely point out expressly that, with the decisions of the council in the fifteenth chapter, must be abandoned, not only the appeal of James to these resolutions, but likewise Paul's course of procedure, which our book sets forth in a perfectly correct point of view as a ratification of them.

But if Paul can in no case have performed the Nazarite sacrifice from the motive and for the object stated by the Acts,[1] it is very doubtful whether he performed it at all. Schneckenburger (p. 65) is indeed of opinion that we have no reason to doubt this, for "more minute explanations may have preceded it." Only it cannot be seen what other explanations were needful or possible in addition to the completely unquestionable one given by James. As the Acts represent the affair, the only motive for Paul's procedure is the one stated; but if this is unhistorical, the general possibility would still remain, that what the Apostle cannot have done for this reason, he may yet have done for some other reason unknown to us. But before making this conjecture, we must first know that he actually did it, and, moreover, we must know it on some authority extraneous to our book. Here Paul's Nazarite sacrifice has undeniably the sole significance of testifying his adhesion to the Mosaic Law. If it is incredible that it was offered by Paul with this object, the only question can be, which is most likely, that the author imparted to a real transaction of the Apostle a motive suitable only to himself, not to the historical Paul; or that, from his idea of the Apostle's whole character, he ascribed to him a corresponding course of procedure? Now we see from the whole representation of our book, that this idea of Paul's character and his relation to Mosaism was firmly established in the author's mind, quite independently of the narrative before us; whereas we are nowhere informed that the story of the Nazarite sacrifice existed

[1] As even *Thiersch* acknowledges (The Church in the Apostolic Age, 172), who easily enough surmounts the difficulty of this admission by the remarkable and genuinely Irvingite hypothesis that Paul did not recognize this motive, but, being at Jerusalem in the episcopal domain of James, it was his duty to comply with his directions.

independently of the story before us. Under these circumstances, the preponderating probability is, that the story is derived from this very representation, and is, therefore, without any foundation in fact. That Paul was arrested in the Temple at Jerusalem, in consequence of an insurrection, may nevertheless be correct; for he might well have visited the Temple without this particular object.[1]

Because of the following account of Paul's arrest (xxi. 27—xxii. 29), Baur (pp. 208 ff.) has justly questioned the authenticity of the Apostle's discourse in xxii. 1 ff. It is already suspicious that, contrary to all rules of prudence, the Roman Tribune so readily granted him permission to make this address. "Is it likely," we must ask with Baur, "that the Tribune, having arrested the Apostle in the midst of a most tumultuous scene, should grant to a prisoner, whom a moment before he had held to be an insurgent of the most dangerous description, and of

[1] A peculiar difficulty arises in this narrative, from the words of James, v. 20, *θεωρεῖς, ἀδελφὲ, πόσαι μυριάδες εἰσὶν Ἰουδαίων τῶν πεπιστευκότων*, &c., for so many myriads of Jewish Christians can never have been at Jerusalem; and even if, with *Neander* (p. 483), we reckon also the visitors to the feast, the expression still appears too strong. The simplest thing would be to refer it not only to the Jewish Christians of Jerusalem, but to the total number; only it is opposed by the *θεωρεῖς* and the whole context of the passage, which, without an intimation of a change of subject, continues to speak of the Jerusalemites. Thus we have here a strong hyperbole, and no one can be hindered from seeing in this unhistorical exaggeration a symptom that our author (from whom alone, according to what has been said, the words of James can have been derived) was here contemplating not only the believing Jews in Jerusalem, but the Jewish Christians collectively, who certainly amounted to several myriads. In the further remark, that these were all zealous of the Law, and were full of mistrust respecting Paul, *Baur* (p. 200) recognizes an involuntary admission on the part of the author of the real disposition of the Jerusalemites. This is undoubtedly correct, and we may assuredly take the words, *πάντες ζηλωταὶ τοῦ νόμου ὑπάρχουσιν*, in their strictest interpretation. On the other hand, the observation that this admission is in contradiction with the general representation of our book, needs some limitation. For verse 21 does not say that the Jewish Christians already positively hold Paul as a renegade from the Law, but that they *suspect* him of this apostacy, and that it would be appropriate to refute such an unfounded suspicion; the words, verse 21, *κατηχήθησαν περὶ σοῦ*, must not be translated, as by *Baumgarten*, p. 144, "they have been informed," for this would assume the truth of the accusation, but in accordance with the proper signification of *κατηχεῖν*, "it has come to their ears." If Paul indeed pursued the course ascribed to him in the Acts, it is difficult to conceive how even such a suspicion should have originated.

whom he knew nothing but what he had heard from himself, permission to make a public address, of which it was impossible to foresee the effect on the already highly excited people?" Even if we overlook the first calmness of the auditors, it is still very remarkable "that this speech also, like that of Stephen and the speech of the Apostle before the Areopagus, is so methodically arranged that the speaker is interrupted at a particular point, but only at the moment when he has already said everything which, under such circumstances, he can have intended to say in favour of his main object." If we are finally obliged to admit that Paul, under the given circumstances, might have spoken as he does, and if the omission of what was really the main question, his relation to the Mosaic Law, may here be considered more probable than in xxvi., our previous investigation respecting the Apostle's conversion makes the present representation of the event, and the occurrences which followed it, to appear so suspicious in several not unimportant points, that for this reason alone we are not able to credit the authenticity of the words attributed to Paul. According to all indications, this speech is also the author's free composition.

Passing over what immediately follows, we now turn to the noteworthy examination of the Apostle before the Jewish Sanhedrim, xxii. 30—xxiii. 10. For this narrative also, Baur (pp. 202 ff.), and Schneckenburger before him (pp. 143 ff.), has so firmly fixed the decisive points of view, that it is difficult to evade his deductions. Of the two utterances of Paul here recorded, both contain much that is striking. Even if he is credited with the passionate word against the high-priest, verse 3, yet the apology in verse 5 (οὐκ ᾔδειν, ἀδελφοί, ὅτι ἐστὶν ἀρχιερεύς· γέγραπται γάρ· ἄρχοντα τοῦ λαοῦ σου οὐκ ἐρεῖς κακῶς) must, from a purely historical standpoint, raise scruples in those who do not share the prejudice of an apostolic sinlessness. That Paul really did not know to whom he had addressed the words of the third verse, can hardly be imagined; an old disciple of the rabbis must have been aware that none but the high-priest was wont to preside in the Sanhedrim; and the evasion, that he may not have looked at the speaker, is expressly excluded by the ἀτενίσας of verse 1, and the πρὸς αὐτὸν, verse 3. It has, therefore, been attempted in various ways to escape the natural interpretation by which Paul denies having recognized the high-priest; οὐκ ᾔδειν is supposed to mean, "I can or could not acknowledge him as legitimate high-priest;"[1] but οἶδα does not mean *agnosco*, and Ananias is styled high-priest by our author himself in verse 2; or else οὐκ ᾔδειν is to be translated, "I had not *considered*,"[2] which, again, the word cannot mean, and does not mean in Acts vii. 18; 1 Cor. i. 16; Eph. vi. 7;[3] or else the answer is intended ironically;[4] whereas the earnest pacificatory ἀδελφοὶ, and the passage of Scripture with which Paul enforces his explanation, exclude such irony, which in any case would be very inappropriate and difficult to understand.[5] The violence of these evasions can only serve to display the impossibility of any other view than that which is given above. But then it certainly follows that, according to our narrative, Paul extricated himself from the dilemma by a falsehood. That this actually occurred cannot, it is true, be pronounced absolutely impossible; even a Paul might, perhaps, in a weak moment, be overtaken by such denial of the truth; yet as we have no single positive instance of his being so overtaken, and as, on the other hand, we have a considerable number of inaccurate statements in our book, it is most probable that the Apostle did not employ this subterfuge himself, but that it is attributed to him

[1] The reason of this non-recognition is explained differently by each individual.

[2] So still *Neander*, 3rd ed. p. 421, 4th ed. p. 489; in the former, appealing to the alleged, but likewise undemonstrable, signification of יָדַע; in the latter, with the remark that "it is unnecessary to torment oneself with the word ᾔδειν—such stress need not be laid upon the words." We have already seen in xxi. 21 the real meaning of this liberality in not laying stress upon the words.

[3] Moreover, according to *Baumgarten's* just remark, p. 199, the expression, τοῖχε κεκονιαμένε, indicates the official dignity of the person addressed.

[4] *Meyer* on this passage, and others; in substance also *Baumgarten*, pp. 199 f.

[5] For οὐκ ᾔδειν does not mean, I *could* not know, but I *did not know*. This word could only be understood by the hearers to signify that Paul really intended to deny having known the high-priest, granting even that they did not believe him.

only by our historian. What induced him to do so cannot be ascertained with certainty; still it is quite possible that he found the tradition of Paul's passionate reply, verse 3, and that, to justify his Apostle, he made use of a certainly not very credible subterfuge.[1]

Verse 6, however, places the Apostle in a still more ambiguous light. In order to win over the Pharisees in the Sanhedrim, and incite a division between them and the Sadducees, he here exclaims, ἄνδρες ἀδελφοὶ, ἐγὼ Φαρισαῖός εἰμι, υἱὸς Φαρισαίου· περὶ ἐλπίδος καὶ ἀναστάσεως νεκρῶν ἐγὼ κρίνομαι. It is only cloaking the difficulty of this passage to say, with Neander, p. 490, "Paul might say, in accordance with truth, that he stood before the judgment-seat because he had borne witness to the hope of the people of Israel (ἐλπὶς cannot mean this; it is ἐλπὶς ἀναστάσεως) concerning the expected resurrection of the dead, for he had indeed preached Jesus as him through whom this hope was to be fulfilled." Just the very point of dispute between Christians and Jews, whether the hope of the people was to be fulfilled through *Jesus* of Nazareth, whether *his* resurrection was the prototype of the general resurrection, would be concealed in his representation; and instead of it, a question about which the two parties were not contending, and as to which Paul was not undergoing judgment—the question of the future resurrection of all—was substituted in a sophistical manner, while not a syllable is said of the special accusation against the Apostle, which had alone occasioned the proceedings against him (xxi. 28), i. e. his attack upon the enduring validity of the Mosaic Law. The chief

[1] As regards the command given by the high-priest, *B. Bauer*, Apostel-geschichte, 106, believes it to be an imitation of the statements in the Gospels of the blows on the cheeks received by Jesus. In this case it must be assumed that our narrative had originally a tendency adverse to Paul; the passionate reply of Paul must have been contrasted with the meekness of Christ when undergoing the corresponding ill-usage. But the more distinct statement of the blows on the cheeks and the answer of Jesus is first found in John xix. 22 f.; while Matt. xxvi. 67, Mark xiv. 65, are too general to allow us to trace our narrative to them. This would therefore necessitate the assumption that a narrative allied to that of John already existed in one of the older Gospels.

difficulty does not, however, consist in this expression about the resurrection—the most suspicious thing is the introductory words, ἐγὼ Φαρισαῖός εἰμι. How could Paul say this of himself with even a semblance of truth? He certainly had been a Pharisee; but was he *at that time still* a Pharisee,—he who unremittingly waged war against the observance of the Law, the groundwork of this Jewish orthodoxy? Paul might certainly call himself an *Israelite,* as he does in a passage, Rom. xi. 1, which was perhaps in the mind of the author; for this name primarily denotes his parentage; but now and never more could he call himself a Pharisee, for this is the designation of a religious creed. Is it credible that Paul should have been guilty of such a direct denial of his religious convictions, of hypocrisy in comparison with which the insincerity of Peter at Antioch, so sharply reproved by him, would shrink into insignificance? But scarcely less improbable is the effect which the craftiness of the Apostle is supposed to have produced. How can it be supposed, we must inquire with Baur (pp. 204 ff.), that the Apostle's palpable stratagem should suddenly have kindled such a passionate conflict between the two parties, who must have been long accustomed to each other's existence, so far at least as not to fly at one another on every slight allusion to their points of difference? that the Pharisees came forward as the champions of his cause, and admitted as possible even the apparition of Christ at Damascus? that in the hollow semblance of identity between his faith and theirs, they entirely lost sight of what must have been the most offensive point in his character, the way in which he undermined the authority of the Law? Is it not also, we must add with Schneckenburger (p. 146), obviously incompatible with the further course of the affair? for although the Pharisees take the part of Paul, and although they always had the majority in the Sanhedrim, he is indicted only a few days later by the chief-priest and the presbytery before the Procurator Felix; and even the day after his innocence has been proclaimed by the brilliant testimony of our ninth verse, we find the Sanhedrists implicated in a treasonable attempt upon his life. It is scarcely possible to answer these considerations in a manner more unsatisfactory than Neander does, p. 291, with the observation that "it might perhaps be that in the tumultuous manner in which the affair with Paul was carried on, the chief persons among the people had not yet learned what constituted the *corpus delicti* in his case; and as the Pharisees *always* (they had, therefore, already heard him more than once, and yet knew nothing of him?) heard him begin by saying that the risen Jesus had appeared to him, they kept to that alone, allowing other things to pass, since the point in dispute with the Sadducees—to them far more important—was here brought under discussion." That it should have seemed to them "far more important," and that the mere mention of it should have been capable of inciting them to such a wild outburst against a party with which they must, nevertheless, have lived for several generations—this is just the improbability which does not become more probable by mere repetition without proof. It is also equally incredible that Christianity was still unknown to the Sanhedrists of Jerusalem in the year 60 A.D., when it had already disturbed the whole Jewish world for a long time; or that, according to Baumgarten's opinion (p. 207), in the perplexity of the moment (for which, from their standpoint, they had no cause), they should have forgotten that Paul, the former Pharisee, had for twenty to twenty-five years laboured with alarming results to extinguish the Jewish Law by the new faith in the Messiah. If the objections to our narrative can only be refuted by such assumptions as these, they will probably hold their ground. Only it must not be said (as Schneckenburger does) that Luke need not, therefore, have given a false account; that Pharisaically-disposed persons spoke in behalf of Paul, and that they threw the apple of discord about the resurrection before the judges. Granting it to be so, Luke would, nevertheless, have given a false report of the chief point if, as he does here, he makes Paul avow himself a Pharisee persecuted for his belief in the resurrection, and in this manner induce the Pharisees to espouse his cause. But who is to guarantee the historical character of the small portion of our narrative which Schneckenburger wishes to maintain? If the essential purport and whole tendency of a record is proved to be unhistorical, it is manifest that we cannot uphold single subordinate circumstances as historical on the sole testimony of the record; but the most we can say is, "It is possible—in our case not even is it probable—that the unhistorical representation is founded on this or that historical fact."

This decided verdict can only be pronounced on the narratives before us, if we apply to them the standard of the Apostle's character as it is known to us from his Epistles. If we confine ourselves to the representation of the Acts, we should indeed still wonder at single points, such as the incongruity of the Pharisees taking part with Paul, and their subsequent conduct; yet the most offensive points might be set aside. The Paul of the Acts may certainly say of himself, Φαρισαῖός εἰμι; for he is, indeed, a Jew as zealous of the Law as are the Pharisaic Jewish Christians of Jerusalem (see below, and xxi. 24); in case of need, he can even assert that he is attacked solely on account of his faith in the resurrection—primarily, indeed, in the resurrection of Jesus; for the real stumbling-block, his Antinomianism, is wanting here; it is mere calumny to say that he seduces the Jews to renounce the Law; in his case it can be imagined that the Pharisees, who seem, in general, not to have persecuted the Jewish Christians, may have taken his side against the Sadducees. But if it is here by no means a part momentarily assumed by Paul, if he represents himself as believing in the Messiah indeed, yet as a Jew none the less obedient to the Law,—again, two years later, he has nothing else to say of himself, and, in truth, as the Acts represents him, he has no cause. This certainly does not prove that Paul was really another man than what his Epistles exhibit him to us, and that a representation such as that under discussion can be historical; all the more so that it is most closely bound up with the whole tendency of the Acts, and is therefore to be explained, not as an accidental misunderstanding, but solely from the standpoint and character of the book.

The short but significant account of the proceedings before the Sanhedrim is followed, in xxiii. 11—36, by an epically broad account of the Apostle's abduction to Cæsarea, in consequence of a Jewish conspiracy against his life. In itself the affair contains no improbability; one can only wonder how all these details could be so accurately known to the author; at least, one would think, he cannot have had a copy of the letter from Lysias to Felix. It is true, Meyer, with whom De Wette also agrees, sees a proof of authenticity in the statement, ver. 27, that Lysias rescued Paul from the Jews because he learnt that he was a Roman.[1] By this "crafty alteration of facts," the Tribune endeavours to veil his mistake.[2] But it does not appear what reproach could be applied to Lysias, even if he spoke nothing but the truth. Our book certainly says, as early as xxii. 29, that when the Tribune became aware that Paul was a Roman citizen, he was alarmed at having put him in fetters. But this is in glaring contradiction to his removing the fetters only on the following morning, according to ver. 30. And in itself also this statement is improbable. Lysias was not bound to consider Paul's privilege as a citizen before he was aware of it; but as soon as he had heard of it, he would have suspended penal proceedings. This statement must therefore be judged like the analogous one in xvi. 38; and if Meyer may have rightly guessed the motive of the 27th verse, we could only regard it as an inference of our author's, but in no way as a proof of the truth of his representation.

The further transactions of xxiv.—xxvi., likewise given at great length, with the exception of the conversion of the Apostle already discussed, afford little material for remark. Paul's vindicatory addresses, which (xxiv. 10 ff., xxv. 8, xxvi.) are repeatedly reported, now in detail, now more briefly, all turn on the

[1] The solution of the *μαθὼν* by *καὶ ἔμαθον* seems in this case verbally unreliable.

[2] So also *Riehm*, De font. Act. Apost. p. 111.

self-same point—that he is a faithful adherent of the Jewish religion (xxiv. 14 ff., xxv. 8, xxvi. 4 ff.[1]); and that it is only the old belief in the Messiah, of which he announces the fulfilment (xxiv. 14 f., xxvi. 6, 22 f.). No mention is made, either by his Jewish accusers or by himself, of the real subject of complaint against the Apostle, i.e. his position with reference to the Law; for even the false charge in xxiv., that he had attempted to desecrate the Temple, does not belong here, and only tends to conceal what might have been said with truth concerning his relation to the ceremonial of the Temple. The recognition of the Apostle's innocence is repeated with equal regularity in every instance; after Lysias (xxiii. 29) has borne witness that he is not guilty of any punishable action, Felix (xxiv. 22) manifests the same conviction;[2] Festus not only refuses the Jews' designing petition for a trial at Jerusalem,[3] but, after a formal investigation, repeats (xxv. 18, 25) the former favourable opinions concerning the Apostle. That a Jewish testimony might not be wanting to these heathen ones, Agrippa, whose voice acquires double weight from his familiarity with the Jewish laws (xxv. 26, xxvi. 2 f., 26), declares his judgment, significantly placed at the end of the whole paragraph, that, save the appeal to Cæsar, there was no impediment to Paul's release. The entire assembly coincides in this opinion. If, therefore, Paul is not released, and is obliged to appeal to Cæsar, the cause must lie in the base motives of selfishness and subservience on the part of his judges (xxiv. 26, xxv. 9), which serve themselves the purpose of a higher providence, xxiii. 11. The whole description is doubtless

[1] This passage ought also to be quoted here: Paul's appeal to his observance of the Law is not intended as in Gal. i. 14, Phil. iii. 5, to point the contrast between his Christian and his previous Jewish standpoint; there is no intimation of this contrast, but it is to serve as positive evidence that he continues to be a good Jew. This is clearly shown by the context of verses 5 and 6. We must judge xxii. 3, from the same point of view.

[2] Verses 23 and 26 especially show that the postponement of the verdict is intended to be favourable to Paul.

[3] It is remarkable that here, xxv. 2 ff., exactly the same plot should be repeated which was already employed in xxiii. 12 ff.

admirably adapted to the object of making the Apostle appear innocent, even from the standpoint of strict Jewish law; but whether it is historically accurate we may question, in spite of several traits taken from life (such as xxiv. 19, the aristocratic ignorance of the Roman; xxvi. 28, Agrippa's answer to Paul's urgency); in the first place, because the various speeches in our book, both in style and arrangement, flowed unmistakably from one and the same pen, and those of Paul show no mark of the characteristic language of the Apostle; but, still more, because it is quite improbable that in the charge against Paul, instead of the actual subject of complaint, i.e. his attack on the Law of his people, it is always the faith in the Messiah which is mentioned against him. How far the whole story of the Apostle's imprisonment and trial before Felix and Festus is affected by this doubt can scarcely be decided with certainty. It is certainly remarkable[1] that Felix and Festus, from the same motive, i.e. to confer a favour on the Jews (χάριν καταθέσθαι), should have arrested or brought Paul into danger (xxiv. 27, xxv. 9), just as Pilate, for similar reasons, had consented to the execution of Jesus (comp. Acts xxiv. 22; Matt. xxvi. 18); that Paul has to answer for himself before Herod Agrippa, as Jesus before Herod, and with the same result (Luke xxiii. 15; Acts xxvi. 31); and in the last-mentioned narrative the symmetrical hand of our author really seems to betray itself even in the style of expression; otherwise, conduct such as that of the two Procurators is too natural under existing circumstances, not merely in the pragmatic assumption of the author, but also in reality, for its repeated occurrence to be surprising; it is everywhere the custom of unscrupulous officials, by complaisance, at the expense of others to appease those to whom they have in other ways given just cause for complaint. At all events, an incorrect conjecture on the part of the author respecting the causes of the Apostle's long imprisonment in Cæsarea does not upset the fact of that imprisonment, for the invention of which no sufficient motives are to be found. On the other

[1] Comp. *B. Bauer*, Apostelg. 106.

hand, we must defer investigating the state of the case with regard to the individual trials, and especially the hearing before Agrippa, as these are too closely connected with the double interest of recording repeated vindications and free-spoken judgments.

6. Paul on the Way to Rome and at Rome.

The account of the journey in the 27th and 28th chapters forms incontestably one of the most ancient portions of the Acts, yet some unhistorical elements have apparently insinuated themselves here also. So much is not incredible that, notwithstanding his examinations, Paul, by the force of his character, may have attained the reputation with which he appears in this record (xxvii. 10, 21 ff., 33), and the dream-vision of verses 23 ff. is also susceptible of a natural interpretation; Paul, reflecting on the significance of his journey, may have prayed for his own and his companion's rescue, and his firm reliance that his petition would be granted might take the form of a vision. That the result corresponded with the expectation is by no means incredible. The observation of the 33rd verse, that, out of consideration for Paul, the centurion obstructed the design of killing the prisoners, might be attributed to a somewhat one-sided interpretation. Humane as he appears to have been (verse 3), for the sake of the other prisoners he must have put a stop to such needless barbarity; and if, on one side, it may be said that his interest in Paul constituted his first and chief motive, on the other side the possibility cannot be denied that this brief observation, which might be omitted without injury to the construction or context, may have been added, only by a later hand, to the primitive record, in order to set forth the impression made by the Apostle even on the Romans, whose prisoner he was. But the conjecture is more distinctly suggested by some traits in the narrative, xxviii. 1—10. Although the incident with the viper, verse 3, which our author indeed wishes to be regarded as a miracle, might in itself be explained by supposing either that a really poisonous serpent crept on to Paul's hand without biting, or that the bystanders mistook a harmless serpent for a poisonous one; still the statement of the 6th verse, that the natives, finding him uninjured by the supposed bite of the viper, regarded him as a god, is too much in the miraculous style of the 14th chapter (verse 11) not to give rise to similar scruples. For when a person supposed to have been bitten by a viper escapes unharmed, the first idea which arises is not that he is a supernatural being; and the people of Melita must have been sufficiently acquainted with these indigenous serpents to be aware that, besides the poisonous, there were also non-poisonous vipers. Thus, even if the other narratives should be correct, the remark in verse 6 probably contains an unhistorical addition. Still more decidedly does the healing of the sick father of Publius bear this character, especially if we include the further statement that all the other (οἱ λοιποὶ) sick people on the island were healed by the Apostle—an assurance which so strikingly recalls the other exaggerated descriptions of apostolic miracles (ii. 43, v. 15 f., xix. 11 f.), that we can only pronounce the same opinion on them as on the others.

After recording the Apostle's journey from Jerusalem to Rome, the last paragraph of our book (xxviii. 16 ff.) concludes with an account of his dealings with the most respected members of the Roman Jewish population. If we have been obliged to regard the previous accounts with a feeling of mistrust, we cannot now abandon this mistrust. What first of all surprises us is the conduct of Paul himself. Scarcely arrived at Rome, he summons the most respected Jews to inform them that he is not judged either on account of a transgression against the Jewish people or the Law, nor yet as the accuser of his people, but singly and solely on account of his truly Jewish faith in the Messiah. After he has thus conferred with his fellow-countrymen for a whole day, and endeavoured to win them over to Christianity, he dismisses them with the declaration that, as the Jewish people in their stubbornness turn away from the Messianic salvation, it shall be offered to the Gentiles.

Can it be credited of Paul, as we otherwise know him, that he should have pursued such a course? Of the Paul of the Acts certainly, but scarcely of the historical Paul. If we contemplate the account in our book in an unprejudiced manner, a two-fold object presents itself for the conference with the Jews; in the first place, the Apostle wishes to refute the bad opinion which they might have of him as an enemy of the Law; and, secondly, to make a first attempt of preaching the gospel to them according to his principle (xiii. 45), to which verse 28 likewise distinctly refers, of invariably turning to the Jews first, and only if they despise the gospel, to the Gentiles. But even if we are further on compelled to think it unlikely that he should really have acted in accordance with this principle, the eagerness to justify himself to the Jews before he can have made closer acquaintance with the Christian community, after which he so greatly yearns in the Epistle to the Romans (i. 11 ff.), is far more befitting the Jewish Christian, whose great object it is not to lose the reputation of orthodoxy among his fellow-countrymen, than to a man conscious, as Paul was, of so thorough antagonism to the Jewish standpoint. With what conscience could he have asserted that he had in no way acted in opposition to the ἔθη πατρῷα, the Mosaic institutions[1]—he whose entire ministry tended to nothing but to suppress these institutions by faith in Christ, whose whole religious consciousness centred in the removal of the Law by the Gospel?

But if Paul's conduct is incomprehensible, that of the Jews is almost more so. They not only come to him twice at his residence and listen to his discourse for a whole day, but in verse 21 they expressly bear him witness: ἡμεῖς οὔτε γράμματα περὶ σοῦ ἐδεξάμεθα ἀπὸ τῆς Ἰουδαίας, οὔτε παραγενόμενός τις τῶν ἀδελφῶν ἀνήγγειλεν ἢ ἐλάλησέ τι περὶ σοῦ πονηρόν. Nay, it is not enough

[1] Comp., on the meaning of this expression, vi. 14, xv. 1, xxi. 21, also xvi. 21.

that they should have heard nothing to his disadvantage; of Christianity altogether they seem to know no details: ἀξιοῦμεν παρά σου ἀκοῦσαι ἃ φρονεῖς, περὶ μὲν γὰρ τῆς αἱρέσεως ταύτης γνωστόν ἐστιν ἡμῖν, ὅτι πανταχοῦ ἀντιλέγεται. This is not the way in which it is usual to speak of a phenomenon which has been before one's eyes for years, respecting which information has been derived by direct intercourse. Therefore, if the Roman Jews speak thus, it must be assumed that only a vague report of the Christian sect had reached their ears. That this was actually the case has been considered so improbable, even by those interpreters who do not wish to impugn the credibility of our book, that they have been able to explain the assertion of the Jews only as a pretence.[1] But what could have been the object of this dissimulation? Schneckenburger thinks that they wished thereby to give themselves a greater show of impartiality. But they had no particular object in giving themselves this appearance; and if they had, the falsehood was not at all requisite. It would have been fully sufficient to inform Paul that, although they had as yet been unable to convince themselves of the truth of the Christian faith, they were, nevertheless, disposed to receive instruction; whereas, according to this view, they open their acquaintance with the Apostle with a lie, which is much too palpable for him not to have seen through it at once. But our author evidently treats the assertion of the Jews as being not at all untrue. They are so much in earnest about it, that on this very account they fix a day for conferring with Paul, in order to learn from him, what they do not know as yet, in what the doctrine of the Christians really consists; and the Apostle on his side enters into the matter with an earnestness which shows clearly enough that he gives full credence to the statement of the Jews. And as far as their declaration respecting the Apostle is concerned, it accords perfectly with the state of the case as represented in our book. Does he not also say of himself that he has in no way offended against the Jewish people or the Law?

[1] *Schneckenburger*, p. 86.

Does he not persistently appear in our book as a faithful observer of the Law? According to this, is the testimony rendered to him anything but the formal confirmation of this state of affairs from the mouth of the Jews themselves, indirectly even of the Jerusalemites, the reiteration of the verdict already pronounced by a Lysias, a Felix, a Festus, an Agrippa, and even by the orthodox party in the Sanhedrim? And after all this, can we doubt that our author wishes this declaration, and of necessity the 22nd verse connected with it, to be regarded as strict truth? But that it really is so, we cannot admit. First, as concerns the supposition that the Roman Jews had not yet heard any particulars of the Christian sect, that is quite incredible under the circumstances of the time. We know, from the Epistle to the Romans, that for years past a not inconsiderable community of Christians had existed in Rome, a community of which Paul says, in Rom. i. 8, that its faith was spoken of in all parts of the world (ἐν ὅλῳ τῷ κόσμῳ). We also see, from the same authority, that, even though the majority may have been Gentile Christians by descent, this community nevertheless contained a still more important Judaizing element,[1] whence it follows that it cannot have been disconnected with the Jews of Rome. What! and can the most distinguished members of Roman Judaism have known nothing further of such a community than that their doctrine was everywhere evil-spoken of? What was known to all the world out of Rome, is supposed to have been unknown only to those whom it most nearly concerned. Only two years later the Neronian persecution of the Christians took place, on which occasion Tacitus testifies that the reputed infamous deeds of the Christians at Rome were in the mouths of the people. "How is it possible," we must ask, with Baur (p. 370), "that two years earlier Christianity in Rome was still so unknown as we must suppose from the account given in the Acts? or how is it possible to imagine that the Jews alone did not know what was

[1] See especially ix.—xi. vii. 1 ff., and *Baur's* inquiry respecting the object of the Epistle to the Romans, Paul. pp. 234 ff.; and also *Schneckenburger*, pp. 89 ff.

known to every one else in Rome?" Baur has already sufficiently refuted Olshausen's evasion, that the Roman Christians may have separated themselves from the Jews in consequence of the persecution of the Jews under Claudius; and that the newly immigrated Jews may have remained unaware of the existence of the Christian community at Rome. Conversely, Kling[1] is of opinion that the Jews broke off intercourse with the Christians on account of the disturbances which Christianity had occasioned among them, and which had produced the edict of Claudius. But then they would not either have acted on the invitation of Paul, nor could they have spoken to him as they do; for they talk as if they knew no details respecting the Christians; and how could they do this if it was precisely a doctrinal dispute with the Christians which had induced them to withdraw from them? There is nothing to recommend Neander's observation (p. 497), that in so large a town the existence of the Christian community might easily have escaped the knowledge of the rich Jews, especially as the main stock of that community were Gentiles, and as these Jews may well have been more occupied about other things than about matters of religion. If the city of Rome was large, neither was the Christian community small; its existence was known even to the heathen population, how much more to the πρώτοις τῶν Ἰουδαίων; for that they did not concern themselves about religious matters is contradicted by their repeated visits to the Apostle, and their conference with him, which lasted from morning until evening; and it has already been shown that the Christian communities maintained intercourse with the Jews of that city; even without this, it would have had at least sufficient interest for them not to be totally ignored. In our time, would even the smallest German Catholic community remain unknown to the Catholics of the same city; and would not a numerous Christian community at Rome have an importance for the Jews far greater

[1] Theol. Studies and Criticisms, 1837, II. 302.

than that of all German Catholic societies together for the Catholicism of the present day?

Equally incredible is it that the Jews, according to verse 21, should have heard nothing disadvantageous to Paul even from Judæa. The man who for decades past had laboured for the downfall of Judaism, who had gained for the hated sect of Christians innumerable adherents from the Eastern to the borders of the Western world, who was everywhere in conflict with the Jews, and with whom they were in mortal combat—this man was an adversary far too important for the Jews of the metropolis of the world not to have been long acquainted with his name, and, when their fellow-believers spoke of him, it was naturally in an unfavourable sense. It is indeed said here that nothing evil had been reported against him *from Judæa*. But, in the first place, verse 22 shows that, according to our author, they know nothing whatever about him, and that Judæa is expressly mentioned merely because the preceding history attributed to the Jews of Palestine alone the attack upon the Apostle, who was supposed to be in no way adverse to Judaism in general; secondly, this qualified declaration is extremely improbable. It is said, indeed (Meyer, on the passage), that before the appeal of Paul, the Sanhedrists had no occasion to make any report about him to Rome, as they hoped to be quit of him in Palestine; after his appeal, probably no opportunity, as the sea-passage, according to xxvii. 9, was already closed; it has even been supposed[1] that the party in Palestine purposely concealed their hatred against Paul (against whom they had brought accusations imperilling life and limb!), in order to ruin him the more readily. But did it require an official report to make the Jews in Rome aware of the events which took place in Palestine? It is known what lively intercourse existed between the provincial capitals and Rome, what extensive relations were formed between Rome and Jerusalem by religion,

[1] *Lange*, Apost. Zeit. I. 106.

commerce, and political circumstances; how, in addition to the innumerable private connections, political agents of the Jewish nobles and priesthood were almost continually at Rome. Moreover, just at the time when Paul was imprisoned at Cæsarea, the most considerable of the Cæsarean Jews came to Rome with an accusation against the Procurator Felix (Jos., Ant. xx. 8, 9). And yet during the three years which had elapsed since the arrest of the Apostle, the πρῶτοι τῶν Ἰουδαίων at Rome are supposed not to have heard a word of the events which had occurred in their own country, of the imprisonment and probable condemnation of the most odious and dangerous enemy of their faith; and we are expected to be satisfied with Meyer's observation, that *accidentally* evil tidings concerning Paul had not reached the Roman Jews either by private correspondence or by travellers! *Credat Judæus Apella!* The unhistorical character of our record is plain, only in this case it cannot be limited to the individual features in which it first becomes evident; much rather if, on the one hand, the whole conduct of Paul, and, on the other hand, the whole conduct of the Jews, was improbable, the meeting of the two, which is only to be explained by their behaviour towards each other, loses its foundation. Natural as it is that at Rome Paul should have come in contact with his fellow-countrymen among others, and have attempted to make an impression upon them, we are yet unable to regard as historical the formal intercourse with the chiefs of the Roman Jews which opened, it is supposed, immediately after his arrival.

7. The Doctrine and Public Character of Paul according to the Representation of the Acts.

Having hitherto taken the narratives of our book concerning the Apostle Paul into consideration individually, it is incumbent upon us, in conclusion, to unite the scattered features of the description into a general picture, and to compare it with the representation of himself given by the Apostle in his Epistles.

If we begin with the side which is most directly adapted to this comparison, i. e. the *doctrine* of the Apostle, his numerous discourses in the Acts promise sufficient material for establishing it. On closer examination, however, we shall find ourselves in a great measure disappointed in this expectation. Of these discourses, those of chapters xxii. xxiv. and xxvi., as well as the shorter speeches of xxiii. 6, xxv. 8, are apologetic in purport; and likewise, according to what we have already said, the address at Miletus, xx.; hence there remain only the two missionary discourses at Antioch in Pisidia, xiii. 16—41, and at Athens, xvii.; besides the short address to the Lystrians, xiv. 15—17, the summary account of the transactions with the Jews in Thessalonica, xvii. 3, and the more detailed description of the conference with those at Rome. This absence of doctrinal discourse in comparison with self-vindication has been justly deemed significant by Schneckenburger (p. 128). In reality, the exposition of the doctrine of salvation, the explanation and vindication of the peculiarities which constitute the Pauline view of it, must, after all, have formed the chief import of the apostolic addresses; and in this respect the discourses cannot have differed essentially from the Epistles, of which the Epistle to the Romans especially shows us how Paul spoke to those to whom his doctrine was still new. If our author records so little of this, and, on the other hand, so much of the vindicatory addresses which, for the most part, offer nothing at all characteristic, we obtain a distorted representation of the Apostle's ministry, and its dogmatical significance is unduly cast into the background. But if we examine more closely into the purport of his doctrinal addresses, and if, for this purpose, we consider the two greater, at Antioch and Athens, it seems to us as if the author wished to present in each the model of a whole species of Pauline doctrinal addresses. In Athens the Apostle has an exclusively Grecian, in Antioch a Jewish audience; the speeches which he makes in these two places represent the Apostle's missionary sermons; in general, the former to the Gentiles, the latter to the Jews. Nevertheless, neither the one nor the other corresponds to the expectations which we must form of Paul's doctrinal addresses. Respecting the Athenian discourse (the authenticity of which became doubtful, for reasons shown above), Schneckenburger (p. 129) correctly considers that it contains as little that is characteristically Pauline as the Lystrian speech; it is merely the great conception of heathenism itself; both speeches might have been made by a person not agreeing with the Apostle in his Christian doctrine of salvation—nay, with the exception of the very last words in the Athenian discourse, by a liberal and profoundly-thinking Jew. In both, it is only Monotheism which is opposed to Polytheism, not the need and consciousness of salvation opposed to the wordly and sinful life of Paganism; but nothing is said in these discourses of the Pauline view of Christianity, as it is expressed, for instance, in the Epistle to the Romans in presence of Paganism, or of going back to the moral root of religion; even the belief in the Messiah is only mentioned once (xvii. 31) in passing. The speech at Antioch certainly makes not only the general Christian, but also the Pauline doctrine to appear more distinctly. But even in this instance, how mild, and to the Jews themselves how inoffensive, is the allusion to the peculiar import of the Pauline doctrines! When Paul has spoken in detail of the early guidance of the people of Israel, of John the Baptist, of the execution and resurrection of Jesus, and has proved his Messiahship from the Old Testament, he adds in verse 38, *Γνωστὸν οὖν ἔστω ὑμῖν, ὅτι διὰ τούτου ὑμῖν ἄφεσις ἁμαρτιῶν καταγγέλλεται· καὶ ἀπὸ πάντων ὧν οὐκ ἠδυνήθητε ἐν τῷ νόμῳ Μωϋσέως δικαιωθῆναι ἐν τούτῳ πᾶς ὁ πιστεύων δικαιοῦται.* But this does not distinctly *substitute* justification by faith for justification by law; it may just as well be regarded[1] as a supplementing of the latter, in the synergistic sense of Jewish

[1] James ii. 22, *ἡ πίστις συνήργει τοῖς ἔργοις αὐτοῦ.*

Christianity.[1] Any one not previously acquainted with the Pauline doctrines of Justification and Law would certainly not glean them from this fleeting indication. This is, moreover, the *only* passage in *all* the speeches ascribed to Paul in the Acts in which any reference to his doctrine is to be found. In all his other sayings, without exception, we find only the same announcement of the risen Jesus, the same evidence from the Old Testament of his Messiahship, as in the speeches of a Peter. It is solely on this question that Paul disputes with the Jews at Thessalonica, xvii. 2 f., when he proves from Scripture, ὅτι τὸν Χριστὸν ἔδει παθεῖν καὶ ἀναστῆναι ἐκ νεκρῶν, καὶ ὅτι οὗτός ἐστιν ὁ Χριστὸς Ἰησοῦς; of this alone he treats, xxviii., for a whole day at Rome, πείθων αὐτοὺς τὰ περὶ τοῦ Ἰησοῦ, ἀπό τε τοῦ νόμου Μωϋσέως καὶ τῶν προφητῶν; of this alone he reminds the Ephesian elders when he unreservedly epitomizes (xx. 21) the doctrine which he preaches as the μετάνοια εἰς τόν θεὸν and the πίστις εἰς τὸν κύριον ἡμῶν Ἰησοῦν Χριστὸν; and scarcely does a light tinge of the expression (εὐαγγέλιον τῆς χάριτος, verse 24) recall to the initiated the Pauline view of the doctrine of salvation. We have already partially seen that the Apostle likewise maintains no other point of view in his declarations in presence of the Sanhedrim (xxiii. 6), of Felix (xxiv. 14), of Festus (xxv. 8), and of Agrippa (xxvi. 19—23). In all these speeches, Paul disclaims, on the part of his doctrine, any hostile relation to Mosaism, and asseverates that the only difference between himself and the Jews is with reference to the Messiahship of Jesus, and the accomplishment of the Old Testament prophecies by his death and resurrection (comp. especially xxvi. 22); whereas not only his warfare against the validity of the Law, but also the doctrine of justification by faith alone, are not indistinctly denied when, in xxvi. 20, he

[1] The immediate sense of the words ἀπὸ πάντων, &c., can only be, that the believers in Christ obtain forgiveness for that for which the Law can procure them. Now this may certainly mean, they obtain forgiveness for *all* sins by faith, for by the Law they cannot all be forgiven; but it may also imply that they obtain this forgiveness for that portion of their sins for which the Law afforded none.

states as the purport of his discourses, ἀπήγγειλον μετανοεῖν καὶ ἐπιστρέφειν ἐπὶ τὸν θεὸν, ἄξια τῆς μετανοίας ἔργα πράσσοντας. This μετάνοια, this ἐπιστρέφειν ἐπὶ τὸν θεὸν, which consists in an altered behaviour, reminds us much more of the Baptist's preaching unto repentance, and the καρποὺς ἀξίους τῆς μετανοίας[1] required by him, or of Peter's μετανοήσατε καὶ ἐπιστρέψατε (iii. 19, comp. verse 29, ii. 38, v. 31), than of Paul's doctrine of faith and re-creation of the inner man, to which the very word μετάνοια is foreign.[2] How little the feeble echo of the Pauline dogmatics, in the discourse of the 13th chapter, guarantees the really Pauline character of this speech, and of the whole doctrine put into the mouth of Paul by our book, is evident from the circumstance that Peter goes quite as far in his speeches as Paul, the former speaking of the forgiveness of sins more frequently than the latter (see ii. 38, iii. 19, iv. 12, v. 31, x. 43); and if Paul propounds that the Jews cannot be completely justified by the Law, Peter declares (xv. 10) the Law a yoke which neither they nor their fathers were able to bear; and in the same passage acknowledges the principle that Gentiles and Jews are saved in the same manner by grace. But this state of the case appears still more distinctly from the relation pointed out by Schneckenburger[3]

[1] Luke iii. 8, where the ποιεῖν is not wanting for the complete reminiscence of this passage; similarly the ἐπιστρέφειν ἐπὶ τὸν θεὸν, with reference to John, is to be found in Luke i. 16, πολλοὺς τῶν υἱῶν Ἰσραὴλ ἐπιστρέψει ἐπὶ κύριον τὸν θεὸν αὐτῶν.

[2] Paul never uses this word (with him always rare) as applied to the reception of the Christian faith, but only with regard to moral improvement. See Rom. ii. 4; 2 Cor. vii. 9 f., xii. 21.

[3] *Schneckenburger*, p. 130: "This speech is only an echo of the discourses of Peter and Stephen. The same glorification of the Jewish forefathers in the introduction (xiii. 17—22, comp. vii. 2 ff.); the Messiah is the son of David (xiii. 23—26, comp. iii. 13 ff.), testified of by John. His rejection by the Jews of Jerusalem from ignorance fulfils the Divine counsels (xiii. 27 ff., iii. 14 ff.). Therefore is salvation now offered to those outside (xiii. 26, comp. iii. 26). The evidence of the Old Testament (xiii. 34—38, comp. ii. 25—32), which expressly shows that a passage in the Psalm cannot refer to David, but to Christ—the admonitions and the threats, just as with Peter (xiii. 40, comp. ii. 19 ff.). If we recall the otherwise well-known dogmas of Paul, we cannot avoid thinking it remarkable that Paul here, like Peter in the first part, lays the whole stress on the resurrection, not on the death; nay, that if he does not directly trace the ἄφεσις τῶν ἁμαρτιῶν to the resurrection, he connects it with the Messiahship in general, which is attested in his view by the resurrection itself."

and Baur between the speech at Antioch and those of the first part, which has led these scholars to the opinion that it is a mere echo of those of Peter and Stephen. After this evidence, it can no longer be supposed that we have anything in the 13th chapter but a free invention of the narrator's.[1] And if it is so with the speech which has most of the Pauline complexion, the case will not be different with regard to the others. How could we believe that in his doctrinal addresses the Apostle should so entirely have forgotten his whole theological system, as must have been the case according to the representation given in our book, when, of all the ideas which form the turning-point of his religious convictions—universal sin, justification by faith, apart from merit by works, the cessation of the Law—nothing but one or two half intelligible echoes should occur in all the speeches recorded in our book? Finally, how that could be true which the Acts makes him so repeatedly and emphatically assert (xxiii. 6, xxiv. 14, xxv. 8, xxvi. 22 f., xxviii. 17, see above), that he does not at all oppose the Mosaic Law, that he continues to be an orthodox Jew and a Pharisee? It is obvious that in all these respects the real kernel of the Pauline doctrine is not only passed over in silence, but altered in a Judaistic sense.

What Paul asserts of himself in the passages above quoted, what James says when avowing his agreement with him (xxi. 24), what even his Jewish opponents are obliged tacitly to admit (xxviii. 21, see above), that he is a faithful observer of the Law, is, according to the representation of the Acts, corroborated by his whole conduct. If we first contemplate his *personal* behaviour, our author has not failed to draw attention to it by sundry small traits. First among these are the repeated journeys to Jerusalem. It is usual to attribute such journeys to various other objects more nearly connected with Paul's apostolic labours. But if he allows even the tempting

[1] For no one will think it credible that Paul should have formed his speech on the model of Stephen's vindication, which he had heard so many years before. (*Heinrichs*, Comm. 338; *Riehm*, De font. Act. Ap. 57, 196.)

opportunity of a fruitful ministry at Ephesus to pass by merely because he is resolved at all costs to spend the next festival at Jerusalem,[1] where, judging by the silence of our book, except the visit to the feast, he has nothing at all to do.[2] If subsequently (xix. 21), in the midst of his Ephesian ministry, he similarly determines to travel to Jerusalem, without mention being made of any definite occasion for this journey; if he then (xxi. 6, 16) spends at Philippi the feast of the Passover, when no pious Jew would like to travel, and hastens past Ephesus, for many years the scene of his labours, which he is never again to visit, merely not to miss the feast of Pentecost at Jerusalem; if, in plain words, he says in xxiv. 11, 17, that he has come to Jerusalem to pray and to sacrifice; if our book so repeatedly and unmistakably indicates how it intends these journeys to be interpreted, we must not take them in any other sense, but must repeat our previous assent to Schneckenburger's observation respecting the record. We have now not only assured ourselves that in his last journey Paul had another object not mentioned in the Acts, and that he could not have been firmly resolved upon it even at Ephesus as our book represents, but we also know, from our investigation respecting the so-called apostolic council, that the account given in the Epistle to the Galatians leaves no room for the visit to Jerusalem described in our eleventh chapter. We cannot think otherwise with regard to the journey of the eighteenth chapter. That this visit is not mentioned in the Epistle to the Galatians is certainly not quite decisive; it cannot be proved that Paul intended to enumerate all the journeys to Jerusalem

[1] *Δεῖ με πάντως τὴν ἑορτὴν τὴν ἐρχομένην ποιῆσαι εἰς Ἱεροσόλυμα.* The genuineness of these words, which Meyer and De Wette justly defend, is rendered probable by their use in the Clementine Recognitions, p. 60.

[2] Verse 22 : *Καὶ ἀνήχθη ἀπὸ τῆς Ἐφέσου· καὶ κατελθὼν εἰς Καισάρειαν, ἀναβὰς καὶ ἀσπασάμενος τὴν ἐκκλησίαν κατέβη εἰς Ἀντιόχειαν.* These words, so directly connected with verse 21, can only give the impression that nothing further is added about the object and result of the journey, because it consisted merely in what was described in the 21st verse.

which he had made before the composition of the Epistle, but only that he recounted those which preceded the decisive acknowledgment of his independence by the party at Jerusalem (ii. 1); it is likewise possible that he intended to specify one journey more, and only lost sight of it in the discussions of the second chapter. On the other hand, the account of the Acts respecting this journey is of the sort that makes its reality appear dubious. The object of the journey—a visit to a Jewish festival—accords ill with the Apostle's opinions, and could only recommend itself to the Jewish-Christian readers of our book;[1] that Paul for this object should have neglected the sphere of work opened to him at Ephesus, shows indeed how much he was bent upon this pious object, but for this very reason it is not probable; what our book relates of the journey itself is merely that Paul made it; for the sojourn at Antioch, and the peregrinations through Galatia and Phrygia, verse 23, arose out of it easily enough. And yet one can but think that, if the Apostle withdrew himself from his extensive missionary labours at Ephesus in order to go to Jerusalem, if he made such a sacrifice of time and means, he cannot have done it without an important aim and object. If, moreover, we see from the example of the eleventh chapter that our author was capable of inventing a journey for Paul from dogmatic motives, there is a preponderating probability that he did so also in the case before us.[2]

With the Apostle's journeys to Jerusalem, our book also connects some further proofs of his Jewish piety; with the last, it adduces the Nazarite sacrifice discussed above; and before that of the eighteenth chapter, he fulfils a vow (verse 18) by shaving his head. The latter passage, it is true, is now, as

[1] This is seen especially from the circumstance just observed, that the Clementine Recognitions, i. 10, appropriate to themselves the words, xviii. 21, and the Homilies also give a similar explanation.

[2] The brevity with which the Acts treats our journey has of itself given rise to a doubt whether it actually intends to record a journey to Jerusalem; but this is unmistakably implied in the ἀναβάς, verse 22.

before, applied by many,[1] not to Paul, but to Aquila. The sole reason, however, that can be given for this is, that in the words, ὁ Παῦλος . . . . ἐξέπλει εἰς τὴν Συρίαν καὶ σὺν αὐτῷ Πρίσκιλλα καὶ Ἀκύλας, κειράμενος τὴν κεφαλὴν ἐν Κεγχρεαῖς· εἶχε γὰρ εὐχήν, the otherwise unsuitable precedence of Priscilla before her husband seems to be chosen for the purpose of enabling the κειράμενος to be immediately connected with its subject Ἀκύλας. This reason cannot prove anything; in Rom. xvi. 3, 2 Tim. iv. 19, and perhaps in our chapter itself, verse 26, Priscilla stands first. On the other hand, it seems to apply to Paul, first, because an express reference to Aquila, perhaps by an οὗτος δὲ before the κειράμενος, to connect the apposition with another than the chief subject of the sentence, should be expected; and, secondly, because one cannot rightly see why this observation respecting Aquila should be here. Schneckenburger thinks it is intended to serve as an indirect vindication of Paul against the accusation that he taught the Jews apostasy from the Law; but this seems to be very far-fetched. Wieseler contents himself with saying that we are not sufficiently acquainted with the particular circumstances of the shaving of the head to be capable of judging whether it was not in some way connected with the history of Paul; whether, for instance, his departure was not delayed by the fulfilment of a vow. But, for the very reason that the previous history gives no intimation of these circumstances, the author would necessarily have added some explanatory hint to a notice respecting Aquila, if it was not to remain incomprehensible and purposeless. In Paul, this vow would indeed be surprising; even Meyer is of opinion that it would be very strange to see the liberal-minded man taking part in voluntarily sensuous Jewish ceremonials, without any higher motive externally induced; such conduct of his is nowhere else to be found, however great may have been the inducements to make vows. As our statement runs, we cannot imagine anything but a vow to allow his hair

[1] *Meyer* on the place; *Schneckenburger*, p. 66; *Wieseler*, Chron. d. ap. Zeit. pp. 203 f.

to grow till a certain period, perhaps till his departure from Corinth—something analogous to the vow of the Nazarites;[1] but this would be, as Neander expresses himself (p. 349), such a "purposeless folly," that he cannot credit it even of Aquila.[2] He therefore assumes that, for some reason or other, Paul determined to give public expression to his gratitude to God in the Temple at Jerusalem; in the spirit of Christian wisdom, he had no scruple in adopting for this purpose the Jewish form of a vow; on setting out, he therefore begins to fulfil his vow by cutting his hair, in order to let it grow till it should be solemnly shaved at Jerusalem. But even without considering that our book ignores this respect for the Jews as completely as the accomplishment of the vow at Jerusalem, what is gained by the hypothesis? Does that which in Corinth would have been a purposeless folly, become a work of Christian wisdom because it takes place at Jerusalem? And would it not be still more repulsive that the Apostle should appear before the Jews and the Jewish Christians of Jerusalem in a part which would not in any way correspond to his real character; for individually he did not require either shaving of his head or the Temple in order to testify his thanks to God; he could at the most regard the vow as an indifferent ceremony; but by undertaking it he would have led others to think that he, like themselves, saw in it an act of piety, and that he was still the pious Jew which he had formerly been. Would not this have been a more reprehensible hypocrisy than that which he so greatly reprehends in Peter? And is it sufficient as a counter argument always to appeal to the Apostle's declaration in 1 Cor. ix. 20, that he was a Jew to the Jews? Does this declaration then imply, not only that under particular circumstances he refrained

[1] It cannot have been a real Nazarite vow, for that could only be fulfilled by a sacrifice in the Temple at Jerusalem.

[2] *Baumgarten*, indeed (ii. a. 302 ff.), has an expedient here also. Paul might undertake a Nazarite vow; for Samson was a Nazarite, and Samson, by his alliance with a heathen woman, is the type of Paul, the Apostle of the Gentiles. But this is a creed which is no longer easy in these days.

from what was repulsive to them, but that he likewise undertook specific works of the Law, such as Nazaritism, without any urgent inducement? This, it is true, applies only to the historical Paul. In the Paul of the Acts, the Corinthian vow can appear no more strange than the Nazarite sacrifice at Jerusalem; and if he undertakes it to show that he himself adheres faithfully to the Law, why should he not, even without any such object, from simple legal piety, have occasionally made a vow?

As with Judaism, Paul in the Acts stands in a connection with Jewish Christianity and with its metropolis, which we cannot look upon as historical as it is represented. Immediately after his conversion, our book makes him go to Jerusalem, and there enter into the closest intercourse with the Christian community (ix. 26 ff.); that this journey only took place three years after his conversion to Christianity, that the visit in Jerusalem was to Peter alone and lasted only fourteen days, is passed by in silence. A second journey to the same place is related in the 11th, a third in the 15th, a fourth in the 18th chapter. We have seen above that, of these three journeys, probably only the middle one is true. Our author does not omit to record in each of them an amicable intercourse with the primitive Church. The first is occasioned by the delivery of a charitable contribution; in the second, Paul not only receives for his official labours the full acquiescence of the Jerusalemites and their chiefs, but also, as an individual, the most flattering recognition (xv. 26); in the third, the extremely short record (xviii. 22) of it at least points out expressly that he exchanged greetings with the community at Jerusalem. In his last journey, the Apostle of the Gentiles is amicably received (xxi. 20), however great may be the prejudice against him, which is, moreover, at once brilliantly refuted by the testimony of James (xxi. 24) and by the avowal of Paul himself. We also find Paul in a connection with other individuals of the Jewish Christian circle, which we cannot indeed declare unhistorical, but the mention of which we can the less regard as unintentional, as silence is at the same time observed respecting his relation with those in less repute there; with Ananias, the Israelite pious in the Law (ix. 10 ff., xxii. 12); with Agabus, the prophet from Jerusalem (xi. 27 f., xxi. 10); with Philip and his soothsaying daughters (xxi. 8 f.), whose reputation is testified by the Judaist Papias (Eus. K. G. iii. 39, 4), Polycrates (the same, iii. 31, 2, v. 24, 1), and the Montanist Proclus (the same, iii. 31, 4).[1] On the other hand, every reminiscence of the well-known hostile relations to the Jewish Christians is avoided. Our book does not once mention Titus, the Apostle's faithful companion, for which occasions were not wanting; it entirely ignores the vehement struggle which Paul had to endure on his account; not a syllable is said of the scene with Peter at Antioch. Perchance because these things and persons were unknown to our author. They could not have remained unknown either to him who was for many years Paul's companion, or to the later one, who doubtless had the Epistle to the Galatians before him, and who even without it must have known of a man so celebrated as Titus, and of incidents which must have come often and much under discussion in the conflict of parties. The silence of our book is obviously intentional; the delineation of Paul's legal piety is not to be disturbed by any heterogeneous feature.[2]

If Paul individually is such a faithful adherent of Judaism, neither can any adverse position to it be expected in his *apostolic ministry*, and accordingly his opposition to Jewish particularism, and to the introduction of the Law into Christianity, is not only softened in the account given in the Acts, but is altered into the very reverse. Most significant in this respect is the fact that

[1] Respecting the identity of our Philip and the Philip celebrated in the tradition of Asia Minor, see above. *Schneckenburger's* conjecture (p. 161) that Philip and his family may have been one of Luke's chief sources of evangelical and apostolic history, stands or falls with the authenticity of Luke's writings; but if he considers the mention of the soothsaying daughters as a trace of that connection, the more obvious explanation consists in the reputation which these young women enjoyed among the Jewish Christians.

[2] More on this in the third Part, section 31.

(as Baur has exhaustively proved in his treatise on the Epistle to the Romans, and now again in Paul. pp. 362 f.) Paul, according to the Acts, turns only by compulsion to the Gentile mission, and does not anywhere consider himself justified in preaching the gospel to the heathen until the Jews have rendered his ministry among themselves impossible. While Paul himself regards the Apostolate to the Gentiles to be his vocation from the beginning (God revealed His Son in me, ἵνα εὐαγγελίζωμαι αὐτὸν ἐν τοῖς ἔθνεσιν, Gal. i. 16), he appears in the Acts (ix. 20 ff.) first in the Jewish synagogue at Damascus; and no mention is made of the journey to Arabia, of which, indeed, we do not know whether it was a missionary journey or not. Driven from Damascus by the Jews, he renews his efforts to convert his own people in Jerusalem and the neighbourhood (ix. 28), nay, as we are assured (xxvi. 20), in all Judæa. According to one account (ix. 29), he is expelled from this sphere of labour also by Jewish conspiracies against his life; according to the other (xxii. 17), Christ commands him in a vision to forsake it, because his preaching will be despised; but his attachment to the Jewish mission is so great that he at first allows himself to make objections even to the words of his Lord,[1] and yields only to a reiterated and distinct command. Even now it still requires fresh revelations to make the Apostle actually enter on his field of labour among the Gentiles, and our author does not neglect repeatedly and purposely to call attention to the fact that he only did so by the express will of God (xiii. 2, 4). Nevertheless, after all these antecedents, he never seems to feel quite secure in his right as Apostle of the Gentiles. Although he now preaches the gospel to the heathens also, wherever it is possible he still turns first to the Jews, and only if they despise it to the Gentiles. That we may have no doubt how much importance our author attaches to the observance of this principle, he passes over with cursory statements or in silence the most important missionary regions where he is unable to apply it, in order to allow the attention of

[1] Verses 19, &c., can only be understood in this way.

the reader to dwell exclusively on those which serve him as evidence. Immediately on the first appearance of Paul and Barnabas in Cyprus (xiii. 5), it is remarked that they preached the word of God, ἐν ταῖς συναγωγαῖς τῶν Ἰουδαίων; Sergius Paulus, the first-fruits of their mission, is also gained only by victory over a Jewish impostor. The next scene of their labours of which we hear any details is the synagogue of Antioch in Pisidia; when the Jews will not hear them, they turn to the heathen with the explicit declaration, xiii. 46, ὑμῖν ἦν ἀναγκαῖον πρῶτον λαληθῆναι τὸν λόγον τοῦ θεοῦ· ἐπειδὴ δὲ ἀπωθεῖσθε αὐτὸν, . . . ἰδοὺ στρεφόμεθα εἰς τὰ ἔθνη. Hence, if the Jews had not despised the gospel, they would have respected the privilege of the people of God, and would not have offered the Messianic salvation to the Gentiles, for whom it was not originally designed. The Gentiles have therefore every reason to rejoice at the course of events (ἀκούοντα δὲ τὰ ἔθνη ἔχαιρον καὶ ἐδόξαζον τὸν λόγον τοῦ κυρίου, verse 48). At the next station, too, in Iconium, it is the synagogue in which they speak (xiv. 1); a persecution emanating from the Jews compels them to fly to Lystra and Derbe, and here, indeed, they preach to the heathen population; but this is only a consequence of the hostility of the Jews of Iconium. Otherwise, no details are recorded of any other point at which they touch in this first journey. The same spectacle is repeated in the second. Respecting the foundation of the important communities in Galatia and Phrygia, we learn nothing, undoubtedly because there was here no opportunity of recording antecedent negociations with the Jews;[1] at Philippi, the first place concerning which any details are given, it is the Jewish προσευχὴ in which the Apostles make discourses on the Sabbath-days; the next station is Thessalonica, ὅπου ἦν ἡ συναγωγὴ τῶν Ἰουδαίων (xvii. 1); Paul here speaks on three Sabbaths, in presence of Jews and proselytes, until the Jews drive him out by means of a popular insurrection. He flies to Berea, and his first resort is again εἰς τὴν συναγωγὴν τῶν Ἰουδαίων (xvii. 10). Expelled also

[1] *Schneckenburger*, pp. 102 ff.; *Hilgenfeld*, Galaterbr. 24 ff.

from this by his old enemies, he wanders on to Athens, and even here we find him in the synagogue in conversation with Jews and their companions; that he turned to the Gentiles also is almost imperceptibly indicated in the words, διελέγετο ἐν τῇ ἀγορᾷ πρὸς τοὺς παρατυγχάνοντας, and is likewise specially ascribed, in a manner doubtless inoffensive to the Jews, to the wrath of the Apostle at the πόλις κατείδωλος. Before the Areopagus he certainly makes a speech to a pagan audience; but is it not as if the author expressly wished to prevent the suspicion that he had done this voluntarily, when he attributes a speech for which Paul had sufficient inducement in his apostolic vocation, merely to the urgency of the multitude which leads him before the Areopagus, and to the improbable transaction before the tribunal? The more protracted sojourn in Corinth comes next. Here Paul speaks in the synagogue every Sabbath-day, and wins over Ἰουδαίους καὶ Ἕλληνας (by which in this context we can only understand σεβόμενοι); after the arrival of Silas and Timothy he strives still more, διαμαρτυρόμενος τοῖς Ἰουδαίοις τὸν Χριστόν. Not until the Jews despise and reject him does he declare, as before at Antioch, τὸ αἷμα ὑμῶν ἐπὶ τὴν κεφαλὴν ὑμῶν καθαρὸς ἐγὼ ἀπὸ τοῦ νῦν (he would therefore not have allowed himself to do so before) εἰς τὰ ἔθνη πορεύσομαι, xviii. 6. Notwithstanding this experience at Corinth, the same procedure is repeated at Ephesus; after Paul visited the synagogue there on his first coming, and only deserted it when called away by the duty of visiting Jerusalem at the feast, on his second arrival he at once adjourns to the synagogue and teaches there for nearly three months; it is only the obstinacy and scorn of the Jews (xix. 9) which compel him, just as at Corinth, to seek another scene and another audience for his discourses. Even at the last moment of his ministry he is not unfaithful to this procedure; at Rome also his first step (xxviii. 17) is to summon the chiefs of the Jews; and here again the negociation ends with the declaration that, as the people of Israel would not hear the Messianic message of salvation, nothing remained but to turn with it to the Gentiles (xxviii. 25 ff., ἀκοῇ ἀκούσετε καὶ οὐ μὴ συνῆτε, &c. Γνωστὸν οὖν ἔστω ὑμῖν, ὅτι τοῖς ἔθνεσιν ἀπεστάλη τὸ σωτήριον τοῦ θεοῦ· αὐτοὶ καὶ ἀκούσονται). Can it be believed that Paul in reality followed these principles in the promulgation of the gospel? It is true, the theocratic privileges of his people were not indifferent even to the Apostle of the Gentiles. He admits that divine revelation was first confided to them; that by this means a prospect of attaining the promised salvation was opened to them (Rom. iii. 1 ff.); he extols them as the people of the covenant and of adoption, as the original owners of the Law, of the true divine worship and of the promise (Rom. ix. 4); he declares that although the Gospel, like the Law, is just as much intended for the Gentiles as for the Jews, it is, nevertheless, for the latter before the former.[1] Thus even in the midst of his labours among the Gentiles he does not lose sight of his own people; he protests that he would readily sacrifice his own salvation for theirs (Rom. ix. 3); he considers it the greatest triumph of his apostolic ministry to call forth the emulation of the Jews by its results in the heathen world (Rom. xi. 13 f.). According to these declarations we are obliged to assume, and from the existence of the Epistle to the Romans, which is certainly addressed also to Jewish Christians, we can likewise prove, that Paul did not exclude the Jews of the Dispersion from the vocation to the Gentiles which he recognized as his. It is likewise quite probable that he gladly made use of the point of contact which the synagogues offered to his ministry among the Gentiles.[2] But does it also follow that he could acknowledge it as a *principle* not to turn to the Gentiles until the unbelief of the Jews had entitled him to do so; that for months he could refrain, as at Ephesus and Corinth, from all influence upon the Gentiles in order to teach in the synagogue alone as long as it was not closed to him; that he could so entirely, without an exception, pursue the

[1] Ἰουδαίῳ τε πρῶτον καὶ Ἕλληνι, Rom. i. 16, ii. 9 f., wherein the τε καὶ expresses the equal position of the two on the part of God, the πρῶτον the precedence of the Jews in the order of time, their earlier entrance into the economy of salvation.

[2] Comp. *Schneckenburger*, pp. 79 ff.; *Kling*, Stud. und Krit. 1837, ii. 303 f.

course ascribed to him by the Acts, as he does here? If there is, strictly speaking, no single case recorded in which he voluntarily acts otherwise—if, moreover, at the beginning, the middle, and the end of his ministry he emphatically repeats declarations similar to those adduced—what else can the reader suppose but that he observed this principle in every place in which circumstances in any way allowed it? But can he really have done so? can he who from the first knew himself to be called the ἀπόστολος ἀκροβυστίας, have striven, as our book records, against entering on this vocation? can he have made the evangelization of the Gentiles dependent on the unbelief of the Jews? We should be obliged to reply in the negative to these questions, even if the narratives on which the descriptions of our book are supported were in other respects more firmly established than is the case with many of them, according to the investigations hitherto made. But if in the same context with the expression respecting the privileges of the Jewish people, Paul says that there is no difference between Jews and Gentiles, all men are alike sinners, and all may alike be saved by grace and faith (Rom. iii. 23 ff.; comp. 1 Cor. 1 24), the contrast between Jews and Greeks is unknown to Christianity (Gal. iii. 28)—if he founds these maxims on the fact that God is as much the God of the Gentiles as of the Jews (Rom. iii. 29 f.)—he nevertheless emphatically contrasts the spiritual sons of Abraham, in whom carnal descent is of no importance, with his descendants according to the flesh (Gal. iv. 21 ff.; Rom. ii. 28 f., iv. 11, 16); he declares that as an Apostle he feels bound to preach the gospel to all, to Greeks and barbarians without distinction (Rom. i. 14); he considers that to preach Christ to the Gentiles is the vocation of his life and the object of his election (Gal. i. 16, ii. 7). With these principles, how is it credible that he should have acted as is recorded in the Acts? If the gospel is designed alike for Gentiles and Jews, it must be preached in the same manner to both, and its promulgation to the Gentiles cannot be conditional on the failure of its announcement to the Jews; the messenger may address himself in the first instance either to Gentiles or to Jews, or to both at once, according to circumstances; but he cannot possibly make it a rule always to address himself first to the Jews, and only if no Jews are found, or if they reject him, to the Gentiles. And this is in no way altered by the πρῶτον of the Epistle to the Romans, of which we are reminded ad nauseam. The gospel belongs first to the Jews, because by their historical position they are first brought into contact with it; but by the will of God it is to the same extent and as unconditionally designed to be the only means of salvation for the Gentiles, and is therefore to be preached to them quite unconditionally, and without any regard to the conduct of the Jews. The Acts indeed also obliterates the characteristic of Paul's mission to the heathen in making him to a certain degree uphold the Mosaic Law, not only as regards himself individually, but also as regards his converts. Although in the 15th chapter the primitive community concedes the liberation of the Gentile Christians from circumcision, they are, on the other hand, bound by the Noachic precepts; but the Jewish Christians, after as well as before, are to be subject to the Law and circumcision. According to our book, Paul observed these principles so conscientiously that calumny alone could accuse him of alienating the Jewish Christians from the Law and circumcision (xxi. 21 ff.); and even where the individual only half belonged to the Jewish people by descent, like Timothy, he readily imparted to such an one the ceremony of circumcision out of consideration for his people. We have already inquired what is to be thought of the truth of such statements; only so much the more clearly does it appear how important they are in the eyes of the author of our book, if he found it necessary to contradict historical fact in a matter so well known, in order to carry out the portrait of the Apostle as he pictured it to himself.

It is certainly not surprising that a ministry of this nature experienced no opposition of consequence on the part of the Jewish Christians. What would they have lost by it—which of their rights, which of their convictions, would have been offended by it? Nothing but unfounded prejudice could have set them against the Apostle of the Gentiles; but *this* Paul had no reason to expect such a general and stubborn antagonism as the Pauline Epistles show to us. Accordingly, the opposition against him which we find in the Acts actually goes no further. The Apostle has some trouble here also with the prejudices of the Jewish Christians at Jerusalem (xxi. 20 ff.); but how trifling is this evil report, soon allayed, when compared to the unremitting conflicts with Judaism which the Pauline Epistles leave us to surmise? How entirely our book ignores the factions in Corinth, and the sufferings brought upon the Apostle by his opponents in Galatia and Ephesus; how little does it lead us to suspect that at Rome also he had to struggle with a party whose attachment to Judaism, as well as their prejudices against his own Christianity, Paul renders sufficiently transparent in the Epistle which he wrote to silence these prejudices! Whence this complete silence respecting the incidents which would give a glimpse of the dissensions between the Apostle of the Gentiles and the primitive Church, such as the occurrence at Antioch and the dispute about the circumcision of Titus; why not a word respecting the object of the last journey to Jerusalem? Perchance, merely because the author already made use of the collection for the 11th chapter, or also because this collection reminded him that a dissension existed between the Gentile and the Jewish Christians, for the reconciliation of which this love-offering was designed, to all appearance in vain. Everything which indicates party opposition within the Christian communities is most scrupulously obliterated in our book, and only so much remains as was utterly indispensable as a motive for the pacificatory decisions which it communicates. "Nowhere," observes Schneckenburger, in his excellent disquisition on this point, p. 100, "during the whole period of his apostolic ministry, does Paul, according to the Acts, experience any Judaistic attacks after the discords at Antioch are once appeased (and even they did not concern him in particular, but had broken out before the commencement of his real and independent apostolic labours), and after the resolutions taken by the Apostles and the primitive community of Jerusalem, granting recognition to the Gentile Christians." "It is only the unbelieving Jews (in Jerusalem) who hate and attack him. It is Jews alone who in foreign lands lay in wait for him everywhere; at Corinth (xx. 3), at Ephesus (xix. 3, 39), in the cities of Macedonia (xvii. 5, 13) and Lycaonia (xiv. 3, 13). He nowhere meets with heretical teachers contradicting him, casting suspicion on his doctrine and falsifying it, but he only foresees their coming (xx. 29 f.) after his decease. How does this harmonize with the pseudo-Apostles of Galatia, the anti-Paulinists of Corinth? Obviously, Luke has not merely omitted a certain number of facts in Paul's history, but those very ones which referred to the continued divisions between the Judaists and the Gentile Christians in the Christian communities, by which Paul was placed in conflict with the former party." The portrait of the Apostle given in our book is thus, in this respect also, brought into harmony with itself; his conduct towards the Jewish Christian party corresponds with their conduct towards him; no actual party opposition exists, and the unbelieving Jews alone are the common opponents of Christianity.

But the less we are able to acknowledge this description as a faithful delineation of historical truth, the more is there opened up to us on the other side an insight into the internal connection of the individual features of which this portrait is composed, and so much the more imperative becomes the task of tracing the leading points of view by which this description is characterized. This will be the chief business of the third division of our work.

Third Part.

THE ORIGIN OF THE ACTS OF THE APOSTLES.

FIRST DIVISION.

ON THE OBJECT OF THE ACTS.

1. THE ACTS A TENDENCY-WRITING.

To the hypothesis that our book has no merely historical motive, is opposed, in the first instance, the prologue of Luke's Gospel, which it was supposed might justifiably be referred to the Acts also, on account of its commencement. As the author specifies only the narration of facts as the object of his representation, it is said,[1] and as the same destination must likewise apply to our book, so it is unreasonable caprice to substitute another object for the one expressed by the author himself. This conclusion is, however, more than uncertain. It cannot in any way be proved that, in the composition of the Gospel, Luke had the Acts in his eye; there is no reference in the former to the latter; and in its history of the ascension, our book commences afresh in a manner utterly incapable of being harmonized with the conclusion of the Gospel; besides which, the history of the Apostles cannot be reckoned among the πεπληροφορημένα ἐν ἡμῖν πράγματα, the histories in which Theophilus was instructed, the

[1] For instance, *Credner*, Intro. p. 268. If I therefore treat this remark as one actually existing, it will not be quite so "absurd" as it is considered by *Lange*, Apost. Age, I. 89, who, it is true, makes the trifling confusion of mistaking that which I maintain with that which I dispute.

incidents which the author is to relate merely on the authority of others, and not as an eye-witness.[1] But what is the consequence if we assume, what is certainly not improbable, that, although while employed upon the Gospel the author was not contemplating the Acts, he nevertheless intended to intimate, by the incomplete opening sentence of his second book, that this was to be a history of the Apostles and their labours, just as the first was the history of Jesus? Does the object of an historical narrative, then, exclude the further design of producing a specific effect by this narrative? Or is our author to inform his readers, like the prologue in the Midsummer Night's Dream, that what he gives them as history is no real history, and that his Paul is not the real Paul? And even if he were fully conscious that he was sacrificing historical truth to his other objects, no intimation of the kind could be expected of him; but he might and must give that which he narrates as the simple representation of history.[2] Plato also gives as history his unhistorical delineations of Socrates, which he more than once even expressly introduces with the question respecting an historical progress. But it has still to be examined whether and how far the author of the Acts possessed this consciousness. After what we have already seen, we must at any rate assume it as probable that his notions of the duty of historical truth were different from ours.

An answer is thus given to those who meet the whole investigation with the question of conscience, How can we suspect extraneous motives in an historical narrative so "ingenuous?"

[1] See on this *Schneckenburger*, Zweck d. Apg. 7 ff.

[2] It is therefore the strangest objection to our view when it is said, with *Lekebusch*, Die Comp. und Ensteh. d. Apg. p. 253, that of a book written for a special object it must be expected that it would plainly and distinctly state this object; if, therefore, the Acts in the first instance gives the impression of a simple historical narrative, and if critics are not agreed as to its motive, neither are we justified in ascribing to it a definite dogmatic object, "otherwise the author would not attain his end with the majority of readers." As if he would not most securely attain his end if his whole representation were accepted as an historically true picture of the apostolic age; as if by this argument the purely historical character of the Clementine writings, or of the εἰκὼν βασιλική, or any similar party writing, might not be proved equally well.

how can we attribute an intentional perversion of truth to a writer so conscientious as Luke? This question is simply senseless, so far as it is to decide the matter previous to any examination of details. Whether the representation be thus ingenuous; whether our author be this conscientious, or, more correctly, this critical historian; whether the perversion of tradition for party purposes necessarily appeared to him as reprehensible as it does to us—all this can be made out only by an examination of our book itself; both the book and its author are what they are supposed to be, if in their narration of history they pursue no unhistorical objects; but whether this be so can only be shown by the investigation of details; to assume that they are not without further ceremony, is to cut off all discussion by a dogmatical prepossession.

But that we really have reason to ascribe to the Acts other than merely historical objects has been sufficiently demonstrated by Schneckenburger in his frequently mentioned work on the Object of the Acts. The critic, with perfect right, appeals to the manner in which our author treats his subject; to the remarkable parallel between Paul and the primitive Apostles, which is here obtained only by omitting many features in the portrait of Paul known to us from other sources, and placing others in a one-sided light; by similarity in the miracles as well as in the sufferings, in the doctrine and the demeanour of the two parties; by the stress laid on everything adapted to recommend Paul to the Jewish Christians, and to remove their prejudices against the Apostle of the Gentiles and his work; by slurring over such things as might serve to foster those prejudices; by the entire selection and arrangement of the historical material, which is incomprehensible from a purely historical point of view, and perfectly explicable by the apologetic interests of a Paulinist. These reasons receive great additional weight if we have become convinced that our author not only selects and arranges the historical material in a particular direction, but that he has also allowed himself the most vital deviations from actual history. For example, what would be striking in the similarity of the Pauline and Petrine miracles, even if all these miracles had actually occurred? Would it not even be evident that these very things were especially attractive to our author? Finally, might it not be the guidance of a higher dispensation that the two Apostles should have worked in an entirely similar manner? Is it strange if our book makes Paul everywhere begin by preaching to the Jews, and turn to the Gentiles only by compulsion, when most strenuous protestations are at the same time made by Schneckenburger (p. 79) against the accusation of an apologetic fiction on this occasion. Why should we seek for a special design in the account of the Apostle's speeches if these speeches are essentially historical? From this standpoint it is only the omission of sundry historical traits which retains anything striking; but part at least of these omissions might be excused by the possible ignorance of the author, and of the remainder, it might be granted that he omitted what was not according to his taste; but these data alone would scarcely be sufficient foundation for a distinct bias methodically pursued. It was, therefore, not merely a reaction of his sound critical judgment against the apologetics forced upon him, but also a result of his view of the object of the Acts, which induced Schneckenburger himself to admit all the doubts as to the credibility of this writing, which have been so acutely pointed out to him by Baur (Paul. pp. 9 f.). For this very reason a complete insight into the motives and internal constitution of our book can be gained only if we have first ascertained the historical truth of its statements by a historico-critical method, and have thus obtained a freedom of view for which our earlier discussions ought to furnish a foundation.[1]

[1] Hence we do not doubt the historical credibility of the Acts because the book is arranged on a systematic plan; but because, by testing the details, we have assured ourselves of the partially unhistorical character of its representation, we seek for the motives by which this representation may be explained. Therefore, when *Lange* (on the Apost. Age, i. 54) maintains that I argue, from the well-considered plan of the Acts, against its historical character, his assertion can only be characterized as a perversion.

Let us review the state of the case as established by the investigations we have hitherto made. The Acts relates in one part the history of the primitive Apostles and the community of Jerusalem, together with the promulgation of Christianity emanating from them until the independent appearance of Paul; in another part it relates the history of Paul. In this narrative there exists, in the first place, the most remarkable harmony between the *actions* and *destinies* of Peter and the older Apostles on the one side, and of Paul on the other. The two parts are not only similar in the description of their miraculous works (ii. 43, v. 16, viii. 6 f.; comp. xviii. 12, xix. 11, xxviii. 9), but there is also no species of Petrine miracle in the first part which is not attributed to Paul in the second.[1] If Peter opens his miraculous activity (iii. 2) with the healing of the man lame from his birth, Paul's first miracle of healing (xiv. 8) is likewise a χωλὸς ἐκ κοιλίας μητρὸς αὐτοῦ.[2] If Peter himself worked miracles by his shadow (v. 15), the aprons and handkerchiefs (xix. 12) of Paul exhibit no smaller degree of miraculous effect at a distance. If the expulsion of devils is specially recorded of Peter and his party, the evil spirit at Ephesus himself testifies (xix. 15), and the expulsion of the Python at Philippi (xvi. 18) and of other demons (xix. 11, xxviii. 9) confirms the fact how much the name of Paul was dreaded among them. No less awful is Paul to those allies of the evil spirits, the magicians, and to the whole magic-world (Elymas, xiii. 6 ff.; Ephesian sorcery, xix. 13 ff.); and in this he may well be placed in juxtaposition with the highly-extolled conqueror of Simon Magus (viii. 14 ff.). Of the Pauline (xiii. 6 ff.; comp. xix. 13 ff.) as of the Petrine (v. 1 ff.) judicial miracles, the Acts relates one example. Finally, that the acme of miraculous works should not be lacking, the raising of

[1] See *Schneckenburger*, pp. 52 f.; *Schwegler*, Nachap. Zeit. ii. 56.

[2] Respecting the perfect resemblance of these two narratives, even in expression, see above; the healing of the paralytic by Peter, ix. 33, with which Scheckenburger not quite appropriately parallels the cure of a man ill with a fever by Paul, xxviii., belongs to the general category of the healing of the lame, and therefore requires no special parallel.

Eutychus (xx. 9) on the Pauline side is set over against the raising of Tabitha by Peter (ix. 36 ff.). What can be more natural than that by these results Paul should have gained for himself the same veneration as Peter and his associates, only that this veneration can be more strongly expressed in the province of his labours than theirs? If the primitive Apostles are extolled and feared in the capital of monotheism, so that no one ventures to approach them, so likewise does no slighter awe[1] take possession of a pagan capital in consequence of the miracles which bear witness to Paul; if the semi-monotheistic Cornelius receives Peter with a *προσκύνησις*,[2] Paul is likewise called a god by the pagan population of Malta (xxviii. 6); and the Lystrians are on the point of sacrificing to him and Barnabas (xiv. 11 ff.), an honour which is naturally refused, and in almost the words employed by Peter[3] in the former passage.

This whole parallel, however—and just herein consists its importance in the present question—lies, not in the facts as such, for in these miracles, as has been already shown, we are on an entirely unhistorical basis. Neither is it possible to suppose that such a parallelism of the Pauline and Petrine miracles was already perfected in the tradition which our author found in existence. For as no given type pre-existed on which tradition could be modelled respecting the Apostles, as was the case with regard to Messianic legend, it would have been more than extraordinary if the innumerable sources which more or

[1] ii. 43, *ἐγένετο δε πάσῃ ψυχῇ φόβος*; v. 11, 13, *καὶ ἐγένετο φόβος μέγας ἐφ' ὅλην τὴν ἐκκλησίαν καὶ ἐπὶ πάντας τοὺς ἀκούοντας ταῦτα . . . . . τῶν δὲ λοιπῶν οὐδεὶς ἐτόλμα κολλᾶσθαι αὐτοῖς, ἀλλ' ἐμεγάλυνεν αὐτοὺς ὁ λαός.* This effect of the judicial miracle of Ananias and Sapphira corresponds perfectly with what is told in xix. 17, as the immediate result of the punishment of the Jewish exorcists, *ἐπέπεσε φόβος ἐπὶ πάντας αὐτοὺς καὶ ἐμεγαλύνετο τὸ ὄνομα Ἰησοῦ.* If to this be added that the legendary miracles recorded in v. 15 f., xix. 11, correspond most exactly, it is obvious that the second passage is an imitation of the first.

[2] Which cannot be softened down, as by *Lekebusch* (p. 260), into the customary Eastern form of greeting, otherwise Peter's words would be unmeaning (v. 26); comp. also Rev. xxii. 8.

[3] Peter, x. 26, *ἀνάστηθι, κἀγὼ αὐτὸς ἄνθρωπός εἰμι*; xiv. 15, Paul and Barnabas, *ἄνδρες, τι ταῦτα ποιεῖτε; καὶ ἡμεῖς ὁμοιοπαθεῖς ἐσμεν ὑμῖν ἄνθρωποι.*

less contributed to form the apostolic tradition should have stored up materials entirely similar for the stories of the two chief Apostles. Rather does a representation unmistakably moulded by a single interest, and carried out on a uniform plan, presuppose unity of authorship also. Of course, this does not exclude the possibility that a part, perhaps a large part, of the author's material was already supplied by tradition—how this was will be examined later; but whatever he may have derived from it, he must have made his selection from a definite point of view, and have examined, metamorphosed, and amplified it; otherwise this uniform whole could not have resulted from it. Several of these miraculous stories, moreover, actually bear distinct traces of this individual activity. If, for instance, the two healings of the lame men correspond, feature by feature, both as to fact and expression, if almost the same words are employed in x. 26 and xiv. 15, who will seek the reason anywhere but in identity of author? If in those general descriptions, which at any rate chiefly belong to the author himself, the same or strikingly similar statements are repeated (as in v. 15 f.; comp. xxviii. 9, xix. 11), from whom but him should this similarity be derived? Thus, in the story of John's disciples (xix.), and in the story of Apollos (xviii.), two accounts, standing in no immediate connection, which cannot have belonged originally to the same tradition, and of which the second especially bears no legendary impress, we found the same features, which, though not in accordance with truth, still serve the purpose of proving the disciples of John to be fit for the Pauline impartation of the Spirit. Can it be supposed that these features are derived from legend, and not much rather from our author? The parallelism of the Pauline and Petrine miracles must therefore be at any rate regarded as his own work.

As Paul is in no way behind Peter in the glory conferred by miracles, so are Peter and the primitive community in no degree inferior to Paul in sufferings and adversities, so that this parallel likewise must be essentially laid to the charge, not of history or tradition, but of our author. If we first take Paul into consideration, mention is repeatedly made of the calumnies of the Jews from whom he is obliged to fly (ix. 24, 30, xiv. 5, xx. 3), or he is driven out of a place by the Jews (xiii. 50, xvii. 10, 13 f.); and if this feature itself is required by the pragmatism of our book (see above), in none of the cases stated does Paul suffer any actual maltreatment. As little is this the case in xviii. 12 ff. and in xix. 21 ff., for in the first passage the accusation against him was dismissed, even before his defence by Gallio, and the chief accuser himself is beaten by the people; and in the second the noisy insurrection of Demetrius is ended, without any personal danger to the Apostle, by a similar pacificatory speech. Thus there remain but three cases in which Paul suffers real injury; i.e. the stoning at Lystra (xiv. 19), the arrest at Philippi (xvi. 16 ff.), the imprisonment in Palestine and Rome. As a fourth peril we may also add the shipwreck (xxvii. 20 ff.). But of all these sufferings there is not one, according to the representation of our book, which does not prove a triumph to the Apostle. In Philippi he is more than compensated for his previous maltreatment by his nocturnal liberation and the apology of the duumvirs; at Lystra (which Schneckenburger, p. 60, without reason excludes from the above canon) the divine providence watching over him is shown by his rising and going his way, as it seems, uninjured, immediately after being stoned; the marvellous rescue from the shipwreck, and from the danger at Melita (xxvii. 23, xxviii. 6), is a clear proof of a higher guidance; and at the same time the peril at sea affords him a brilliant opportunity of displaying his pre-eminent wisdom and his trust in God (xxvii. 21, 30 ff.). The imprisonment in Palestine becomes the medium of a series of apologies, which have the effect of eliciting an acknowledgment of his innocence from all the Jewish and Pagan authorities of the country, from the Pharisees of the Sanhedrim (xxiii. 9), king Agrippa (xxvi. 31 f.), the tribune Lysias (xxiii. 29), and the two procurators (xxiv. 22 ff., xxv. 18). Finally, the manner in which the author wishes the Roman imprisonment to be regarded is best shown by the circumstance that he is silent respecting its tragic conclusion, whereas he lays great stress on the liberty of preaching which is granted to the Apostle at Rome (xxviii. 30 f.), and the design of the dispensations which led him to this scene of his ministry (xxiii. 11, xxvii. 23, comp. xix. 21). If with these sufferings of Paul, which must all conduce to his glory, we compare those of the primitive community and its Apostles, it will be seen that they have no advantage over their younger colleague. If Paul is cast into prison and brought to judgment, the same occurred first to Peter and John (iv.), then to all the Apostles (v. 17 ff.), and again to Peter alone; if Paul received stripes at Philippi, the primitive Apostles received them previously at Jerusalem; if Paul was stoned, so was Stephen, the highly esteemed member of the community at Jerusalem, stoned to death; if Paul dies the death of a martyr (although our author does not mention it), not only did Stephen precede him in the same path, but also James, and he is an instance among the original Apostles of the manner of his death, namely, decapitation by the order of an impious despot (xii. 2, 20 ff.). Neither did the model church at Jerusalem remain free from internal altercations such as are not recorded of the Pauline communities; a murmur arose even against the Apostles (vi. 1 f.), and the golden age of the community of goods is stained by the transgression of Ananias and Sapphira. If, on the other hand, the Apostles of Palestine were the object of a special divine providence, Paul enjoys it to a no less extent; if an angel liberates Peter from close custody (xii. 7 ff.), if, similarly (v. 20), all the Apostles are led out of prison by an angel, so does a miraculous earthquake loose the bonds of Paul and his companion; if the angel of the Lord speaks to Philip (viii. 26), so does he appear to Paul also (xxvii. 23); if, according to the notions of later times, the Apostles were secured against venomous serpents (Luke x. 19; Mark xvi. 18), so is Paul the only one of whom our author confirms the fact by actual example. Paul's career is not more full of suffering, not less marked by divine providences, than is that of Peter and his associates.

Does this correspond with historical truth? or do we not learn much more of the Apostle's sufferings from the few indications given in the Pauline Epistles, than from this presumptively complete history? Where in our narrative are the greater number of those troubles and maltreatments recorded in the Second Epistle to the Corinthians, xi. 23 ff., comp. vi. 4 ff.,—the *many* imprisonments (before the last), the many perils of death, the five-fold scourging by the Jews, two out of the three scourgings, the three shipwrecks? Why no word of the vehement conflicts in the interior of the churches in Galatia, at Corinth, at Ephesus (1 Cor. xvi. 9)? Why is the *θηριομαχεῖν ἐν Ἐφέσῳ* (1 Cor. xv. 30) either entirely omitted, or distorted beyond recognition, in the insurrection of Demetrius? Why no word to explain the Apostle's complaints of the weakness of his flesh (1 Cor. iv. 9 ff.; 2 Cor. i. 8 f.; Gal. iv. 13), the *σκόλοψ ἐν τῇ σαρκὶ* (2 Cor. xii. 7 ff.)? Why this silence about the death of Paul, of which we see, from xx. 25, 38, that it had already taken place?[1] Is it at all likely that the author was *able* to say nothing of all these matters? If he was Paul's travelling companion, obviously not; but even if he was another person of more recent date, the remembrance of things made known to us in the Apostle's letters cannot have been effaced, one or two generations after his death, so completely that no tidings of them should have reached the ears of the historian. Many of these things, and, above all, the party conflicts in the leading communi-

[1] It is a very insufficient answer to these questions when it is said, with *Lekebusch*, Die Comp. d. Apg. p. 263, that the Acts mentions only the sufferings of Paul which influenced the spread of Christianity, for the greater number of those enumerated above obviously belong to the same category as those recorded in the Acts. Equally little does it avail to appeal with the same author to the slanders of the Jews, which drove the Apostle from one place to another, for this feature was indispensable to our author, for whose pragmatism it will be shown to form a main pivot; but the striking thing is that they are only slanders, of which but a few result in actual maltreatment.

ties, penetrated the religious life of that period far too profoundly not to leave a mark upon tradition; and the letters of the Apostle cannot possibly have been unknown to a later biographer. Hence we can only explain the silence of our book as proving that the author did not choose to say anything about the greater portion of the Apostle's sufferings. If this is sufficient to demonstrate the tendency-character of the writing, it appears still more distinctly from an observation made (pp. 232 ff.) earlier, quite independently of the present question, that the three alleged persecutions of the primitive Apostles, those of the 3rd and 4th, of the 5th and 12th chapters, are in reality reduced to one, the last-named, the first two being only imitations of this, in all appearance the produce of reflection rather than of legend. Let it only be considered what a situation this reveals. We find in our book a striking similarity between the sufferings undergone by Paul and the primitive community. But this parallelism became possible only by the omission of a great portion of those experienced by Paul, while those which befel the primitive Apostles are doubled and trebled. Now which is most probable, that tradition should have undertaken these alterations of historical material quite independently of the object of this parallelism; that by chance the persecution of the primitive community reached the ears of the author increased three-fold, while only a third of those endured by Paul came to his knowledge; or that these alterations were from the first directed to the effect attained by them, i.e. the similarity of the sufferings endured by the primitive Apostles and by Paul; that they are simply to be explained by the design and special object of the writer? The answer cannot be doubtful. Even the individual narratives are likewise, in a measure, calculated for this parallel, or at least are developed in the same spirit and in the same manner. For example, let us compare the story of Paul's imprisonment at Philippi with that of our fifth chapter. In both narratives, an imprisonment of the Apostle in consequence of a miraculous cure; in both, a two-fold liberation from imprisonment,—a supernatural one, which is, however, completely useless in its final result, and another, apparently natural, which, nevertheless, on nearer inspection proves to be equally improbable; in both, corporal punishment of the prisoners, only that in one case it is before, in the other after, the imprisonment; and in xvi. 24, moreover, the feature taken from the narrative, which served likewise as a model of the 5th chapter, a feature not wholly wanting here in ver. 23, namely, that the captives were guarded in an *ἐσωτέρα φυλακή*, in bonds seemingly impossible to unloose;—who can believe that the whole of this resemblance rests only on the accidental coincidence of the traditions or even of the historical incidents, and not much rather on the definite design of the author, who, for the object of the parallel, copied one narrative from the other, or—this may remain undecided for the present—invented both in the same interest? Nor is it otherwise with the two scenes before the Sanhedrim in the 5th and the 23rd chapters. If in both these the Pharisees take the side of the accused Apostles, and even grant the possibility that they may be real instruments of revelation;[1] and if this course has proved itself as unlikely in one case as in the other; if, moreover, in both cases the whole transaction in all probability never took place at all,—what can be more evident than that the two similar and equally unhistorical accounts proceeded from the same originator, namely, our author? In his representations alone do the chief Jewish parties occupy the position towards Christianity and to each other which is attributed to them alike in the 4th, 5th, and 23rd chapters; he alone makes the Sadducees the sole accusers, the Pharisees the defenders, of the Christians, and hence transforms Annas and Caiaphas into Sadducees; how can the design of this pragmatism and the tendency-character of our representation be mistaken?

[1] v. 39, where the categorical *εἰ ἐκ θεοῦ ἐστιν* should be noticed in contrast to the problematical *ἐὰν ἐξ ἀνθρώπων ᾖ*, and xxiii. 9, where the resemblance to ch. v. impressed itself so strongly on the transcribers that some transferred the *μὴ θεομαχῶμεν* thence.

This character appears even more strongly in the manner in which the doctrine and demeanour of the Apostle are depicted in our book. We have already pointed out (pp. 91 ff.) how remarkably the *doctrine* of Paul is cast into the background in its records, what a comparatively small space doctrinal discourse occupies in his addresses altogether; and how even this little does not bear the characteristic Pauline stamp. In all the Apostle's speeches, only a single timid reference to his doctrine of the law and justification (xiii. 38 ff.), and likewise only one cursory indication of the doctrine of atonement (xx. 28); elsewhere merely the proclamation of monotheism in opposition to pagan polytheism, the preaching of the resurrection and Messiahship of Jesus, of conversion and good works, "of righteousness, temperance, and judgment to come" (xxiv. 25); nothing of universal sinfulness, and reconciliation by the blood of Christ, of the cessation of the religion of the law, of justification by faith alone, of all the ideas which constitute the centre of Pauline Christianity. We hear but the maxims of Jewish Christianity from the lips of the Apostle of the Gentiles,[1] only the same evidence for the Messiahship of the risen Jesus, the same call to μετάνοια which previously came from Peter (ii. 22 ff. 38, iii. 13 ff., v. 30 ff., x. 37 ff.). The forgiveness of sins also, instead of its Pauline connection with the atoning death, is put in the same relation (in xiii. 38) to faith in the risen and glorified Jesus as in the first part by Peter (ii. 38 ff., iii. 19, v. 31, x. 43), or even on purely Jewish ground (Luke i. 77) by Zacharias. And that the similarity of this and the Jewish Christian standpoint may not escape us, the Pauline speech, which contains the most minute development of doctrine, so much resembles the earlier addresses of Peter and of Stephen, that we were already obliged (p. 95) to acquiesce in the opinion of those who regard it only as an echo of those discourses. So much of the Pauline doctrine as is communicated to us, our author makes Peter, Stephen, and even James, pro-

[1] Comp. on this also, *Schwegler*, Nach-ap. Zeitalter, p. 96.

claim more distinctly than Paul himself. Peter says[1] that before God there is no difference between Jews and Gentiles, for the Gentiles, the unclean, are cleansed by faith (xv. 9; comp. Gal. iii. 28); he calls the Law a burden which neither they nor their fathers have been able to bear; he declares (xv. 11; comp. iv. 11, and also Rom. ix. 32 f.) that Jews as well as Gentiles can be saved only by the grace of Christ; Stephen refers (vii. 48 ff.) to the end of worship in the Temple; James professes (xv. 17) Pauline universalism, although without the complete foundation of the doctrine of law; in the Paul of the Acts these principles are difficult to discover. But if Paul cannot have spoken in a manner so un-Pauline, neither can Peter and James have spoken in a manner so Pauline; nor can the well-known historical character of his heroes have been so strange to our author as to allow him to have imagined that they had really spoken thus; his representation is to be explained by nothing but an intentional and biassed alteration of historical fact.

We are led to the same conclusion by the account which he gives of the conduct of Paul on the one side, and the original Apostles on the other. If Paul appears here as an Israelite pious in the Law; if, even amidst the greatest urgency of the affairs of his apostolic office, he will not abandon the old journeys to the national sanctuary; if he not only undertakes vows and Nazaritism (or a Nazarite offering), but does so also with the express object of refuting the calumny that he teaches apostasy from the Law; if he values the theocratical privileges of his people so highly, that from the beginning to the end of his apostolic ministry he always preaches first to the Jews, and to the Gentiles only when compelled by the former's unbelief, by divine commands, or by special circumstances; if at the apostolic council he binds himself to acquiesce in the Law and circumcision among the Jews, and to impose at least the Noachic precepts upon the Gentile Christians; if he himself circumcises

[1] See *Schneckenburger*, pp. 187 ff.

Timothy, the Gentile Christian, out of consideration for his Jewish fellow-countrymen;[1] if, on the other side, the men of the primitive Church not only most readily acknowledge the principle of Gentile baptism, but are also the first to avow this principle and act in accordance with it; if Peter, even in his first speech, while admitting the prerogatives of the theocratic nation, at the same time alludes to the possibility of forfeiting them;[2] if Philip preached to the semi-pagan Samaritans; and Peter and John, commissioned by the Twelve, imparted the final consecration to those whom he baptized; if Peter, in consequence of the clearest revelations, baptized the Gentile Cornelius with the consent of the Jerusalemites; if, even before the appearance of Paul, the Gentile Christian community of Antioch arose and was recognized by the pious (xi. 24), well-approved (iv. 36) plenipotentiary of the primitive community; finally, if, on the recommendation of Peter and James, the assembled Jerusalemites issued a charter which emancipates them from the Law and circumcision—if Paul and the party of Palestine exchanged parts in this manner —it requires, in truth, very little critical candour to suspect, even previous to any examination of details, that some distinct tendency underlies such a striking transformation of characters. And if the full conviction has been gained that this representation was rendered possible only by means of a series of thorough historical contradictions; that of the five journeys to Jerusalem known to the Acts, only three are historical, and of these three not one had originally the object which our book attributes at least to the last (xxiv. 11, 17); that Paul cannot have undertaken either the Corinthian vow (xviii. 18) or the services contrived for him in xxi. 23, least of all from the motives here stated; that the method respecting the instruction of the Gentiles and the Jews, which, according to our represen-

[1] See above, Vol. II. p. 32.

[2] iii. 26: *ὑμῖν πρῶτον ὁ θεὸς ἀπέστειλεν αὐτὸν* ('Ιησοῦν), which obviously implies, what is announced by Paul and Barnabas, xiii. 46: *ὑμῖν ἦν ἀναγκαῖον πρῶτον λαληθῆναι τὸν λόγον τοῦ θεοῦ, ἐπειδὴ δὲ ἀπωθεῖσθε αὐτὸν, στρεφόμεθα εἰς τὰ ἔθνη.*

tation, he imposed upon himself as a duty, belongs to the author alone and not to him; that scenes such as that with the Roman Jews lack all historical possibility; if, likewise, the universalism of Peter and James has been found more than suspicious, and in the story of the conversion of Cornelius not only single unhistorical elements have been seen, but, from beginning to end, nothing except what is unlikely and incredible; if, finally, with the assistance of the Epistle to the Galatians, a proper appreciation of the apostolic council has been arrived at, Paul's supposed concessions to Judaism put aside, and those of the original Apostles to Paul reduced to their true standard,—not the slightest doubt can remain that it is not history, not even legend, but pure pragmatizing reflection which produced the remarkable harmony between the conduct of Paul and the primitive community, which turned the Apostle of the Gentiles into a Petrinist, the Apostles of the Jews into Paulinists. What we have remarked above with reference to the stories of the sufferings of Paul and of the primitive community, of the difference between the formation of legend and the composition of tendency-history, might be repeated here.

With respect to their *apostolic authorization* also, there is no essential difference[1] between Paul and the original Apostles. If, with the latter, it was founded on their personal relation to Christ, the want of which was very early a main argument for refusing to Paul the dignity of an Apostle,[2] and was also employed by the Ebionite party for this object far into the second century;[3] if, on the other side, Paul himself encounters his antagonists with the question (1 Cor. ix. 1), οὐκ εἰμὶ ἀπόστολος; οὐχὶ Ἰησοῦν Χριστὸν τὸν κύριον ἡμῶν ἑώρακα,—this is the very attestation by the personal appearance of Christ which the Acts proclaims with unmistakable emphasis, inasmuch as it records the conversion of the Apostle no less than three times, and moreover relates (xxii. 18, xviii. 9, xxiii. 11; comp. also

[1] See on this especially, *Schwegler*, pp. 77 ff.

[2] 2 Cor. v. 16, x. 7, xi. 5.

[3] Clem. Hom. xvii. 13 f.

xvi. 9, xxvii. 23) or hints at (xxvi. 16) still further appearances of Christ, so that Paul, no less than the συνελθόντες τοῖς ἀποστόλοις ἐν παντὶ χρόνῳ (i. 21), bears testimony in his evangelical preaching to what he himself heard and saw (xxii. 15, xxvi. 16; comp. iv. 20). He too is a μάρτυς τῆς ἀναστάσεως Ἰησοῦ (i. 22, x. 41), a valid witness of the fact to which the Acts reduces the whole characteristic doctrine of Christianity.[1] But as this visionary species of credentials was not recognized by the Ebionite party,[2] it was necessary for the Jewish Christian authorities to lead the way; the appearances of the risen Lord vouchsafed to the older Apostles are likewise represented by our book in the guise of visions (ὀπτανόμενος, i. 3; ὤφθη, xiii. 30), and so far, after the Apostle's own example (1 Cor. xv. 5 ff.), on a level with the οὐράνιος ὀπτασία (xxvi. 19) at Damascus;[3] Stephen also sees the Lord in a visionary manner (vii. 55), but it is Peter especially who prepares the way for Paul, for he is similarly charged by a vision with the ἀποστολὴ ἐθνῶν. It is just this latter narrative which especially proves the designedness of the whole parallel. For if the conviction has already been forced upon us that this incident is unhistorical, it bears, on the other hand, plain indications of having been copied from the course of events occurring at the conversion of Paul. Not only is the object—a call to the mission to the Gentiles—the same, but also the form of the two visions, according to Schneckenburger's (p. 170) subtle observation, is strikingly similar: both times two inter-connected visions, those of Paul and Ananias, of Peter and Cornelius; both

[1] *Lekebusch* overlooked this (comp. d. Apg. 373) when he considers that speeches such as i. 21 f., x. 41, must have been most offensive to the Gentile Christians, as they institute a criterion of apostolic authorization inapplicable to Paul. Our author removes this stumbling-block, inasmuch as he claims this for Paul as regards the main point, the μαρτυρία τῆς ἀναστάσεως, for it was impossible for him to reject the criterion itself if he did not wish to cut off every point of agreement with the Jewish Christians.

[2] Clem. Hom. in another place; also *Baur*, Paul. pp. 84 ff.; *Schneckenburger*, p. 170.

[3] Similarly the Gospel of Luke, xxiv. 34, comp. ver. 23; whereas neither Matthew nor Mark apply to the risen Jesus this expression, elsewhere employed only with reference to the appearances of angels and spirits. John ignores the word entirely.

times the express testimony of what was seen by the beholder's own narrative (xi. 5 ff., xxii. and xxvi.). The voice, too, which spoke to Peter seems (x. 14) to be described as the voice of Christ.[1] It would, in truth, be marvellous if this accordance of the two things were not founded upon the positive intention of representing them as similar, which appears again distinctly in the twice-repeated narration of the one, and the three-fold repetition of the other. But if, after all these proofs, Paul's equality with the original Apostles should still be a subject of doubt, every hesitation must disappear when we see, from xix. 1 ff., that the Apostle of the Gentiles was not wanting in the token which Jewish Christian tradition held to be the most characteristic privilege of the apostolic office, shared by no other preacher of the gospel, however distinguished; that he as well as Peter (viii. 14 ff.) possessed the full power of communicating the Holy Ghost by the imposition of hands. This at the same time constituted the most triumphant refutation of the Ebionite calumny expressed in the legend of Simon; it incontrovertibly proved that Paul was not the intruder who had begged this gift from the Palestinians, and had begged in vain; in case the legend of Simon had already turned the sorcerer into the disciple of John, the trait that it was the disciples of John to whom Paul imparted the final consecration contained a further refutation of the hostile slander.

Finally, if we examine what the Acts records of the *personal* relations between Paul and the Jewish Christian party, it has been already observed by others, and shown in this book, p. 100, Vol. II., how friendly they are here represented to have been. Of the Apostle's ceaseless conflicts with the Judaists, scarcely a trace; not a syllable is said of the Corinthian, Galatian, Ephesian, and Roman adversaries, who, according to his Epistles, drove Paul to desperation; the παρείσακτοι ψευδαδέλφοι, whom he was obliged to

[1] For although the title, κύριε or κύριοι, undoubtedly occurs elsewhere (for instance, x. 4, xvi. 30), the case is quite different when it is applied, not to a person present, but to a voice from heaven.

oppose so decidedly at Jerusalem (Gal. ii. 4), are mentioned in the mildest manner (xv. 5); the passionate hatred of the zealous Jewish Christians against the assailant of the Law is softened in xxi. 20 into a suspicion easily refuted; even in places such as Ephesus (1 Cor. xvi. 19) and Corinth, where Paul was most certainly troubled by the enmity of the Jewish Christians, the unbelieving Jews are his only antagonists (xx. 19, 3).[1] Similarly, on the other hand, everything irritating which might have been recorded of the Pauline side is carefully cast into the background; Titus, the faithful fellow-worker of Paul, who was, however, uncircumcised, and the cause of the dispute in Jerusalem, are merely named here; the impetuous scene with Peter, for which even the Clementine writings cannot forgive Paul,[2] is passed over in profound silence, and only the squabble with Barnabas (xv. 37) is mentioned instead, at any rate a far less important occurrence. So much the more expressly emphasized is Paul's amicable intercourse with the community of Jerusalem and the whole Jewish Christian party. Immediately after his conversion, it is Ananias, ἀνὴρ εὐσεβὴς κατὰ τὸν νόμον, μαρτυρούμενος ὑπὸ πάντων τῶν Ἰουδαίων (xxii. 12), who receives and baptizes him at Damascus; soon afterwards he himself hastens

[1] That such a representation was not adapted to draw the Jewish and Gentile Christians together (*Schneckenburger*, p. 223) is an assertion that *Lekebusch* (p. 369) should not have repeated. This would indeed have failed if the author had invented the Jews' attacks upon Paul without any traditional motive, but it will not be asserted by any one who shares our view. The case was rather that the enmity between Paul and the Jews (including the Jewish Christians) was well established in general tradition. Under such circumstances, it was incontestably a very suitable version to separate the cause of the Jewish Christians from that of the Jews; for the Paulines to say that the Apostle of the Gentiles was not persecuted by their Jewish fellow-christians, the Jewish Christians by their Christian forefathers and fellow-countrymen; and that these attacks were made much more by the unbelieving portion only of the Jews, by the same people and in the same manner as on the original Apostles. It is most overwhelmingly proved that Gentile and Jewish Christians together constituted one party, and found their common antagonism in unbelieving Judaism. Our author pursues the same course in this respect as, for example, the friends of the Evangelical Union now-a-days, when they postpone the antagonism of Lutheran and Reformed to that of Catholic and Protestant.

[2] Hom. xxii. 3.

to Jerusalem, and stands on the most confidential terms with the Twelve, the revered Barnabas having made himself responsible for him (ix. 26 ff.); three further journeys are so many proofs of his good agreement with the primitive community. So also in the last of his pious pilgrimages to the national sanctuary, he is hospitably entertained before his arrival by the esteemed Philip and his daughters, warned by Agabus, the prophet of Jerusalem (xxi. 8 ff.), and joyfully received by the brethren at Jerusalem (xxi. 17 ff.). A similarly friendly and honourable reception awaits him (xxviii. 17 ff.) on the part of the Roman Christians, of whom, however, the author is strangely unable to record anything further than that they went some stations outside the city to meet Paul. The design pervading this representation is shown by the doubling of the journeys to Jerusalem (see above), the unhistorical delineation of incidents (ix. 19 ff.), and the silence respecting Titus and the scene at Antioch. As regards these journeys, we have already seen how little historical foundation there is for two of them, and how they look as if they were copied without any definite occasion from the historical journeys. Now if we have ascertained the particular object which our author must have had in an imitation of this sort, it can scarcely be subject to doubt that this imitation originated only in himself, and not in any traditional source. The same applies, as has been already observed, to the narrative of the 9th chapter. Finally, the transactions about Titus and the dispute with Peter, matters universally known in primitive Christian times, which from their nature ought to be as little wanting in a history of the Acts as, for instance, the religious debate at Marburg in a history of the German Reformation, could only be omitted with a special object; and in this, as in everything else, our book proves itself a decided tendency-writing.

This is, of course, not to be understood as if the similarity of Palestinian and Pauline parts was carried out to the complete similarity of each individual feature. Such a slavish resemblance of the two descriptions would be scarcely possible to a writer not utterly devoid of art or taste, even in a matter of entirely free invention; but it is much more incredible when a perfectly new building is carried out by one who does not invent freely on vacant ground, but employs an existing tradition, and respects it, as much as possible, even when most thoroughly metamorphosed. In this case nothing else can be expected but that the writer should allow much to stand which did not directly serve his dogmatic purpose; that he should not always expunge even what contradicted his own standpoint; but frequently content himself with rounding off the dangerous points by minute alterations, or with neutralizing their effect by juxtaposition with narratives of opposite tendency. We shall ascertain later that our author was in the last-mentioned position. Hence, if the narratives of Paul and the original Apostles offer much that is peculiar as well as cognate, this affords no ground for disputing the correctness of the above-named parallels and the force of its evidence; but the question must still remain whether, in the fundamental features of the picture we obtain of Paul and Paulinism on the one side, and of Jewish Christianity and its Apostles on the other, a resemblance exists which it was impossible to reach without thorough alteration of the historical position. Now that this was actually the case, we believe we have shown not only in the present section of this work, but throughout our whole criticism of the apostolic history. So long as this is not refuted in its main points, the assertion that the Acts is a tendency-writing is fully justified.[1]

[1] According to this, what can it prove against our view if *Lekebusch* (d. Comp. u. Ensteh. d. Apg. p. 258) demonstrates with cheap wit in a straggling discussion, that the similarity of the Pauline and Petrine narratives is not absolute? Peter works through his "unsubstantial shadow," Paul by his "material aprons and handkerchiefs;" the former performs his judicial miracle on Christians, the latter on a Jewish impostor; Peter, in x. 25, speaks only a few words to Cornelius, Paul makes a long speech at Lystra, xiv. 15 (of three verses); Peter and John in Samaria impart the Holy Spirit to persons baptized, Paul to mere disciples of John, &c. This is no question of minor deviations such as these, but merely whether the two parts are made to appear *essentially* alike, and whether this resemblance corresponds to actual history or not. That in the latter case it can only be explained by the bias assumed by us, *Lekebusch* repeatedly admits; but what he produces as proofs of the truth of the

When it is therefore usually supposed that the author of the Acts intended his writing merely as an historical description, and that his dogmatical point of view or his regard for special readers was of subordinate importance in the selection and arrangement of the historical material, we are compelled entirely to contradict this view. The actual nature of our book cannot thus be accounted for. If the Acts is a history of the Church in the apostolic age, as the majority still assume,—if the author puts together in his book everything that was known to him of the history of the Apostles and the apostolic communities,—it still remains incomprehensible that on the appearance of Paul the original Apostles and the community at Jerusalem should fall so completely into the background, and be mentioned only where they come in contact with Paul. Not less remarkable are the numerous gaps in the history of Paul, the silence of our book respecting the majority of the sufferings mentioned by the Apostle in 1 Cor. xi., the ceaseless conflicts with Judaizing

representation now under consideration is so feeble, that I can scarcely regret having received his work at a time when the MS., as far as the second division of the present work, was no longer in my hands. It is there denied that in iv. 15, a healing power was attributed to Peter's shadow (p. 257), although in ver. 16 it is said, ἐθεραπεύοντο ἅπαντες, and although the representation of the Acts would be entirely misleading and perplexing if the author had not intended these words to be referred to ver. 15; with a contemptuous shaking of the shoulders it is lamented that in the raising of Eutychus it is not certain whether it actually was a raising of the dead (p. 259), although *Lekebusch* himself subsequently admits (p. 381) that the author certainly "intended to relate a miracle;" not only are the expulsion of the soothsaying spirit at Philippi and the incident with the viper, xxviii. 3 ff., but also the earthquake, xvi. 26, and its effects, and the healing of a man sick of a fever, xxviii. 8, supposed to be not actual miracles, but the fulfilment of prayer such "as have taken place in all ages, and take place still," such as may be perfectly understood also by a "sound philosophy"! On xxviii. 9, *Lekebusch* even makes the sensible remark that Luke the physician may have had his share in these cures (see pp. 380 ff.). We may be allowed to dispense with answering such evasions, or with demonstrating again, in opposition to *Lekebusch*, what we have already minutely proved in opposition to *Neander*, that Paul wished circumcision to be abolished even for Jewish Christians; neither shall we enter upon the summary questions, Why should not first Peter and John, and then all the Apostles, have been taken prisoners? (p. 264). Why should it be incredible that Peter received Cornelius into the Christian community without previous circumcision? If our earlier criticism has not brought conviction, neither would further discussion be able to do so. We have, however, not found any new remarks in *Lekebusch* which require a fresh rejoinder.

antagonists, the internal condition of the Pauline communities, the foundation of the Galatian churches, the journey to Arabia, the dispute about Titus, the scene at Antioch, the great collection of alms, the result of the imprisonment at Rome. We cannot attribute this phenomenon to the incompleteness of the sources; whether the author was or was not that companion of Paul which tradition proclaims him to have been. For in the first case, as far as Paul is concerned, he must necessarily have known by personal observation and inquiry much more than he communicates to us; and even of the history of the original community and its Apostles he must, without any special investigation, have heard much, during the year and a half at Cæsarea, which he has not mentioned. In the other case he doubtless had before him the Pauline Epistles, or at any rate a tradition far too developed not to apprize him of matters which he has passed over; wherever he could collect what he imparts, he must also have had opportunities of acquiring more. The information of any one capable of relating the earlier history of Peter in so much detail would assuredly not cease all at once with the appearance of Paul. Any one so narrowly acquainted with all the negociations between Paul and the Jerusalemites must surely have heard something of the circumstances of the community at Jerusalem, the incident at Antioch, and so many other matters. But our author himself betrays in more than one passage (xviii. 23, xx. 25, xxiv. 17) that he knows more than he thinks fit to communicate. Are we to suppose that he considered what he excludes to be less important than what he accepts?[1] the celebrated dispute with Peter as less important than the squabble with Barnabas about Mark? the non-circumcision of Titus as less significant than the alleged circumcision of Timothy? a second and a third repetition of the accounts of Paul's conversion, the speeches of the 23rd chapter, and the letter from Lysias to Festus, the elaborate detail of the story of Cornelius, as more

[1] The point of view from which *Baumgarten*, in various passages of his Commentary, seeks to justify the selection of materials in our book.

necessary than any statements respecting the Galatian and Corinthian party conflicts, the condition of the Christian community in the metropolis of the world, the protracted ministry of Paul in the capital of Achaia? This is not credible. Neither is it more credible that the author, as Meyer (p. 5) and others insist, should have passed over some things because he assumed them to be already known to the reader; for what was more widely known than Paul's conversion, and yet he relates it three times? what is better known to the reader of the 10th chapter than the visions, which are, nevertheless, repeated in full detail in the 11th? and what sort of historian would he be who does not even briefly allude to subjects with which the reader may perchance be acquainted, but passes them over in perfect silence? This silence would not be explicable even if the author intended to write a τρίτος λόγος, a continuation of our book;[1] for of the events which fall within the range of our narrative only a very small portion could in any case be subsequently supplied, the gaps in our description could not be filled up by them.[2]

But if the usual view of the object of the Acts cannot be carried out even on the traditional premisses respecting its historical credibility, it loses all foundation when it is seen how much that is unhistorical it records, and how much of this unhistorical material can be explained only by reflection on the part of the author, and not by purposeless legend. If the description is from the commencement adapted to the parallel between Peter and Paul, and if this parallel is obtained only by a thorough alteration of history, by unhistorical episodes, additions, and changes in the historical material, it is quite obvious that the writer with whom this description originated has some other object in view than the mere transmission of history.

The same reasons are also opposed to the hypotheses which

[1] *Credner*, Einleitung, i. 277 ff.

[2] Neither is this *Credner's* opinion; it is only the abrupt termination of the Acts which caused him to suppose the intention of continuing the history.

assume for our book a more special but still essentially historical object; such as that the author relates only what he himself saw or had heard from eye-witnesses;[1] that he intended to give a history of Peter and Paul,[2] or a Christian missionary history,[3] or more especially a history of the spread of Christianity from Jerusalem to Rome.[4] After all that has gone before, we are altogether unable to impute such purely historical motives to our author; and even, independently of this, the internal construction of the Acts cannot be explained by any of the objects adduced. It seems to us beyond doubt that very few of the narratives in the book are traceable to eye-witnesses; that, moreover, other things which must have been known to any companion of Paul are here passed over. Our book certainly gives us a history of Peter and Paul, but this history is neither so faithful nor so complete as we should expect; and neither its deficiencies nor its partial untruthfulness can be explained merely by the nature of the sources employed by its author. From a general history of Christian missions, we should necessarily expect tidings of the spread of Christianity in Eastern countries, of the foundation of the Galatian and Roman churches,[5] of Paul's ministry at Corinth, of the internal condition of the infant communities; and even a special history, as Meyerhoff, not without some inkling of the truth, assumes it to be, ought not to pass over the greater number of these points; while, on the other hand, neither had any direct reason for giving the minute accounts of the trial of Stephen, Paul's vindicatory speeches, the occurrences in his captivity, the reiterated narration

[1] *Michaelis*, Einleit. ins N. T. ii. 1179; comp. the evidences in *Credner's* Einleit. ins N. T. i. 283.

[2] *Grotius*, in his Commentary, on the Superscription.

[3] *Ziegler*, in *Gabler's* neuestem Theol. Journal, vii. 1, 125; *Eichhorn's* Einleit. ins N. T. ii. 19; *De Wette's* Einleit. ins N. T. 4 Div. p. 221 and others.

[4] *Meyerhoff's* Einleit. in d. petrin. Schriften, p. 5; *Baumgarten* on the Acts; *Lekebusch* on the Comp. and Origin of the Acts, 199 ff., 364 ff.

[5] For of course no one who regards our book as purely historical can admit that it considers Paul as the actual founder of the latter.

of the conversions of Paul and Cornelius. But if, besides the external and internal spread of the Church, its limitations and internal formation are also (as by Meyerhoff) to be included among the objects of our book, it would be equivalent to abandoning the speciality of its object, and returning to the vague notion of a history of the primitive Christian Church. The main point is, that the phenomena which we have exhibited in the parallelism of the Petrine and Pauline portions, and in the unhistorical foundation of this parallelism, are incomprehensible on the supposition of a history of apostolic missions.

It is usually believed that the peculiarities which go beyond any purely historical object in our book, are to be explained partly by its destination for Theophilus, partly by the acknowledged Paulinism of the author.[1] The two explanations in fact coincide; for of Theophilus, of whom, indeed, we know nothing, it is assumed that he was a Gentile Christian; consideration for Theophilus would therefore, like his own Paulinism, have induced the author to lay most stress on the subjects most interesting to Gentile Christians, i. e. the concerns of the Apostle of the Gentiles, the communities founded by him, his conduct and his principles. But precisely for Gentile readers would it have been least necessary, and in his Paulinism would there have been the smallest inducement *to judaize* the Apostle of the Gentiles; to Gentile Christians and Paulinists the internal condition of the Pauline communities would surely have been no less instructive than the three imprisonments of Peter; an account of the struggles which Paul had to undergo there with antagonists, and the errorists whom he had to conquer, would have been no less valuable than a second and third repetition of the story of his conversion. A history of the founding of purely Gentile Christian churches would not have been more uninteresting than the similar recurring incidents in the mixed communities, the maintenance of Gentile Christian liberty in the case of Titus no less

[1] Comp. *Olshausen*, Comm. Einl. p. 542; *Meyer*, Erkl. d. Apg. p. 5; *Credner*, Einl. i. 269.

important than its sacrifice in the case of Timothy. If our book is supposed to have been written especially for Gentile Christians and from a Pauline standpoint, everything remains inexplicable which serves either to conceal the characteristics of this standpoint, to diminish its contrast to Judaism, or to place the Apostle of the Gentiles in a position towards the Jewish Apostles and their party at variance with his own statements. But, above all, the freedom of its treatment of history (which alone made the parallel between Peter and Paul possible) presupposes that dogmatical points of view do not merely play into one another in it, that its representation is not only modified by the author's standpoint and the character of the reader, but is essentially determined by them; that we are here not dealing with an historical narrative having a dogmatical background, but with a free employment and metamorphosis of history for dogmatical purposes.

This point of view must, however, be more fully worked out, and these purposes must be more accurately and correctly defined, than has been done by the older commentators. If it be said, for instance, that our book is intended to prove the divinity of Christianity by its miraculous extension,[1] it is in fact equivalent to regarding it as a missionary history of the apostolic age; its peculiar character is as little explained by one hypothesis as the other. If we consider its object to be the justification of Pauline universalism,[2] it might not unreasonably be objected[3] that the book contains much which does not serve this purpose, such as the description of the community at Jeru-

[1] *Eckermann*, Erkl. aller dunkeln Stellen des N. T. ii. 165. *Hänlein*, Einl. iii. 165. Similar definitions of earlier exegesists, but which are not applied to the explanation of the peculiarities in style of the Acts, those of Chrysostom, Luther, Flavius, &c., in *Credner*, Einl. ii. 271 f., 269.

[2] Paulus *de consilio, quo scriptor, in actis apost. concinnandis ductus fuerit*, Jen. 1794, printed in the *capita selectiora introductionis* in the N. T. 283 ff. It is doubtlessly the same dissertation which is quoted by ancients and moderns under Griesbach's name, but alike in title, the place in which it is printed, in date, and in import.

[3] *Eichhorn*, Einl. ii. 23 ff.; *Kuinöl*, Comment. Proll. xvi.

salem, the stories of Ananias and Sapphira, of Stephen, the execution of James, Peter's imprisonment, Simon Magus, and the imprisonment of Paul; and although we shall certainly find that even of these subjects the greater number are connected with the Pauline interest, yet, in the first place, it is not to Pauline universalism that they immediately refer; and, secondly, this connection becomes probable only if our author be credited with a handling of the historical material incomparably freer than is supposed by the originators of the view of which we are speaking. But what stands most in the way of such view in its older aspect is the circumstance that neither the similarity of the fates of Paul and the original Apostles, nor the partial sacrifice of pure Paulinism, can be thus explained; and Pauline universalism likewise suffers very essential limitations by the apostolic decree, the circumcision of Timothy, Paul's observance of the Law, and his principles as to the authorization of the Gentile mission.

Still less can we agree with those who attribute various objects to the main divisions, or even to the single narratives, of our book;[1] for the mutual reference of these divisions, the evenness of details, the unity of presentation, which our investigation of the Acts has partially exhibited already, and will partially exhibit further on, are all incompatible with this hypothesis. Our task will much rather be that of discovering the idea which will supply an explanation of the book as a whole; to point out the motive which influenced the selection and arrangement of the historical material, the manifold deviations of our representation from accredited or probable history, and the relation of its parts. That the entire contents of our book should admit of

[1] *Michaelis*, Einl. ins N. T. ii. 1178, where the first part is supposed to relate the outpouring of the Holy Spirit and the miracles which serve to accredit the Christian religion, the second to be a confirmation of universalism. *Gfrörer*, die heilige Sage, i. 383; the narratives of the first part are intended to glorify the Judaistic tendency and the original Apostles (compare especially p. 417); the second is a simple narration of history, with a legendary colouring only in parts. *Schrader*, in the fifth volume of his Apostle Paul, in his observations on the individual narrative, brings together the most varied and contradictory motives.

explanation by this motive is certainly not to be expected, as its records are at any rate based on historical traditions and legends; but we may hope thereby to explain the peculiar working of such tendency, since the investigations already made have shown how much of the narratives before us must be laid to the score of the author, and how little of the episodes, additions, and alterations essential to the parallel between Paul and the original Apostles, can be the work of history or even of legend.

2. The Relation of the Acts to the Parties in the Primitive Church.

If we first inquire generally in what locality we are to seek the centre point of our book, the Acts itself leaves us not a moment's doubt on this subject. A book of the post-apostolic period, which treats the history of the Apostles with the most decided design from the standpoint of a parallel between Paul and the original Apostles, and which in important cases sacrifices historical fidelity to this tendency,—the object of such a book can obviously be only to produce a specific effect on those who did not put Paul and the original Apostles on the same level, and who, with this contrast of the two sorts of Apostles, combined also an antithetic aspect of Christianity; in other words, the still conflicting parties of the Paulinists and the Petrine Judaists. Now this object might be understood as either relating to the person or the matter; our author might be striving to gain appreciation either for the personal character and historical importance of the Apostles, or for a particular view of apostolic doctrine — in short, of Christianity. In fact, however, to make such a separation of the two points of view would be to mistake the whole character of the primitive Christian as well as of every religious party conflict. For as, on the one side, the question respecting the view of Christianity cannot be parted from that respecting the importance of these individuals; as the exaltation of Peter and James, and the depreciation of Paul and animosity against him, were natural and necessary to the Judaist; the equality of the Apostle of the Gentiles to the Apostles of the Jews to the moderate, the Gnostic rejection of the latter to the extreme, Paulinist; so, on the other side, the dispute respecting the individuals was not separated from that respecting the cause; it occurred to no one, from purely historical interest, to discuss the pre-eminence of Paul or Peter; but whoever glorified Paul glorified him just because in him he recognized his Apostle, and in Pauline Christianity his own—whoever preferred Peter or James, and contrasted them with him, ranked Jewish Christianity above or contrasted it with Paulinism. If Peter was in question, it was a question of Petrinism; if Paul, of Paulinism: this is testified by all the documents concerning this dispute, from the Epistles of Paul to the Clementine writings and the second Epistle of Peter; it is testified by the legends of Peter's ministry at Rome; it is testified by the attitude of a Hegesippus, a Papias, and a Justin, towards the Apostle of the Gentiles; of a Marcion and other Gnostics against the Jewish Apostles. Our book, therefore, is not a mere historical work, not a mere historical tendency-writing, but it places itself in the midst of the party antagonisms of the primitive Christian period, and endeavours to work decisively, not only upon the leading *idea* entertained of Paul and the primitive Apostles, but by means of this idea upon the position of the parties themselves. In what direction we must now inquire.

A representation such as that in the Acts might in general have a three-fold object; if Paul and the original Apostles are paralleled in order to favour some tendency, this might occur either in the Petrine, the Pauline, or the common interest; i.e. it might be either to recommend the Jewish Apostles and Jewish Christianity to the Paulinists, or Paul and Paulinism to the Judaists, or, finally, to merge the whole antagonism into a third and common cause. Of these possibilities, however, the first is at once silenced by the observation that the author of our book is obviously a Paulinist; and that in this representation the interest of Paul and Pauline Christianity preponderates. B. Bauer, indeed, opines that, far from opposing Judaism, the Acts first raised it to supremacy within the Church, and that in the interests of this Judaism it falsified the history of Paul.[1] But as he explains at the same time that by Judaism he understands, not historical Judaism nor Jewish Christianity, but conservatism and counter-revolution in general,—as he maintains that at the period when the Acts was written nothing was known either of Paulinists or Jewish Christians, and that no Jewish Christians ever existed who were offended by Paulinism,—as, in a word, he withdraws all historical foundation from his investigation, and seems to be altogether ignorant of the requirements of a historical demonstration,—we may be allowed to spare ourselves any further refutation of his theses.[2] If we hold by historical data, we cannot doubt the essentially Pauline character of its author. Not to forestal details about to be given, we will here merely recall the position of the primitive Apostolic and Pauline parties. The former occupy only the first and smaller half of the whole; on the appearance of Paul, Peter and his comrades vanish from the scene of the apostolic ministry, and reappear only twice, at the apostolic council and at Paul's last journey to Jerusalem; in the first case to issue their charter to Paul and his churches, in the latter to receive him among themselves. All independent interest in them ends at Paul's entrance on office; after this epoch there is not the slightest record of their ministry. How could this be possible were a recommendation of them the author's original motive? In that case, must not most be related precisely of that portion of their ministry which was contemporaneous with that of Paul? must it not have been shown that they were in no way behind the Apostle of the Gentiles and his bril-

[1] Die Apostelgeschichte, p. 122.

[2] A detailed examination of it may be seen in the Theol. Jahrb. 1852, 148 ff.

liant successes? must not the concluding effect of the whole have been concentrated on Peter rather than on Paul? Hence this alternative may be completely laid aside.

Incomparably more weighty reasons may be adduced in favour of the second of the above alternatives, namely, that our book intends to be a recommendation, or, more correctly, a vindication, of the Apostle Paul and Paulinism. This view is recommended, above all, by the circumstance that its effect is obviously centred in Paul and his ministry; that the party in Palestine serve as a background to him, not he to them. Let us now enter upon details; and if, at the beginning, we again view the apostolic miracles, it may be assumed as probable that apostolic miraculous legends must have belonged pre-eminently to the Judaistic, not to the Pauline side. As the Jews tormented Jesus to display miraculous signs, so also as Christians did they regard miracle as an essential mark of apostolic dignity; and Paul himself gives us to understand how the lack of this mark was advanced against him: *Ἰουδαῖοι σημεῖα αἰτοῦσιν, ἡμεῖς δὲ κηρύσσομεν Χριστὸν ἐσταυρωμένον* (1 Cor. i. 22). On the Jewish side, the demand for signs; on the Pauline, the doctrine of the atonement. It is, therefore, only towards his Judaistic opponents that he appeals to his miracles, because they could not imagine an Apostle without miracles.[1] Thus we also know of the most famous of Peter's feats, the conquest over Simon Magus, that it was celebrated in Petrine legend independently of our book; whereas this is not known of Paul's conflicts with Elymas and the Ephesian jugglers. Similarly, the indistinct account of John's disciples has quite the appearance of an intentional pragmatic fiction, which, copied from the narrative of Peter's ministry in Samaria, can only be occasioned by the wish not to allow Paul to remain behind his predecessors in anything. The healing of the lame man at Lystra, xiv. 8 ff., of

[1] 2 Cor. xii. 11: *οὐδὲν ὑστέρησα τῶν ὑπερλίαν ἀποστόλων· τὰ μὲν σημεῖα τοῦ ἀποστόλου κατειργάσθη ἐν ὑμῖν*, &c.

which we have already observed the striking resemblance to the Petrine miracle, iii. 1 ff., shows by its brevity alone, and by the lack of all characteristic features, that it is not original, but an imitation. If we finally compare the two instances of raising from the dead, ix. 36 ff. and xx. 9 ff., it is true that the first bears more distinct traces of a completely unhistorical origin than the second, but it has its prototype (see above) not in this, but in the raisings from the dead in Old Testament and Gospel history, and, indeed, after the manner of the Petrine Gospel of Mark; whereas the other, although it seems to have an historical occasion, attains the character of an actual raising from the dead by intermingling features which again point to those sources; and in other respects it is related to the narrative of the 9th chapter in the same manner as the healing of the lame man at Lystra is related to the healing of the cripple at Jerusalem. If from all this it can scarcely be doubted that in our book the Pauline are adapted to the Petrine miracles, and not vice versa,—that hence the object of the parallel before us is not to rank Peter with Paul, but, on the contrary, Paul with Peter,—it is the reverse as to the sufferings and persecutions which befall both parties. It has already been demonstrated that the equality of the respective experiences was attained only by a remarkable diminution of Paul's misfortunes, and an unhistorical increase of those encountered by the original Apostles. Now it might certainly appear that this alteration was not made in Paul's interest; for as, from the Christian standpoint, suffering for Christ's sake, μαρτυρία, could only be regarded as something creditable, some portion of the credit due to the Apostle of the Gentiles would thereby be withdrawn from him and transferred to the Jewish Apostles. But undeniable as is this view of suffering and persecution, and well as it corresponds with the Ebionite standpoint in particular (comp., for instance, Luke vi. 20 ff.), still the adversities with which Paul had to struggle admitted of another interpretation, not far removed also from Jewish thought; the cause which met with contradiction on every side could not be God's cause; a man so little rejoicing in divine assistance could not be the true ambassador of the Messiah. That Paul himself had to contend against this stumbling-block transpires from several passages in his Epistles. When he praises the Galatians for not having despised and ridiculed the πειρασμὸς in his flesh (Gal. iv. 14), the conclusion is natural that others may have done so; when he contrasts his weakness and misery with the brilliant position of the Corinthians (1 Cor. iv. 9 ff.), even the irony of his expressions points to the self-exaltation with which some looked down upon his ἀσθένεια; if in 1 Cor. iv. 7 ff. he demonstrates how his sufferings are compatible with his apostolic calling, it may not have been superfluous to oppose the prejudices against them; if he repeatedly maintains that he will boast of his weakness, this does not seem to be said only against those who boasted of their own supposed strength, but quite as much also against those who despised him for his weakness; and then he is also obliged expressly to make the Corinthians observe (2 Cor. xiii. 3) that, in spite of his weakness, Christ was mighty in him. All this indicates that not only the apparent dejectedness of his personal appearance, but even his sufferings also, were employed against him, that the παρουσία τοῦ σώματος ἀσθενὴς (2 Cor. x. 10), with which he was reproached, points to the same depressed condition. Our description also appears to bear similar reproaches in view. For if the remarkable alteration of historical facts contained in it can be explained only by the design of ranking the men of the primitive community on a level with Paul as to sufferings and persecutions, and this itself might occur either for vindication of the Apostle of the Gentiles or for glorification of the Jewish Apostles, the former motive must be attributed to our author; and the same is indicated by the fact that the death of Paul, known though it was to our author according to xx. 25, 38, is nevertheless not further mentioned. Finally, one feature which we have already demonstrated is quite decisive; if not one of Paul's adversities is recounted which does not result in his glorification, and if at least in one case (the liberation from the prison at Philippi) we find an evident imitation of Petrine narratives, no doubt can exist that our description is not designed for the glorification of the original Apostles, but to recommend and vindicate Paul.

This appears still more plainly from several other features. So especially with regard to the Pauline speeches. If the greater part of these speeches is directly devoted to the vindication of the Apostle; if even in the doctrinal addresses what is characteristically Pauline withdraws completely in favour of the generalities of Jewish monotheism and the Jewish Christian belief in the Messiah; if Pauline universalism and scattered reminiscences of the Pauline doctrine of justification appear incomparably more often and more emphatically in the mouths of Peter and James than in that of the Apostle of the Gentiles himself; and if in this the author has neither followed actual history, nor can have intended to follow it,—it is obvious that in such representation of the Pauline doctrine his only object must have been to make this doctrine acceptable to those to whom he thought no authority could better recommend it than that of the Jewish Apostles, but to whom even in this form he did not think fit to present Paulinism simple and entire, but only mutilated and external; in a word, that his representation is influenced by apologetic consideration for Judaistic anti-Paulinists. With this is connected the fact that of the results of the Pauline mission to the heathen nothing is recorded with so much emphasis as the expulsion of polytheism by monotheism. As to the pagan audience at Lystra (xiv. 14 ff.) nothing else is preached but the conversion from idols to the true God; as at Athens it is indignation against idolatry which chiefly opens Paul's mouth (xvii. 16), so are the results of his ministry in Asia Minor united into one scene which affords the most triumphant testimony to the damage inflicted upon polytheism by Paul, the Apostle accused by

Jewish Christian zealots of secession to Paganism.[1] We need scarcely point out how the same interest explains the unhistorical portrayal of the Apostle of the Gentiles as a Jew pious in the Law. Neither shall we be able to judge differently of the profoundly significant feature that Paul, according to the unvarying pragmatism of our book, turns only by compulsion to the Gentiles; that the principle of Gentile conversion is, on the contrary, revealed first to Peter, and by him brought to actual recognition; that here Peter is made the actual Apostle of the Gentiles. Many, indeed, endeavour to explain this representation by the anti-Pauline interest of transferring to Peter the glory of the conversion of the Gentiles, and in this respect rendering Paul apparently dependent on him and the original Apostles. But if this is in itself incredible in our author, otherwise so Pauline in his opinions, the readers for whom he wrote were hardly of the kind in whose eyes the Pauline mission to the Gentiles would have been anything creditable, and not much rather a temerity needing excuse. Schrader considers that the story of the conversion of Cornelius is adapted to Gentile Christians, to whom the Jewish Apostle Peter is to be commended. But, according to Schneckenburger's just observation, it allows an entirely different design to appear as its ultimate object when it epitomizes its final result in the exclamatory avowal of the Jewish Christians of Jerusalem (xi. 18), *ἄραγε καὶ τοῖς ἔθνεσιν ὁ θεὸς τὴν μετάνοιαν ἔδωκεν εἰς ζωήν.* If we may justly assume that the effect with which a narrative concludes is likewise its ultimate object, we have in these words the distinct declaration that it only aims at obtaining a recognition of the principle of the Gentile mission; and that so it intends to be an apology for Pauline universalism against the narrow bigotry of Jewish Christianity. This alone necessitated the inter-connected visions, evidences of the most express divine command; for this alone

[1] Comp. *Baur*, Paul. p. 218, and what we have said above on the occasion of the legend of Simon Magus.

avail the reiterated and minute notices of these visions; and for this object alone is the incident with Cornelius, x. 7 ff., employed. It is in no way an affair of Peter's merit, but of the admissibility of Gentile conversion; not the matter of a person, but a principle. Still less can the same tendency be mistaken in the improbable statements respecting Paul's conduct towards Jews and Gentiles, in the unhistorical motives given for his ministry to the Gentiles.[1] What other object could this representation have but that of concealing the side of the Apostle's ministry which was offensive to Judaism; of making his mission to the Gentiles appear not as the work of his own free choice, but as an affair of necessity, as produced by the unbelief of the Jews, by the most distinct commission from Jesus, by the most obvious divine leadings, and so to justify it? After our earlier discussions, we need not further demonstrate how perfectly the narratives of Paul's visions, on the one side, and those of Peter and his comrades, on the other, serve the apologetic object of vindicating the apostolic dignity of Paul; how emphatically our author for this same reason points out that he was called by Jesus in person, and that he testified what he had himself experienced. It is equally obvious what a favourable light his friendly relations with the primitive community must throw upon the Apostle of the Gentiles in the eyes of Jewish Christians. Finally, if the primitive community (in xv.) issues a formal charter to the Gentile Christians gained over by Paul and Barnabas, this seems likewise to harmonize admirably with the apologetic object of our book.

Meanwhile, however, more than one feature exists which forbids us to rest content with this definition of its object. We have already demonstrated above that the Paul of our book is not the historical Paul; that the standpoint which he occupies in doctrine and conduct is not pure unadulterated Paulinism; that it not only maintains silence respecting the centre-point of its hero's whole thought and effort, the repeal of the Law by the

[1] ix. 29 f., xxii. 2, 46, &c.

Gospel, but directly denies it in word and deed, alluding either slightly or not at all to his fundamental doctrines respecting sin, redemption, and justification; that it makes him accommodate himself both in doctrine and in conduct to the example and demands of the Jewish Apostles, and even transfers to Peter the greater portion of his peculiar merit, the principle of Gentile conversion, and the practical realization of this principle. Why this misrepresentation of historical fact if the author was concerned with nothing beyond the vindication of the Apostle of the Gentiles? Would not a faithful delineation of his character, his principles, and his services, have been the best apology that could be made for him? To these questions only one of two answers can be given: either that the author himself had this un-Pauline idea of Paul, or that he did not expect to attain his apologetic object with the readers without sacrificing the true character and the pure doctrine of the Apostle. Certainly, if he was the companion of the Apostle that he asserts himself to be, he must necessarily have been better acquainted with his master, and the most important adventures of that master; and if he was not, it is scarcely credible that no further particulars were known to him of the vehement party conflicts, of the still open wounds which he himself wishes to assist to close by means of his representation; that at least the Apostle's own Epistles, traces of which permeate Christian literature as far as it extends, should not have revealed their true character. Thus the first hypothesis is at any rate subject to important limitations. But even should our author not have grasped his Apostle's principles clearly and sharply, this assumption is far from sufficient to explain so elaborate and artificial a metamorphosis of history as we have here; which serves, moreover, one and the same interest. If an author, in accordance with some tendency, doubles or trebles stories, as ours does the persecutions of Peter and Paul's journeys to Jerusalem; if he passes over things universally known, like the dispute at Antioch, in order to substitute less important ones; if he freely composes, not single speeches only, but entire transactions, with a particular tendency, such as those of the 15th and 23rd chapters; if his whole representation teems with such liberties, and betrays its design also by the deliberate arrangement of its material,—this cannot be explained by a preconceived opinion of the character of the persons concerned, but solely and absolutely by a special purpose; and whether the author himself was or was not fully conscious of the unhistorical nature of his procedure is a very subordinate question for the present investigation; in one case, as in the other, we have in the Acts a tendency-writing which not only attempts to justify the Apostle Paul, his doctrine and his ministry, but at the same time to substitute an essentially altered portrait of him in the place of one historically true. How would this have been necessary if the genuine Paul and pure Paulinism had satisfied its author; if he was only concerned with a defence of him, and not with conciliation with the opposite standpoint? But if it is said that the apologetic object itself, consideration for the anti-Pauline or at least non-Pauline reader, required these concessions; that is, in other words, to abandon the limitation of our book to a merely apologetic object. For how could the author omit such essential features in the portrait of the Apostle, if not because they did not appear essential to him, because he had forsaken pure Paulinism, or had at least abandoned the hope of carrying it out? Any one who clung to this would never have transformed the Pauline into a Petrine doctrine, nor stamped Paul as an Israelite pious in the Law, and renounced the abrogation of circumcision and the Law for the Jewish Christians. If a Paulinist made such concessions, it is that, in order to save what is most essential to him in his Paulinism, he abandons something in itself most important; his book is a proposal of peace to the opposite party, based on mutual concessions. And this it would remain even if it were said that the ultimate object of the author was only the universal acknowledgment of his Apostle, and that all concessions with reference to his doctrine and conduct were merely a means to this object. In that case too, a portion of the Pauline doctrines and principles, and therewith a series of essential features in the portrait of the Apostle, would be sacrificed to gain recognition for what our author in his Paulinism most highly valued, the apostolic authority of Paul. Meanwhile, we have already seen how little the personal question can be separated from the cause; and that this has not been done in our book we can easily demonstrate.

If we narrowly examine how far it goes in its concessions, and, on the other hand, how much that is Pauline it maintains, two closely connected points appear of which it never loses sight, for which it so emphatically seeks recognition that we can unreservedly designate them as the final word of his Paulinism. On the one hand, the personal recognition of Paul as of equal authority with the other Apostles; on the other hand, a matter of fact which could not be abandoned without forsaking the whole basis of Paulinism, i. e. Pauline universalism. How urgently our book enforces the recognition of Paul, and how the whole historical parallel between him and the original Apostles aims at this, has been already shown after Schneckenburger. But the second point has no less significance towards the same end. The very opening scene unmistakably assumes that tendency; the disciples inquire, previous to the ascension (i. 6), after the restoration of the kingdom of Israel, but the Lord refers them to the promulgation of the gospel, ἔν τε Ἰερουσαλὴμ καὶ ἐν πάσῃ τῇ Ἰουδαίᾳ καὶ Σαμαρείᾳ καὶ ἕως ἐσχάτου τῆς γῆς. With this object, they are forthwith endowed on the day of Pentecost with the languages of all nations (ii. 5); and a new and more distinct indication is hereby given of the universal destination of the new faith, which is expressly acknowledged by Peter also, when in his address to the assembled people he significantly adds to the proclamation of the Messianic salvation for the Israelites (ii. 39), ὑμῖν γάρ ἐστιν ἡ ἐπαγγελία καὶ τοῖς τέκνοις ὑμῶν, καὶ πᾶσι τοῖς εἰς μακρὰν, ὅσους ἂν προσκαλέσηται κύριος ὁ θεὸς ἡμῶν—so that even this first proclamation of the gospel from the lips of the Jewish-christian prince of the Apostles, converts the particularism of the Jewish faith in the Messiah into a universal view which renders access to the Messianic salvation dependent not on nationality, but solely on divine election (as Paul in Rom. ix. 8, 16, &c.). After Peter has gently, indeed, but unmistakably, referred in his second discourse, iii. 26, to the possible transfer of salvation from the unbelieving Jews to the Gentiles, and has testified before the Sanhedrim, in Pauline fashion (Rom. ix. 33), to the culpability of the Jews and to salvation in the name of Jesus, Stephen contrasts (vii.) in yet sharper parallel the mercy of God and the stubbornness of the people; and with the termination of the Temple service proclaims the end of Jewish particularism also. To this prophecy is immediately attached the commencement of its fulfilment, of which it becomes itself the means; the persecution after Stephen's death occasions the extension of Christianity to Samaria (ch. viii.); of the three localities designated by the Lord in his final charge, it steps beyond the first (Ἰερουσαλὴμ καὶ Ἰουδαία) into the second (Σαμάρεια), and is already making ready to proceed to the third (ἔσχατον τῆς γῆς); the typical conversion of the Ethiopian by Philip is followed by the first real Gentile baptism performed on Cornelius by Peter, and herewith the most incontrovertible divine revelation, the most formal apostolic acknowledgment of universalistic principles; but between the two our author places (ix.) the story of the conversion of the great Apostle of the Gentiles. His anxiety even now, before the beginning of the actual Gentile mission, to impress upon his readers its legitimacy and divine preparation, is shown in his account of Paul's conversion, when, according to one representation in the vision at Damascus, in another in a subsequent appearance of Christ, the Apostle is expressly sent to the Gentiles (xxvi. 17, τῶν ἐθνῶν εἰς οὓς νῦν σε ἀποστέλλω; xxii. 21, ἐγὼ εἰς ἔθνη μακρὰν ἐξαποστελῶ σε), and when Jesus reveals to Ananias, ix. 15, respecting him, ὅτι σκεῦος ἐκλογῆς μοί ἐστιν οὗτος τοῦ βαστάσαι τὸ ὄνομά μου ἐνώπιον ἐθνῶν καὶ βασιλέων. This interest appears still more strikingly in the story of the conversion of

Cornelius, which fact, together with the antecedent occurrences, is the most brilliant vindication of the Gentile mission of a Paul. God himself, by His messengers, reveals to the Gentile Cornelius that he is to summon Peter. Christ himself declares to the latter that the distinction of clean and unclean, of heathenism and Judaism, is abrogated in the sight of God; the outpouring of the Spirit and the gift of tongues are the solemn and palpable confirmation of these declarations. Peter understands that every God-fearing man, without distinction of nationality, is admitted to salvation, and he bestows baptism on this Gentile full of the Spirit; the scruples of the Jerusalemites are triumphantly overcome by Peter's evidence, and all unite in the joyful acknowledgment, *ἄραγε καὶ τοῖς ἔθνεσιν ὁ θεὸς τὴν μετάνοιαν ἔδωκεν εἰς ζωήν.* Could there be a more brilliant and explicit vindication of the Pauline Gentile mission, for those at least who regarded Peter as the highest authority, a revelation, its ultimate testimony? Hence the author now for the first time ventures to relate the founding of a Gentile Christian community, and to introduce Paul into his new field of labour (xi. 19 ff.). But as if all that went before were still insufficient, his work must needs receive the express assent of the primitive church, and result in the formal acknowledgment of Gentile Christianity at Jerusalem (xv.); though the author did not fail to observe previously, and repeatedly with reference to the first missionary journey of Paul and Barnabas, that they went forth to the work only by special divine command, and with the benedictions of their fellow-christians (xiii. 2, iv. 47, xiv. 26); what a happy effect its successful result produced in the newly converted (xiii. 48, 52); how it was the decree of God himself that led them to the Christian faith (xiii. 48). Finally, if after the 15th chapter the direct vindication of Gentile conversion disappears, its indirect vindication is repeated with all the greater regularity, consisting in the hard-heartedness of the Jews which drives the preachers of the gospel to the Gentiles; and that we may not be left in the dark as to the meaning of this trait, the author himself collects the impression of his whole description of Paul's missionary labours, xxviii. 28, into the final declaration, γνωστὸν οὖν ἔστω ὑμῖν, ὅτι τοῖς ἔθνεσιν ἀπεστάλη τὸ σωτήριον τοῦ θεοῦ, αὐτοὶ καὶ ἀκούσονται. From this accumulation of marks pervading our whole book, no doubt can remain as to what constitutes its chief interest, and to what the author clings as the essential element of his Paulinism—the universal destination of Christianity, the just title of a Gentile Christianity free from the Law side by side with Jewish Christianity. In order to carry out this, he is willing to make all those concessions to Judaism with which we are already acquainted; he sets aside the main portions of the Pauline doctrine, leaves to the Jews Law and circumcision, makes Paul himself a zealous servant of the Law, makes him enter upon his most characteristic ministry only by compulsion, and under the protection of Peter, with the permission of the Jerusalemites. Thus it is the author's main object to convince the reader of the just title of Gentile Christianity, and to say this is to assume that these readers disputed the title, i. e. that they were votaries of a Judaistic particularism. On this side, our book therefore seems an attempt to obtain the recognition of Gentile Christianity in its independence and freedom from Law, by means of concessions to the Judaistic party.

This object our book nowhere proclaims more unreservedly than in the 15th chapter. The less this account of the so-called apostolic council corresponds with historical truth, so much the more distinct becomes the design of influencing the author's own times; on the other hand, the greater the importance which he assigns to this transaction by its central position immediately before Paul's great missionary journey, and by the subsequent references to it in xvi. 4, xxi. 25, the more plainly do we see how anxious he was that the relations of the Christian parties should be formed according to the directions here given. Now what are these directions? On the Jewish Christian side it is demanded (ver. 5) that the Gentile Christians also should be held to circumcision and the observance of the Law; the Apostles, on the contrary, and the assembled community decide that, as in the past so in the future, the Jewish Christians shall remain subject to the Law; the Gentile Christians, on the other hand, are to remain free from it, and to observe only the so-called Noachic ordinances. If we translate these decisions from the past, in which the author has placed them, into the present time, their purport is that harmony betwixt the Gentile and the Jewish Christians is possible, as well as the recognition of the former by the latter if each of the two parties restricts its demands to itself. Still forbearance is recommended to the Gentile Christians, that like the proselytes of the gate they may refrain from the habits most obnoxious to Jews and Jewish Christians. Thus if the strictly Pauline side required the total repeal of the Law, and the strictly Judaistic side required its extension to all believers in the Messiah, our author wishes to allay the strife by a division of territory, to grant the demands of the one side for the Gentile, those of the other for the Jewish Christians, and by mutual forbearance to establish peace between the two parties. The consistency of Paulinism is sacrificed to the practical carrying out of its universalism, to the idea of catholicity.

According to all this, we can have no scruple in describing the tendency of the Acts as conciliatory, and itself as an attempt at mediation between Judaists and Paulinists. Not, indeed, as if the author, standing personally aloof, balanced their claims against each other like a disinterested arbitrator. No; he is himself a Paulinist; his interest is the interest of Paulinism; and so far his book may be regarded as an apology for the Apostle of the Gentiles and his cause. But inasmuch as it is not the standpoint of pure Paulinism which he occupies, or at least which he attempts to carry out—inasmuch as he knows no other means of justifying Paul than by making him a Petrinist, and subordinate to the Jewish Apostles even with regard to his most indisputable merit, the conversion of the Gentiles; and of vindicating Paulinism by veiling everything harsh or prejudicial to the Jewish Christians, by directly denying its polemical position towards the Law, and of all its principles maintaining only the one element of universalism,—so far does his work lose the character of a simple apology, and become a proposal of conciliation founded on mutual concessions. It is the project of a treaty of peace submitted to the Judaists by the Paulinist side. The author wishes to reconcile the Jewish Christians to Paulinism, while he holds up to them in the primitive history of the two parties, in the relations and the destinies of their chiefs, the essential equality of their authorization and their principles, their original concord and the conditions of it. But, on the other side, this assumes that he also wanted to influence his own party in the interest of such reconciliation; for what did it avail to make propositions of peace to his opponents if his friends did not recognize these propositions? How could he hope to accomplish anything by his representation of Paul and Paulinism, if the predominating idea of his fellow-partizans respecting their Apostle, and therewith their view of Christianity in general, was quite different? The design of our book for the author's own party would have been improbable only if his view of Paulinism had been at that period quite universal among them. But how little this was the case a whole century after the Apostle's death is shown, not only by the extreme Paulinism of the Gnostics, which on this hypothesis would lack all historical explanation, but also by the general fact of the continued party strife in the Christian Church. If the Pauline side had been unanimous in allowing the Law and circumcision to the Jewish Christians—if the tradition of the party had attributed that very principle to its founder—this unquenchable hatred of the Ebionites against the destroyer of the Law, the whole vehemence of its antagonism to Pauline Christianity, the need of apologetic writings such as ours, would have been incomprehensible. Mere jealousy of the Gentile Christians and their admission to the Messianic salvation obviously affords no sufficient explanation, in case the Jewish Christians did not find themselves insulted in their own interests and convictions by the opposite party. But this hatred against the Apostle of the Gentiles, the ἐχθρὸς ἄνθρωπος, still meets us at a period at which, on the side of the Ebionites, the circumcision of the Gentile Christians had long been renounced in the Clementine writings, and even later. Only see how monuments, which are at any rate no older than our book, such as the Epistle of Barnabas and the Epistle to Diognetus, express themselves respecting Judaism and circumcision. Nay, all ecclesiastical practice after the middle of the second century did not go nearly so far in its concessions to Judaism as our author; for the circumcision of the descendants of baptized Jews was dropped. This would be quite incredible if these concessions had at any time been universally made by the Pauline side itself. But if they were not made, if a considerable proportion of the Paulinists maintained a harsher opposition towards Jewish Christianity than our author, it was in the nature of the case that in his propositions of peace he should endeavour to influence not only the opposite, but also his own party. And, indeed many features exist which are not only consistent with this design, but are otherwise incapable of being fully explained. Among these must be reckoned everything which serves as evidence of Paul's amicable relations to the primitive Church. Although this representation has a good meaning, even if it were only an affair of disposing the Judaists more favourably towards the Apostle of the Gentiles, it becomes incomparably more significant when with it is combined the design of showing the Paulinists, by the example of their chief, what behaviour was due to the opposite party. Conversely, the universalistic speeches of a Peter and a James, the descriptions of the apostolic council, and the conversion of Cornelius, served not only the main purpose of justifying to the Jews the Pauline mission to the Gentiles, but also the further one of allowing the members of the primitive Church to appear under a more favourable light to the Paulinists. Moreover, the profound silence with which all hostilities of the Jews against the Apostle of the Gentiles are passed over, and the unbelieving Jews represented as his only antagonists, is probably calculated as much for one of the conflicting parties as the other. But here again the most decisive thing is what is said of the main point in dispute between the two parties, the relation of Christians to the Law. When our book repeatedly points out that the liberation of the Gentile Christians from Law and circumcision applies to them only; that the obligation of the Jewish Christians, on the other hand, is not in the least lessened by it (xv. 21, xxi. 20 ff.); when it seeks in every way to obviate the suspicion that Paul had likewise endeavoured to alienate the Jews from the Law of their fathers (see above), is it likely that the author had no other design than to anticipate his opponents' prejudices against Paul, and not the ulterior one of blunting the edge which Paulinism presented towards Judaism, of telling his fellow-partizans how much of their claims they must abandon if peaceable relations with the other party were to be rendered possible? When Paul, in his own person as a born Jew, not only observes the Law and more than the Law (xviii. 18, xxi. 26), but likewise circumcises the semi-Jew Timothy, *διὰ τοὺς Ἰουδαίους* (xvi. 4), is it not as if it was to be made very evident to his devotees what sacrifices they should make for peace? For whom this emphatic inculcation of the so-called Noachic ordinances, if not for those from whom their observance was required? The four things from which the Gentile Christians were to abstain are first of all enumerated by James (xv. 20); the same enumeration is repeated in the apostolic decree (xv. 28), with a double appendix[1] urging the imperative necessity of these points; it is forthwith recorded of Paul and Silas that they imposed the observance of the apostolic decisions on the Lycaonian communities, which, at least for the Gentile Christians among them, could refer only to the Noachic ordinances; nevertheless, in xxi. 25, these ordinances are again specified by James. Who required this urgent inculcation of those decisions? The Jewish Christian readers, that they might not forget they must limit their demands on the Gentile Christians

[1] *Πλὴν τῶν ἐπάναγκες τούτων . . . ἐξ ὧν διατηροῦντες ἑαυτοὺς εὐ πράξετε.*

to the points stated? But these do not contain a moderate lowering of Judaistic claims, but rather the reverse, a restriction of Gentile Christian liberties; they do not specify the limits which the former, but which the latter must not exceed. Or did the same readers require it in order to convince themselves that the claims of the Law upon the Gentile Christians were fully guaranteed by the apostolic decree? For that also it was unnecessary to urge the indispensability of these ordinances; and altogether it seems that it would have been less requisite to prove to the Jewish Christians that they were uninjured in their rights by the Jerusalemites than by Paul and the Gentile communities; if it was appropriate that the liberation of the Gentile Christians from the Law should be proclaimed by James and the Jerusalemites, on the other hand their subjection to the Noachic ordinances ought to have been testified by the conduct of Paul and his adherents. So much the more important may it have appeared to the author to lay these precepts to the heart of the Pauline party. We know how little Paul himself urged their observance; we encounter in the Apocalypse an apparently not unimportant party passionately hated by the Jewish Christian prophet, and having no other mark than the φαγεῖν εἰδωλόθυτα καὶ πορνεύειν;[1] we find in many long after a vehement denial of these demands; if at this particular period we meet a representation which, in historical form indeed, but in an obviously unhistorical manner, most emphatically inculcates their necessity, what else can we think but that this representation is calculated for the express purpose of opposing that resistance? And if, on this single point alone, the tendency of our book against rugged Paulinism irrefutably forces itself upon us, why should we refuse to acknowledge this tendency in other points, which, though in themselves capable of other interpretations, are nevertheless best explained by this one? But if the point in question should appear too insignificant to afford an explanation of the whole tendency of our book, it would be to overlook

[1] See on this my observations in the Tübingen Theol. Journal, 1842, p. 713.

the importance of its bearings on the whole question. Our author establishes the Noachic ordinances as an essential part of the Jerusalemite compact between Jewish and Gentile Christians; the liberation of the Gentile Christians from Law and circumcision is qualified on their side by the observance of these ordinances; and to enforce their importance, they are fully enumerated no less than three times. Moreover, trivial as they may now appear, at that period they actually possessed this importance; and we ought not to be surprised when we consider that, in religious as in other affairs, a deviation in external customs is usually far more repulsive to the mass of mankind than a deviation in principles; in Corinth, at least, the question of *εἰδωλόθυτα* must have raised great commotion, otherwise Paul would scarcely have treated it so minutely (1 Cor. viii.—x.) and with so much caution; to the author of the Apocalypse, the consumption of sacrificial meat and the transgression of the Mosaic marriage laws, which he terms *πορνεία*, must have appeared more scandalous than what was in his eyes their diabolical gnosis, for the former are its established tokens (ii. 14, 20; comp. ver. 6), the latter is only once cursorily touched upon (ii. 24). Justin[1] also declares that a believing Gentile would rather be tortured to death than eat food offered to idols; and the assertion that a Christian might do this without injury, he calls a doctrine of devils. The Clementine writings also place our Noachic ordinances on a level with the most essential religious duties.[2] The transgression of these ordinances seemed to the Jewish Christians as sheer paganism, as a *μεταλαμβάνειν τραπέζης δαιμόνων*; how could any one who wished to negociate peace between them and the Paulinists fail to attempt to obtain from the latter the removal of this stumbling-block?

Hence, what our author wishes to give is such a representa-

[1] Trypho, xxiv.; Schl. xxxv.

[2] Hom. vii.: *ἡ δὲ ὑπ' αὐτοῦ ὁρισθεῖσα θρησκεία ἐστὶν αὕτη, τὸ μόνον αὐτὸν σέβειν, καὶ τῷ τῆς ἀληθείας μόνῳ πιστεύειν προφήτῃ, καὶ εἰς ἄφεσιν ἁμαρτιῶν βαπτισθῆναι . . . τραπέζης δαιμόνων μὴ μεταλαμβάνειν, λέγω δὲ εἰδωλοθύτων, νεκρῶν, πνικτῶν, θηριαλώτων, αἵματος*, and so on. See further *Baur's* Paul. p. 140.

tion of Paul in his relations to the primitive community and the Jewish Christian Apostles as not only to justify the Apostle individually against the accusations and prejudices of the Judaists, but also to prepare the way for a reconciliation as regards Pauline Christianity. For this purpose, not only are Paul and his cause to be commended to the Jewish Christians, but on the Pauline side also a view of Christianity and an idea of the character and doctrine of Paul are to be spread abroad, which, by setting aside or concealing the most obnoxious aspects of Paulinism, should adapt it for union with Jewish Christianity. Our book is the proposal of peace from a Paulinist who wishes to purchase the recognition of Gentile Christianity from the Jewish Christian party by concessions to Judaism, and is desirous of influencing both parties in that sense.[1]

[1] We can here consider only briefly what *De Wette*, Comm. p. 3, retorts against Schneckenburger, but which would in the main apply likewise to the view here expounded. It is denied, in spite of the plain word of the author, that the Acts is the second part of the Gospel. This has already been previously answered. Further, it is unappropriate that an apology written for Judaists should be dedicated to a Gentile Christian such as Theophilus. This objection would indeed disappear according to our view, inasmuch as by this the Acts is not intended for Judaists only; but it is altogether without foundation. To whom could a narrative of the deeds of the Apostle of the Gentiles be more suitably dedicated than to a Gentile Christian? He is not hereby stamped as an opponent of the Judaists; there were likewise Judaistic Gentile Christians, for instance, in Galatia and at Rome itself (Rom. i. 13, comp. with vii. 1 ff.); and this is not a mere exception to the rule, as *Lekebusch* thinks (Comp. of the Acts, p. 372), but it must have been a very frequent case, if Judaism was able to attain such importance in Rome and Galatia as by the evidence of history it actually possessed. Besides, how do we know that Theophilus was a Gentile Christian? We assume it, and the Fathers of the Church assumed it, merely because the writings of Luke are dedicated to him. If it be deemed unappropriate that they should be dedicated to a Gentile Christian, we might imagine Theophilus to be a proselyte. But it is not so much a Gentile Christian in general as a *Roman* Christian whom the author addresses in his Theophilus (hence the κράτιστος, which indicates the noble Roman, as Θεόφιλος does a Christian). And to whom could a writing intended for the Roman Church be more appropriately addressed than to a Roman? Finally, De Wette considers that narratives of more general import, such as i.—vi., xii., are merely forced into the apologetic scheme; other parts which do not suit, such as xvii. 16—34, xviii. 24—28, xiv. 1—7, 20—28, xvi. 5—8, 14 f., xviii. 23, xix. 22, xx. 1—6, 13—15, xxi. 1—3, are passed over in silence; to other parts, such as xix. 23—40, xx. 7—12, a remote or unstable purpose is attributed; finally, the omissions, such as the silence respecting sundry of Paul's sufferings, the foundation of the Galatians, &c., are explained in a most improbable manner. But whether these

3. The Reference of the Acts to the Roman Church.

The reconciliation of the Jewish Christian and Pauline parties is to be regarded as the general and essential object of the Acts. This does not, however, at all prevent the object from being modified in detail according to the standpoint of a particular community or neighbourhood; moreover, as we are obliged to consider primitive Christian literature in general as local, elicited by local conditions and requirements, we must likewise assume, in works of more general significance, that the traces of their proximate destination have not been entirely lost. The trouble of following up these traces is rewarded by a more minute knowledge of their origin.

A preliminary indication of this is furnished by several features which we have not hitherto investigated. We find in xvi. 20, at the transaction at Philippi, in a context historically insecure (see above), the following accusation against Paul and Silas: οὗτοι οἱ ἄνθρωποι ἐκταράσσουσιν ἡμῶν τὴν πόλιν Ἰουδαῖοι ὑπάρχοντες, καὶ καταγγέλλουσιν ἔθη, ἃ οὐκ ἔξεστιν ἡμῖν παραδέχεσθαι οὐδὲ ποιεῖν Ῥωμαίοις οὖσι—in a word, an accusation of proselytizing, of promulgating a *religio illicita et peregrina*. The accused are actually punished on these grounds, and without any regular legal proceedings; it appears, however, that it is Romans, and not Jews, who were concerned; and their judges are compelled to make a humiliating apology. The same accusation, politically

explanations be actually so forced can only be ascertained by an investigation of details, and most of the accusations have already been answered above. It has been shown, for instance, how well the Athenian speech suits the whole representation of Paul in our book; how perfectly narratives such as xiv. 1—7, 19 ff., harmonize with its pragmatism; how clearly the history of the primitive community betrays its premeditated purpose by the three-fold multiplication of the Petrine persecutions. That every detail can be explained by this design is not to be expected; whoever maintains the existence of the design does not suppose that the author evolved his whole narrative from it, but merely that he arranged and metamorphosed given materials according to a practico-dogmatic point of view. For indispensable parts of the history, such as xvi. 5—8, no demonstration of a special purpose can be required; yet we have seen even here that the brevity with which the author passes over this portion of the Gentile mission can scarcely be unintentional.

applied, is repeated in Thessalonica, xvii. 6: *οἱ τὴν οἰκουμένην ἀναστατώσαντες οὗτοι καὶ ἐνθάδε πάρεισιν· καὶ οὗτοι πάντες ἀπέναντι τῶν δογμάτων Καίσαρος πράττουσι, βασιλέα λέγοντες ἕτερον εἶναι, Ἰησοῦν.* Here also, however, it seems to have been without result. Still more decidedly is the charge against Paul, *ὅτι παρὰ τὸν νόμον οὗτος ἀναπείθει τοὺς ἀνθρώπους σέβεσθαι τὸν θεὸν* (xviii. 13), repelled by Gallio at Corinth with the declaration that it is a *ζήτημα περὶ λόγου καὶ ὀνομάτων καὶ νόμου τοῦ καθ' ὑμᾶς*, a purely religious point of dispute among the Jews, in no way concerning the civic authorities. The clamour of the Ephesian insurgents respecting the injury to public worship (the *desolatio templorum* of Pliny, ep. 96), is similarly answered by the town-clerk, xix. 37: the Christians have neither robbed churches nor been guilty of blasphemy; they ought to be brought before the ordinary tribunals. Finally, when Paul is under arrest by the Romans, the Tribune Lysias declares in his report to Felix (xxiii. 29): *εὗρον ἐγκαλούμενον περὶ ζητημάτων τοῦ νόμου αὐτῶν, μηδὲν δὲ ἄξιον θανάτου ἢ δεσμῶν ἔγκλημα ἔχοντα.* Notwithstanding the political colouring which the Jews give to their accusation (xxiv. 5), Felix by his conduct (xxiv. 22 ff.) clearly enough betrays the same conviction; and finally Festus avows (xxv. 18 f.) that the charge against Paul was a question not of any crime, but merely of some Jewish points of dispute, and Agrippa likewise confirms the Apostle's innocence (vers. 31 f.). These traits may perhaps at first sight appear quite purposeless. It was in the nature of the case, and is also evident from 2 Cor. xi. 25, that Paul was several times brought to justice; therefore, why should there not have been occasion for the view of the Christian cause which we meet with here, i.e. the consideration of it as a private affair of the Jews, having no civil importance, especially as Christianity had not then attained such consequence as to rouse political apprehensions? But it likewise transpires from this passage that Paul did not deal solely with such reasonable pagan authorities as those our book introduces to us; why does it persistently relate encounters of this sort only with non-Jewish magistrates, terminating with an honourable vindication of the Apostle? We may have convinced ourselves, further, from our whole investigation that the account is not altogether of a purely historical nature; and that a feature which is repeated in it with such persistency as the above-mentioned one, must always point to some special tendency. This is finally placed beyond doubt in the case before us when we observe that these declarations, so favourable to Paul and to Christianity in general, are not always obtained in an historical manner. We have already seen how improbable is the scene at Philippi. It was similarly observed that the accusation of the Thessalonian Jews bears the colouring of a later period. The decision of xviii. 13 is indeed put into the mouth of Seneca's brother, a person known to history; yet it is striking that the Roman proconsul should reject without investigation a charge of a legally punishable crime, the promulgation of a *religio illicita*,[1] as a Jewish war of words. Finally, as regards the declarations in favour of Paul during his arrest in Cæsarea, one must reasonably wonder whence the author obtained this minute information concerning the letter of Lysias to Felix, and the conversations between Festus and Agrippa; and, after all the results of our previous investigations, no one can refuse to attribute these expressions to the author rather than to the persons concerned. When it is added that in our book account is taken precisely of those reproaches against Christianity which make it appear politically dangerous and contrary to law, the charge of introducing a prohibited cultus to the prejudice of the national religion, of revolutionary tendencies (the *Christiani hostes Cæsarum*), there is every probability that the author, with his accumulation of stories of the rejection of these accusations by the pagan authorities, was endeavouring to refute the political suspicions against Christianity; and for this

[1] For the accusation, if it be historical, must have referred to this, since we must not suppose the chief of the Jews, in a town like Corinth, to be so ignorant of their privileges as to have complained before a Roman of secession from the Mosaic faith. Our author indeed, in ver. 15, explains the *παρὰ τὸν νόμον* of the 13th verse as *περὶ νόμου τοῦ καθ' ὑμᾶς*.

we shall also have to appeal to a fact in the first portion of our book, which we have already been obliged to declare unhistorical on other grounds, i.e. the famous speech of Gamaliel, v. 38; for the policy he recommends of waiting and allowing it to mature, comprises everything that the Christian apologists demanded from the Roman Government.

But if this feature has a purpose, it certainly points, whatever may be the interpretation put upon it, to the circumstances of a time and place at which Christianity was already at variance with the Roman administration. The most natural conjecture in this case will of course be, that the author wished to refute the accusations of pagan opponents; and it cannot be said that this design would be incredible as regards his Christian readers, for he may have thought it expedient to supply them with a ready answer to pagan accusations; and, moreover, it is not essential that in his book our author should have contemplated Christian readers alone, especially as at that period of the most varied civil and social connections between Christians and heathens, the respective circles of readers could not have been completely separated.

Schneckenburger's conjecture is certainly not improbable (pp. 244 ff.), i. e. that the intentionally political absolution which Paul receives is more closely connected with the main object of our book, and is likewise calculated for Jewish Christians. If it was primarily exclusive pride and the instinct of self-preservation that rendered the Jews averse to the wholesale conversion of the Gentiles effected by Paul, the ulterior motive might also be added that, by this very extension of faith in the Messiah within the domains of pagan religions, they came in conflict with the laws against proselytism; and little as the most zealous Judaism regarded these laws (Matt. xxiii. 15, and others), there was none the less readiness to lay upon Paul the responsibility of the perils to Christianity which he had caused; nay, the more vehement Jewish Christians might even throw all the reproaches raised against Christianity exclusively on the Paulinists, as those who had alone transgressed the legal prerogatives of Judaism and invaded the domain of the State religion, raising a commotion among the people by addresses not confined to the synagogue.[1] After the Neronian persecution of the Christians especially, and in the place where it had raged, the idea might be agitated among the Jewish believers in the Messiah of cutting off all further cause for persecution by proclaiming their independence of those on whom the State religion might lay hold, and who on their side had, as they considered, no right to the Messianic salvation. Such a relation of our book to the Jewish Christians is rendered extremely probable by the circumstance that the political charges against Paul are put chiefly into the mouths of Jews (xvii. 5, xviii. 12, xxiii. 27 ff., xxiv. 5), whereas the pagan authorities protect him. But at any rate the unmistakable purpose of these charges points to the condition of a community which had already suffered from political persecutions. And we should seek it with preponderating probability in the west of the Roman Empire, as it was precisely here, in the strictly Roman world, that the political accusations against Christianity emphasized by our book were prevalent; whereas in eastern countries disputes turned more on theoretical questions of a religious nature. Meanwhile, we shall forthwith meet with more evident indications of the place for which our book was destined; indications which are not noticed here for the first time.[2]

In xix. 21, it is recorded that, after a protracted ministry at Ephesus, Paul undertook a journey to Jerusalem, *εἰπών, ὅτι μετὰ τὸ γενέσθαι με ἐκεῖ δεῖ με καὶ Ῥώμην ἰδεῖν.* What he here announces as his own intention proves subsequently to be the will of God; also in xxiii. 11, Jesus says to him, *ὡς διεμαρτύρω τὰ περὶ ἐμοῦ εἰς Ἱερουσαλήμ, οὕτω σε δεῖ καὶ εἰς Ῥώμην μαρτυρῆσαι*; and on the perilous voyage an angel encourages him, in xxvii. 24, with the

[1] The Fathers of the Church act in this manner when they impute the pagan accusations against the Christians to the Gnostics; for instance, *Justin*, Apol. i. 26.

[2] Comp. *Schneckenburger*, pp. 123 ff.

words, *μὴ φοβοῦ, Παῦλε· Καίσαρί σε δεῖ παραστῆναι.* Nay, even in the words of Jesus about Paul, in ix. 15, *σκεῦος ἐκλογῆς μοί ἐστιν οὗτος τοῦ βαστάσαι τὸ ὄνομά μου ἐνώπιον ἐθνῶν καὶ βασιλέων υἱῶν τε Ἰσραήλ, βασιλεὺς,* signifying here in the context with *ἔθνη*, pagan princes, might indicate the Emperor Cæsar, the only one mentioned in our book. Fact corresponds with this interpretation. Paul himself rejects all warnings against the journey to Jerusalem (xx. 22 ff., xxi. 10 ff.), which by a higher dispensation was to become the means of his reaching Rome; and by his appeal to Cæsar (xxv. 10 ff.), which would not have been at all necessary for himself, he brings about his abduction to Rome. On the other hand, such conspicuous proofs of a controlling Providence watching over him are connected with these revelations, that no doubt can remain that it was the hand of God himself which brought him to Rome; immediately after the nocturnal vision, xxiii. 11, follows the story of the Apostle's rescue from a serious danger, which in this context we can regard only as material evidence that Paul might be assured that God's purpose, which was likewise his own, the *μαρτυρῆσαι εἰς Ῥώμην*, would be accomplished in spite of all hindrances. At the second revelation, xxvii. 24, the angel himself says that Paul and his fellow-travellers should be saved, because he was destined to appear before the throne of Cæsar. The point of view under which the Apostle's Roman imprisonment is here placed deserves the greatest consideration. It is not a misfortune which befals him, not an event unexpected by him and counteracting his project; but merely the accomplishment of his own voluntary decision, merely the means to attain the goal appointed for him by God. Hence, far from evading it, he freely goes to meet it, and himself takes the step which occasions it. Similarly, on the part of God, everything occurs in order to bring him to the place whither he is destined to go; and neither the deadly malice of his enemies nor the fury of the elements can impede him. The Apostle's sojourn at Rome appears to be the point to which his whole life has tended, after which he himself has striven, and to which he has been guided by Providence. But if we inquire what was the Apostle's destiny at Rome, our book does not refer us to the event which we should naturally contemplate, i. e. his martyrdom; on the contrary, respecting this it is silent, little as, from xx. 24 f., the writer can have been ignorant of it;[1] but to his activity in promulgating Christianity at Rome. This alone is recalled in the μαρτυρῆσαι εἰς Ῥώμην, xxiii. 11, although martyrdom seems to ring in the expression; but the conclusion of our book reveals positively that it is to this that the whole narrative respecting Paul has tended. He arrives at Rome as a prisoner under the heaviest accusation. What could interest the reader more than to learn in the first instance the fate which befel him? But of this not a word. Only so much is recorded, that he was there for two years without being debarred from intercourse with others; that he preached the gospel "with all confidence, no man hindering him." If we take this conclusion of the book along with the previous representation, what other impression can we receive but that the promulgation of the gospel at Rome was the end to which Paul was to be conducted through all his adventures subsequent to his departure from Ephesus, and which he had from the first acknowledged[2] as the fulfilment of his apostolic career (δεῖ με καὶ Ῥώμην ἰδεῖν, xix. 21)?[3] We shall be the less able to regard this impression as the purposeless result of an historical representation, the oftener we are forced to confess that it is not attained in a purely historical manner. This might be assumed in a general way, if only from the thorough tendency-character of our book. We find, besides, the very first reference to Rome, xix. 21, in a context which we cannot regard as entirely his-

[1] See *Schneckenburger*, p. 125, who justly remarks that the numerous prophetic warnings of the πνεῦμα elsewhere would not have been quite suitable if they referred only to a temporary imprisonment.

[2] Comp. *Schneckenburger's* excellent exposition, p. 126.

[3] τελειῶσαι τὸν δρόμον μου καὶ τὴν διακονίαν ἣν ἔλαβον παρὰ τοῦ κυρίου Ἰησοῦ, διαμαρτύρασθαι τὸ εὐαγγέλιον τῆς χάριτος τοῦ θεοῦ, xx. 24.

torical, because, according to his Epistles, Paul while at Ephesus cannot so decidedly have announced his determination to go to Jerusalem. Furthermore, if the two visions (xxiii. 11, xxvii. 23) are not in themselves incredible, still the recurrence of such psychological phenomena, in direct combination with rescues from death which serve as their confirmation, are too improbable to be upheld from any other standpoint but the belief in miracle—at least in our book, the historical credibility of which has been otherwise too severely shaken to allow its authority to counterbalance any such improbability. It is quite clear, finally, that the silence respecting Paul's death can only be intentional; for we have already seen that it was known to the author; and it is utterly incredible that he did not allude to it because he might assume it as known to his readers; otherwise he must have kept silence respecting the Apostle's conversion and a hundred other things. And why should it have been void of interest to even Roman contemporaries to possess an accurate record of the last words and fate of their Apostle? Hence a definite purpose lies at the basis of our representation: Paul's ministry at Rome is the goal of the whole book, towards which the Apostle is brought, not by his own steadfast determination alone, but likewise by the most unmistakable divine guidance.

In the same category must be reckoned Paul's dealings with the Roman Jews, the truth of which we have been already obliged to question, after the example of Baur; but whose importance in our author's eyes only becomes the more conspicuous. Although it is his unvarying custom always to make Paul attempt the conversion of Jews before he turns to the Gentiles, the very minuteness of our record, quite needless after so many similar scenes, shows his anxiety to mark this procedure in Rome especially. But here, according to Schneckenburger's excellent remark (p. 85), the thing proceeds not only more minutely, but more comprehensively, than in the description of the same thing in previous scenes. Those present are not only upbraided for their personal obduracy against the gospel, but the Apostle makes the prophet Isaiah bear witness that this is the invariable conduct of the Jewish people; the unsusceptibility of the Jews and the right of preaching to the Gentiles are deduced from an accidental individual case; the two are contrasted in a general way as an universal law, and receive higher confirmation from the words of the prophet. "This final scene at Rome is at the same time the conclusion of an empirical induction for the divine design of the gospel toward the Gentiles." But how is it that the author only now arrives at this conclusion, that Paul is for years obliged to make one and the same experience, only at the end of his course to become aware for the first time in this fundamental manner of his right to the ἀποστολὴ τῆς ἀκροβυστίας? Is it because his history is now at an end, and the author has no further opportunity of recounting the course of it in other towns? Or does not the very significant termination of our book in this particular scene, and its contrast between the conspicuous obduracy of the Jews depicted in its universal necessity, and the Apostle's unchecked evangelization of the Gentiles, show that the final impression intended to be carried away by the reader from this representation is, that Paul, brought to Rome by Divine Providence, and here also despised by his own people, preaches the gospel to the Gentiles in the world's metropolis? Does not the striking silence respecting the Roman community [1] of Christians point to such design? The importance of this community even before the Apostle's arrival is still more incontrovertibly evinced by the Epistle to the Romans than by the definite statement in Rom. i. 8 ff., for its intrinsic consequence alone could induce Paul to prepare for his personal advent by a letter thus uniting in itself all the fruits of his prolific mind. Even for this reason it is impossible to imagine that our author—whoever he might be, and to whatever age he belonged—was not aware of the notorious fact (Rom. i. 8) of the early existence of the Roman community. Nevertheless, in the narrative of Paul's

[1] Comp. *Schneckenburger*, pp. 120 ff.

arrival there is not a word about this community, only the cursory notice (xxviii. 15) that the brethren from Rome came a certain distance to meet him; but these brethren might likewise be some stray believers; the existence of a church is not implied in the expression. Is it not clear that the author says no more of the community because he *chooses* to say no more? And why does he not choose? Hardly because Paul's connection with the Romans was too unfriendly to be mentioned by him (Schneckenburger); for in that case what prevented him from substituting a more friendly in place of the unfriendly reception, as he does with regard to Paul's relations to the Jerusalemites and the Jewish Christians in general? It seems much rather that the Roman community of Christians is thrown into the background previous to the arrival of Paul, in order to make him appear its actual founder; and similarly the fundamental rupture with Judaism is, on the other hand, transferred to Rome, in order to introduce him here for the first time into his complete ministry as Apostle of the Gentiles. With this it perfectly accords that, immediately after his arrival, Paul summons not the chiefs of the Christian community, as might be naturally expected, but the most revered leaders of the Jews, and that they know as yet no details of Christianity. On the basis of real historical circumstances, this must be striking in the highest degree, as has been already shown; but by our author's account it appears quite consistent. According to him, a Christian community does not as yet exist at Rome; it is first founded by Paul. Rome is then the ultimate goal towards which Paul's whole course is directed. Perils and rescues, hindrances and persecutions, conspire to lead him hither, that he may be enabled to found the Roman Church among the Gentiles.

What is related of Paul's citizenship seems likewise to have a special reference to the Romans. I should indeed be reluctant to say with Schneckenburger (p. 243), that an acquaintance with the privileges of a Roman citizen is assumed in the readers of the book, such as could be most readily expected of *Roman*

Jewish Christians; for the advantages in this respect of the conquerors over the conquered was probably known throughout the whole of the Roman Empire. So much the less does the two-fold mention of this citizenship appear to be purposeless. However the case may be with regard to its reality, at any rate a very improbable application of it is made (xvi. 37 ff.); and that, besides Paul, Silas also was a Roman citizen is scarcely likely. Hence in this trait, or at least in the manner in which it is employed, we are justified in supposing design. Is it not really as if it were merely to give a tangible answer to the accusation in v. 20, οὗτοι οἱ ἄνθρωποι ἐκταράσσουσιν ἡμῶν τὴν πόλιν, Ἰουδαῖοι ὑπάρχοντες? and does not even analogy render it probable that the narrative in xxii. 25, is not without similar design? Be it observed how everything conduces to give effect to the Roman citizenship. First, the contrast between the Roman Tribune who was able to obtain it only at great cost, and the prisoner who possesses it by birth; then, instant liberation by means of this talisman; finally, the terror of the Tribune, who had in reality no cause for alarm. This cannot be reckoned a perfectly simple historical narrative. And if it have a tendency, what other is more suitable than that of commending the Apostle to the Romans as a born Roman? On these premisses, what an insight do we obtain into the pragmatism of our book! Paul is not the intruder his antagonists represented him to be (comp. the Legend of Simon and the Apology, Rom. xv. 20 ff.); he belongs to Rome from his birth; in the most critical situations and with the most brilliant result he made use of his Roman citizenship; precisely on account of his character as a Roman citizen, and under the most evident protection of Divine Providence,[1] he has come to Rome, where, compelled to do so by the Jews themselves, he has established a Gentile church in unrestrained

[1] xxiii. 11 ff., xxvii. 21 ff., xxviii. 3 ff., where the reflection, ver. 4, plainly expresses the intended impression of the οὐδὲν ἔπαθεν, which it is meant to strengthen by the contrast.

activity;—what is still lacking to the proof that, according to all laws, divine and human, he was to be regarded as the Apostle of the Roman community; and in a representation which concludes with this result, how can we mistake its special relation to the Christian community at Rome?

This special purpose is not related to the general object of our book—the establishment of peace between Gentile and Jewish Christians—so as to run independently by its side, but only to define it more closely. That which specially refers to the Roman community is likewise treated with the reconciliation of parties, with the eulogy of the Apostle of the Gentiles and his ministry; only that the writer does not here pursue this object in the abstract, but primarily in its application to the circumstances existing at Rome. Herewith we obtain a notable disclosure respecting the whole scheme of our book. Even in itself there is no inherent probability that a work such as the one before us should have been evolved from an abstract contemplation of ecclesiastical circumstances and requirements; as it rather attempts to work directly on the practical conduct of parties (comp. xv.), it may be assumed as probable that an immediate practical need, the condition of a particular community, primarily occasioned its composition and determined the details. This of course does not prevent the author from having grappled with his task in a more general way; and as the points in dispute between the parties were probably more or less the same, a book which primarily intended to work upon a single community in that sense must, by the nature of the case, become a general tendency-writing. Yet it may be expected that it will not disown the traces of its immediate destination. Appearances confirm this. Paul and Paulinism are here placed in a parallelism with the primitive community and its Christianity adapted to the peaceable aims of our author. The universality of Gentile baptism, with him the main point of Paulinism, is vindicated; but since the career of the

Apostle of the Gentiles reaches its predestined conclusion precisely at Rome, and this attainment of its goal is prepared with all care and observable, the general naturally merges in the special object; and while the Gentile Christianity of Paulinism essentially converges to Rome as its proper metropolis, the Apostle of the Gentiles as such being necessarily the Apostle of the Romans (δεῖ με Ῥώμην ἰδεῖν, &c.), so conversely Roman Christianity is essentially Paulinism, and the Roman a Pauline community, to which all that the author has said in commendation of Paul and his standpoint finds its special application, where peace with the Paulinists should not for a moment be contested. That the circumstances at Rome were of a nature to give rise to such a description as ours must be shown later on.

4. The Composition of the Acts explained by the Object for which it was designed.

The task on which we have hitherto been employed was to arrive in an analytical method, by the accumulation and comparison of single indications, at the idea which floated before the mind of its author as the object of the book, forming the internal point of unity in the whole, and dominating its individual parts. It still remains for us to pursue the same course backwards, and to develop synthetically how the details in it proceeded out of that original unity.

In order to prepare friendly relations between the conflicting parties of Christendom, the Paulinists and the Judaists, primarily for the Roman Church, the author wishes to portray Paul and Paulinism in harmony with and of equal authority to primitive Christianity and its Apostles. With this design he shows how the Christianity of the first church was transmitted, essentially unchanged by Paul as a fully authorized, universally accredited and acknowledged Apostle, with the knowledge and consent of the primitive community, under the most unmistakable guidance of God, to the Gentile Christians in general, and especially to the Gentile Christian community at Rome.[1] By this fundamental idea of our book, the purport and connection of its principal parts are mainly determined. The commencement necessarily gives a description of the primitive community; but the real object is the portraiture of Paul and his ministry among the Gentiles. The former the author has given in the first five chapters, the latter from the 13th chapter forwards; but between these two parts he interposes a section which, by the remarkable limitation of the Pauline and Jerusalemite portions, shows that it is intended to constitute the transition from the first to the second.[2] A splendid introduction is supplied by the narration of how the Lord himself, departing in the glory of Messianic sovereignty, intimates beforehand the course of his doctrine from Jerusalem to the ἔσχατον τῆς γῆς, to the far West, the extreme limit reached by an Apostle, the τέρμα τῆς δύσεως (Clem. 1 Cor.). Then follows the portrait of the primitive community in the *first* part: first, its founding by the Apostles and the outpouring of the Spirit; then the description of its internal condition, its miracles and its persecutions. But as the miracle of Pentecost prefigures the extension of Christianity among all nations recorded in the third part, and as the speeches of Peter point to it, so also the subsequent sufferings of Paul and the animosities against him are foreshadowed in the external persecutions and the inward disturbances to which the community at Jerusalem with its Apostles was exposed. The description of the primitive community itself is symmetrically divided into two groups (ii. 42—iv. 31, and iv. 32—v. 12), in which each of the three points above indicated follows in the given order: first, a panegyrical representation of the piety, harmony, and community of goods in the primitive Christian society (ii. 42—47, iv. 32—

[1] The Pauline community at Rome (see above) is obviously placed among the ἔθνη, as may be seen by comparison of xxviii. 28 with vers. 30 f. Comp. Rom. i. 13, 14.

[2] Connecting i. with viii., one might likewise represent this connection thus: of the stations for the extension of Christianity, Judæa and pagan countries, the first part treats the first, the next the second, the last the third; but this would not be geographically correct.

37), then a miracle minutely related, iii. 1—10, a miracle of healing, v. 1—11, a judicial miracle; after this, the persecutions, iii. 11 ff., v. 17 ff. In all three points, moreover, a gradation is to be observed in the second group of what has been related in the first: the εἶχον ἅπαντα κοινὰ, ii. 44, is increased in iv. 32 by the negative expression, οὐδὲ εἷς τι τῶν ὑπαρχόντων αὐτῷ ἔλεγεν ἴδιον εἶναι; and similarly what is said in ii. 45 of the sale and partition of goods, by the more minute description in iv. 34, and the ἦσαν ἐπὶ τὸ αὐτὸ in ii. 44, by the καρδία καὶ ψυχὴ μία in iv. 32. Of the two persecutions, we have already seen that the second is merely a more forcible repetition of the first; instead of the single healing of the lame man, iii. 1 ff., we have in v., besides the judicial miracle on Ananias and Sapphira, a mass of the most extraordinary miracles of healing (vers. 12, 15). Thus everything here develops itself according to a very simple pragmatism. Between the actions, Petrine discourses are interwoven at the Feast of Pentecost and the two persecutions.

Far more complicated and artistic is the construction of the second part. The beginning is constituted by an event which was in all probability the indirect cause of the extension of Christianity to the Gentiles, and at the same time of the conversion of the Apostle of the Gentiles, i. e. the persecution of Stephen. This incident is treated with visible regard to the main object of the book. If Stephen was undoubtedly in historical truth a precursor of Paul, he here appears as his actual prototype in the primitive community. First, a highly distinguished position is allotted to him within it; as even at the deacons' election, vi. 5, he is named among the most trusted men with the most pointed epithets (ἄνδρα πλήρη πίστεως καὶ πνεύματος ἁγίου), so does he appear in vi. 8 working miracles[1] in apostolic fashion. In his trial and death, it is impossible to mistake the parallel with the

[1] vi. 8: Στέφανος δὲ πλήρης χάριτος καὶ δυνάμεως ἐποίει τέρατα καὶ σημεῖα μεγάλα ἐν τῷ λαῷ. iv. 33: μεγάλῃ δυνάμει ἀπεδίδουν τὸ μαρτύριον οἱ ἀπόστολοι, χάρις τε μεγάλη ἦν ἐπὶ πάντας αὐτούς. v. 12: Διὰ δὲ τῶν χειρῶν τῶν ἀποστόλων ἐγίνετο σημεῖα καὶ τέρατα ἐν τῷ λαῷ πολλά.

accused and dying Christ, whose glorified appearance is vouchsafed to him in the hour of death;[1] after his execution, as a clear proof of his blamelessness in the eye of the Law, he is buried by men pious in the Law, who in this context, after the flight of all the Christians (ver. 1), can only be understood as Jews. At the same time, this hero of the primitive community occupies, not in his fate alone, but also in his doctrine, a kindred relation to Paul, which, as it here appears, we cannot possibly explain otherwise than by the two having been purposely formed on the same model. If Paul was decried as the destroyer of the Law, the accusation against Stephen also turns on blasphemy against the Law and the proclamation of its abolition through Jesus; and against the service of the Temple, at least, he expresses himself strongly enough in his speech. If the former transferred the Messianic salvation from the Jews to the Gentiles, the latter also declares that the people of Israel had at all times rendered themselves unworthy and unsusceptible of manifestations of divine favour. If Paul finally succumbed to the hatred of the Jews, Stephen still more obviously fell a sacrifice to it. That this parallel does not consist only in historical fact, but is consciously and purposely pursued by the author, is evinced by the freely composed vindicatory address of Stephen, and its relation to the addresses of Paul at Antioch and Athens. Stephen thus forms the proper link between Paul and the primitive church; in character and fate he is the type of the Gentile Apostle.

A double series of narratives now follows the persecution against Stephen, all having reference to Paul and his appear-

[1] Our narrative has likewise a striking resemblance to the Ebionite legend of the death of James the Just (*Heg.* b. *Eus.* K. G. ix. 23, 6 f.); as Stephen beholds Christ sitting on the right hand of God, so does James exclaim: *τί με ἐπερωτᾶτε περὶ Ἰησοῦ τοῦ υἱοῦ τοῦ ἀνθρώπου; καὶ αὐτὸς κάθηται ἐν τῷ οὐρανῷ ἐκ δεξιῶν τῆς μεγάλης δυνάμεως καὶ μέλλει ἔρχεσθαι ἐπὶ τῶν νεφελῶν τοῦ οὐρανοῦ* (an obvious imitation of the speech of Jesus, Matt. xxvi. 64); as Stephen intercedes on his knees for his murderers, vii. 60, so there, § 7, James, *ἔθηκε τὰ γόνατα λέγων· κύριε θεὲ πάτερ ἄφες αὐτοῖς· οὐ γὰρ οἴδασι τί ποιουσιν* (L. xxiii. 34). This coincidence, which is scarcely likely to be accidental, proves at any rate how much our narrative is according to Ebionite taste.

ance; those which concern him directly and personally, and those which include preparations for his appearance, on the part of the Jerusalemites. The two species of narrative are characteristically intertwined; but although the second class far preponderates in extent, not only does their whole nature show that in them Paul is the real object, but he also constantly reappears at such important points in the history, that it is evident how little the author has lost sight of him in the interval. A brief mention of Saul and his zeal in persecuting, viii. 1, 31, is not followed, as might be expected, by the next event in chronological sequence, i. e. his conversion, but by the conversions effected by Philip and Peter in Samaria, and that of the Ethiopian. Before the Apostle of the Gentiles is called, the second part of the Lord's injunctions, i. 8, the promulgation of the gospel in Samaria, must have commenced, and Simon Magus, that Ebionite caricature of Paul, must have played out his part, to render any confusion impossible. Paul only now joins the Christian association, and that under circumstances which represent him from the first in close connection with the primitive community; he is baptized by Ananias, pious in the Law; the long-tried Barnabas introduces him at Jerusalem; he himself, far from the conduct on which he prides himself in Gal. i. 16, hastens from Damascus to Jerusalem; lives for a long time with the Twelve as a preacher of the gospel at Jerusalem and in all Judæa, xxvi. 20; and only reluctantly allows himself to be driven, whether it be by the murderous attempt of the Jews, or by the appearance of Jesus (xxii. 17), to the mission to the Gentiles. Nevertheless, before he actually enters upon it, Peter must prepare the way for him; Paul betakes himself from Jerusalem to his own country, and only reappears in xi. 25. Any one acquainted with our book only could not but suppose that in the interval he had sat completely still, especially as the first mention of a Gentile community occurs at Antioch. If, on the contrary, we listen to Gal. i. 16, 21, it is extremely improbable that the newly-converted enthusiast, who in his vocation as Apostle of the Gentiles went not only to Tarsus, but to the κλίματα τῆς Συρίας καὶ τῆς Κιλικίας, should not have been busy, acting with zealous energy. Our author's plan, however, involves silence on this point; before Paul can work, his work must have been authorized by the precedent of Peter (x. f.), to which the narratives in ix. 31 ff. serve as a prelude, and by the Jerusalemites' toleration of Gentile conversion, xi. Not till now are we apprized of the founding of a community of Gentile Christians (xi. 20), although this seems to have been chronologically antecedent to the conversion of Cornelius; Paul labours in it (xi. 25), but has not yet appeared independently as a converter of Gentiles and a founder of churches; Barnabas has only introduced him as coadjutor in a community already existing. He is first exhibited in his independent apostolic ministry when the history of the primitive church is brought to an end. This is accomplished by the narrative of the twelfth chapter. While the persecution against Stephen had not affected the Apostles, one of them is now executed, another is snatched from impending death only by the most conspicuous miracle; and while, in viii. 1, they remained at Jerusalem during the general flight, the history of Peter closes, xii. 17, with ἐξελθὼν ἐπορεύθη εἰς ἕτερον τόπον. Jerusalem, hitherto the fixed centre of Christian history, ceases to be so with the flight of the prince of the Apostles; and Paul's journeys thither alone recall the existence and importance of the primitive community. The less can we regard it as undesigned that the final narrative is framed between one of Paul's journeys to Jerusalem, xi. 27, and his departure thence, xii. 25; as Peter retires from the scene, he to whom he has opened the barriers by his last apostolic act is at hand to enter on his vocation, now prepared and authorized on all sides. The history of the primitive church is at an end, and that of the Apostle of the Gentiles begins. Hence he only now receives the name under which he was known to the Gentile Christian world (xiii. 9).

The arrangement of the third part, embracing the history of Paul, appears simpler on the whole. Here the events themselves prescribed the general course of the narrative to the author, who in this part, no doubt, more than in the earlier ones, has adhered to given historical sources. First, the shorter missionary journey of Paul and Barnabas; hereupon the apostolic council; then the great missionary journey of Paul and Silas; finally, the last journey to Jerusalem and the imprisonment of the Apostle. This is doubtless the actual sequence of events. It is also in part attested by Paul's Epistles. Thus the Epistle to the Galatians (ii. 1) allots to the apostolic council the same position which it here occupies; for according to i. 21, it cannot be assumed that Paul had already permanently passed beyond the limits of Syria and Cilicia; while in ii. 7 f. results in the pagan world are presupposed of sufficient importance to place Paul as Apostle of the Gentiles by the side of Peter the Apostle of the Jews, and to wring from the Jerusalemites the recognition of his authorization and conduct. These results on their side necessitate a missionary activity such as that of which ch. xiv. and xv. give us examples. It appears, however, very natural that Paul should wish to make his footing secure by negociations with the Jerusalemites before extending his mission so successfully begun, over Asia Minor and Europe; and if, in Gal. ii. 2, he went to Jerusalem in consequence of a revelation, we must probably trace this to the feeling which he expresses with full consciousness in the same passage (μήπως εἰς κενὸν τρέχω ἢ ἔδραμον). But although the author has on the whole adhered to the actual course of history, he has not failed, partly by the selection and arrangement of what is related, partly by the transformation and amplification of the material transmitted, and partly by sundry slighter hints, so to carry out his pragmatism, that even in the present part we recognize the plan of the whole. This has been already demonstrated in the historical material. The arrangement of the whole, and the indications of the general plan afforded by the several parts, must now be examined from the same point of view. The first thing that strikes us with regard to the two missionary journeys, besides the complete similarity of what is said on both occasions of Paul's conduct towards the Jews and of the Jews towards him, is, that in each only one long doctrinal discourse is recorded; in the first, before a Jewish, in the second, before a pagan audience. As the authenticity of these speeches is not to be thought of, after all that has gone before, and as, moreover, it cannot be supposed that among so many Pauline speeches only these two should have reached our author, it is obvious that he wished to give a sample of each kind of such missionary addresses. It is in itself quite proper, also quite in accordance with his special pragmatism, that the transaction with the Jews stands first; not merely because it was only on the second journey that Paul reached the spiritual focus of the pagan world, but also because, as our book portrays him, he is primarily an Apostle of the Jews, and only secondarily the Apostle of the Gentiles, and is hence to be represented as engaged in the former ministry earlier than in the latter. Further, the brevity deserves consideration with which on the second journey the Apostle's labours, prior to his arrival in Europe, are passed over; scarcely from mere want of sources (mention is made, xvi. 1 ff. 6 f., of isolated particulars of this journey), but because the author, with his interest directed to the West, cannot sufficiently hasten to exhibit the Apostle in his European sphere of labour,—an interest which seems likewise to cast uncertainty on the statement of his inaction in Western Asia Minor, xvi. 6 f., little as we might deem it improbable in itself. It has already been shown how this interest is embodied in the vision, xvi. 9; how, in xvi. 37, preparation is already made for Paul's connection with the Roman community; how the object of the book is served by the conduct of the Apostle towards Jews and Gentiles, the trial scenes, the miracles, the journey to Jerusalem, and the vow, xviii. 18; how this whole section concludes in the Miletus discourse with an elaborate apology by the Apostle, and in the final scene, xx. 36 ff., with an effect confirmatory of this apology. If we finally contemplate that which intervenes between the two missionary journeys, namely, the apostolic council; apart from the essential portion of the description, its chronological position is undoubtedly correct, but that must not induce us to overlook how the author strives to transfer this fact also to the locality where it would accomplish most for his object. According to Gal. ii. 7, we must assume that, previous to his visit to Jerusalem, Paul had laboured in the pagan world for a considerable period, with such effect that as the Apostle of the Gentiles, κατ' ἐξοχὴν, he might demand for himself a recognition not second to that of Peter, the Apostle of the Jews. But now let us ask ourselves whether such a notion of his importance at this epoch could be obtained from our book. Until xii. he appears only as the coadjutor of Barnabas at Antioch; in xiii. he makes a missionary journey with Barnabas, which is certainly accompanied by important results, and in which, in our account also, he is decidedly the chief person, although it is here difficult to comprehend how it could procure for him alone, as contrasted with the older and more highly revered Barnabas, the position in which he appears in the Epistle to the Galatians. But neither does he in our book as yet occupy this position; where this Epistle represents Paul as dealing in his own name (ii. 1 ff., ἀνέβην μετὰ Βαρνάβα, ἀνεθέμην τὸ εὐαγγέλιον, πεπίστευμαι τὸ εὐαγγέλιον τῆς ἀκροβυστίας, &c.), in the Acts the transactions of the two, Paul and Barnabas (xv. 4, 12), are entirely in common; both come commissioned by the community at Antioch; both stand in a subordinate position towards the Jerusalemites; both are equally (xv. 26) ἄνθρωποι παραδεδωκότες τὰς ψυχὰς αὐτῶν ὑπὲρ τοῦ ὀνόματος Ἰησοῦ; of Paul's distinguished position no conception is obtained. Thus our book causes the consequence he had attained previous to the so-called apostolic council to disappear. With this intention, as it seems, it has contracted Paul's previous missionary labours of several years into the single proselytizing journey which he makes in common with Barnabas, in order that he may appear in the full glory of the Apostle of the Gentiles only after the official sanction of the primitive church has been obtained for this work.

In the record of the last journey to Jerusalem and the Apostle's imprisonment, the disproportionately greater minuteness must strike us, as compared with what has gone before. This may be partially explained by the circumstance, that here (see below) the notes of an eye-witness were in all probability employed. Meanwhile, the explanation in question does not suffice when we have already assured ourselves that the whole section, from xxi. 18—xxvi. 32, bears no trace of ocular testimony; that the negociations with James respecting the Nazarite sacrifice, the trial scenes, and the vindicatory discourses, betray the unhistorical pragmatism of the author far too clearly to be derived from any authentic source; and that even for the narrative xxiii. 11 ff., no sort of guarantee of authenticity is afforded. Hence we can explain the minuteness with which these portions are treated only by the design of the author to make everything which could conduce to the vindication of his Apostle find play, especially in Palestine in the presence of his chief opponents; and by the result of this vindication to place his innocence in the brightest light. Hence the repeated apologies before the people, the Sanhedrim, king Agrippa on the Jewish, Lysias, Felix, and Festus, on the Roman side,—apologies which make Paul appear an orthodox Jew, observing the Law and innocent in every respect; such apologies place the reality of his divine appointment beyond doubt, and in every instance elicit an acknowledgment of his innocence. This narrative, primarily intended for the Judaistic readers of the book, is immediately followed in the record of the journey by a section, xxvii. f., which makes Paul's destination as Apostle of the Romans conspicuous by the divine guidance and the miracles which accompany his passage to Rome; and after the final scene with the Roman Jews has brought the relation of the Jewish people to the gospel to a fundamental decision, our book concludes with the account of Paul's unchecked entrance on his Roman ministry.

If from hence we cast a retrospective glance at the whole of the description under discussion, we cannot deny the design and artificiality of its plan. From the first beginnings of the Christian Church, everything converges to the point in which the author concentrated the final effect of his book. The concluding commission of the departing Messiah to publish his gospel to the ends of the earth is already *typically* fulfilled in the miracle of Pentecost, *actually* in the primitive community of Jerusalem first, which, however, in its doctrine, its miracles, and its fate, already prefigures the Apostle of the Gentiles. The stubbornness of the Jewish people, testified by Stephen, drives Christianity beyond the boundaries of Judæa by the murderous violence with which it bursts out against him; while it spreads in Samaria, the most vehement persecutor of the Christians is transformed by a miracle into an Apostle; his destination among the distant heathens is pointed out to him beforehand, and, notwithstanding all his efforts, he is led to it by the will of Christ and the contumacy of the Jews. Yet before he actually enters upon this vocation, the right of Gentile conversion must be assured by the example of Peter, in consequence of the most distinct revelations, with the assent of the primitive community; and the history of the Jerusalemites must be closed by the flight of Peter. The transfer of salvation to the pagan world is now prepared on all sides, and Paul may begin his work; at first, however, only under the protecting companionship of Barnabas, and on a more limited domain; not till after a final negociation at Jerusalem has established the right and conditions of Gentile Christianity does he turn in complete independence to his chief sphere of labour in the Greco-Roman world. The doctrine which he preaches is merely the old primitive Christian doctrine; he himself is a faithful observer of the Law; his miracles are in no way inferior, his sufferings no greater than those of the original Apostles; he is altogether the true counterpart of Peter; his relations to the original Apostles are most cordial; Paulinism is the original primitive Christianity, brought to the Gentiles by the most conspicuous divine dispensations. That he should prove this to be the case, that the apology of Paul should be exhaustively argued before Jewish Christians (xxi. 20 ff.), Jews, and Gentiles, is accomplished by the Apostle's last sojourn in Palestine; but this likewise becomes the means of realizing what had long been recognized as necessary by Paul, determined by the divine counsels, nay, prepared from the first by the civil position of the Apostle. Brought to Rome as prisoner, and here also at the last hour rejected by his fellow-countrymen, Paul becomes the Apostle of the Roman Gentiles. His history has now reached the goal to which the author wished to bring it; for which reason it concludes without alluding to his death.

After this elucidation of the motive and plan of our book, we shall now for the first time be in a position to examine the question regarding its author, and the circumstances in which it originated.

Second Division.

THE AUTHOR OF THE ACTS; THE TIME AND PLACE OF ITS ORIGIN.

1. The Acts is the Work of a Single Author.

The investigation concerning the author of the Acts will most conveniently commence with the question, whether the book, as it now exists, is to be regarded as the work of a single author, or possibly an aggregate of separate compositions or fragments loosely bound together. If the former becomes probable, we must forthwith endeavour to ascertain the character, or at least the age and general circumstances of the author; and it is only in the third line that the question will arise respecting the sources employed; in the other case, on the contrary, the various elements of our book would have to be distinguished and their origin examined before we could inquire in what manner and by whom they were merged into the whole which they now constitute; for of course we must not understand the above dilemma as if the unity of the author entirely excluded a variety of aids, or the slight connection of the parts a single collector. The problem is merely whether the individual from whom our book is derived worked up his materials himself, or whether he only strung together more ancient records essentially unaltered in form and contents. So far the hypothesis of a single author embraces several possibilities; he might have created the contents entirely or in essence; on the other hand, he might, with historical fidelity as to the contents, have only remodelled extant traditions; thirdly and finally, he might also have combined the two methods and united tradition with invention. Which of these alternatives actually took place cannot be ascertained till later; we shall first consider the question of the author's unity only in the general way above stated.

For the solution of this problem three criteria offer themselves in the Acts itself: the language and representation, the contents and composition, the prospective or retrospective reference of different passages to each other. Even if decisive marks are not to be found in all these points, we must nevertheless attend to them all, if only that we may not overlook any argument that might conflict with our view.

One of the most important marks available in favour of the unity of our book is its uniformity in language and in style. It is true we may perceive peculiarities of language in individual sections also; but it will be shown that they are far too insignificant to prove anything contrary to the identity of their author, even if in some cases they may render it probable that special sources were employed. On the other hand, the whole book is pervaded throughout by a multitude of peculiar words and expressions such as are possible only in the work of one and the same author. I shall attempt to indicate the most conspicuous of these peculiarities, gratefully making use of the fundamental investigations of Gersdorf[1] and Credner.[2]

Much that is peculiar in this respect is exhibited even in the use of single words. The Acts contains, partly alone, partly in common with the third Gospel, a whole series of words which pervade every part of it; while in the other books of the New Testament they occur either not at all or comparatively seldom. Among these words are not a few which, by their remarkably frequent employment in our book, appear to be favourite expressions of the author, and are hence striking evidence of his identity throughout all sections of the work.[3] Among them are the substantive αἵρεσις, sect, in various parts of the Acts six, in the rest of the New Testament only three times; ἀπειλὴ and βία, the former peculiar to the Acts and the Epistle to the Ephesians, the latter to the Acts alone; βουλὴ and γένος, both indeed occurring elsewhere, but here with remarkable frequency (βουλὴ τοῦ θεοῦ appears only in Luke vii. 30; Acts ii. 23, iv. 28, xiii. 36, xx. 27); δῆμος, as well as δημόσιος and δημοσίᾳ, in the New Testament belonging only to our book; διάλεκτος only here, and that six times; ἔκστασις, with the verb ἐξίστασθαι, two words the frequent use of which can the less be deemed accidental, as both the mention of ecstasy and the description of violent affections are constant features with our author (ἐξίστασθαι, however, is to be found only in the 12th chapter; it appears elsewhere three times in Luke, oftener in Mark, and twice more in Matthew and Paul); ἐπιβουλὴ and ἐνέδρα here only, the former four times in different places, the latter in xxiii. 16, xxv. 3; ἐπαγγελία in the Pauline and pseudo-Pauline Epistles, as in the Acts, frequently,

[1] Beiträge zur Sprachcharacteristik der Schriftsteller des N. T., Erster Theil, pp. 160—272.

[2] Einleit. ins N. T. i. 132—142. Comp. also *Meyerhoff*, Einleit. in die Petrinischen Schriften, pp. 22—29.

[3] The próofs of the following are given, so far as they are not expressly stated, in *Schmid's* Ταμιεῖον, improved by *Bruder*, under the words in question.

in the Gospels only once, in Luke; ἐργασία, xvi. 16, xix. 19, 24 f., both times in the combination ἐργασίαν παρέχειν, and signifying gain; also with a different signification, Luke xii. 58, Eph. iv. 19; ζήτημα and συζήτησις, both peculiar to the Acts and comparatively frequent; whereas the simpler ζήτησις (Gospel and Epistles of John) is here more rare; the plural forms, καιροὶ, i. 7, iii. 20, xiv. 17, xvii. 26, Luke xxi. 24, and μέρη (parts), which are indeed to be found elsewhere; κλῆρος, καρδιογνώστης (only here, i. 24, xv. 8); νεανίας, which always stands as νεανίσκος in other parts of the New Testament; οἰκουμένη, οἶκος, especially as signifying family; ὅραμα, besides Matt. xvii. 9, in the Acts only, and that eleven times; σωτὴρ, with its derivatives σωτηρία and σωτήριον, words which are indeed not rare in the New Testament, but which, like χάρις, also very frequent in the works of Luke, belong especially to the idiom of Paul and his school (Epistles, Heb., 1 Peter), and are, on the contrary, entirely wanting in the two first Gospels; ἄφεσις ἁμαρτιῶν also is especially frequent in Luke. Of adjectives may be remarked, ἀγοραῖος, xvii. 5, and ἀγόραιος, xix. 38; ἀκατάκριτος, xvi. 37, xxii. 5; ἄξιος, frequent in Luke and Acts; ἀναντίῤῥητος, xix. 37, and also its adverb ἀναντιῤῥήτως, x. 29; ἅπας in all the rest of the New Testament only nine times, in the Acts fourteen times, Luke nineteen times; ἀσφαλὴς, xxi. 34, xxii. 30, xxv. 26, with ἀσφαλῶς, ii. 36, xvi. 23, ἀσφαλίζειν, xvi. 24, ἀσφάλεια, v. 23, Luke i. 4, all four rare elsewhere; γνωστὸς, in the Acts ten times, mostly in the combination γνωστόν ἐστιν (ἔστω, ἐγένετο), elsewhere twice in Luke and three times in John and Paul; ἔμφοβος and ἔντρομος, both almost exclusively in the Acts, the former also in Luke's Gospel, always in the context ἔμφοβον or ἔντρομον γίγνεσθαι; εὐλαβὴς, only in Luke; εὐσχήμων (xiii. 50, xvii. 12, both times γυναῖκες εὐσχήμονες), ὁ ἡγούμενος (vii. 10, xiv. 12, xv. 22, comp. Luke xxii. 26); ἱκανὸς, signifying "many," Acts eighteen times, Luke six times, elsewhere in the New Testament only three times; τεσσαρακονταετὴς, in the New Testament in the Acts only, both times in combination with χρόνος; χειροποίητος,

vii. 48, xvii. 24, both times in the same context: ὁ θεὸς οὐκ ἐν χειροποιήτοις (xvii. 24, χειρ. ναοῖς) κατοικεῖ. But greater still is the number of verbs, the use of which in different parts of the Acts attests the individuality of its linguistic character; comp. the words, ἅλλεσθαι, ἀνάγειν (Acts seventeen times, Luke four times, elsewhere in the New Testament three times), ἀναιρεῖν, ἀνακρίνειν, ἀναλαμβάνειν, the intransitive ἀναστρέφειν, ἀνατρέφειν, the transitive ἀνιστάναι, ἀποδέχεσθαι, ἀποφθέγγεσθαι, ἀπωθεῖσθαι, the frequent ἀτενίζειν, αὐξάνειν, ἀφιστάναι, βοᾷν; the δεῖ, *oportet*, a favourite in the Gospel and the Acts; διαλέγεσθαι (xvii.—xxiv., seventeen times, elsewhere in the New Testament three times more), διανοίγειν (in Luke and Mark only besides), διαμαρτύρεσθαι and διατρίβειν (each nine times, elsewhere rarely), διαπονεῖσθαι, διαπορεῖν, διαπρίεσθαι, διασπείρειν (always in Aor. pass. σπαρῆναι), four words to be found in the Acts only, διαπορεῖν also in Luke's Gospel; διερχέσθαι (Luke eleven times, Acts twenty-one times, elsewhere eleven times), διελθεῖν ἕως (only in Luke ii. 15, Acts ix. 38, xi. 19), δοκεῖν,[1] εἰσάγειν and ἐξάγειν, εἰσιέναι, ἐκτίθεσθαι, ἐξαιρεῖν, ἐξαποστέλλειν, ἐξηγεῖσθαι, ἐπιλαμβάνεσθαι, ἐπικαλεῖσθαι (signifying *to name*, nine times; signifying *to call*, eight times in the Acts; in the rest of the New Testament both together ten times), εὐαγγελίζεθαι, ἐφιστάναι (Luke seven times, Acts eleven times, elsewhere only twice), ἔχειν, in the sense of to be (Luke twice, Acts seven times), κακοῦν, καταγγέλλειν and παραγγέλλειν, κατάγειν, καταλαμβάνεσθαι, in the middle, κατανοεῖν, κατέρχεσθαι (Acts thirteen times, Luke twice, elsewhere only once in James), κελεύειν (eighteen times), λατρεύειν, μαρτυρεῖσθαι, signifying having a good character; μεγαλύνειν, μένειν, signifying to dwell (Credner, Nr. 50), μετακαλεῖσθαι and μεταπέμπεσθαι, μεταλαμβάνειν, especially μ. τροφῆς, νομίζειν, ὁρίζειν, παραγίνεσθαι (Acts twenty-one times, Luke eight times, elsewhere in the whole New Testament eight or nine times), παύεσθαι, προσέχειν, προχειρίζεσθαι, the fre-

[1] The impersonal δοκεῖ τινὶ is to be found in the New Testament, Luke once, Acts five times; elsewhere six times, in Matthew and John, but only in both in the question, τί σοι δοκεῖ.

quent πείθειν and πείθεσθαι (on the other hand, never πεποιθέναι), σέβεσθαι (xiii.—xix. eight times), στερεοῦν, συγκαλεῖν, συγχέειν, or —ύνειν (here only six times, σύγχυσις, xix. 29), συμβάλλειν, συμπαραλαμβάνειν, συναρπάζειν, σύρειν, ὑπάρχειν (Luke seven times, Acts twenty-four times, elsewhere in the New Testament fifteen times more), ὑποστρέφειν (eleven times, Luke twenty-two times, in the rest of the New Testament three times). Especially worthy of notice is the author's preference for verbs compounded with prepositions, with which the majority of the other New Testament writers are much less conversant than classic Greek; thus, in addition to those already quoted—that we may not enumerate them all—he is acquainted with the following compounds of ἀνά: ἀναβαίνειν, ἀναβάλλεσθαι,—βλέπειν,—γινώσκειν,—γνωρίζειν,—δεικνύναι,—δέχεσθαι,—διδόναι,—ζητεῖν,—θεωρεῖν, καθίζειν,—κάμπτειν,—πείθειν,—σκευάζειν,—σπᾶν,—στατοῦν,—στρέφειν,—τίθεσθαι,—τρέφειν,—φαίνεσθαι,—χωρεῖν, ἀνετάζειν, ἀνευρίσκειν, ἀνέχεσθαι, ἀνιέναι, ἀνιστάναι, ἀνοικοδομεῖν, ἀνορθοῦν; with διά: διαβαίνειν, διαγγέλλειν, διαγίνεσθαι,—γινώσκειν,—δέχεσθαι,—διδόναι,—κατελέγχεσθαι, διακούειν, διακρίνειν,—λύειν,—μάχεσθαι,—μερίζειν,—νέμειν, διανύειν, διαπερᾶν,—πλέειν,—πορεύεσθαι,—σκορπίζειν,—σπᾶν,—στέλλεσθαι,—στρέφειν, σώζειν,—τάσσειν,—τελεῖν,—τηρεῖν,—τίθεσθαι,—φέρειν,—φεύγειν,—χειρίζεσθαι,—χλευάζειν, διενθυμεῖσθαι, διερμηνεύειν, διερωτᾷν, διηγεῖσθαι, διϊστάναι, διϊσχυρίζεσθαι, διοδεύειν. Compare further the compounds with ἐπὶ, σὺν, &c., especially the compound verbs in the concordance. Although a portion only of these words is peculiar to the Acts, another portion to be found there only in one or few passages, yet the frequent occurrence of such compounds in all parts of the book proves a similar tendency of expression. There is something peculiar too in the use of the adverbs, prepositions, and particles. The Acts, and to a less degree the third Gospel, are partial to adverbs derived from πάς: πανταχοῦ (ῇ), πάντῃ, πάντως, διαπαντὸς, comp. also πανοικί, xvi. 34; adverbs which denote a sequence, ἑξῆς and καθεξῆς, both in Luke only; the otherwise rare κἀκεῖ and κἀκεῖθέν, which occur in the Acts, the former five, the latter nine times; ἐνθάδε, besides two passages in John's Gospel, only in one in Luke's Gospel and five in the Acts; ἄχρι, in Matthew once, in Mark and John never, Luke four times, Acts sixteen times, especially in the context ἄχρι ἧς ἡμέρας (Acts i. 2; Luke i. 20, xvii. 27), or ἀ. τῆς ἡμ. ταύτης (Acts ii. 29, xxiii. 1, xxvi. 22); adverbs which express the idea of suddenness: ἄφνω, ἐξαυτῆς, ἐξαίφνης, παραχρῆμα (the two first are wanting in the Gospel; on the other hand, besides the four passages in Luke's Gospel and the Acts, ἐξ. appears only in Mark xiii. 36, παραχρ., besides ten passages in Luke's Gospel and six in the Acts, only twice in Matthew); the prepositions σὺν and ἐνώπιον, of which the former occurs in Luke twenty-four times, Acts fifty times, elsewhere, except in the Pauline Epistles, rarely in the New Testament; the latter in Luke twenty times, in Acts twelve times; on the other hand, in Matthew and Mark never, in John once; the combinations ἐν τάχει (Luke xviii. 8, Acts xii. 7, xxii. 18, xxv. 4), ἐν ὀλίγῳ (Acts xxvi. 28 f.), ἐν μέσῳ (Gospel eight times, Acts five times, more rarely ἐκ μέσου), ἐπ' ἀληθείας (Luke's Gospel three times, Acts twice, elsewhere twice in Mark; on the other hand, the otherwise customary ἐν ἀληθείᾳ); ὃν τρόπον (Acts i. 11, vii. 28, Luke xiii. 34, elsewhere twice) and καθ' ὃν τρόπον (only in Acts xv. 11, xxvii. 25); κατά πρόσωπον, in the New Testament only in Luke ii. 31, Acts iii. 13, xxv. 16, 1 Cor. x. 1, 7, Gal. ii. 11; in the New Testament, only the Gospel and the Acts have the particle καθότι, the former twice, the latter four times; with the otherwise frequent καθὼς and ὡς they often place (Luke nine times, Acts eight times) the more rare ὡσεί. The Acts alone, besides Rom., xv. 6, is acquainted with the word ὁμοθυμαδὸν, which, not very usual even out of the New Testament, occurs here in nearly every part, altogether ten times; the Acts alone makes use, in addition to the frequent νῦν, of the compound τανῦν, whereas here, as in the Gospel, the ἄρτι, frequent in Matthew and John, is entirely wanting; it is partial to the combinations of particles μὲν οὖν and μέν γὰρ, of which the former especially is extremely frequent (see Bruder under the word μὲν), and the anomalous μὲν without the following δὲ (see i. 1, xviii. 2, 11, iii. 13, 21, iv. 16, v. 41, xiii. 4, xvii. 30, xxiii. 22, xxvi. 4, 9, xxvii. 21, xxviii. 22. Finally, the Acts alone makes use, and indeed equally in all its parts, of the conjunction τε to the same extent as the classic Greek. While this particle occurs in all the remaining books of the New Testament only fifty-three times (including twenty-one times in Hebrews and fifteen times in Romans), the Acts alone has it no less than from 140—150 times (the reading is not always certain). An idiom so unique in the New Testament, and at the same time so marked, can scarcely be explained otherwise than by unity of authorship.[1]

To this must be added many peculiarities in the form and combination of words, the construction, and phraseology. Thus the Acts and the Gospel of Luke employ the form Ἱερουσαλήμ far more frequently than the Ἱεροσόλυμα, otherwise habitual in the Gospels; both invariably employ as part. perf. of ἵστημι, and the verbs compounded from ἵστημι, the abbreviated form ἑστως, never ἑστηκὼς (see Bruder, s. v., Credner, p. 140, Nr. 45); the infinitive future ἔσεσθαι occurs in the New Testament only in Acts xi. 28, xxiii. 30, xxiv. 15 (25), xvii. 10, and always in the combination μέλλειν ἔσεσθαι; both are partial to the optative,[2] otherwise rare in the New Testament; both, the periphrasis of the substantive by the neuter of a participle, as τὸ εἰωθὸς, Acts xvii. 2, Luke iv. 2, comp. ii. 27; τὸ γεγονὸς, Acts iv. 21, v. 7, xiii. 12, Luke viii. 34, 35, 36; τὸ συμβεβηκὸς, Acts iii. 10, Luke xxiv. 14; τὰ κατεστραμμένα, Acts xx. 30; τὸ διατεταγμένον, Acts xxiii. 31; τὸ ὡρισμένον, Luke xxii. 22; τὸ γεννώμενον, Luke i. 35; both, especially the Acts (ii. 3, 6, xvii. 27, xx. 31, xxi. 19, 26), have the otherwise somewhat rare εἷς ἕκαστος (it occurs besides in Matt. xxvi. 22, not quite certainly, 1 Cor. xii. 18, Eph.

[1] A fuller catalogue of words common to the two writings of Luke is given by *Lekebusch*, The Composition and Origin of the Acts (Gotha, 1854), pp. 37—74; but he ought to have more carefully distinguished the various cases of the employment of the words, especially proof and non-proof examples. We confine ourselves purposely to the above evidence.

[2] *De Wette's* Int. to the N. T. § 115, a. Anm. 6.

iv. 7, 16, Col. iv. 6, 1 Thess. ii. 11, 2 Thess. i. 11); both alone, with the Philippians and Colossians, among the books of the New Testament employ the periphrasis τὰ περί τινος (Ἰησοῦ, ἐμου), Luke xxii. 3, 7, xxiv. 19, 27, Acts i. 3, viii. 12, xviii. 25, xix. 8, xxiii. 11, 15, xxiv. 10, 22, xxviii. 15, 23, 31; and with Mark, the periphrasis οἱ περί τινα, Luke xxii. 49, Acts xiii. 13, xxviii. 7; both not unfrequently employ the interrogative τίς ἄν (Luke i. 62, vi. 11, ix. 46, Acts v. 24, x. 17, xvii. 18, 20, xxi. 33); the Acts repeatedly (xvii. 18, 20) in the formula τί ἄν θελοι εἶναι or λέγειν, which without ἄν (according to others with ἄν) recurs in ii. 12; both, especially the Acts, have the attraction of the relative more frequently than the other books of the New Testament;[1] the Acts also several times refers the relative ὅ to a whole sentence (ii. 32, iii. 15, xi. 30, xxiv. 18, xxvi. 10, 12); both introduce interrogations with the article τὸ, Luke i. 62, xix. 48, ix. 46, xxii. 2, iv. 23, 24, Acts iv. 21, xxii. 30 (elsewhere only Rom. viii. 26); both are partial to the certainly not rare τοῦ, διά τὸ, μετὰ τὸ, πρὸ του· and the like before infinitives (Gersdorf, 208 f., 217, 243 f.); both after νομίζειν place the accusative with the infinitive, which is rare in the New Testament after this word (Gersdorf, 265); both frequently append to a verb accompanied by a participle a second designation also in the participle, without uniting them with a καὶ (Luke iv. 20, Acts xii. 4, 25; many other instances in Gersdorf, p. 258 f.); both by the *constructio ad sensum* frequently place the plural of the verb in connection with a previous πλῆθος, and similar words (ibid. p. 188 f.); both often use the augmentative δὲ καὶ, which appears in Luke twenty-nine times, in Acts nine times (see Bruder, s. v. δὲ); both like to say καὶ αὐτος (Acts viii. 13, xxi. 24, xxii. 20, xxiv. 16, xxv. 22, Luke very often), καὶ αὐτοὶ (Acts ii. 22, xv. 32, xxvii. 26, Luke often), καὶ αὐτοὺς (Acts xv. 27), αὐτῇ τῇ ὥρᾳ (Acts xvi. 18, xxii. 13, in Luke as αὐτὸς ὁ in general, frequently, see Bruder p. 116), ἐπὶ τὸ αὐτὸ or κατὰ τὸ αὐτό (Acts i. 15, ii. 1, 44, iii. 1, iv. 26, xiv. 1, Luke xvii. 35,

[1] Proofs in *Gersdorf*, 241; *Bruder*, p. 691 f.; *Lekebusch*, p. 75 f.

comp. vi. 23, 26). Both are partial to the periphrasis with *πρόσωπον* and *χείρ*;[1] both, especially the Acts, with *ἡμέρα*, in the expressions *καθ' ἡμέραν*, *πᾶσαν ἡμέραν*, *μετὰ ταύτας τὰς ἡμέρας*, *ἐν ταῖς ἡμέραις ταύταις* (instead of which, elsewhere always *ἐν ἐκείναις τ. ἡμ.*, in John *ἐν ἐκείνῃ τ. ἡμ.*), see Bruder s. v. *ἡμέρα*; the Acts alone has *ἄχρι τῆς ἡμέρας ταύτης* (ii. 29, xxvi. 22), or *ἀ. ταύτ. τ. ἡμ* (xxiii. 1); the Acts alone, altogether five times, *τῇ ἐπιούσῃ*, and (xx. 15, xxi. 26, comp. xiii. 44, *τῷ ἐχομένῳ σαββάτῳ*) Luke (xiii. 33), *τῇ ἐχομένῃ*. The verbs *εἰπεῖν* and *λαλεῖν* are in both writings of Luke; *φάναι* in the Acts, usually construed with *πρὸς* (*εἰπεῖν πρός τινα*), which is rare in the rest of the New Testament, less often with the otherwise customary dative of the person addressed; this preposition, to which Luke is partial,[2] stands also with *ἀποκρίνεσθαι*, *ἀπαγγέλλειν*, *λέγειν*, *διαλέγεσθαι*, *συζητεῖν*; *τίθεσθαι*, in the sense of putting somewhere, he construes sometimes, like the rest of the New Testament, with *ἐν* (*ἐν φυλακῇ τίθ*, and so forth), sometimes with *εἰς*; the former, Luke, i. 66, Acts v. 4, xviii. 25, xix. 21; the latter, the Gospel of Luke ix. 44, Acts iv. 3, xii. 4; the Acts has *τίθεσθαι* pretty often. *At the feet of one*, in the Acts iv. 35, 37, v. 2, 10, vii. 58, xxii. 3, Luke vii. 38, viii. 35, 41, x. 39, xvii. 16, is *παρὰ τοὺς πόδας*; in the rest of the New Testament, except Matt. xv. 30, always *πρὸς τ. π.* and the like; to sit at the feet of any one (in order to learn from him) occurs only in Luke, Gospel viii. 35, x. 39, Acts xxii. 3. In address, the Acts extremely often employs *ἄνδρες*, twice (vii. 2, xxii. 1) in the similar form *ἄνδρες ἀδελφοὶ καὶ πατέρες*. Like the Gospel, it is apt to introduce the mention of a name with *ὀνόματι* (this it has in all places together

[1] *Προ προσώπου* stands four times in Luke, once in the Acts; *ἀπὸ πρός·*, Acts three times; *κατὰ πρός·*, Luke and Acts once each; *ἐκ χειρὸς* or *δ. χειρῶν*, Acts seven times (comp. especially xi. 30, *ἀποστείλαντες διὰ χειρὸς Βαρνάβα*, &c., with xv. 23, *γράψαντες διὰ χ. αὐτῶν*); *ἐν χειρὶ*, Acts once; *εἰς χεῖρας*, Luke three times, Acts twice, with Luke ix. 44, xxiv. 7, comp. Acts xxi. 11, xxviii. 17; also on account of the similarly formed *παραδιδόναι εἰς χεῖρας*.

[2] *Gersdorf*, 180 f., 186; *Credner*, p. 138, Nr. 38 f. Also *λαλεῖν περί τινος* is especially Lukan, *Gersdorf*, 186.

twenty-two times), or it appends to the name a *καλούμενος* (twelve times, Gospel nine times), or *ἐπικαλούμενος, ἐπικληθεὶς, ὃς ἐπικαλεῖται, ὃς ἐπεκλήθη* (Acts eight times). Instead of the simple *Αἴγυπτος*, and so forth, it is, vii. 4, 29, 36, 40, xiii. 17, 19, *γῆ Αἴγυπτος, γῆ Αἰγύπτου, γῆ Μαδιὰμ, γῆ Χαλδαίων*: instead of the simple *ἄζυμα*, which stands in the rest of the New Testament, xii. 3, xx. 6, *αἱ ἡμέραι τῶν ἀζύμων*. The population of a town or a country is constantly introduced by *οἱ κατοικοῦντες*; it is also peculiar to the Acts that it generally says, not *οἱ κατ. ἐν Ἀσίᾳ*, &c., but *οἱ κατ. τὴν Ἀσίαν, τὴν Ἔφεσον*, and so on. A deadly crime is termed, xiii. 28, xxviii. 18, *αἰτία θανάτου*, xxiii. 29, xxv. 11, 25, xxvi. 31, as in Luke xxiii. 15, comp. xii. 48, *ἄξιον θανάτου*; instead of *αἰτία*, Acts xix. 40, Luke xxiii. 4, 14, xxii., *αἴτιον*, which does not occur in the rest of the New Testament. To seize any one is in the Acts three times, in the Gospel twice, expressed by *ἐπιβάλλειν τὰς χεῖρας* (*ἐπιβ. τὴν χ.* stands elsewhere, in Matt. xxvi. 5, Mark xiv. 46, John vii. 30, 44, with a different signification; also in Luke ix. 62). To give oneself out as something important (as a prophet) is termed, v. 36, viii. 9, *λέγειν εἶναί τινα ἑαυτὸν*, or *εἶναι τ. ἑ. μέγαν*. The Acts alone (ix. 2, xix. 9, 23, xxiv. 22, styles Christianity *ἡ ὁδὸς*, without any further epithet. The Acts frequently employs the otherwise rare formula, *ἐπιστρέφειν ἐπὶ τὸν θεὸν (κύριον)*; similarly Luke i. 16. The binding of a prisoner the Acts describes, both in xii. 6, xxi. 33, as *ἁλύσεσι δυσὶ δέειν*; elsewhere only Luke, viii. 29, has *ἁλύσεσι δεσμεῖν*, and Mark in the parallel passage, v. 3 f., *ἁλ. δέειν*. The death of Christ is termed, v. 3, x. 39, *κρεμάσαντες ἐπὶ ξύλου*; the decease of John the Baptist and of Paul, xiii. 25, xx. 24, *πληροῦν τὸν δρόμον* and *τελειοῦν τὸν δρόμον*. The idea of comprehensiveness is paraphrased by *μικρῷ τε καὶ μεγάλῳ* (xxvi. 22), *ἀπὸ μικροῦ ἕως μεγάλου* (viii. 10). The Acts and the Gospel very frequently employ expressions signifying plenitude, such as *πλῆθος, ἅπαν τὸ πλῆθος, πολὺ πλῆθος, πλήρης, πληροῦν, πληθύνειν, πλησθῆναι* (Credner, p. 141); the word *πλῆθος*, in the rest of the New Testament only seven times, appears eight times in the Gospel, seventeen times in the Acts; πλησθῆναι, for which, except in Matt. xxii. 10, we always find πληρωθῆναι, in the Gospel twelve times, in the Acts nine times. In both writings the author is partial to modes of speech compounded with καρδία (Credner, Nr. 6); τίθεσθαι ἐν τῇ καρδίᾳ or εἰς τ. κ. (Luke i. 66, ii. 14, v. 4) is peculiar to him; equally τίθεσθαι εἰς τήρησιν (ἐν τηρ., εἰς φυλακὴν), Acts iv. 3, v. 18, 25, xii. 4. He says, ἀπειλῇ ἀπειλεῖσθαι, παραγγελίᾳ παραγγέλλειν (iv. 17, v. 28, xxiii. 14, Luke xxii. 15, Gersdorf, p. 199), βάπτισμα βαπτίζειν (Luke xii. 50, Acts xix. 4), and so forth; he likes to depict strong passions or exhibitions of passion, and for this he employs by preference the predicate μέγας; comp. φόβος μέγας, χαρα μεγάλη, φωνὴ or κραυγὴ μεγάλη, and so forth (Credner, Nr. 57); the occurrence of extraordinary circumstances he describes by ἐπιπίπτειν (x. 10, xiii. 11, xix. 17, Gospel i. 12); he uses this word especially for the sudden operation of the Spirit, viii. 16, x. 44, xi. 15; elsewhere the Acts (five times) and the Gospel (three times, ch. i.) also say, πλησθῆναι πνεύματος ἁγ.; the former also λαμβάνειν τὸ πν. (i. 8, ii. 38, viii. 15, 17, 19, x. 47, xix. 2; elsewhere only in Paul in the Epistles to the Romans, Corinthians, and Galatians, in John's Gospel, and 1 John ii. 27). The Acts, like the Gospel, frequently paraphrases a finite verb by ἦν or ἦσαν with the participle (Credner, p. 139, Nr. 41); both books, for the sake of picturesqueness, employ the word πορεύεσθαι, which occurs altogether fifty times in the Gospel, thirty-eight times in the Acts; for instance, Acts v. 20, ix. 11, 15, Gospel x. 37, xiii. 31, &c.; for the same purpose a participle is often added to the finite verb, expressing the position or demeanour of the speaker or actor, as ἀναστὰς, ἐπιστὰς, σταθεὶς, ἑστὼς, ἐπιστρέψας, καθίσας, πεσών (instances in Credner, Nr. 40); special mention in this respect is due to the formulæ, θεὶς τὰ γόνατα and κατασείσας τῇ χειρὶ (τὴν χ.), which occur in a perfectly similar form, the former in Acts vii. 60, ix. 40, xx. 36, xxi. 5, Luke xxii. 41, the latter in Acts xii. 17, xiii. 16, xix. 33, comp. xxi. 40, but elsewhere never; only in Mark xv. 19, we read, τιθέντες τὰ γόνατα προσεκύνουν. The phrase, αἴρειν φωνὴν occurs only in Luke xvii. 13, Acts iv, 24; ἐπαίρειν τὴν φωνὴν only in Luke xi. 27, Acts ii. 14, xiv. 11, xxii. 22, and these works generally have ἐπαίρειν pretty often. So also we find φωνὴ γίγνεται, Luke i. 44, iii. 22, ix. 35, 36, Acts ii. 6, vii. 31, x. 13, 15, xix. 34; elsewhere only in the passage of Mark i. 11, derived from Luke iii. 22; comp. ix. 35, and in John xii. 30, Rev. viii. 5, xi. 15, 19, xvi. 18; φόβος ἐγένετο occurs only in Luke i. 65, Acts ii. 43, v. 5, 11; φόβος ἐπέπεσε only in Luke i. 12, Acts xix. 17, comp. Rev. xi. 11. Finally, the formula ἐγένετο δὲ has yet to be mentioned. This formula, frequent in the Lukan writings, occurs in the Acts always followed by an infinitive (see iv. 5, ἐγένετο δὲ συναχθῆναι, ix. 3, 32, 37, 43, x. 25, xi. 26, xiv. 1, xvi. 16, xix. 1, xxi. 1, 5, xxii. 6, 17, xxvii. 44, xxviii. 8, 17); only in v. 7 does the finite verb follow with καὶ (ἐγένετο δὲ ὡς ὡρῶν τριῶν διάστημα καὶ ἡ γυνὴ εἰσῆλθεν), probably owing to the ὡς διάστημα. In the Gospel this latter construction is more frequent. To the Gospel also especially belongs the combination of ἐγένετο with an ἐν τῷ (for instance, Luke xiv. 1, καὶ ἐγένετο ἐν τῷ ἐλθεῖν αὐτὸν . . . . καὶ αὐτοὶ ἦσαν, &c.); nevertheless, we also find it in the Acts, ix. 3, xix. 1, xxvii. 17 (the other passages in Credner, Nr. 1, do not apply here); similarly our book shares with the Gospel the habit of expressing the ideas of "whilst" and "by which" by an ἐν τῷ, with a following infinitive (ii. 1, viii. 6, ix. 3, xi. 15, xix. 1, iii. 26, iv. 30), as it is also accustomed to use the article before the infinitive (Credner, Nr. 14).

Another thing should be mentioned here, i. e. that in the Acts the Old-Testament is always quoted from the LXX.; that this occurs also in ii. 24, will be demonstrated below.

These numerous peculiarities of language and description running through the whole of the Acts, and in great part through the third Gospel, suffice to place it beyond doubt that we must regard our book as the work of a single author, who has stamped it with a characteristic impress of style and manner. We do not deny hereby that the author employed various written authorities, and that from this circumstance are derived sundry peculiarities in individual portions; but, on the other hand, it is irreconcilable with this result that he did not freely reproduce the matter of his sources, but merely put together single portions of the various writings, comparatively unaltered.[1] Were the author such a dependent compiler, the traces of this procedure must necessarily have become evident by a thorough dissimilarity of language and expression; and the dissimilarity must have been the greater if the sources, as in this case we can scarcely avoid assuming, belonged to very different departments, far apart in language and in thought. It would, on the contrary, be quite inexplicable that in all parts of the book we should encounter the same favourite expressions, the same turns, the same lexical and syntactic peculiarities. This phenomenon is intelligible only when the contents of our book have been reduced to their present form by one and the same person; if they have been not merely collected but composed by one man as they lie before us.

The inference is confirmed if we turn from the stylistic form of the book to its contents, which exhibit throughout the whole book a harmony such as we can explain only by unity of authorship. It is true that, in the accounts of Paul's conversion and the period immediately subsequent to that event, variations exist which we found of sufficient importance in estimating its historical value. Yet how little these variations justify us in attributing a different origin to the narratives concerned, is incontrovertibly proved by the circumstance that between the three accounts of Paul's conversion, especially between those in the 9th and 22nd chapters, there is an accordance,[2] in a great

[1] *Schwanbeck*, Ueber die Quellen der Schriften des Lukas, p. 253.

[2]

ix.	xxii.
1: προσελθὼν τῷ ἀρχιερεῖ. 2: ᾐτήσατο παρ᾽ αὐτοῦ ἐπιστολὰς εἰς Δαμασκὸν πρὸς τὰς συναγωγὰς, ὅπως ἐάν τινας εὕρῃ τῆς ὁδοῦ ὄντας,	4 f.: ταύτην τὴν ὁδὸν ἐδίωξα. . δεσμεύων. . ἄνδρας τε καὶ γυναῖκας, ὡς καὶ ὁ ἀρχιερεὺς μαρτυρεῖ μοι . . παρ᾽ ὧν καὶ ἐπιστολὰς δεξάμενος

measure verbal, which renders it impossible to attribute them to different authors. Even should it be assumed that one of these accounts lay before the author in an older book in the same form in which he communicates it, he must still have had this before his eyes in the composition of the two others, and have imitated it in them; hence, if the three accounts contradict each other in individual features, in no case can the blame be attributed to diversity of sources. At the same time we lose the right to infer, from the relation of ix. 29 f. to xxii. 17 ff., a diversity of authors; for if contradictory features were received into the history of the conversion, although in the second of his accounts the author had the first, and in the third the first and the second before him, contradictions may just as well be narrated by the same author respecting the journey to Jerusalem, although the contradicion is less obvious here. In this case minor contradictions between different passages are of less importance if they do not lie directly in the records themselves, but can only be deduced from concrete reflection. Con-

ἄνδρας τε καὶ γυναῖκας δεδεμένους ἀγάγῃ εἰς Ἰερουσαλήμ.

3: ἐν δὲ τῷ πορεύεσθαι ἐγένετο αὐτον ἐγγίζειν τῇ Δαμασκῷ καὶ ἐξαίφνης περιήστραψεν αὐτόν φῶς ἀπὸ τοῦ οὐρανοῦ.

4: καὶ πεσὼν ἐπὶ τὴν γῆν ἤκουσε φωνὴν λέγουσαν αὐτῷ Σαοὺλ, Σαοὺλ, τί με διώκεις;

5: εἶπε δέ τίς εἶ κύριε; ὁ δὲ κύριος εἶπεν ἐγώ εἰμι Ἰησοῦς ὃν σὺ διώκεις.

6: ἀλλὰ ἀνάστηθι καὶ εἴσελθε εἰς τὴν πόλιν καὶ λαληθήσεταί σοι τί σε δεῖ ποιεῖν.

πρὸς τοὺς ἀδελφοὺς εἰς Δαμασκὸν ἐπορευόμην, ἄξων καὶ τοὺς ἐκεῖσε ὄντας δεδεμένους εἰς Ἰερουσαλήμ.

6: ἐγένετο δέ μοι πορευομένῳ καὶ ἐγγίζοντι τῇ Δαμασκῷ . . . ἐξαίφνης ἐκ τοῦ οὐρανοῦ περιαστράψαί φῶς ἱκανὸν περὶ ἐμέ,

7: ἔπεσόν τε εἰς τὸ ἔδαφος καὶ ἤκουσα φωνῆς λεγούσης μοι Σαοὺλ, Σαοὺλ, τί με διώκεις;

8: ἐγὼ δὲ ἀπεκρίθην· τίς εἶ κύριε; εἶπέ τε πρός με· ἐγώ εἰμι Ἰησοῦς ὁ Ναζωραῖος, ὃν σὺ διώκεις.

10: ὁ δὲ κύριος εἶπε πρός με· ἀναστὰς πορεύου εἰς Δαμασκὸν κἀκεῖ λαληθήσεται περὶ πάντων ὧν τέτακταί σοι ποιῆσαι.

xxvi.

14: ἤκουσα φωνὴν λαλοῦσαν πρός με . . Σαοὺλ, Σαοὺλ, τί με διώκεις; σκληρόν σοι πρὸς κέντρα λακτίζειν.

15: ἐγὼ δὲ εἶπον· τίς εἶ κύριε; ὁ δὲ εἶπεν· ἐγώ εἰμι Ἰησοῦς, ὃν σὺ διώκεις.

16: ἀλλὰ ἀνάστηθι καὶ στῆθι ἐπὶ τοὺς πόδας σου.

tradictions of this sort were unavoidable if the narrator, with or without a purpose, allowed himself a general alteration of facts; without, however, metamorphosing the entire historical tradition, with its full train of consequences, from an unhistorical point of view. Thus we must certainly consider it contradictory that a double liberation of the Apostle should be related in v., first the miraculous but purposeless one by an angel, then the other humanly natural, though likewise improbable one, by Gamaliel. Of course we could not hence conclude that the first part of the narrative has a different author from the second, but at the most that an older record might have been employed and further elaborated by a later one. We are not justified in going further, even if irreconcilable features of the same sort belong, not to one and the same, but to different portions of our book. Little accordant as it is, for instance, that after ii. 45, iv. 34, all householders among the Christians of Jerusalem should have sold their property, while, nevertheless, in xii. 12, the house of a Mary, the mother of Mark, is noticed; it does not in the least follow that the author accepted these records unaltered in form and purport from earlier writings, but only that he did not observe their mutual contradictions, or had no interest in avoiding them. Little as the ascension in our book can be reconciled with that in Luke's Gospel, we must not infer from this circumstance either a diversity of authorship or such a dependence of the one author upon his authorities as would transform him, as Schwanbeck insists, from a self-dependent author into a mere collector; but it proves only that he did not possess sufficient historical accuracy or feeling to avoid contradictions which must certainly have struck a more critical eye. It is the same with all those features, the irreconcilability of which we have had occasion to demonstrate in our two first articles; the fact that such features occur we must admit, but must dispute the inferences built upon them; for the assumption that unity of authorship excludes any discrepancy in his records has been substantially refuted.

Still farther, it is just from the contents of our book and the essential harmony of all its parts that the unity of its authorship is most decidedly educed. We will not here reiterate what the previous section has shown in detail, that the whole of the book is pervaded throughout by one fundamental idea, one fundamental interest dominating the whole description; that its very first chapters, even the stories of the primitive community, are influenced by this interest; that through its whole course, from the beginning to the end, it appears with increasing distinctness; that not only is it testified by the selection of what is communicated and the position of the single narratives (especially in the section viii.—xii), but also that the historical facts themselves have been altered in favour of this tendency; that the entire harmony of the speeches of Paul, Stephen, Peter, and even of James, the notable parallelism between the deeds and destinies of Paul on one side, of Peter and the primitive community on the other, can only be explained by the unity of the original plan. If our investigation of the object and plan of the Acts has any foundation at all, it has placed the unity beyond doubt. Only consider the most prominent particulars. Already in the opening scene of our book, i. 8, not only is its main dogmatic point of view, the universal destination of Christianity, announced; but the successive steps in which the realization of this destination is meant to show itself are also indicated in brief outline. In the narration of the miracle of Pentecost this same interest makes itself powerfully influential by referring the speaking with tongues to the languages of all nations. In the portraiture of the primitive church and its adventures, consideration for the Apostle Paul already floats so distinctly before the eyes of the narrator, that by this consideration alone we were able to explain the unhistorical persecutions of the fourth and fifth chapters. Stephen is unmistakably treated as the precursor of Paul; and especially the elaborate speech which is put into his mouth in contradiction to the tumultuous character of the rest of the transaction, can be fully understood only from this point of view. We have already demonstrated at the proper time what close reference the incidents in Samaria and Cæsarea (x. 10 f.) bear to the ministry of the Apostle of the Gentiles subsequently recorded, and especially how the utterly unhistorical conversion of Cornelius is an explicit apology for the Pauline mission to the Gentiles. That the narrative of Paul's conversion, but especially the unhistorical assertions respecting the years immediately following his conversion, his first sojourn with the Jerusalemites and his second journey to Jerusalem (xi. 17), are only the first lines of the picture of the great Apostle of the Gentiles which is sketched in the last portion of the Acts; that here, contrary to his own declarations, he is represented in the same relations of amity and dependence towards the Apostles of the Jews as he is later on, it is scarcely necessary to remark again. Similarly it has been shown how the delineation of the Apostle Paul from xiii. forwards, framed according to a definite and partially unhistorical point of view, harmonizes in all its essential features with itself as well as with the narratives of the first part; how the Pauline miracles are depicted like the Petrine miracles of the first part; how the sufferings of the Apostle of the Gentiles are diminished in the interest of the same parallel; how he himself, contrary to historical fact, appears completely in harmony, both in doctrine and conduct, with the Apostles of the Jews; how xxiii. 1 ff. represents him in the same relation to the Jewish parties as iv. 1, v. 34 ff. the original Apostles; how the plan already laid down in the commencement of our book concludes with the carefully prepared founding of the Roman community by Paul. This unity of plan and object pervading our whole book is the most certain proof of one author. The clearer it appears that this object is not attained by mere arrangement, but by a profound transformation of historical tradition, so much the more obvious does it become that the description which furnishes it must be the work of one man.

It is scarcely necessary, in addition to this main evidence, to demonstrate the unity of our book by the manifold connections existing between individual passages. Yet we must admit De Wette's demonstration of this point[1] to be well founded and meritorious. Quite palpable is, above all, the reference from xi. 16 back to i. 5; since the saying of Jesus there quoted, Ἰωάννης μὲν ἐβάπτισεν ὕδατι, ὑμεῖς δὲ βαπτισθήσεσθε ἐν πνεύματι ἁγίῳ, is found only here. But just as clear is the reference of this saying to the narrative of the second chapter about the outpouring of the Spirit. By this it is proved, in the first place, that the three sections named cannot in their present state belong to different authors, even if they were originally founded on different sources. But the same author must also have had viii. 1 in his narrative, for when it is said in xi. 9, οἱ μὲν οὖν διασπαρέντες ἀπὸ τῆς θλίψεως τῆς γενομένης ἐπὶ Στεφάνῳ διῆλθον ἕως Φοινίκης καὶ Κύπρου καὶ Ἀντιοχείας, the reference to viii. 1 (ἐγένετο δὲ . . . διωγμὸς μέγας . . . πάντες τε διεσπάρησαν κατὰ τὰς χώρας τῆς Ἰουδαίας καὶ Σαμαρείας) is quite obvious, since here alone is the dispersion of the Christians at Jerusalem spoken of. Schwanbeck[2] indeed is of opinion that the reporter of viii. 1, when writing his passage, cannot have known anything of xi. 19; for according to the first passage the Christians are dispersed to Judæa and Samaria, according to the second they go as far as Phœnicia, &c.; still it is evident that the last statement does not in the slightest degree contradict the second, but much rather carries it further: the subjects of persecution, it was first said, fled to Judæa and Samaria, and now, after the events have been recorded (viii. 4—11, 18) which occurred[3] in these two countries, in consequence of this dispersion of the Christians to Judæa and Samaria, ch. xi. 19 proceeds, the dispersed people wandered yet further (διῆλθον)[4]

[1] Com. on Acts, § 2 a; Int. to the N. T. § 115, Observation d.

[2] Work quoted before, p. 52.

[3] Why this is previously interposed, i. e. that the first Gentile conversion by Peter should be related, is shown by *Schneckenburger*, Zweck d. Apg. 175 f.

[4] Respecting the use of the word διέρχεσθαι, comp. Rom. v. 12 and the commentators on this passage: διέρχεσθαι, to go through, to proceed from a given commencement through a whole series, always assumes an ἔρχεσθαι. Thus also our passage, they went further, beyond those places to which, according to viii. 1, they had first gone.

to Phœnicia, &c. The author could not express himself thus if he did not presuppose the first-mentioned dispersion. Ch. xi. 19 is therefore certainly written with reference to viii. 1. That, conversely, there is also in viii. a reference to xi. 19 cannot indeed be asserted, neither can it be required; and it is only a misapprehension of the passages concerned which makes Schwanbeck ask why, if the author in viii. 1 already knew that the Christians had dispersed, some to Judæa, others to Antioch, he did not put them both together in his representation? The author's meaning is not at all that the dispersed Christians went, some to Judæa, others to Syria, &c., but he makes them all go in the first place to Judæa and Samaria, and a part of them (as is naturally understood from xi. 19) thence reached Antioch, Phœnicia, and Cyprus. Still less does xi. 22 favour Schwanbeck's hypothesis; for the contradiction that a community in Jerusalem is mentioned here, whereas viii. 1 notifies the dispersion of all Jerusalemite Christians excepting the Apostles, might be partially removed by the assumption that in the interval a Christian society had re-assembled round the Apostles. But it is only a consequence of historical exaggeration in viii. 1, and can so far prove nothing more in favour of a diversity of authorities than other contradictions in which our book is involved by unhistorical statements.

The resemblance of vi. 8 to iv. 33, v. 12, has been already observed (p. 176). Ch. ix. 1 is expressly referred by the ἔτι to viii. 1—3. The case of the records concerning the conversion of Paul has been partially discussed already, and must be partially touched upon later; whether in ix. 15 is to be understood precisely the audience before Agrippa, xxvi. (De Wette), may be doubted. Ch. x. 41, xiii. 31, term the Apostles, as does vi. 22, μάρτυρες τῆς ἀναστάσεως. In xi. 25 the reference to ix. 22 is obvious, otherwise whence should we know that Paul was to be found at Tarsus? In xii. 24 we meet the same formula as in vi. 7. That the sections xi. 19—30 and xii. 25 are connected with xiii. 1 ff. is admitted even by Schwanbeck. We should wish to limit this concession to xi. 19—26, for the narrative of the journey of Paul and Barnabas to Jerusalem might be omitted without injury to the context; while, on the other hand, xiii. 1 certainly assumes that the existence of a Christian community at Antioch is already known to the reader; and as our book has spoken of it only in xi. 19 ff., we should be entitled to see in xiii. a reference to this passage, even if in other respects the contents of the chapter were derived from another special source. That this could, however, in no case apply to its entire contents, is evident from the demonstration above given, after Schneckenburger and Baur, of the accordance of the Pauline discourse, v. 16—41, with the speeches of Stephen in the seventh, and of Peter in the second and third chapters. This accordance cannot possibly be explained by the real historical state of the matter, but only thus, that the earlier speeches still dwelt in the memory of the author during the composition of the Pauline speech; and even if, so far as we have yet gone, the case were still supposable that it had been derived from special sources, we have ascertained this much, that the author of the speech in xiii. is not separable from the author of our whole book, for he alone can have had the speeches of Peter and of Stephen before him in his work. That the speech before the Areopagus in its arrangement recalls that of Stephen, and that of the 22nd chapter both the others, has been observed at the proper time; the verbal coincidence of xvii. 24 with vii. 48 we have likewise pointed out, and have also convinced ourselves with respect to the narrative in xiv. 8 ff., that its striking affinity to the earlier one in iii. 2—8, extending to the minutest details and to the verbal expression, is intelligible only by the one being copied from the other. Of Peter's utterance in xv. 7—9, the verbal accordance of ver. 8 with x. 47 would alone leave no doubt that it has express reference to the narrative of the conversion of Cornelius in x. and xi.; and the more weighty are the doubts which underlie the veracity of this narrative, the plainer is it that it is not the expression alone which is affected by this reference, but much more that Peter's speech can only have the same author with the narrative of Cornelius. With Schwanbeck (pp. 52, 121 f., 265), to separate this speech from its surroundings, and to insert it as from another source[1] into the record of the 15th chapter, is altogether impossible; for this record constitutes a closely connected whole, and the speech of James immediately following would lose all basis without Peter's speech and allusion to the conversion of Cornelius. Finally, after our previous investigations, it is quite incredible that the author should have found such an obviously unhistorical narrative, so entirely spun out of the tendency of our book, in essentially the same form which it bears, not in one only, but in two of his sources. Schwanbeck could overlook this merely because he undertook to answer the question respecting the sources of the Acts without any previous investigation of the credibility and tendency of its narratives, but purely from the language and literary character of the single sections. By such procedure it was scarcely to be avoided that, to its great injury, his whole investigation proceeded on a mass of baseless assumptions, with the critical examination of which it ought to have commenced. The speech of James, moreover, also contains, besides ver. 14, an unmistakable reminiscence of what precedes; for as Moses in ver. 21 is called κατὰ πᾶν σάββατον ἀναγινωσκόμενος, so it is said in xiii. 27, in one of Paul's speeches, τὰς φωνὰς τῶν προφητῶν τὰς κατὰ πᾶν σάββατον ἀναγινωσκομένας.

As the record of the 15th chapter refers to what has gone before, so is it also most distinctly presupposed, not only in the section, xvi. 1—4, immediately connected with it, but also still later in the words of James in xxi. 25. If this retrospective reference testifies of itself unity of authorship in ch. xv. and xxi., the testimony receives a still greater weight when, adhering to the results already obtained, we abandon the historical veracity of the apostolic ordinance, xv. 28 f.; for if this account of the

[1] The biography of Peter assumed by *Schwanbeck*, whereon more below.

apostolic council belongs not to historical fact, but to the reporter alone, neither can an appeal to it belong to any other person.

Ch. xv. 36 alludes expressly to xiii. f.; the reference of xv. 38 to xiii. 13, notwithstanding Schwanbeck's partial doubts (p. 54), must likewise be still maintained. For the first words of the passage respecting Mark, *Παῦλος δὲ ἠξίου τὸν ἀποστάντα ἀπ' αὐτῶν ἀπὸ Παμφυλίας . . . μὴ συμπαραλαβεῖν τοῦτον*, would be completely incomprehensible to the reader had not xiii. 13 preceded them: *ἦλθον εἰς Πέργην τῆς Παμφυλιας. Ἰωάννης δὲ ἀποχωρήσας ἀπ' αὐτῶν ὑπέστρεψεν εἰς Ἱεροσόλυμα.*

That xviii. 5 glances back at xvii. 15,[1] even Schwanbeck cannot deny; but the reference is supposed to be neutralized by the circumstance that xvii. 15 assumes an immediate departure of Silas and Timotheus at the instance of Paul; whereas in xviii. 5 it seems that this urgency to hasten had not taken place. This is not correct; the whole difficulty consists herein, that in xviii. 1, on the departure of Paul from Athens, it is not expressly remarked that it occurred before the arrival of Silas and Timothy; but what can this prove, above all with such a cursory narrator as our author?[2]

There is less importance in the reference of xix. 1 to xviii. 23, on account of the small distance between the two passages; and also in that of xxi. 8 (*Φιλίππου τοῦ εὐαγγελιστοῦ ὄντος ἐκ τῶν ἑπτὰ*) to vi. 5 (the selection of the seven deacons, and Philip amongst them), as such a trifling addition might have been inserted by an otherwise dependent collector; on the other hand, the connection between xxi. 8 and viii. 40 seems more capable of bearing evidence. In viii. 40, it is said of Philip after the incident with

[1] xvii. 14—16, Paul leaves Beræa while Silas and Timotheus stay behind. From Athens he sends word to them, *ἵνα ὡς τάχιστα ἔλθωσι πρὸς αὐτὸν*; while he awaits them at Athens, the scene in the Areopagus takes place, xviii. 1, *μετὰ ταῦτα χωρισθεὶς ἐκ τῶν Ἀθηνῶν ἦλθεν εις Κόρινθον.* Ver. 5: *ὡς δὲ κατῆλθον ἀπὸ τῆς Μακεδονίας ὅ τε Σίλας καὶ ὁ Τιμόθεος*, &c.

[2] Thus, for example, in viii. 13, it is not expressly observed that Philip returned to Jerusalem, yet it is taken for granted in verse 26.

the eunuch: Φίλιππος δὲ εὑρέθη εἰς Ἄζωτον καὶ διερχόμενος εὐηγγελίζετο τὰς πόλεις πάσας, ἕως τοῦ ἐλθεῖν αὐτὸν εἰς Καισάρειαν. From this time forward Philip is mentioned no more; only in xxi. 8 do we meet him again—at Cæsarea. Now is it to be supposed that the person who wrote viii. 40 had not already this subsequent meeting with Philip in his mind? The evangelist, having wandered through the sea-towns, probably established himself only at a later period permanently at Cæsarea.[1] At any rate, it would be a strange coincidence, when the last and penultimate mention of Philip in our book should fit each other so accurately, if the one had not taken the other into consideration; and if it subsequently becomes probable that xxi. 8 was derived from a more ancient source, we must assume that the general author of the Acts was already acquainted with this source when he wrote viii. 40.

Ch. xx. 4 refers to xix. 29; xxiv. 18 to xxi. 26; xxv. 21, xxvi. 32, xxvii. 24, xxviii. 19, to xxv. 11; that xxi. 29 looks back to xxiv. is very probable, and that the partially verbal coincidence of xxii. 20 with vii. 58, viii. 1,[2] is not the effect of mere chance is apparent. Let it be assumed that the words of Paul in the 22nd chapter are determined by the passage in the 7th and 8th, or conversely, with Schleiermacher[3] and Schwanbeck (p. 56), that these are determined by the speech of Paul, at any rate there is here a relation between remote sections, which can only be derived from the author of the whole. The quotation in xxiii. 6 of Paul's speech in xxiv. 21, would be less important if the result of our earlier investigation respecting the historical veracity of the speech first cited did not give it some weight; for if one of the Apostle's speeches refers to an utterly impro-

[1] *Schneckenburger*, Zweck d. Apg. 162.

[2] Ch. xxii., Paul, with regard to the appearance of Christ at Jerusalem, relates as his own speech: ὅτε ἐξεχεῖτο τὸ αἷμα Στεφάνου τοῦ μάρτυρός σου καὶ αὐτὸς ἤμην ἐφεστὼς καὶ συνευδοκῶν καὶ φυλάσσων τὰ ἱμάτια τῶν ἀναιρούντων αὐτόν. Comp. vii. 58: καὶ οἱ μάρτυρες ἀπέθεντο τὰ ἱμάτια αὐτῶν παρὰ τοὺς πόδας . . . Σαύλου. viii. 1: Σαῦλος δὲ ἦν συνευδοκῶν τῇ ἀναιρέσει αὐτοῦ.

[3] Einleit. ins N. T., edited by *Wolde*, p. 377.

bable fact, this speech can only proceed from a person who had the record of the supposed fact before him; and if this can be explained only by the general tendency of our book, the other also must be traced back to the author of the whole. That Paul's last journey to Jerusalem is prepared by xix. 21, xx. 16, the Roman journey by xix. 21, xxiii. 11, xxv. 10 f., xxvii. 24; that the speech of xx. 23 forestalls what is subsequently related (xxi. 4, 10 ff.); that the declaration in xx. 25 betrays the author's knowledge of the Apostle's death, have been already shown.

The instances which Schwanbeck, pp. 57 ff., opposes to this evidence have but little significance. It is supposed to betray a diversity of reporters, or an omission on the part of the reviser, that Peter after his recorded flight, xii. 17, appears again at Jerusalem, xv. 7, without express mention of his return; but this circumstance is easily explained by the simple negligence of the author, or by a deficiency in his information concerning Peter. Moreover, it is supposed to be incredible that the same person who in viii. 1 makes all the Christians fly from Jerusalem, should immediately after have mentioned, in ver. 2, devout men, and, in ver. 3, the Christians persecuted by Paul. But the meaning of these three verses probably is not that what is recorded by each was chronologically concluded before the commencement of that which is related in the next, but ver. 1 communicates the generalities of the Christian persecution after Stephen's death; to which vers. 2 and 3 add something more special, though certainly not very orderly. The ἄνδρες εὐλαβεῖς of the 2nd verse are, moreover, not Christians, but Jews. It is furthermore asserted (p. 58) that in the beginning of the 16th chapter Paul passes through the same regions, the visitation of which is related in the 14th chapter; both passages are marked by considerable prolixity, and yet no one would guess from the 16th that it had been preceded by a 14th; certainly not necessarily from the 16th chapter, although here also Christian communities in Pamphylia and Lycaonia are mentioned in vers. 2 and 4, but so much the more distinctly from xv. 36: μετὰ δέ τινας ἡμέρας εἶπε Παῦλος πρὸς Βαρνάβαν· ἐπιστρέψαντες δὴ ἐπισκεψώμεθα τοὺς ἀδελφοὺς κατὰ πᾶσαν πόλιν, ἐν αἷς κατηγγείλαμεν τὸν λόγον τοῦ κυρίου. It is a further stumbling-block to Schwanbeck that Gamaliel, in v. 34, appears as the apologist of the Christians, and in xxii. 3, on the contrary, as the instructor of Saul the persecutor of the Christians; these two statements, he thinks, cannot possibly be recorded by the same narrator. This assertion has been already answered: if from historical contradictions we might at once infer a diversity of narrators, the Acts would have a fine number of authors; but as one and the same author may have fallen into such contradictions, and as, at any rate, he actually has made them in all those cases in which they occur in the same narrative, or in two narratives obviously dependent on each other, they cannot in themselves furnish the slightest proof against identity of authorship. In the present case, moreover, the contradiction is not so directly conspicuous that he must necessarily have observed the discrepancy; for Gamaliel is quoted in xxii. 3, not as a persecutor of Christians, but as the representative of Jewish orthodoxy; and it is precisely because he is so that he is able to appear in ch. v. with such effect. Our author can bear much more. What a striking contradiction is it, for instance, that the same Pharisaic Sanhedrim which brings a mortal accusation against Paul (xxiv. 1 and xxv. 2); the same party which immediately before, xxiii. 14, xxv. 3, approves or organizes his assassination, in xxiii. 7 ff. appears on his side against the Sadducees! And yet here even, on account of the reference of xxiv. 21 to xxiii. 6, and because of the close connection of the whole narrative, there can be no idea of a diversity of reporters, and even Schwanbeck does not think of it. This contradiction disturbs the author of the Acts as little as it has disturbed the majority of his commentators to the present day. Still weaker is the argument which Schwanbeck draws from the treatment of the names of Herod and Agrippa in the 12th, 13th and 25th chapters, for which reason we pass it over; there is something more in the fact that on the mention of Mark in xii. 25, the complete description of his name is employed, Ἰωάννην τὸν ἐπικληθέντα Μάρκον, whereas in xii. 12 it had been preceded by Ἰωάννου τοῦ ἐπικαλουμένου Μάρκου; but even if this should betray the employment of another source, the circumstance by no means affords proof of a new author; that in xv. 37, after an interruption of three chapters, the full name, Ἰωάννην τὸν καλούμενον Μάρκον, again appears, is quite unimportant; and it implies equally little that in xv. 39 only Mark is said; in xiii. 5, 13, on the contrary, only John. Likewise in the introduction of Agabus, who appears in xxi. 10 as a person still unknown to the reader, may be found indications of a record in which there was no earlier mention of this prophet; but, on the other hand, our investigation of xi. 27 ff. renders it probable that Agabus and his prophecy found their way into the unhistorical narrative of this small section only from xxi., and thus, by the relation of these two passages, only confirms the general unity of our book, notwithstanding the probable use of more ancient sources.

The evidence adduced by Schleiermacher, pp. 350 ff. of his Introduction to the New Testament, to prove the Acts to be the combination of single narratives, partially knowing nothing of each other, can also scarcely bear examination. He considers it unlikely that any one intending to give a consecutive history should relate the conversion of Paul three times, Peter's visions (x. 11) twice. But it is certainly still more unlikely that two mutually independent narrators should have recorded these facts in great measure verbally alike; if, on the contrary, their stylistic form originates with the collector, he has not merely copied them from his authorities, but has purposely and consciously framed them alike. Herewith every reason disappears for tracing their repetition to a plurality of authorities, which is, moreover, prohibited in the repetitions of x. and xi. by uniformity of narrative; for whoever was capable, for a distinct purpose, of taking three accounts of the same event and rendering them alike, might quite as well, for the same purpose, repeat one account two or three times; hence we have only to inquire what this purpose was. It has already been shown also that the discrepancies in the history of the conversion prove nothing in favour of the fragmentary hypothesis. If, further, the proper coherence is lacking between the third chapter and the end of the second (p. 352), the first question is, whether the author cares at all for this sort of historical coherence; and even, like an artificial historian, if in the beginning of the third chapter traces should be found of a narrative which originally did not directly unite with the preceding one, it would by no means follow that it had been secured and inserted by the author without his own revision. The same applies to Schleiermacher's observation (p. 354), that in xix. 1, the previous sojourn of Paul at Ephesus is entirely ignored; but perhaps we ought to explain this circumstance in another way, i.e. that by the intercalation of the unhistorical journey in xviii. 20, the author converted the Apostle's single visit to Ephesus into a two-fold one. In this case it might certainly indicate that only in xix., after the free composition of xviii. 18 ff., the employment of sources recommenced; that the record employed was not, however, received without revision, but was expressly connected with the narrative of the journey to Jerusalem by the words, *διελθόντα τὰ ἀνωτερικὰ μέρη.* It is doubtless the same with the beginning of xiii., where it is certainly striking that Barnabas and Saul, who have scarcely been mentioned, are suddenly introduced as complete strangers. There is every probability that the author here follows a record which contained nothing of the journey of Paul and Barnabas, xi. 27 ff., xii. 25. Only it must not hence be inferred that he derived this journey from another source, but it is his own unhistorical fiction, which he has neglected to make entirely harmonious with its surroundings. That vi. 1 ff. no longer assumes a community of goods, although its cessation is not recorded (p. 353), is one of the historical discrepancies which have been already discussed;

but that the description in iv. 32 ff. ignores the previous one in ii. 42 ff. is incorrect; much rather the very similar descriptions, unhistorical as they are, can only be derived from the self-same author. It is equally incorrect, according to all probability, that Philip's missionary labours, viii. 4—40, should not have taken place till after the conversion of Cornelius; in our book at least they form a preliminary stage for the latter. If it be finally required that in viii. 1—4, the extension of Christianity to Phœnicia and Syria (xi. 19), and the communities of Galatia (ix. 31), should be already mentioned, and if Schleiermacher likewise takes offence at the silence respecting the earlier conversions in Cyprus, xiii. 4, xv. 39, he attributes to our author an historical accuracy to which he makes no pretence. But even though his book may not in every detail constitute an absolutely harmonious whole, we are by no means justified in stamping it as a mere aggregate of unrevised fragments.

It would be of greater importance in the present investigation if essential differences could also be shown in the language of the various sections; but as we must afterwards enter more minutely on this point, it may be allowed here to refer to that section. For the present, the positive proofs above adduced in favour of the literary unity of our book justify us in tracing it, not to a mere collector, but an author.

Before we proceed from this to the question respecting the time, the circumstances, and the person of this author, it will be useful first to examine a point by which the decision of that question will be in a great measure determined, namely, whether the two books attributed to Luke proceed from one and the same individual. This discussion is, therefore, the next subject which will occupy us.

2. The Acts and the Third Gospel are the Work of a Single Author.

The Acts describes itself at its commencement as a continuation of the third Gospel. Since it cannot, however, be demonstrated that the latter refers to the former, this announcement is not an unqualified proof. It might be supposed that another person had foisted the history of the Apostles on the author of the Gospel. The testimony of ecclesiastical tradition, which knows Luke alone as the author of both writings, likewise affords no absolute proof. For as this evidence with regard to the Acts only begins at the end of the second century, we are entirely ignorant whether it is founded on real historical information or on our book's own statement; whether with respect to it we are not in the same predicament as with respect to the Pastoral Epistles and other writings, which, without any contradiction within the Church,[1] are ascribed to an author to whom neverthelesss in all probability they do not belong. In the present case, however, the identity of the author of the two writings is raised to such a high height of probability that we have every right to consider it as historically proved.

Here again one of the most decisive proofs consists in the language. I have already given elsewhere[2] a list of 134 words[3] and expressions which, among the books of the New Testament, occur exclusively, or nearly exclusively, in the writings of Luke. In the same place I have put together 139 other words which, by their comparatively frequent use in both writings, show themselves to be either the author's favourite expressions, or at least a considerable element in his stock of words. Much of that

[1] Heretics alone rejected the Pastoral Epistles, but the Acts were also missing in the canon of Marcion.

[2] Tübingen Theol. Journal, 1843, 467 ff.

[3] By an oversight, the words *κοινωνὸς* and *κοίτη*, which occur only in the Gospel, and *συνεφιστάναι*, which occurs only in the Acts, have been placed in that list among those common to both; on the other hand, *ἀπαλλάσσεσθαι* was passed by, which occurs, besides Luke xii. 5 and Acts xix. 12, only in an uncertain passage, Heb. ii. 15.

which is in this respect common to both has necessarily been mentioned above already among the lexical proofs of the unity of the Acts itself. While referring to these lists, and partially completing them, I point out the following:

1. Among the words exclusively peculiar to the Acts and the Gospel of Luke are αἴτιον, Gospel three times, Acts once; ἀποδέχεσθαι, Gospel twice, Acts five or six times; the plural form δεσμὰ, Gospel once, Acts twice; διαπορεῖν, Gospel once, Acts three times; διϊστάναι, Gospel twice, Acts once; ἐνεδρεύειν, only once in each, but ἐνέδρα twice more in the Acts; ἑξῆς and καθεξῆς, Gospel twice, Acts three times; ἐπιβιβάζειν, Gospel twice, Acts once; ἐπιφωνεῖν, Gospel once, Acts three times; ἐπιχειρεῖν, Gospel once, Acts twice; ἑσπέρα, the same;[1] εὐλαβὴς, Gospel once, Acts three times; θάμβος, Gospel twice, Acts once; ἴασις, Gospel once, Acts twice; καθιέναι, Gospel once, Acts three times; καθότι, Gospel twice, Acts four times; κράτιστος, Gospel once, Acts three times; ὀδυνᾶσθαι, Gospel three times, Acts once; ὁμιλεῖν, Gospel twice, Acts twice; παραλελυμένος, Gospel once, Acts twice; πολίτης, Gospel twice, Acts once; στρατηγὸς, of the commander of the Temple guard at Jerusalem, Gospel once, Acts twice; also of the duumvirs at Philippi, Acts. xvi., five times; συμβάλλειν, Gospel twice, Acts four times; συμπληροῦν, Gospel twice, Acts once; συναθροίζειν, Gospel once, Acts twice; συναρπάζειν, Gospel once, Acts three times. Luke alone uses (Gospel vii. 7, Acts xv. 38, xxviii. 22) ἀξιοῦν with the following infinitive in the good Greek signification—*to regard as suitable;* the rest of the New Testament, in the four passages in which the word again occurs, always with the genitive following, τιμῆς ἀξιοῦν τινα, and the like. The use of περιλάμπειν may also be remarked, inasmuch as the word, in the only two passages in which it occurs, Gospel ii. 9, Acts xxvi. 13, is on both occasions used

[1] On the other hand, in the Gospel of Luke, as in the Acts, the bad Greek ὀψία is missing; where it stands in Matthew, Luke chooses other formula; comp. Matt. viii. 16, Luke iv. 40; Matt. xiv. 15, Luke ix. 12; Matt. xxvi. 20, Luke xxii. 14; Matt. xxvii. 37, Luke xxiii. 54.

with respect to an appearance of the Schechinah. Even these points of contact are not without significance; for although any two of the New Testament writings of some length will coincide in single expressions foreign to the others, this will probably not recur in so many cases, except when the identity of the author or the dependence of one writing on another as to matter and style can be assumed; still less would a merely accidental coincidence account for the repeated employment of expressions which recur in one or both of the writings concerned with sufficient frequency to be reckoned among the peculiar linguistic treasury of the author. But special consideration in this respect is due to the phenomenon that, in the majority of cases above quoted, it is the Acts which repeatedly employs expressions peculiar to both writings. This would be remarkable in a merely accidental coincidence, but it is very naturally explained by the author's identity; in the Gospel he is more dependent on the style of his predecessors, especially of Matthew; in the Acts he allows his peculiarities of style to appear more freely.

But stronger evidence is afforded both as to number and weight by

2. Those cases in which a word, occurring in other than the Lukan writings, is used by the latter with such comparative frequency that we must consider it as an expression specifically belonging to the author. Part of these have been already mentioned. Thus the substantives, *ἀσφάλεια*, *βουλή*, especially *βουλὴ τοῦ θεοῦ*, *ἔκστασις*, besides *ἐξίστασθαι*, *ἐπαγγελία*, *ἐργασία*, *οἶκος* (Gospel thirty-two times, Acts twenty-five times, in the sense, family; Gospel seven times, Acts nine times; elsewhere also Matt. twice, 1 Cor. once; on the other hand, several times in the Pastoral Epistles and in Hebrews; 1 Peter ii. 5 must not be included here); *οἰκουμένη* (Gospel three times, Acts five times, elsewhere six times), *σωτὴρ*, with its derivatives, *χάρις* and *ἄφεσις ἁμαρτιῶν*; the adjectives, *ἄξιος*, *ἅπας*, *γνωστὸς*, *ἔμφοβος* (Gospel twice, Acts three times, elsewhere only Rev. xi. 43), *ἡγούμενος*, *ἱκανὸς*; the verbs, *ἀνάγρεῖν*, *ἀναιρεῖν* (Gospel twice, Acts nineteen times, elsewhere twice or three times

more), besides ἀναίρεσις, ἀνακρίνειν (in the legal sense, only in Luke xxiii. 14, and in five passages in the Acts; with another meaning, ten times more in the first Epistle to the Corinthians), ἀτενίζειν (Gospel twice, Acts ten times, elsewhere twice in 2 Cor.), αὐξάνειν (Gospel and Acts four times each), ἀφιστάναι (Gospel four times, Acts six times, elsewhere only four times), βοᾷν (besides Old Testament quotations, only in three passages of the Gospel and three or four of the Acts), δεῖ and δοκεῖ, διαμαρτύρεσθαι (besides Luke xvi. 28,[1] and nine passages in the Acts, only four times in the New Testament), διανοίγειν (Gospel and Acts three times each, once more in Mark), διέρχεσθαι, εἰσάγειν (Gospel three times, Acts six times, elsewhere twice more), ἐξαποστέλλειν (Gospel twice, Acts seven times, elsewhere twice more in the Epistle to the Galatians), ἐξηγεῖσθαι (besides John i. 18, only in Luke xxiv. 35, and Acts four times), ἐπιλαμβάνεσθαι (Gospel five times, elsewhere altogether six times, and in one quotation from the Old Testament), εὐαγγελίζεσθαι (Gospel ten times, Acts fifteen times, otherwise chiefly in the Pauline Epistles; Matthew has the word once, Mark and John not at all), ἐφιστάναι (besides Romans x. 6, only Luke v. 11, and in seven passages of the Acts), κατάγειν, κατανοεῖν (Gospel and Acts four times each, elsewhere six times more), κατέρχεσθαι, λατρεύειν (Gospel three times, Acts five times, elsewhere only three times), μένειν, νομίζειν (Gospel twice, Acts seven times, in these writings only ἐνομίζετο), ὁρίζειν (Gospel once, Acts six times, elsewhere only twice), παραγίνεσθαι, παύεσθαι (Gospel three times, Acts six times, elsewhere five or six times more), πλησθῆναι, πορεύεσθαι, συγκαλεῖν (Gospel four times, Acts three times, otherwise once more in Mark), ὑπάρχειν,[2] ὑποστρέφειν; the adverbs, ἐξαίφνης (besides Mark xiii. 36,

[1] A passage in all probability added by the author of the Gospel to the original parable. See Tübingen Theol. Journal, 1843, 62 ; *Schwegler*, Post.-Apost. Period, II. 65.

[2] The participle, τὰ ὑπάρχοντα, employed as a substantive, appears eight times in the Gospel, in the Acts only four times, but in a remarkable manner, as in Luke viii. 3, and probably xii. 15 also, with the dative of the person (τὰ ὑπ. αὐτῷ), instead of which the genitive is always used elsewhere. The word occurs besides only five times in the New Testament.

only Luke and Acts twice each), and παραχρῆμα (Gospel ten times, Acts six times, elsewhere only twice more in Mark); the prepositions σὺν and ἐνώπιον, ἀπ' ἀληθείας and κατὰ πρόσωπον; the particles ὡσεὶ and διό. The partiality of both the Lukan writings for compound verbs has already been remarked, and even if the examples quoted above may apply only partially to both, they nevertheless exhibit a similar tendency in both towards expressions of that sort. To this add, moreover, the following data. Of substantives, the otherwise rare ἀγαλλίασις is to be found in Luke i. 14, 44, Acts ii. 16; ἀδικία, in Matthew and John once each, in Mark never, Luke four times, Acts twice; ἀπόστολος, in the other Gospels only once each, in Luke six times, Acts naturally much oftener; ἀρχισυνάγωγος, elsewhere only in Mark, but in the same narrative in which Luke has it, Gospel twice, Acts three times; βάτος, besides one passage in Mark coincident with Luke, only in Gospel and Acts twice each; ἑκατόνταρχος and ἐλεημοσύνη, besides Gospel and Acts, which latter has both pretty frequently, only in Matthew; ἔθος, Gospel three times, Acts seven times, otherwise only twice more; ἔτος, in the Gospels, elsewhere not frequently, in Luke fifteen times and Acts eleven times; ἐσθὴς, Gospel once, Acts three times, elsewhere only in James; ἱματισμὸς, besides 1 Tim. ii. 9, and the quotation John xix. 24, only Gospel vii. 25, ix. 29, Acts xx. 33; μερὶς, Gospel once, Acts twice; μεσονύκτιον, Gospel once, Acts twice, elsewhere once more in Mark; μνῆμα, elsewhere only in Rev. xi. 9, and (from Luke) Mark v. 3, 5, Gospel three times, Acts twice (on the other hand, the μνημεῖον usual in the Gospels, Luke ten times, but in Acts only once); ὀπτασία, elsewhere only 2 Cor. xii. 1, Gospel twice, Acts once (but in the same also ὀπτάνεσθαι); πρεσβυτέριον, of the Jewish assembly of elders, only Luke xxii. 66, Acts xxii. 5, elsewhere also 1 Tim. iv. 14; ῥύμη, only once more in Matthew, Luke once, Acts twice; στάσις, Gospel twice, Acts five times, elsewhere only twice more; the ἀνάληψις, which is in Luke ix. 51, applied to Christ's ascension, corresponds with Acts i.

2, xi. 22, compare also x. 16, the ἀναλαμβάνεσθαι, elsewhere employed with reference to this event only in Mark xvi. 19, 1 Tim. iii. 16. Of adjectives, compare the following: ἀμφότεροι, elsewhere only in Matthew and Ephesians, occurs in Luke six times, Acts three times; ἄτοπος, elsewhere only in 2 Thess. iii. 2, Gospel once, Acts twice, always in the combination οὐδὲν ἄτ., τί ἄτ.; λαμπρὸς is indeed to be found in Gospel and Acts only once each, but both times in the combination ἐσθὴς λαμπρὰ, in the same combination also James ii. 2, 3, moreover several times in Revelations; ὅλος frequently occurs not only in the Gospel and in the other Synoptics, but also in the Acts twenty-one times; πυκνὸς, elsewhere only in 1 Tim. v. 23, is used twice by Luke in an analogous manner, Gospel v. 33; πυκνὰ (Matt. ix. 14, πολλὰ), Acts xxiv. 26, πυκνότερον; ὕψιστος, except in the writings of Luke, only four times altogether in the New Testament, occurs here, Gospel seven times, Acts twice; it is peculiar to Luke to employ ὁ ὕψιστος, without any apposition, for God, Gospel i. 32, 35, 76, vi. 35, Acts vii. 48; but we also read τοῦ θεοῦ τοῦ ὑψίστου, besides Luke viii. 28 and Acts xvi. 17, only in the corresponding passage of Mark v. 7, probably dependent on Luke, and Heb. vii. 1, from Gen. xiv. 18. As regards the use of verbs in the two Lukan writings, besides those already mentioned, we note, ἄγειν, Gospel fourteen times, Acts twenty-eight times; αἰνεῖν, Gospel four times, Acts three times, elsewhere also Rom. xv. 16; ἀντιλέγειν, Gospel twice, Acts three times, elsewhere only John xix. 12, Tit. i. 9, ii. 9, and in the quotation Rom. x. 21; ἀποτάσσεσθαι, Gospel and Acts twice each, otherwise only twice more; διαπορεύεσθαι, besides Rom. xv. 24, only in Gospel three times, Acts once; διαστρέφειν (Gospel twice, Acts three times, elsewhere twice more, the perf. past. διεστραμμένος); διασώζειν, Gospel once, Acts five times, elsewhere twice more; διατάσσειν, Gospel four times, Acts five times; ἐᾷν, besides Matt. xxiv. 43, 1 Cor. x. 13, only in two passages of the Gospel and seven of Acts; εἰσέρχεσθαι, frequent elsewhere, it is true, but most frequent of all in Luke; εἰσποῥεύεσθαι, often in Mark, elsewhere only once in Matt. and in each of the Lukan writings four times; ἐπισκέπτεσθαι, Gospel three times, Acts four times, elsewhere only three or four times; ἡσυχάζειν, Gospel and Acts twice each, elsewhere only 1 Thess. iv. 11; καθαιρεῖν, Gospel and Acts three times each, elsewhere three times more; καταξιοῦν, Gospel twice, Acts once, elsewhere once more; κατηχεῖν, Gospel once, Acts three times, elsewhere three times more; κολλᾶσθαι, Gospel twice, Acts five times, elsewhere four or five times more; κρεμᾶν, only Luke xxxiii. 39, Acts v. 30, x. 39, and in the quotation, Gal. iii. 13, respecting the crucifixion of Christ, besides twice more in Matt. and Acts xxviii. 4; κτᾶσθαι, Gospel twice, Acts three times, elsewhere only twice more; μεθιστάναι, Gospel once, Acts twice, twice more elsewhere; παρατηρεῖν, Gospel three times, Acts once, elsewhere only Gal. iv. 10, and, in agreement with Luke, Mark iii. 2; πέμπειν, in Luke, in accordance with the idiom of the Acts, far more frequently than with the other Synoptists; πράσσειν, unknown in Matthew and Mark, in Luke six times, Acts thirteen times; προέρχεσθαι, Gospel twice, Acts three times, elsewhere probably only 2 Cor. ix. 5; προσδοκᾷν, Gospel six times, Acts five times, elsewhere only twice in Matthew and three times 2 Peter iii. 12—14 (προσδοκία, only Luke xxi. 26, Acts xii. 11); προστιθέναι, Gospel seven times, Acts six times, elsewhere five times altogether; προσφωνεῖν, besides in Matt. xi. 16, only Luke four times, Acts twice; σαλεύειν, in the Gospel, besides the two parallel passages with Matthew, twice more, Acts four times; σιγᾷν, Gospel and Acts three times each, elsewhere four times in Paul; σπεύδειν, besides 2 Peter iii. 12, only in three passages of the Gospel and two of the Acts; συλλαμβάνειν, Gospel seven times, Acts four times, elsewhere altogether five times; συνευδοκεῖν, rare elsewhere, Gospel once, Acts twice; συναντᾷν, Gospel and Acts each twice, elsewhere only Heb. vii. 1, 10; συνέχειν, Gospel six times, Acts three times, only three times besides; ὑποδεικνύναι, Gospel three times, Acts twice, only once more besides in Matthew; ὑποδέχεσθαι, Gospel twice, Acts once, elsewhere only James ii. 25; ὑπολαμβάνειν, Gospel and Acts twice each, besides 3 John once; χαλᾶν, Gospel twice, Acts three times, elsewhere twice; χαρίζεσθαι, like χάρις, unknown to the Synoptists, in Luke three times, Acts four times. What is common to both in the use of adverbs and adverbial modes of speech, of prepositions and particles, has already for the most part been stated above; here we have only to add the following: the adverb ἀκριβῶς, elsewhere only in three other passages of the New Testament, is found in Luke's Gospel once in the prologue, in the Acts five times; also ἀκριβὴς and ἀκρίβεια, in the Acts only; ἄνωθεν occurs only in Luke i. 3, Acts xxvi. 5, Gal. iv. 9, in the sense of "from the beginning;" βραχὺ or μετὰ βραχὺ, only Luke xxii. 58, Acts v. 34, xxvii. 28, in a temporal sense; ἔναντι and ἐναντίον, only Luke i. 8, xx. 26, xxiv. 19, Acts viii. 21, vii. 10, viii. 32, and once in Mark (ii. 12); ἀνθ' ὧν, besides 2 Thess. ii. 10, only Luke i. 20, xii. 3, xix. 44, Acts xii. 23; διότι, at least in the narrative books of the New Testament, in Luke only. With him alone (Gospel ii. 15, Acts xiii. 2, xv. 36), and with Paul (1 Cor. vi. 20) is to be found the δὴ, altogether rare in the New Testament, employed for the enforcement of a demand; here only the combinations ἰδοὺ γὰρ (Luke i. 44, 48, ii. 10, vi. 23, xvii. 21, Acts ix. 11, 2 Cor. vii. 11) and ἀλλ' οὐδέ (Luke xxiii. 15, Acts xix. 2, and three times in Paul). The use of ὅπως may be mentioned here, which, with Matthew, occurs most frequently in the two writings of Luke.

3. Of the peculiarities common to the third Gospel and the Acts with respect to the form of words, the construction and the phraseology, a great part has necessarily been mentioned already. Here we shall make some further remarks. Both writings of Luke employ the more minute definition of a substantive by means of the genitive of another, even in cases where another expression would be more simple; thus, in Gospel iii. 3, Acts xiii. 24, xix. 4 (elsewhere only in Mark, in the passage coinciding with Luke, i. e., i. 4), the baptism of John is termed βάπτισμα μετανοίας; in Gospel iv. 33, we read, πνεῦμα δαιμονίου ἀκαθάρτου,

Acts xvi. 16, πνεῦμα Πύθωνος. Luke always places the word θυγάτηρ (Gospel i. 5, ii. 36, xiii. 16, xxiii. 28, Acts vii. 21) before the name of the Father without an article (θυγάτηρ Φαραώ, &c.); we find the same besides only in Heb. xi. 24, and in the Old Testament passages, Matt. xxi. 5, John xii. 15; see Gersdorf, p. 171. Instead of ὀλίγος, οὐ πολὺς is substituted; besides Luke xv. 13, Acts i. 5, xxvii. 14, only in John ii. 12; in the two first of these passages it is similarly said, μετ' οὐ πολλὰς ἡμέρας. After the infinitive δοῦναι, Luke generally places (comp. Gersdorf, p. 208) the dative of the person and the accusative of the object,[1] δοῦναι ἡμῖν, &c.; comp. Gospel i. 73, 77, ii. 24, xi. 7, xii. 32, xvii. 18, Acts v. 31, vii. 38, xx. 32, probably also vii. 2; only in Gospel xx. 22, xxiii. 2, is Καίσαρι, similarly xii. 51, εἰρήνην, put first for the sake of emphasis; xxvii. 5, αὐτῷ is also dependent on συνέθεντο, and the arrangement of the words influenced by it; δοῦναι itself is also a special favourite with Luke. Luke alone (Gospel ii. 33, iv. 22, ix. 43, xx. 26, Acts iii. 12), and Mark in the passage, xii. 17, corresponding to Luke xx. 26, says θαυμάζειν ἐπί τινι, Luke alone ποιεῖν τι μετά τινος (עָשָׂה עִם פ״), Gospel i. 58, 72, x. 37, Acts xiv. 27, xv. 4; the χαίρειν ἐν, Luke x. 20, elsewhere only in Phil. and Eph., finds its parallel in εὐφραίνεσθαι ἐν, Acts vii. 41. The word πρὶν ἤ, which is elsewhere always followed by the infinitive, is only in Luke ii. 26 (xxii. 34) followed by the subjunctive; only in Acts xvi. 35, the optative (according to others, the indic. or subjunctive). The pronoun οὗτος is often added by Luke to a word of number or interrogation for more exact definition, without any connecting particle or formula; comp. Gospel xxiv. 21, τρίτην ταύτην ἡμέραν; Acts xxiv. 21, περὶ μιᾶς ταύτης φωνῆς; Acts i. 5, οὐ μετὰ πολλὰς ταύτας ἡμέρας; Gospel xvi. 2, τί τοῦτο ἀκούω, an expression otherwise foreign to the New Testament. The formula τίς ἐστιν ὅς, Acts xix. 35, xxiii. 19, otherwise somewhat rare, corresponds to

[1] That he alone does it is not correct; comp. Matt. xix. 7, xx. 28, xxii. 17, xxvi. 9, whereas another arrangement of words is certainly selected in Matt. vii. 11, xiv. 7, xx. 14.

the double τίς ἐστιν οὗτος ὃς, Luke v. 21, vii. 49 (elsewhere only in John xvi. 17 f.), and the three-fold οὐδείς ἐστιν ὃς, Luke i. 61, xii. 2, xviii. 29, elsewhere in Matt. x. 26, Mark ix. 39, x. 29. Luke only, Gospel ii. 49, Acts v. 4, 9, and Mark, ii. 16, say τί ὅτι; only Luke (Gospel i. 66, viii. 25, xii. 42, xxii. 23, Acts xii. 18) and Matthew in four passages, Mark in one, say τίς ἄρα (on τίς ἄν, see above). Luke uses καὶ more frequently than any other writer in the New Testament, especially καὶ ἰδοὺ to introduce the apodosis (Gospel twelve times, Acts two or three times (see Bruder, p. 455 D.), comp. also the simple ἰδοὺ, Acts xiii. 46); moreover, Gospel twice, Acts once, καὶ in the otherwise somewhat rare sense, when after a preceding designation of time (the same, p. 466); καὶ αὐτὸς has been discussed already. In Luke ii. 48, vii. 25, Acts v. 9, the answer to a question is introduced with ἰδοὺ, which occurs besides only in Matt. xi. 8. In Gospel x. 11, xii. 39, Acts xx. 29, xxiv. 14, Luke makes an ὅτι follow a previous τοῦτο, which the other Evangelists never do;[1] in Gospel i. 43, there is also τοῦτο . . ἵνα, Acts ix. 21, εἰς τοῦτο . . ἵνα. The Gospel as well as the Acts is partial to a periphrasis with εὑρίσκειν and ἔχειν; οὐχ εὑρίσκειν τί or πῶς occurs only in Luke v. 19, xix. 48, Acts iv. 21;[2] the good Greek ἔχειν or οὐκ ἔχειν τι ποιεῖν, not frequent elsewhere in the New Testament, is in Luke vii. 42, ix. 58, xi. 6, xii. 17, xii. 50, xiv. 14, Acts iv. 14, xxv. 26. In Luke alone, or nearly alone, we meet with the expressions, ἀπ' αἰῶνος (Gospel i. 70, Acts iii. 21, xv. 18, elsewhere only Col. i. 26, Eph. iii. 9, ἀπὸ τῶν αἰώνων), εἰς τὰς ἀκοὰς (Gospel vii. 1, Acts xvii. 20), or εἰς τὰ ὦτα (Gospel i. 44, ix. 44, Acts xi. 22, also in James v. 4; Mark vii. 33, does not belong here), ἐκ κοιλίας μητρὸς (Gospel i. 15, Acts iii. 2, xiv. 8, always with the apposition αὐτοῦ, elsewhere also, Gal. i. 15, ἐκ κ. μ. μου, and without a genitive, Matt. xix. 12). The Messiah is called in Luke iv. 34, ὁ ἅγιος τοῦ

[1] Matthew and Mark do not know this expression at all; John has ὅτι only after διὰ τοῦτο, after simple τοῦτο only ἵνα.

[2] Εὑρίσκειν in general is frequent in Luke; χάριν εὑρ., besides Heb. iv. 16, occurs only in Luke i. 30, Acts vii. 46.

θεοῦ, Acts ii. 27, xiii. 35, in the same application of Ps. xvi. 10, ὁ ὅσιος τ. θ.; the same in iv. 27, 30, ὁ ἅγιος παῖς θεοῦ; the first designation is also to be found in the passage undoubtedly derived from Luke, Mark i. 24; but in John, too, vi. 69, where it is the most probable reading, it may be a reminiscence. The predicate ἄγγελοι ἅγιοι (Gospel ix. 26, and probably hence Mark viii. 38, Acts iii. 21, comp. Eph. iii. 5, 2 Peter iii. 2) is also to be remarked. By Luke alone (Gospel i. 17, 35, iv. 14, comp. xxiv. 49, Acts i. 8, x. 38), with the exception of Paul (Rom. i. 4, xv. 13, 19, 1 Cor. ii. 4), πνεῦμα is combined with δύναμις, sometimes in the genitive δύναμις πνεύματος, sometimes in the same case; in him also we meet with the combination of πνεύμα and σοφία (Gospel ii. 40, Acts vi. 3, 10, elsewhere also Eph. i. 17), σοφία and χάρις (only Luke ii. 40, 52, Acts vii. 10). Both the Gospel and Acts use the expressions υἱὸς Ἀβραάμ (Gospel xix. 9, Acts xiii. 26), παῖς θεοῦ = servant of God (Gospel i. 54, of Israel; Gospel i. 69, Acts iv. 25, of David; Acts iii. 13, 26, iv. 27, 30, of Jesus, never elsewhere; παῖς alone stands in the Gospel of Luke and in Matthew several times = δοῦλος); χεὶρ κυρίου (Gospel i. 66, Acts iv. 28, 30, xi. 21, xiii. 11, elsewhere only 1 Peter v. 6, χεὶρ τοῦ θεοῦ); ἡμέρα σαββάτων (Gospel iv. 16, Acts xiii. 14, xvi. 13) or σαββάτου (Gospel xiii. 14, 16, xiv. 5), a circumlocution foreign to the rest of the New Testament; βίβλος ψαλμῶν (Gospel xx. 42, Acts i. 20), β. τῶν προφητῶν (Acts vii. 42), or λόγων τοῦ προφητοῦ (Gospel iii. 4), with which only β. Μωϋσέως, Mark xii. 26, is to be compared; καρπὸς τῆς κοιλίας, or τῆς ὀσφύος (only Gospel i. 42, Acts ii. 30); both make frequent use, not only of the preposition ἐνώπιον in general, but especially of the phrase ἐν. τοῦ θεοῦ (Gospel five times, Acts four or five times, see Bruder, s. v. ἐνώπ.), the formulæ διὰ στόματος (besides Luke i. 70, Acts i. 16, iii. 18, 21, iv. 25, xv. 7, comp. xxii. 14, only Matt. iv. 4, in a quotation) and ἀνοίγειν τὸ στόμα (Gospel i. 64, Acts viii. 35, x. 34, xviii. 14, elsewhere five times more in the New Testament), the combination of ῥῆμα with γίγνεσθαι (only Luke ii. 15, τὸ ῥῆμα τοῦτο τὸ γεγονὸς, Acts x. 37, τὸ γενόμενον ῥῆμα). Further, be it observed, αἶρε =

down with one, exists only in Luke xxiii. 18, Acts xxi. 36, xxii. 22 (John xix. 15, has the aorist ἆρον — or αἴρειν φωνὴν and ἐπαίρειν φ., see above); μὴ φοβοῦ, without any accusative, besides Mark v. 36 (from Luke viii. 50) and Rev. i. 17, only Luke i. 13, ii. 10, v. 10, viii. 50, xii. 7, 32, Acts xviii. 9, xxvii. 24; πληγὰς ἐπιτιθέναι, only Luke x. 30, Acts xvi. 23; ἐκ δεξιῶν ἑστάναι, only Luke i. 11, Acts vii. 55, 56 (though ἐκ δ. καθῆσθαι is frequent); πορεύου εἰς εἰρήνην or ἐν εἰρήνῃ, for which ὕπαγε εἰς εἰρ. or ἐν εἰρ. is elsewhere (Mark v. 34, James ii. 16) substituted, only in Acts xvi. 36, Luke vii. 50, viii. 48); λατρεύειν νύκτα καὶ ἡμέραν, only Luke ii. 37, Acts xxvi. 7 (also in Rev. vii. 15, λατρ. ἡμέρας κ. νυκτὸς), both times with reference to ardent prayer for the coming of the Messiah. Many similar peculiarities of expression have already come under our notice.

4. After what we have seen, it cannot be surprising that not a few passages of the two writings coincide in style in a manner which makes the later appear an imitation (intentional or unintentional) of the earlier one, or both as the product of the same literary idiosyncrasy. In the first place, the appearances of superior spirits are very similarly described, not as to matter alone, but also as to the words. In Acts i. 10, it is said in the narrative of the ascension, ὡς ἀτενίζοντες ἦσαν, &c., καὶ ἰδοὺ ἄνδρες δύο παρειστήκεισαν αὐτοῖς ἐν ἐσθῆτι λευκῇ; likewise x. 30, in the story of Cornelius, καὶ ἰδοὺ ἀνὴρ ἔστη ἐνώπιόν μου ἐν ἐσθῆτι λαμπρᾷ. Very similar in the account of the resurrection, in a feature which Luke alone records in this manner, Gospel xxiv. 4, ἐν τῷ διαπορεῖσθαι αὐτὰς . . . καὶ ἰδοὺ ἄνδρες δύο ἐπέστησαν αὐταῖς ἐν ἐσθήσεσιν ἀστραπτούσαις; and with somewhat less resemblance, which, however, disappears entirely in the parallel passages of the Synoptists, Matt. xvii. 3, Mark ix. 4, in the history of the transfiguration, Luke ix. 30, καὶ ἰδοὺ ἄνδρες δύο συνελάλουν αὐτῷ. The appearances of angels, Acts xii. 7, Gospel i. 9, offer a similar parallel; in the former, καὶ ἰδοὺ ἄγγελος κυρίου ἐπέστη καὶ φῶς ἔλαμψεν ἐν τῷ οἰκήματι; in the latter, καὶ ἰδοὺ ἄγγελος κυρίου ἐπέστη αὐτοῖς καὶ δόξα κυρίου περιέλαμψεν αὐτούς. The resemblance

in the description of angels' disappearance is less striking; Acts x. 7, ὡς δὲ ἀπῆλθεν ὁ ἄγγελος; Gospel i. 38, καὶ ἀπῆλθεν ἀπ' αὐτῆς ὁ ἄγγελος; ii. 15, ὡς ἀπῆλθον ἀπ' αὐτῶν εἰς τὸν οὐρανὸν οἱ ἄγγελοι; yet it must be observed that this departure of the angels is elsewhere expressly mentioned only in Rev. xvi. 2. There is some resemblance of style between Acts i. 15, καὶ ἐν ταῖς ἡμέραις ταύταις ἀναστὰς Πέτρος, and Gospel i. 39, ἀναστᾶσα δὲ Μαριὰμ ἐν ταῖς ἡμέραις ταύτ.; it is slighter between Acts v. 17, ἀναστὰς δὲ ὁ ἀρχιερεὺς καὶ πάντες οἱ σὺν αὐτῷ ἐπλήσθησαν ζήλου, and Gospel xxiii. 1, καὶ ἀναστὰν ἅπαν τὸ πλῆθος αὐτῶν ἤγαγον, &c. With Acts iv. 1, λαλούντων δὲ αὐτῶν πρὸς τὸν λαὸν ἐπέστησαν αὐτοῖς οἱ ἱερεῖς, comp. Gospel xx. 1, διδάσκοντος αὐτοῦ τὸν λαὸν . . . ἐπέστησαν οἱ ἀρχιερεῖς; with Acts vi. 10, οὐκ ἴσχυον ἀντιστῆναι τῇ σοφίᾳ, &c., Luke xxi. 15, ἐγὼ γὰρ δώσω ὑμῖν στόμα καὶ σοφίαν, ᾗ οὐ δυνήσονται ἀντειπεῖν ἢ ἀντιστῆναι, &c.; with Acts viii. 35, καὶ ἀρξάμενος ἀπὸ τῆς γραφῆς ταύτης εὐηγγελίσατο αὐτῷ τὸν Ἰησοῦν· Luke xxiv. 27, καὶ ἀρξάμενος ἀπὸ Μωϋσέως . . . διηρμήνευεν αὐτοῖς, &c.; with Acts x. 37, ἀρξάμενον ἀπὸ τῆς Γαλιλαίας, Luke xxiii. 15, ἀρξάμενος ἀπὸ τῆς Γαλιλαίας; with Acts xvii. 26, ἐπὶ πᾶν τὸ πρόσωπον τῆς γῆς, Luke xxi. 35, ἐπὶ πρόσωπον πάσης τῆς γῆς;[1] with Acts ix. 36, ἦν μαθήτρια . . . αὕτη ἦν πλήρης ἀγαθῶν ἔργων (comp. also xvi. 17), with respect to the construction, Luke ii. 36, καὶ ἦν Ἄννα προφῆτις . . . αὕτη προβεβηκυῖα ἐν ἡμέραις . . .; likewise to xiii. 29, ὡς δὲ ἐτέλεσαν πάντα τὰ περὶ αὐτοῦ γεγραμμένα . . ἔθηκαν εἰς μνημεῖον· ὁ δὲ θεὸς, &c., Luke ii. 39, καὶ ὡς ἐτέλεσαν ἅπαντα τὰ κατὰ τὸν νόμον κυρίου, ὑπέστρεψαν . . . τὸ δὲ παιδίον, &c. The striking similarity in expression and phraseology which exists between Acts xv. 24 f. and the beginning of the Gospel has been already pointed out above; it actually goes so far that there can be no idea of explaining it by accidental coincidence. Also between Acts xxiv. 2, 5 (accusation against Paul), ἤρξατο κατηγορεῖν ὁ Τέρτυλλος λέγων . . . εὑρόντες γὰρ τὸν ἄνδρα τοῦτον λοιμὸν καὶ κινοῦντα στάσιν . . . πρωτοστάτην τε τῆς τῶν Ναζωραίων αἱρέσεως, and Gospel xxiii. 2 (accusation against Jesus,

[1] The periphrasis by πρόσωπον is generally frequent in the Lukan writings.

recorded by Luke alone), ἤρξαντο δὲ κατηγορεῖν αὐτοῦ λέγοντες· τοῦτον εὕρομεν διαστρέφοντα τὸ ἔθνος καὶ κωλύοντα Καίσαρι φόρους διδόναι, λέγοντα ἑαυτὸν Χριστὸν βασιλέα εἶναι (observe the threefold predication of both the accused), not only is the resemblance, but also the actual connection, unmistakable; whereas the analogy of ῥῆμα ἕν, Acts xxviii. 25, with ἕνα λόγον, Luke xx. 3, by itself would prove the less because the latter is in Matt. xii. 24 also.

Not only the style, but the contents of the two books, exhibit unmistakable affinity. It is true that their subject is too different to allow a frequent coincidence to be expected in *single* features; but in the very point which is common to them as the conclusion of one and the commencement of the other, i.e. the ascension, insoluble difficulties are to be found. But as in any case the author had before him the narrative of the Gospel to which his opening words expressly refer, and as we have convinced ourselves that in other cases he is not scrupulous about single historical contradictions, we cannot attribute much importance to this circumstance with regard to the question before us; if his view of an historian's task had rendered it impossible for the author to diverge from his own earlier narrative, the divergence from the narrative of a predecessor with whom he wishes to be considered identical would have been at least equally impossible; if, on the other hand, even in our book itself he has not avoided the manifold contradictions enumerated above, we cannot assume that he must have avoided similar contradictions with an earlier book. It is all the more worthy of remark that in divers details, independently of the opening words, the Acts assumes the existence of the third Gospel. The history of the ascension itself in several features reminds us of Luke. Luke alone (xxiv. 49) knows of Jesus' command not to leave Jerusalem, and the promise of the Holy Spirit connected with it, Acts i. 4, 8; he alone transfers the scene of the ascension to the neighbourhood of Jerusalem; only he and John place there the appearances of the risen Jesus vouchsafed to the Apostles, and especially his final conversation with them; he alone and his dependent Mark, or the interpolator of Mark, make mention of the visible ascension. The words in Luke xxiv. 47 also unmistakably recall Acts i. 8. Acts i. 5 is a faulty quotation of Luke iii. 16, and the concluding verses of the Gospel have also their parallels in the Acts; comp. ver. 52, ὑπέστρεψαν εἰς Ἱερουσαλήμ, with Acts i. 12, τότε ὑπέστρεψαν εἰς Ἱερ.; ver. 53, καὶ ἦσαν διαπαντὸς ἐν τῷ ἱερῷ αἰνοῦντες καὶ εὐλογοῦντες τὸν Θεόν, with Acts i. 14, πάντες ἦσαν προσκαρτεροῦντες ὁμοθυμαδὸν τῇ προσευχῇ, and ii. 44, πάντες δὲ οἱ πιστεύοντες ἦσαν ἐπὶ τὸ αὐτὸ . . . καθ' ἡμέραν τε προσκαρτεροῦντες ὁμοθυμαδόν ἐν τῷ ἱερῷ . . . αἰνοῦντες τὸν Θεόν. The list of Apostles, i. 13, harmonizes with that of Luke's Gospel, vi. 16 ff., against Matt. x. 2 ff. and Mark iii. 16 ff., in naming Judas the son of James instead of Thaddeus, and designating Simon Zelotes, not as κανανίτης (Lachm. Καναναῖος), but as ζηλωτής. This coincidence is the more worthy of attention, as at the same time the trifling deviation in the position of the Apostle's name indicates that it is not founded on the express employment of the Gospel, but in a uniform habit of the author. That several features in the narrative of the trial and death of Stephen may in all probability be explained by Luke's account of the trial and death of Christ, has been already observed. The last words of the dying Stephen are in purport and expression an echo of the words of Jesus, transmitted by Luke alone; as in Luke xxiii. 46, he says, πάτερ, εἰς χεῖράς σου παρατίθεμαι τὸ πνεῦμα μου, so Stephen, Acts vii. 58, κύριε Ἰησοῦ, δέξαι τὸ πνεῦμά μου; as Jesus, Luke xxiii. 34, prays, πάτερ, ἄφες αὐτοῖς,[1] so Stephen, vii. 60, κύριε, μὴ στήσῃς αὐτοῖς τὴν ἁμαρτίαν ταύτην. Also the φωνὴ μεγάλη, with which these words are uttered (ἔκραξε φωνῇ μεγάλῃ), have their prototype in the φωνήσας φωνῇ μεγάλῃ, Luke xxxiii. 46; and though the ἔκραξε may correspond more accurately with the κράξας, Matt. xxvii. 50, yet Luke alone, like the Acts, gives the purport of the φωνή. Where, finally, Stephen, vii. 5, rapturously exclaims, ἰδοὺ θεωρῶ . . . τὸν υἱὸν τοῦ

[1] With the οὐ γὰρ οἴδασι, τί ποιοῦσιν, comp. Acts iii. 17, xiii. 27.

ἀνθρώπου ἐκ δεξιῶν ἑστῶτα τοῦ θεοῦ, he sees therein only the fulfilment of the declaration delivered by Jesus, Luke xxii. 69;[1] whereas the evidence of the *ψευδομάρτυρες* with respect to Stephen's supposed sayings against Temple and Law, Acts vii. 13 f., certainly refers only to Matt. xxvi. 60 f., Mark xiv. 58 (to which Acts vii. 48 may be compared), as Luke, hastening quickly over the trial of Jesus before the Sanhedrim to that before Pilate, has passed over this subject of accusation. A further prototype of several features in this narrative will be found in Luke iv. 28. The passage, Acts iv. 27 (*συνήχθησαν . . . ἐπὶ τὸν ἅγιον παῖδά σου Ἰησοῦν . . . Ἡρώδης τε καὶ Πόντιος Πιλάτος*), takes for granted the scene in the court of Herod, which of all our Gospels is recorded only by the third. That xxvi. also recalls it will be shown later; meanwhile comp. Luke xxiii. 14 f. with Acts xxvi. 31.

Still more frequent are the cases in which narratives in the Acts and the third Gospel, or single features of these narratives, without materially referring to each other, are yet formed on the same type. Thus apparitions of angels are favourites in both writings. While in Matthew, besides the three visions of Joseph (i. 20, ii. 13, 19) only one angel takes part in the Gospel history at the resurrection (xxviii. 2, 5), and at the end of the story of the temptation (iv. 11) the ministry of angels is briefly mentioned; while Mark is also acquainted only with this and the angel of the resurrection (xx. 12),—in Luke appears, first (i. 11), the angel of the Lord to the father of the Baptist; afterwards (i. 26), the angel Gabriel to the Virgin Mary; next (ii. 9), the angel of the Lord and a number of the heavenly host

[1] Even regardless of the other references of the passage to the Gospel of Luke, it is probable that Luke's record was present to the mind of the author of Acts vii. 55; in Matt. xxvi. 64, the words of Jesus run, *ἀπάρτι ὄψεσθε τὸν υἱὸν τοῦ ἀνθρώπου καθήμενον ἐκ δεξιῶν τῆς δυνάμεως καὶ ἐρχόμενον ἐπὶ τῶν νεφελῶν*; they refer to the approaching return of Christ; similarly in Mark; in Luke, on the contrary, it is only said, *ἀπὸ τοῦ νῦν ἔσται ὁ υἱὸς τ. ἀ. καθήμενος ἐκ δεξιῶν τῆς δυνάμεως τοῦ θεοῦ*; the words therefore apply not to the Parusia, but to Christ's sitting at the right hand of God immediately on his exaltation to heaven. Also the *θεοῦ*, which in Luke alone is added to the *δυνάμεως*, reappears in the Acts. But that in the latter Jesus stands, while the Gospel represents him sitting, is either unimportant or is caused by the context. Jesus has risen to receive his confessor after his approaching death.

to the shepherds near Bethlehem; and these three appearances do not take place in dreams, but are objectively real; the ministry of angels after the temptation, it is true, is passed over; but, on the other hand (xxii. 43), an angel appears at Gethsemane; to which must be added (xxiv. 4) two angels of the resurrection. Similarly, the Acts is full of appearances of angels: first, the two angels at the ascension (i. 10); then (v. 19) the angel who liberates all the Apostles; later (xii. 7), the one who releases Peter from prison; further (viii. 26), the angel of the Lord speaks to Philip; x. 3, an angel appears to Cornelius; xii. 23, king Herod is smitten by the angel of the Lord; xxvii. 23, Peter receives a higher communication from an angel. It is the same with the operations of the Spirit; while the appearance of the Spirit at the baptism of Jesus, and the subsequent operation of the Spirit which drives Jesus into the wilderness, stand quite alone in the other books of the New Testament, the two books of Luke are very rich in such supernatural agencies (compare Acts ii. 4, iv. 8, 31, vii. 55, viii. 17, 29, 39, x. 19, 44, xi. 28, xiii. 2, 9, xvi. 6 f., xix. 6, xxi. 4, Gospel i. 41, 67, ii. 27, x. 21). There is also an affinity in the miraculous narratives of the two books. When Luke vi. 19, viii. 46, alone among the Evangelists says that a power went out from Jesus which healed all who touched him; the same magical power emanating from the worker of miracles encounters us (Acts v. 15 f.) in the story of the healing power of Peter's shadow, and indeed with the same universality of effect, οἵτινες ἐθεραπεύοντο ἅπαντες. The kindred story of the aprons and handkerchiefs of Paul (xix. 12) may be also compared. I have already drawn attention to the analogy of Luke xxiv. 31, 36, to Acts viii. 39. If in the latter passage Philip is suddenly transported by the Spirit, the Gospel records a sudden disappearance of Jesus at Emmaus, and an equally sudden appearance at Jerusalem; John also has the last (xx. 19), after his own fashion emphasizing the magic of the miracle by a θυρῶν κεκλεισμένων; but here, as elsewhere, he seems to be dependent on Luke, so that this circumstance cannot be taken into consideration. To the remark, Acts v. 26, that the servants of the Sanhedrim did not venture to take the Apostles by force, because they were afraid of being stoned by the people; Luke, xx. 6, xxii. 2, 6, offers the Gospel parallel in the same fear and precaution of the priests. That the incorrect statement of the Acts, iv. 6, respecting Annas and Caiaphas corresponds to that of the third Gospel, iii. 2, has also been previously observed; as the Acts makes Annas high-priest at a time when it was Caiaphas, the Gospel calls Annas and Caiaphas high-priests at the same time; and even if the notion of two simultaneous high-priests, analogous to the Roman consuls, cannot well be attributed to the author, yet the expression *ἐπὶ ἀρχιερέως Ἄννα καὶ Καϊάφα*, indicates that he did not know which of the two was invested with the functions of high-priest at the period of Jesus' appearance. A similar phenomenon is exhibited by the two statements concerning the census of Quirinus and concerning Theudas, Luke ii. 1 f., Acts v. 36 f. The Gospel places the census ten years too early; the Acts makes an insurgent who is half a century more recent appear before it. Hence both know of the census and make use of it for their narrative, but both also prove themselves no further instructed respecting the circumstances of that period. If we compare the narrative in the Acts of the centurion Cornelius with that in Luke's Gospel of the centurion of Capernaum, it may at the first glance appear far-fetched; nevertheless, if we have already reached the conviction how little historical foundation the story of Cornelius possesses, it is natural to seek a prototype for this personage, and it is certainly remarkable that the very points in the description of the centurion at Capernaum in which Luke deviates from Matthew, coincide with the description of Cornelius in the Acts. In Matt. viii. 5 ff., the centurion is treated simply as a Gentile, who humbly and trustfully applies to Jesus, and whose petition is granted. Luke, vii. 2 ff., likewise represents him as a Gentile, but at the same time he interweaves several traits which connect him more closely with the Jews and their religion; he loves the Jews, and has even built them a synagogue; the Jewish elders therefore intercede with Jesus in his behalf. How much he resembles Cornelius, who is also a Gentile, but εὐσεβὴς καὶ φοβούμενος τὸν Θεὸν, ποιῶν τε ἐλεημοσύνας πολλὰς τῷ λαῷ! It is not even wanting that, according to Luke's representation, Jesus is invited to his house by the centurion, as Peter is by Cornelius, through the intervention of messengers, incompatible as this is with the entreaty, derived from Matthew, that he should not trouble himself to come (ver. 6). Of course, any one who considers the story of Cornelius in the Acts to be historical will attach no importance to this; but one who does not will hardly be able to regard the coincidence as accidental. The same applies to the narrative in Acts xxviii. 7 ff., in its relation to the healing of Peter's mother-in-law, recounted by all the three Synoptists (Matt. viii. 14, Mark i. 30, Luke iv. 28). As Jesus heals the mother-in-law, so Paul heals the father of his host of fever, and consequently, in both cases, sick people flock in and are all healed. If the story in the Acts is not historical, as it cannot possibly be, the hypothesis that it is an imitation of the Gospel story has much to recommend it. That in this case the later one was derived from Luke is both probable in itself and is rendered more so by coincidence in expression; while Matthew and Mark say of the sick woman, εἶδε πυρέσσουσαν and κατέκειτο πυρέσσουσα, it is said in Luke, ἦν συνεχομένη πυρετῷ μεγάλῳ, which is obviously nearer the expression, Acts xxviii. 8, πυρετοῖς καὶ δυσεντερίᾳ συνεχόμενον. The words of Paul to his fellow-travellers, xxvii. 34, οὐδενὸς γὰρ ὑμῶν θρὶξ ἐκ τῆς κεφαλῆς ἀπολεῖται (or πεσεῖται), have the most striking resemblance to the speech of Jesus transmitted by Luke alone (xxi. 18), θρὶξ ἐκ τῆς κεφαλῆς ὑμῶν οὐ μὴ ἀπόληται. The resemblance between Acts xxvi. 20 and Luke iii. 8, has already been observed. Also the remarkable feature that Paul is always driven to the Gentile mission only by the unbelief of the Jews, has, according to

Köstlin's accurate observation,[1] its unmistakable prototype in the narrative with which Luke so significantly opens the public appearance of Jesus, of his rejection in his own *πατρὶς*. The offensive turn taken by Christ's discourse (iv. 23), apparently without sufficient cause, and the effect which it produces, correspond perfectly with the representations of the Acts, such as vii. 48 ff., xiii. 40 ff., 45 f., xxii. 22, xxviii. 25 ff.; and the identity of the fashioning hand is betrayed by the striking resemblance of the features, especially in the story of Stephen, that type of the Apostle of the Gentiles, and the Jews' conduct towards him.[2] Finally, the relation of the christological passage, Luke xxiv. 19, to several sayings in the Acts, must be noticed in this place. When Christ is here described as *ἀνὴρ προφήτης δυνατὸς ἐν ἔργῳ καὶ λόγῳ*, there is no passage in the New Testament which comes nearer to this than the two speeches of Peter, ii. 22, *Ἰησοῦν Ναζωραῖον, ἄνδρα ἀπὸ τοῦ θεοῦ ἀποδεδειγμένον εἰς ὑμᾶς δυνάμεσι*, and x. 38, *Ἰησοῦν τὸν ἀπὸ Ναζαρὲτ ὡς ἔχρισεν αὐτὸν ὁ θεὸς πνεύματι ἁγίῳ καί δυνάμει* (compare also iii. 22 ff., iv. 30), and these very passages connect the death of Jesus with this description of his person and ministry in the same way as the Gospel. Also what follows in Luke xxiv. 25 ff., 44, that the suffering and glorification of Christ were predicted by the prophets, like the appeal to the prophets peculiar to Luke in the announcement of his sufferings, xviii. 31 (Matt. xx. 18, Mark x. 33), has its closest parallels in the Acts, xiii. 27, xxvi. 22, compare also x. 43, ii. 23; the essentially similar christological view in these passages cannot be mistaken.

Still more decisively is the identity of authorship of the two books proved by the affinity of their object and their whole dogmatic character. I have already demonstrated[3] that the third

[1] D. Ursprung u. d. Comp. d. Synopt. Evang. 204.

[2] Luke iv. 28 f., *καὶ ἐπλήσθησαν πάντες θυμοῦ ἐν τῇ συναγωγῇ ἀκούοντες ταῦτα. Καὶ ἀναστάντες ἐξέβαλον αὐτὸν ἔξω τῆς πόλεως . . . . ὥστε κατακρημνίσαι αὐτόν.* Acts vii. 54, 57 f., *ἀκούοντες δὲ ταῦτα διεπρίοντο ταῖς καρδίαις αὐτῶν . . . καὶ ὥρμησαν ὁμοθυμαδὸν ἐπ' αὐτόν· καὶ ἐκβαλόντες ἔξω τῆς πόλεως ἐλιθοβόλουν.*

[3] Tübingen Theol. Journal, 1843, 59 ff.

Gospel, like the Acts, interposes itself, in the interest of Pauline universalism, between Jewish Christianity and Paulinism, and in parts alters the Jewish-Christian tradition of Christ itself in a Pauline sense, in parts enriches it with a series of Pauline elements. Schwegler has established this view with greater detail,[1] and Baur has carried it out farther in several features.[2] In this respect the Saxon Anonymus had preceded him;[3] but he endeavours to explain the peculiarities of our canonical Gospel of Luke exclusively by the Paulinism of its author, and at the same time he attributes to this Paulinism a constant reference to Paul's personal relations to the primitive Apostles, on which basis he interprets a number of single features in a manner which I certainly cannot adopt. Without owning allegiance to him in this, Hilgenfeld[4] also believes himself bound to maintain the exclusively Pauline character of our Luke; and Volckmar[5] labours to demonstrate the Pauline impress of even those portions which Schwegler and Baur had designated Judaistic; whereas Schwanbeck, on the contrary,[6] holds the Pauline view discerned in the Gospel to be factitious. If, however, we are able to answer the latter otherwise groundless judgment by a simple reference to the investigations given above, it appears, on the other hand, one-sided to consider the Gospel of Luke merely as a Pauline polemical writing, and to disregard all the concessions to Judaism. Now there do undeniably exist in the Gospel sundry elements which do not allow of explanation either by their purely Pauline character or by their adherence to the common Gospel tradition, nor yet by mere chance, the adoption

[1] Nachap. Zeit. II. 39—73.

[2] Krit. Untersuch. über die kanon. Evang. pp. 427 ff., 501 ff. Further, comp. *Köstlin*, Or. and Comp. of the Synopt. Gosp., 182, 216, 262.

[3] In the book, "The Gospels: their Spirit, their Authors," &c.

[4] "The Gospel of Justin, the Clem. Hom. and Mark," p. 474. Nevertheless, Hilgenfeld approaches my opinion very nearly when, in p. 472, he terms it a characteristic feature of the Acts that it adopts Judaistic elements, but contrives, nevertheless, to neutralize them adroitly.

[5] Tübingen Theol. Journal, 1850, 215 ff.; Mark's Gospel, 228 f.

[6] Quellen der Apg. p. 127.

of which, therefore, points either to the author's own Judaistic mode of thought, or to an accommodation to the Judaism of others. To this belongs, above all, the greater part of the first two chapters. Volckmar,[1] it is true, denies what is otherwise universally acknowledged, that these two chapters bear a predominant Jewish impress. Let us only ask ourselves who could have an interest in recording so minutely the birth of John the Baptist, Mary's visit to Elizabeth, the speeches and songs of thanksgiving uttered on this occasion, the accomplishment of the circumcision, and the presentation of the offering for the first-born,—who could thus accumulate the Old Testament designations of the Messiah, the Old Testament thanksgivings for the Messianic salvation, but some one to whom all these things were edifying, or who deemed them edifying to his readers? And whom could they serve for edification if not some one generally interested in the Messiah's connection with Judaism, in the Old Testament idea of the Messiah? Independently of this, where was the advantage of being so circumstantially instructed concerning the birth, not only of the Messiah, but also of his forerunner, the last of the Jewish prophets; not only to be most accurately informed of Mary's visit to the mother of this prophet, but also of the words which they exchanged; to ascertain as explicitly as possible, what would, however, have been understood of itself, that with respect to the Christian Messiah none of the precepts of the Law were neglected (*ὡς ἐτέλεσαν ἅπαντα τὰ κατὰ τὸν νόμον κυρίου*, ii. 39); to hear these Old Testament songs of thanksgiving, in which the characteristically Christian purport is so extremely small? That the personages of the preliminary history really lived and moved in Jewish fashion (Volckmar), explains nothing, for it does not in the least follow that the Evangelist was obliged, in the interest of history, to spread before us in all detail these Jewish ways. And are we at all justified in assuming for the author the historical interest of representing these personages according to historical reality?

[1] Theol. Jahrb. 216 f.; Gospel of Mark, 228 ff.

That his representation cannot be a true one is obvious, and that need not now be proved to Volckmar by referring him to Strauss; but that he did not even adhere more closely to an older representation, that the speeches especially are his own free composition, is made evident by the striking similarity of the language and mode of expression in these two chapters to those of the rest of the Gospel and of the Acts.[1] It would hence only remain, and this is probably Volckmar's opinion, that for the sake of poetical truth to nature the author represented the personages of the preliminary history in the way in which he has represented them. How little does this harmonize with the object and character of a Gospel! Little as such a writing is a simple historical record, as little is it a free and objectless work of art; it is essentially a *didactic religious work;* what it relates, it relates not merely to gratify the desire for knowledge by an actual or poetically embellished history, but it relates it as a normal precedent for religious belief and conduct. In this sense the Gospels have at all times been employed by the Church, and for this object they also originated; traditions of the Messiah were collected, not only from a desire to know something of the Founder of the Church, but to learn something for themselves from the personages of holy Scripture; people collected them, as Luke also expressly says of himself, i. 4, in order to learn something certain respecting the Christian doctrine, or, as Papias (Eus. iii. 39, 2) describes the same object, for the sake of their *utility,* their doctrinal and practical bearing. Hence the speeches which are put in the mouths of the personages of the Gospel history, the actions which are recorded of them, possess an essentially dogmatic significance. Historical and poetical truth to nature were comparatively left out of the account, as is proved by a hundred examples.[2] Thus this motive

[1] On which comp. *Gersdorf,* Beiträge, &c., pp. 160 ff.

[1] How little probable are, for instance, the speeches of John the Baptist—nay, very many speeches of Jesus himself in the fourth Gospel! How improbable are, in the Acts, many things in the speeches and conduct of Paul; how improbable the speech of

does not at all suffice to explain Luke's introductory history, but we must suppose that he conceded an enduring authority in Christianity to the Jewish standpoint which here encounters us; that he wished it at least to be received as an element of the Christian standpoint. But we cannot believe Volckmar, that in this respect he did not differ from Paul. Paul, indeed, also knows that Christ was subject to the Law; but is it credible that he would have recorded the fulfilment of all the precepts of the Law in his person, not in order thereby to show the termination of the Law, but simply in the tone of one to whom this ceremonial possessed intrinsic significance of its own? The general assertion of Christ's necessary subjection to the Law is, moreover, mentioned only in the context, *ἵνα τοὺς ὑπὸ νόμον ἐξαγοράσῃ* (Gal. iv. 5). Paul, indeed, assumes the general Jewish idea of the Messiah; but it by no means follows that a conception exists in his mind adhering to this Jewish idea of the Messiah, utterly and entirely a conception that knows the Messiah only as one on whom God bestowed the throne of his father David, as one who will for ever reign over the house of Jacob (Luke i. 32 f.), through whom God has accepted His servant Israel, fulfilled the promises to the patriarchs, procured salvation for the people of God (i. 54 f., 68 ff.), &c.; for if mention is likewise, ii. 32, made of the *φῶς εἰς ἀποκάλυψιν ἐθνῶν*, it in no respect extends beyond the Old Testament conception of the Messiah; but in the other passages adduced by Volckmar (i. 48, 51, 53, 79, ii. 10, 34), when correctly interpreted, there is not the slightest trace to be found of an universal or even anti-Jewish destination of the Messiah. Moreover, what interest could Paul, who would not know even Christ according to the flesh, have in the lengthy family history of the forerunner, and the personal intercourse which took place between Mary and Elizabeth? No; we here find ourselves on different ground from that of Pauline Christianity. Even the genealogy cannot refuse its Jewish-Christian

James at the Apostolic Council; and yet the fear of making his Gentiles into "*monstra*" has not restrained the author from representing them as he does.

origin, which is rendered evident by its indirect contradiction of the story of the supernatural conception of Christ; and here again it avails little to recall the Pauline ἐκ σπέρματος Δαβὶδ κατὰ σάρκα (Rom. i. 3), for to this υἱὸς Δαβὶδ the υἱὸς θεοῦ κατὰ πνεῦμα is emphatically opposed. Whoever, on the other hand, composed the genealogy, can have made it originally only in the interest of founding the Messianic dignity of Jesus on his descent from David; in order that he might be acknowledged as the lawful heir of David's throne, his right of succession must be shown. Now, along with this showing, Luke not only establishes the descent of Jesus from the protoplast Adam, which makes the Son of David appear at the same time the Son of Man in a higher sense—the national Messiah of the Jews as the Messiah of mankind in general; but, like Matthew, he again renders it illusory by terminating the genealogy, not in Mary, but in Joseph; are we hence, as the Saxon Anonymus insists (p. 240), to suppose that Luke's pedigree is merely a mockery of the Jewish genealogies, or, on the contrary, that it may, as Volckmar believes, have been composed by the Paulinist Luke to satisfy his own "entirely Pauline" requirement of a reference of Christ to the Old Testament? The former is prohibited by the corresponding genealogy of Joseph in Matthew, and as decidedly by the whole character of the Gospel, in which nothing is to be found of all the attacks, invectives, animosities, and derisions against Judaism which are there sought for by the Anonymus; the latter hypothesis founders on the circumstance that he who interrupted the connection between Jesus and Joseph by the story of the supernatural conception, could have no further interest in circumstantially demonstrating Joseph's connection with David; much rather the genealogy can be originally derived only from some one with whom, instead of the ὤν, ὡς ἐνομίζετο of our Luke, stood a simple ὤν or ἦν. That the author of the Gospel nevertheless accepts this genealogical evidence of the Messiahship of Jesus, although he explicitly deprives it of its original significance by his ὤν, ὡς ἐνομίζετο, and by its continuation to Adam, can be explained only by the desire to leave room in his representation for the Jewish-Christian view of Christ; and if in this respect we are more inclined to assume in Matthew an unconscious co-existence of two different views of Christ, both, however, produced on Jewish soil,[1] the older one which considers Christ only as the Son of David, the later one which considers him in a physical sense as the Son of God; in Luke the position of the genealogy after the story of the supernatural conception, by which it is paralysed, the ὡς ἐνομίζετο, the prolongation of the pedigree up to Adam, incompatible as it is with the exclusively Jewish object of the genealogy,—all unite to show that he is perfectly conscious of the relation which this Jewish record bears to his own description. If, therefore, he adopts it notwithstanding, he could only be induced to do so by a regard for persons judaistically disposed. Further, when Schwegler and I have considered as Ebionite the strong emphasizing of the contrast between the αἰὼν οὗτος and the αἰὼν μέλλων, many sayings respecting the value of poverty and the detriment of riches, and the expressions that have a reward-seeking tone, in Luke vi. 35, xvi. 9, here Baur also opposes us for the sake of the "original Luke;"[2] yet I cannot consider our opinion on this subject to be really refuted even by his penetrating remarks. It is quite true the contrast between this and the future world expresses nothing but the primitive Christian view of life; but when this contrast is so sharply stretched and so objectively grasped that one and the same individual cannot belong to both; that he who fares well here below will for that very reason be tormented in the other world; that the poor are blessed as such, the rich as such condemned; if there is utterly no distinction

[1] When *Volckmar*, Gospel of Mark, 230, attributes to the supernatural conception of Jesus the view of liberating Christ from connection with the Jewish people, this is indeed more credible than the further conjecture that it is in behoof of the doctrine of original sin, of which there is no trace in Luke; but that the original motive of the story does not consist in this is evident from its Jewish-Christian origin, to which Matthew clearly testifies.

[2] Krit. Untersuch. pp. 446—455.

between the outward condition and the inward disposition; if the unworldly disposition is recognized *only* by the outward renunciation of the world,—is not this primitive Christianity that same primitive Christian Ebionitism above which Paul raised himself essentially? For I have already shown elsewhere,[1] that in passages such as 2 Cor. vi. 10, 1 Cor. vii. 29 ff., an entirely different estimate of riches and poverty is displayed, and an incomparably greater freedom of self-consciousness towards these outward circumstances. Less decisive indeed are the passages, vi. 23, 35, xvi. 9, both because the former are derived from Matthew, who speaks much more than Luke of future recompence, and because such a view is also not entirely unknown to Paul either (see 1 Cor. ix. 17, 2 Cor. ix. 6); yet these sayings in the context of Luke's version of the Sermon on the Mount certainly do not give the impression that they presuppose the Pauline standpoint, and in no case would Paul have taught, like Luke in the parable of the unjust steward, that it was possible to gain admission to the σκηναὶ αἰώνιοι, to the Messianic kingdom, by works of benevolence; to these the reward he promises to such works cannot possibly refer. The Lukan sayings rather remind us of James than of Paul, as also the whole doctrine of the third Gospel respecting poverty, wealth, and alms (on which xii. 15 ff., xii. 23, should also be compared), most resembles that of James.[2] Herein, again, the Acts coincides with it: see ix. 36, x. 2 ff., xx. 33 ff. That likewise in the christology of the Gospel and the Acts the Ebionite view of Christ as the Prophet appears more strongly than anywhere else in the New Testament, I have already remarked.

All these features appear to me to justify us in continuing to assert, besides the characteristically Pauline, a smaller amount of Ebionite elements in the third Gospel; and the less the accept-

[1] Tübingen Theol. Journal, 1850, 457 ff.

[2] On this and on all the Ebionite elements of the Gospel of Luke, *Köstlin* especially (Urspr. u. Comp. d. Synopt. Evang. 220 ff.) should be compared, though all the conjectures of this scholar respecting the origin of the individual narratives may not be equally tenable.

ance of these elements can be reckoned accidental, the more obviously the author shows that he labours in several points, especially such as the genealogy and the parable of Lazarus and Dives, to metamorphose them in the interest of Pauline ideas, or, as in xvi. 16, to accompany them with sayings and narratives of the opposite character; so much the more plainly does the general tendency of his entire description become apparent. This Gospel certainly serves essentially the interests of Pauline Christianity, and especially of Pauline universalism; it endeavours to adapt the judaistic image of the Messiah in the older Gospel tradition to the Pauline views which, instead of a national Messiah of the Jews, require a universal Messiah; but it strives to accomplish this, not by direct polemics against the older ideas, but rather, while acknowledging and partially appropriating them, by adding Pauline elements in preponderating numbers, and thus, as far as possible, rendering the whole Pauline. In a word, his tendency is conciliatory, not indeed in the sense that the two views of the Messiah—the judaistic and the universalistic—are placed side by side as of equal authority, but that the later is unmistakably more strongly emphasized and treated as the highest, to which the former must adapt itself. Yet the older one is not therefore to be excluded, but to be taken over into the higher one. Here then is a relation analogous to that in the Acts between Jewish Christianity and Paulinism; as in the latter the recognition of Pauline universalism is the object towards which the whole description tends, yet this standpoint itself is not represented in opposition to the Jewish Christianity of the primitive community, but as essentially identical with it; so in the Gospel it is one and the same Christ who is portrayed as the Jewish Messiah, as the Son of David, as God's ambassador to the twelve tribes of Israel, as the surety for the eternal duration of the Mosaic Law,[1] and who by word and deed, in

[1] Luke xvi. 17, a passage which obviously goes far beyond the Pauline *νόμον ἱστῶμεν* (Rom. iii. 31); in the latter an eternal validity of the Law as such, with all its minute definitions, cannot be thought of.

plain language and in parables, proclaims the universal destination of his work, the end of the Law, the superiority of faithful devotion to Jewish righteousness by works, the salvation of all repentant sinners.[1] But as the Acts sacrifices essential features in the character and doctrine of Paul to its conciliatory object, so also in the Gospel we see, not the pure Pauline view of Christ and Christianity, but only Pauline universalism predominantly. In conjunction with this exist traces of the Ebionite aspect of life incompatible with the spirit of pure Paulinism. Thus, amid all the difference of their contents, the two books exhibit in their whole tendency, and in the manner in which they pursue that tendency by presenting history, an affinity explicable only by identity of authorship.

The very arrangement of the two books has a remarkable resemblance. Complete similarity of composition was naturally hindered by difference of subject. The Acts is essentially influenced by the parallel between Paul and the primitive Apostles; the Gospel must necessarily take a different shape in many respects, owing to the unity of its principal personage and his history. Yet the Gospel, with the exception of the preliminary history, is also divided into three parts; in iii. 1—ix. 50, we see Jesus wandering about in Galilee; in ix. 51—xix. 27, he is on the way to Jerusalem;[2] with xix. 28, begins the last part of his history in Jerusalem. As Christianity, according to the Acts, extends from Jerusalem by Samaria to the Gentiles, and each of these three movements corresponds with a particular portion of the book, so, conversely, its founder wends his way from the Γαλιλαία ἐθνῶν, by Samaria to Jerusalem; and similarly to each of these points a particular part of the book is devoted. But their strongest characteristics are chiefly concentrated in the second part, which opens so significantly with the sending out of those second universal apostles, the seventy disciples. That a parallel to the preliminary history of the Gospel may not be

[1] For more minute evidence, see my above quoted treatise and *Schwegler*.

[2] See *Baur*, Krit. Untersuch. pp. 431 ff.

wanting in the Acts, this latter is connected with the pre-apostolic period by the account of the ascension, in a manner similar to that in which the Gospel is connected with the pre-Christian age by its first two chapters. As a special instance of notable resemblance, may be mentioned the treatment in both writings of the two apostolic names, Peter and Paul. It was long ago remarked that Paul is persistently called Saul until xii. 9, and henceforward with equal persistency Paul; which was regarded as an indication that on this occasion he first assumed the latter name. The conjecture is confirmed by the observation that, in a perfectly similar manner, Peter in the Gospel bears exclusively the name of Simon until vi. 14, and indeed, with the exception of the single passage, v. 8, which even then records an adumbration of his subsequent position, always (seven times) without the addition of Peter; in vi. 14, the name of Peter is introduced with the words, Σίμωνα ὂν καὶ ὠνόμασε Πέτρον (compare xiii. 9, Σαῦλος δὲ ὁ καὶ Παῦλος), and Peter keeps this name with equal persistency, and similarly always (seventeen times) without an antecedent Σίμων. The latter occurs only twice more, in xxii. 31, where the Σίμων, Σίμων, in the warning of the denial is probably intended to indicate that the person addressed was still the old Simon, and not only Peter the rock of faith; and in xxiv. 34, in a speech of the Jerusalemites, where the more familiar name seems as dramatic as in the Acts, which never says Simon except in x. 5, xviii. 32, xi. 12, the Σίμων, ὃς ἐπικαλεῖται Πέτρος, and in xv. 14, the Hebraising Συμεών.[1] Insignificant as is this feature in itself, it nevertheless allows us to cast an instructive glance into the similarity of the literary procedure adopted in the two books.

[1] The same phenomenon recurs in Mark; Peter is here exclusively called Simon till iii. 16, where the bestowal of the name of Peter is related, henceforward only once, xiv. 37, in the Σίμων καθεύδεις, which likewise recounts a weakness. Matthew, on the contrary, changes between Peter and the more rare Simon and Simon Peter; and John makes use of the latter term as often as of the simple Peter. It is not improbable that Mark was dependent on Luke for his procedure; at any rate the introduction of the name of Peter in Luke more resembles that of the name of Paul in the Acts than it does in Mark.

If we collect all the grounds furnished us by the language and representation of the two books, their contents, their tendency, their composition, the direct or indirect reference of one to the other, we have every reason to give credence to the deposition of the Acts and to the unanimous evidence of tradition as to the identity of their authors. The only objection that can be made arises from certain linguistic, especially lexical, peculiarities, which we may perceive in both, notwithstanding the essentially similar character of their language.[1] I have already given a considerable number of words and expressions of which some belong to the Gospel and not to the Acts, others to the Acts and not to the Gospel;[2] and I can increase this list in the foot-note with still further examples.[3] Still these peculiarities

[1] With respect to the contents, besides the variations already discussed in the history of the ascension, the most important divergence is that the Gospel seems repeatedly (xiv. 14, xx. 35) to restrict the resurrection to the righteous, whereas Acts xxiv. 15 expressly teaches an *ἀνάστασις δικαίων τε καὶ ἀδίκων*. As, however, the rest of the New Testament vacillates between these two determinations, and as not infrequently one and the same writer enunciates both without showing their compatibility (for instance, Paul, if we compare 1 Cor. xv. 35 ff., Rom. viii. 11, and similar passages, with Rom. ii. 16, 2 Cor. v. 10; and John, if we compare vi. 39 f., 44, 54, with v. 28 f.), neither can this circumstance prove anything in the present case.

[2] Tübingen Theol. Journal, 1843, 450 ff., 461 ff., 471 ff.

[3] Besides those already cited, the Gospel has the following words, which are wanting in the Acts, *ἔντιμος, προσψαύειν, φιλάργυρος, ψηφίζειν* (these four occur elsewhere by mistake among the stock of words peculiar to the Acts), *ἀγάπᾶν* (thirteen times), *ἀλλ' ἤ, ἀλλάγε, ἀλλότριος* (Acts only in one quotation), *ἥκειν* (namely, if in Acts xxviii. 23 is to be read *ἦλθον*), *καλὸς, κλίνειν* (four times, twice *ἡμέρα κλίνει*), *κοινωνὸς, κοίτη, παλαιός*. *'Απολλύναι*, Gospel four times, is only twice in the Acts; *διατί*, there six times, here once; *διδάσκαλος*, there seventeen times, here once; *δοῦλος*, twenty-six times there, here two or three times; *ἑτοιμάζειν*, there thirteen times, here once; *εὐλογεῖν*, there fourteen times, here once; *μακάριος*, there thirteen times, here twice; *ὅταν*, there twenty-nine times, here twice; *οὐχὶ*, there fifteen times, here twice; *σῶμα*, there thirteen times, here once; the Gospel alone has the neuter in the substantive sense, *τὸ ἀγαθὸν*; the plural forms *αἱ ἔρημοι, τὰ ἔσχατα*; the future *ἐρεῖν*; the combinations *ἀπὸ τότε, ἀπὸ μακρόθεν, ἀπὸ μιᾶς, σὺν τούτοις, ἐν ἐξουσίᾳ*; the construction of *ἐὰν* with the indicative (vi. 34, xii. 19, 40, not quite certain), and of *θέλειν* with a conjunctive following it (with or without *ἵνα*); the comparative *ἤ* with an antecedent positive, xv. 7, xvii. 2; the Gospel alone has the expressions, *ἀκολουθεῖν μετά τινος, εἰπεῖν ἐν ἑαυτῷ* or *ἐν τῇ καρδίᾳ, λέγειν ἐν ἑαυτῷ* or *πρὸς ἑαυτὸν, ἔρχεσθαι ὀπίσω τ., ἐρχ. εἰς ἑαυτὸν, εἰς φανερόν, ὁμολογεῖν ἔν τινι, κακῶς ἔχειν, αἰὼν οὗτος, αἰ. ἐρχόμενος, ὁ πατὴρ ὁ ἐξ οὐρανοῦ* (xi. 13), *βασιλεὺς* of Christ, *εἰρήνη ὑμῖν, ἔγειρε*

are not of a nature to prove anything against the same origin of the two writings. For, in the first place, from the words and expressions enumerated, we must subtract all those which occur once or only rarely in the same context in the book which contains them; for there is no reason why expressions which are not repeated in the same book should not be repeated by the author in another book of somewhat different contents. To this class belong by far the greater number of the examples adduced; in the Acts alone I have counted more than six hundred words not contained in the Gospel, which occur only in one passage, and mostly only once. Such expressions could be taken into consideration only if their number in one writing were incomparably greater than in the other; for this would be a positive indication that the author of the former had a richer supply of words at his command; but even then it would be necessary to examine whether the disproportion could not be accounted for by the nature of the subject or the influence of the sources employed. In our case, however, no such dis-

(*ἐγείρου* and such-like, the *ἔγειρε*, Acts iii. 6, is very uncertain); *υἱὸς Δαβὶδ* exists only in the Gospel; *υἱ. ανθρώπου* and *υἱ. θεοῦ* (*ὑψίστου*), each of which only once in the Acts, are found in the Gospel, the former twenty-three times, the latter thirteen times; also the combinations *υἱὸς φωτὸς*, *εἰρήνης* and so on, not infrequent in the Gospel, find an analogy in the Acts only in iv. 36; the periphrasis *ἄρχεσθαὶ* is far more frequent in the Gospel than in the Acts; *βασιλεία θεοῦ* occurs in the Gospel thirty-four times, in Acts seven times; *ὃς ἂν* (*ἐὰν*) Gospel twenty times, Acts once, and three times in quotations; *καὶ ὂυτος*, Gospel i. 36, viii. 41, xvi. 1, xix. 2, xx. 28, ii. 37, viii. 42, Acts only xvii. 7. The Gospel more frequently has *καὶ* before the apodosis, and oftener continues the narrative with *καὶ* than the Acts; see *Bruder*, pp. 455, 460 ff. On the other hand, besides those already enumerated, the following are peculiar to Acts as compared with the Gospel: the words *ἁγνίζειν*, *ἀδύνατος* as signifying feeble; *ἀεὶ*, *δαιμόνιον* in the sense of divinity; *δέον ἐστὶ*, *ἔχειν* = *ἀπέχειν* (i. 12); *καθὼς* in a temporal sense (vii. 17); *μαρτυρεῖσθαι* in the sense of having a good reputation; *ἡ ὁδὸς*, without any apposition, for the Christian religion; the verbal forms *ἤμην* and *ἔσεσθαι*; the expressions *ἐν γωνίᾳ*, *ἐκ δευτέρου*; the beginning of sentences with *ὡς δὲ* and *ὅτε δὲ* (the Gospel has only *καὶ ὡς*, *καὶ ὅτε*, which latter occurs only twice in the Acts, see *Gersdorf* elsewhere, p. 242); the comparatively frequent use of *δέειν* (Gospel twice, Acts twelve times), *ἐπαγγελία* (Gospel once, Acts eight times), *μάρτυς* (Gospel once, Acts thirteen times), *μόνον* (Gospel once, Acts eight times), the use of *μὲν* without a subsequent adversative particle (Acts i. 1, 18, ii. 41, iii. 13 (?), v. 41, xiii. 4, xvii. 30, xxiii. 22, xxvi. 4, xxvii. 24, xxviii. 22).

proportion exists. Of the differences remaining after the subtraction of those expressions which occur only once, a large portion are explicable by the variety of the sources employed in the Gospel and in the Acts. On the occasion of the lexical catalogue, Tübingen Theol. Journal, 1843, 533 f., already mentioned, I pointed out a not inconsiderable number of words and expressions foreign to the Acts, and occurring in the third Gospel only in those passages in which Matthew has them also, and which were probably borrowed from him. It is the same with several others. Thus, ἀποκτανθῆναι, ἀποκτέννειν, two forms wanting in the Acts, occur in Luke ix. 22, xii. 4, after Matt. xvi. 21, x. 28; ὁ ἐρχόμενος βασιλεὺς, of Christ, Luke xix. 38, after Matt. xxi. 5, 9; τὰ ἔσχατα, Luke xi. 26, after Matt. xii. 4, 5; κεραία, Luke xvi. 17, after Matt. v. 18; κληρονόμος, Luke xx. 14, after Matt. xxi. 38, ὁμολογεῖν ἔν τινι, xii. 8, after Matt. x. 32; παλαιὸς, v. 36, 37, after Matt. ix. 16 f. whence it appears to have been taken into the probably "spurious" addition ver. 39;[1] ὁ ἐρχόμενος, without any apposition, vii. 19, after Matt. xi. 3; the same observation may also be made with respect to many of the words elsewhere enumerated. As to other expressions, it is probable that even if the author used them in partial independence of his sources, they were primarily suggested by them. This applies chiefly to such words and phrases as were frequent in the earlier Gospel writings, or which constitute the leadings words of Gospel tradition, such as βασιλεία θεοῦ, υἱὸς ἀνθρώπου, αἰὼν οὗτος, νομικὸς, διδάσκαλος, δοῦλος, ἁμαρτωλὸς, τελώνης, ἀποκαλύπτειν, κληρονομεῖν ζωὴν αἰώνιον (comp. Luke x. 25, xviii. 18, to Matt. xix. 29), μακάριος, μεριμνᾷν, and others, or of which the use was directly conditioned by the subject; such as the frequent παιδίον in the histories of the childhood. It may be the same with those idioms which, less closely bound up with the substance of Gospel history, were nevertheless current in the older Jewish-Christian representations. Thus, by the influence of these representations

[1] See Vol. I. p. 102.

upon the style of the third Evangelist, we might account for the Gospel's having a stronger Hebraistic colouring than the Acts; for the periphrasis by the participles ἐγερθεὶς and πορευθεὶς, very frequent in Matthew, occurring in the former only and not in the latter (the verbs themselves, ἐγείρ. and πορ. are frequent in the Acts also), that with ἄρχεσθαι in the Gospel is more frequent; for the Gospel's far more frequent use of the ὃς ἂν or ὃς ἐὰν, a favourite with the Hellenists, and the Hebraistic καὶ οὗτος, than the Acts; for its putting καὶ where the Acts has δὲ (καὶ ἐγένετο, and ἐγ. δὲ, καὶ ὡς, καὶ ὅτε and ὡς δὲ, ὅτε δὲ); for its being more partial than the Acts to καὶ in introducing an apodosis and continuing the narrative, though the καὶ in δὲ καὶ, καὶ αὐτὸς, καὶ αὐτοὶ, is far more frequent in the Gospel than in the Acts (see above); for, on the contrary, the good Greek particle τε, occurring twenty times oftener in the Acts than in the Gospel; for the Acts being altogether better written. We are the more justified in this hypothesis, because in the Acts itself the style is somewhat unequal, and because, moreover, those portions in which the author evidently does not rigidly adhere to his sources, such as the speeches of Peter, are distinguished from the others by a more Hebraistic tone of language. If to this we add, what has already been observed,[1] that of the characteristic expressions of the two books not a few belong to a similar, as others to a common stock,[2] and several more are formed on the same type,[3] —that both are partial to combinations with prepositions, and especially to compound verbs, both to verbal adjectives, compound substantives, to periphrases by adverbs with the help of prepositions,—that thus, notwithstanding material differences,

[1] Tübingen Theol. Journal, 1843, 537.

[2] Comp. the words, ἀκριβὴς, ἀκρίβεια, ἀκριβῶς, ἀσφαλὴς, -λεια, -λῶς, -λίζειν, καλὸς and καλῶς, ἄγνωστος, γνώστης, γνῶσις, γνωστὸς, ἀγάπη, ἀγαπᾷν, ἀγαπητὸς, ἀλλογενὴς and ἀλλόφυλος, ἀναδεικνύναι and ἀνάδειξις, ἀποκρίνεσθαι and ἀπόκρισις, πρόσωπον λαμβάνειν and προσωπολήπτης. στρατόπεδον and στρατοπεδάρχης, &c. &c.

[3] Thus, for instance, the Gospel only has ἀπὸ τότε and ἀπὸ μακρόθεν, but the Acts has ἀπὸ πρωῒ and ἀπὸ τοῦ νῦν. Further evidence see above.

the similar character of the whole mode of expression is not abandoned,—we have every reason not to allow the number of expressions peculiar to each of the two books to disturb us in the conviction of authorship-unity. More striking, however, is the circumstance that individual expressions and idioms occur with extreme frequency in one book, and in the other only seldom or not at all;[1] but, for this also, with the otherwise preponderating similarity of their linguistic character, the explanation will suffice that the author, in style as in contents, adheres to what he found before him; and even where he is not directly dependent on documental authorities, he still to a certain degree adapts his language to the character of the speakers and the spirit of the individual narratives, and that hence even the comparative variety and dissimilarity of expression form part of his literary peculiarities.

These observations, it is true, apply to the two books of Luke only in their present form. What they demonstrate is in the first instance merely this, that as the works are now constituted they proceed from the same author in their essential elements, and irrespective of some possible single interpolations. Nevertheless, it remains conceivable that one or the other belonged in an earlier form to another author. When, therefore, Baur supposes a more ancient Gospel of Luke, in which the introductory history and some other portions were wanting, and which was similarly and almost simultaneously elaborated by the author of the Acts in an ecclesiastical, by Marcion in a Gnostic sense,[2]—when he accordingly distinguishes between the author of the Acts and the original author of the Gospel,—this hypothesis still requires special investigation. If we first examine the

[1] As to the Gospel compare our catalogue above; as to the Acts, besides what is adduced respecting *μὲν* and *δέ*, the use of the words *αἵρεσις*, *ἐπαγγελία*, *ὅραμα*, *τέρας*, *ζήτημα* and *συζήτησις*; in the address *ἄνδρες*; of the verbs *διαλέγεσθαι*, *διαμαρτύρεσθαι*, *διατρίβειν*, *ἐπικαλεῖσθαι*, *καταγγέλλειν*, *καταντᾷν*, *κελεύειν*, *τηρεῖν*, *πείθειν*, and *πείθεσθαι*; the adverbs and particles *ὁμοθυμαδὸν*, *τανῦν*, *τὲ*, *κἀκεῖ*, and *κἀκεῖθεν*.

[2] Marcusevang. 223 ff.

reasons adduced in its favour, our previous inquiry respecting Marcion's Gospel has already deprived it of the support which the text of this Gnostic appears to warrant. As on dogmatic grounds Marcion avowedly altered or removed many portions of the Gospel that lay before him, we cannot attribute sufficient weight to his testimony to entitle us, on his account, to conjecture a later origin for the paragraphs which are wanting in him. A further reason for the severance of the Gospel from the Acts may be derived from the linguistic differences of the two books. But these differences are of such a subordinate kind in comparison with the whole of their linguistic character, that they are quite incapable of counterbalancing the otherwise far-reaching similarity in expression and mode of presentation; and even if the supposed two authors were both Paulinists, and the second had imitated the first, we should be scarcely able to explain the similarity. This is much more considerable than we are wont to find it in the works of different authors even when one is imitated by the other,[1] and, moreover, the linguistic and literary peculiarities by which the third Evangelist is distinguished from the other Synoptists are more richly and freely developed in the Acts than in the Gospel;[2] while in the relation of an imitator to his model, exactly the reverse is usually the case, and the features common to both bear a less free and more dependent character in the place where they are merely second-hand. Thus, from the language and mode of representation in the two books, we get the impression much rather of one and the same literary idiosyncrasy, which in the Gospel is more hampered by dependence on its documental authorities and only attains a freer development in the Acts, than of two individualities, of which the more powerful and independent produced the Gospel, the less independent the Acts. Neither, after our previous

[1] *Baur*, 225.

[2] Consider, for instance, the more frequent Hebraisms of the Gospel and the superior Greek of the Acts. For the rest, the evidence for the above position is contained in the previous investigation.

disquisition, can the diversity of the two books in the history of the ascension prove diversity of authors. It would be far more decisive if in the whole view of Christianity, in the whole standpoint and tendency of the two representations of the original Gospel of Luke, on the one side,—of the Acts and the revised Gospel on the other,—a difference existed thorough enough to render identity of author improbable. "In the original Gospel of Luke," observes Baur, "the Pauline spirit expresses itself chiefly in the antithesis to the primitive Apostles as the Twelve, who in different ways are cast into the shade, and have their true apostolic counterpart in the Seventy disciples. In the second author, as we know him principally from the Acts, the antithetical tendency attacks Judaism alone, in order to describe the unbelief of the Jews in its harsh contrast to Christianity, and to portray its enmity and love of persecution as the reason why the promulgation of the gospel was diverted from them to the Gentiles. The more all opposition is thrown back upon the Jews, so much the more conciliation can be shown within the limits of Christianity. The sharp anti-judaistic spirit which in the original Gospel of Luke evinces itself most in the point wherein lies the chief nucleus of its peculiarity ch. ix. and x., is not the element in which the author of the Acts and the later portions of the Gospel is wont to move." These observations must undergo some restriction. That the twelve original Apostles are purposely cast into the shade in the three Gospels we must admit, and must acknowledge as correct the greater part of what Baur has before[1] observed in this respect; but it does not appear to us that the Gospel goes further in this direction than we can credit the author of the Acts with. The most striking proof of this tendency consists in the narrative of the seventy disciples, when we compare it with the preceding account of the sending out of the Apostles. The greater portion of what Jesus says in Matthew x. to the Twelve, Luke

[1] Krit. Untersuch. ueber die Evang. 435 ff.

has reserved for instructions to the Seventy; they are the labourers (x. 2) whom the Lord sends forth to his harvest (in Matt. ix. 37, it is the Twelve); they receive the universally applicable precepts and promises (x. 16, 20) of the apostolic office; their return occasions that animated speech which in Matthew xi. 25 ff., we can only apply primarily to the known disciples of Christ, and to a blessing (x. 23) which in Matthew (xiii. 16) also applies only to the *μαθηταὶ*, without any subordinate designation. It cannot be mistaken that the Seventy are here exalted above the Twelve; in other words, a higher significance is ascribed to those whom they represent, i.e. the Apostle of the Gentiles and his coadjutors, than to the Apostles of the Jews, because by them the dominion of Christ over the whole world was first realized (the *πάντα μοι παρεδόθη*, Luke x. 22); by them the true knowledge of God, which, notwithstanding their acquaintance with divine revelation, had remained hid from the Jews (the *σοφοὶ* of ver. 21), was imparted to those who had hitherto dwelt in profoundest ignorance (the *νήπιοι*). By several further traits, the Evangelist also shows that he ranks the twelve original Apostles lower than was the case in Jewish-Christian tradition. Even if the strong accusation against the *γενεὰ ἄπιστος καὶ διεστραμμένη* applies as little in Luke ix. 41 to the Apostles[1] as in Matt. xvii. 17; on the other hand the third Evangelist repeatedly and expressly points out how little even the Apostles understood their Master; at the transfiguration, ix. 32 f., they are heavy with sleep, so that Peter does not know what he is saying; at the announcement of the passion, ix. 45, where Matthew, xvii. 23, only speaks of the grief of the disciples, Luke knows not how to express himself strongly enough about the obtuseness of their understanding; the same feature is repeated in xviii. 34, xxiv. 25 f.; in Luke alone also, on the occa-

[1] Still less the *ἐκβαλὼν ἔξω πάντας*, viii. 54, which probably first found its way into Luke's text from the parallel passage, Mark v. 40, and is at any rate to be explained only by the standard of this passage and in correspondence with the *πάντες*, ver. 52.

sion of the appearance in Samaria (ix. 51 ff.), which again is given only by him, the sons of Zebedee are asked if they know what spirit they are of; Luke xxii. 32, seems to indicate an apostasy on the part of the disciples such as is known to Justin;[1] and after the resurrection, notwithstanding all that has previously occurred, Jesus (xxiv. 37 ff.) has difficulty in assuring them of the fact.[2] Now it perfectly corresponds with this when several features conducive to the Apostle's honour are partly omitted, partly softened down. Thus when Jesus, according to Matthew xii. 49, expressly terms his disciples his nearest relations, Luke, viii. 21, substitutes for the μαθηταὶ all who hear and obey his word; thus the latter wants the speech by which in Matt. xviii. 18 f., power is granted to the Apostles to bind and to loose; and when he records Peter's confession, ix. 20, it still sounds in him so cold compared with Matt. xvi. 16, and the omission of the lofty promise here connected with it appears so intentional, that we cannot doubt that the position which Peter here assumes was repugnant to Luke; he does not wish the Church to be founded on Peter, nor the keys of heaven to be delivered to him alone. Nevertheless, we cannot assume an actual enmity on his part to the original Apostles, for he has likewise taken what redound to their honour, even in cases where Matthew has not got it; and has also suppressed what might place them in an unfavourable light. The call of Peter and the sons of Zebedee is described in v. 1 more minutely than by Matthew (iv. 18 ff.), and with additions which illustrate the faith and readiness of Peter. The words of Jesus to the disciples, that it was given to them to know the mysteries of the kingdom of God, Luke records in viii. 10, like Matthew in xiii. 11. The promise, Matt. xix. 28, which is here, xviii. 29, wanting, is afterwards adduced, at least in our text, in xxii. 28 ff.; and if these

[1] Apol. i. 50, Tr. 53.

[2] Less seems proved by other points, such as the pusillanimity in the storm on the lake, viii. 24 f., which is essentially similar in Matt. viii. 26 f.; as are also Peter's query, viii. 45, Matt. ix. 31; the hesitation at the feeding of the five thousand, ix. 12 f., Matt. xiv. 15 f.

verses were missing in Marcion, the dogmatic reason for the omission is too obvious to enable it to prove anything. The Apostles' petition to increase their faith, which is related by Luke alone, at any rate testifies their susceptibility; while in Matt. xvii. 20, on the contrary, the speech about faith like a grain of mustard-seed is connected with a censure of the disciples' unbelief. In the narrative of the agony at Gethsemane, although our three Synoptists are aware of the disciples' sleep at that important moment, Luke makes this weakness appear in a much milder light than the two others; with him, it is explained by their grief at the impending fate of Jesus; the disciples are found sleeping, not three times, but only once; the words of Jesus sound milder; and Peter, to whom in Matthew (xxvi. 40) and Mark (xiv. 37) they are chiefly addressed, is not named. Peter's backsliding at his denial likewise appears less in Luke xxii. 54 ff. than in Matt. xxvi. 69 ff. where with protestations and curses he affirms that he knows not Jesus. The severe reproof of this Apostle, *ὕπαγε ὀπίσω μου σατανᾶ, σκάνδαλόν μου εἶ*, &c. (Matt. xvi. 23), Luke has suppressed, as also the petition of the sons of Zebedee (Matt. xx. 20 ff.). On the other hand, he alone (xxii. 32) records the important promise that Peter's faith shall not fail, and alone among the Synoptists mentions the zeal of Peter in visiting the tomb of Christ (xxiv. 12), as well as the pre-eminence conferred upon him above the others by the first appearance of the risen Lord (xxiv. 34); the latter certainly in imitation of Paul, 1 Cor. xv. 5. These traits contradict the hypothesis that he was endeavouring to degrade the original Apostles. When, therefore, he expunged from the Gospel tradition some things honourable to them, and added others to their prejudice, he must have had some other motive for so doing. He suppresses those declarations which seemed to confer upon the Twelve a pre-eminent position at the head of the Church to the exclusion of others, and to limit the apostolic privileges to them; he makes it emphatically conspicuous that the Seventy, the representatives of the mission to the Gentiles, were not merely not behind the Apostles of the Jews, but that the solicitude and pleasure of their Lord turned to them by preference; that by them first the object of the proclamation of the gospel was truly attained; he shows by the example of the original Apostles that, taken by itself, personal intercourse with Christ during his earthly life did not lead to the apprehension of his words; that to them also the risen Lord, the same whom Paul had seen, was obliged to expound the meaning of the Scriptures (xxiv. 45); that notwithstanding their personal intercourse with Jesus, the Spirit, whose coming they were obliged quietly to await at Jerusalem,[1] was alone able to qualify them, as well as the others, for the apostolic ministry (xxiv. 49). In this he does nothing essentially different from the author of the Acts, for the latter book also decidedly endeavours to rank Paul, notwithstanding his apparent subordination at the apostolic council, as in every respect equal with the original Apostles; it could not endure stories which founded a primacy for Peter and the Twelve; it carefully strives to prune away any pre-eminence deduced from their personal relation to Christ; here also the Apostles of the Jews are obliged to withdraw as soon as the Apostle of the Gentiles appears in that character; and the last result of its representation, i.e. as enunciated by the concluding scene at Rome, is the transfer of salvation from the Jews to the Gentiles, the same which is symbolically indicated by the story of the mission and success of the seventy disciples. An incapacity to comprehend the truths of salvation, such as the Gospel repeatedly ascribes to the Apostles, would certainly be no longer appropriate in the Acts; but the Evangelist also does not treat it as lasting; it is only at the period previous to the resurrection that they did not understand Jesus; that it was otherwise after the appearances of their risen Lord, and the outpouring of the Spirit, is already said by the Gospel, xxiv. 31, 45, 49; and that

[1] Καθίσατε, which here, as in the previously discussed sayings of Justin (p. 47, 1), involves the additional signification of inactivity.

Marcion only had these verses in part can prove nothing against their originality. The adduced characteristics of the Gospel are, therefore, as it seems to me, not incompatible with the standpoint of the Acts; and we are not obliged for their sake to make a distinction between the authors of the two books, whose identity is indicated by everything else.

3. By whom, when, and where was the Acts written?

The Acts is universally ascribed to Luke, a companion of Paul. Its author describes himself as a temporary follower of the Apostle, since he (xvi. 10—18, xx. 5—15, xxi. 1—18, xxvii. 1—xxviii. 18) speaks of Paul and his companions in the first person plural. That this occurs here only may be explained by the usual hypothesis that he first joined the company of the Apostle at Troas, xvi. 10; when Paul fled from Philippi, xvi. 40, he remained behind; subsequently he again attached himself to Paul at Philippi (xx. 5), and accompanied him to Jerusalem (xxi. 17); and after spending the period of the imprisonment at Cæsarea in his vicinity, he made with him the journey from Cæsarea to Jerusalem (xxvii. 1, xxviii. 18). As regards the sections xx. 17—38, xxi. 19—xxvi. 32, the ἡμεῖς is here suspended because the author did not wish to represent himself as a personal sharer, as in the journey and its events. But it has been recently questioned on various sides whether the "we" is at all intended to designate the author of our book as one of Paul's companions; Schleiermacher in his Lectures suggested the opinion[1] that the Acts as well as the third Gospel was merely a collection of scattered essays, and that the "we" was derived from one of these, which was, moreover, written not by Luke, but by Timothy. This hypothesis seemed to many a welcome

[1] The same view is now developed in the printed Lectures on the Int. to the N. T., p. 347, but with merely an incidental allusion to the conjecture respecting Timothy as the author of the record of the journey (p. 354).

expedient for combining belief in the personal testimony of the reporter with the recognition of later elements in our book. Bleek,[1] Ulrich,[2] and De Wette,[3] entered the lists in its behalf, after Mayerhoff[4] had already ascribed the whole of the Acts to Timothy. From the same fundamental view, Schwanbeck, in his frequently-mentioned work,[5] endeavours to demonstrate that the section with "we" is the memorandum of a travelling companion of Paul, of Silas in fact, from which indeed nearly the whole of the second part of the Acts, from xv. 1 onwards, is supposed to be derived. Meanwhile the establishment of these hypotheses has failed, as well as the invalidation of the objections opposed to them, to Ulrich by Kraus,[6] to Mayerhoff by Strauss,[7] and by Schwanbeck to the whole theory of Timothy.[8] Most of the reasons by which it is attempted to prove the separation of the diary of the journey from the rest of our book, and the origin of the former in Timothy or Silas, are quite unimportant. It is considered strange that the author who names all the other companions of Paul should not have named himself; but by the "I" which is implied in the ἡμεῖς he would have designated himself sufficiently, for the title of the book must have told the readers who was intended by this "I." It is said that if Luke speaks in xvi. 11 ff., he must also have told what became of himself on the arrest of Paul and Silas; but this reason would be equally applicable against any other companion of Paul, and especially against Timothy and Silas, as the former

[1] Stud. und Krit. 1836, 4, 1025 ff., 1046 ff.

[2] The same, 1837, 2, 367 ff.; 1840, 4, 1003 ff.

[3] Einleit ins N. T. § 114 f. Commentar zur Apg. Einl. § 2 a. Explanation of xvi. 10, 19, xx. 5.

[4] Einleit. in die Petrin. Schriften, pp. 6 ff.

[5] Pp. 63 ff., 140 ff., 186 ff.

[6] Essays by the Evangelical Clergy of Würtemberg, x. 2, 122 ff., xiii. 2, 106 ff.

[7] In his review of the book mentioned, now Characteristiken und Kritiken, pp. 286 ff.

[8] Zweck d. Apg. pp. 19 ff. Further, the minute refutation of the hypotheses of Timotheus and Silas by *Lekebusch*, Comp. d. Apg. 140 ff., should be compared.

disappears, without any remark, for a considerable period in xvi. 18, xxi. 17; the latter in xviii. 5, xxi. 17. Moreover, it is supposed to be improbable that Paul should have already found a Christian at Troas, whither he had first brought Christianity; as we, however, do not learn from xvi. 10 how or whence the reporter encountered Paul, whether he was first won over to Christianity at Troas, or whether he was a Christian previously, a wide margin is left for conjectures. The same applies to the further consideration why Luke should have remained at Philippi, which was not his home (xvi. 15), or otherwise how a purely accidental meeting could be imagined at the same place at which he had left him. He might have all sorts of reasons for staying at Philippi—for instance, to work there in the place of the Apostle who had fled; but he might also have returned from Philippi to Troas, or wherever else he came from, and have purposely met Paul again at Philippi. If further evidence is required, from the Epistles to the Thessalonians and Philippians, of Luke's remaining behind at Philippi, or if it is deduced from Col. iv. 14 that he first became acquainted with Paul at Rome, one of these assertions is as weak as the other; for the order of the greetings in the Epistle to the Colossians, even assuming its authenticity, is not meant to be regulated by seniority of service (to speak with Schneckenburger); that Luke was with Paul when he wrote the Epistle to the Philippians cannot be proved; and, finally, the Epistles to the Thessalonians, even independently of the question of their origin, afford no particular opportunity for mentioning Luke. Bleek indeed thought (p. 1033) that the reckoning of the Jewish feasts, xx. 6, xxvii. 9, would not suit the Gentile Christian Luke (but how do we know that Luke was a Gentile Christian?); and even Schwanbeck (p. 144) has acknowledged that they must have been familiar to any of Paul's companions. That on which Mayerhoff (pp. 8 f., and also Ulrich, 1837, 373) lays great weight is likewise inaccurate, namely, that wherever Timothy is present the narrative is distinguished by its picturesqueness, whereas this ceases as soon as he has parted from the company; xvii. 16—34 describes very graphically also, though Timothy was not then at Athens (xvii. 14, 16, xviii. 5); the account in xxiii. 11 ff. is likewise picturesque enough, though Timothy neither saw nor heard what it records; in xix. 23 ff. we also obtain a very graphic description of the insurrection of Demetrius, though Timothy had at that time (verse 22) gone on in advance to Macedonia.[1] To all these and similar reasons I should therefore be reluctant to assign any weight. The single real difficulty in the usual hypothesis rather consists in the fact, that in xvi. 10 the first person appears abruptly and unannounced, vanishes in ver. 17 equally without notice, and appears again in xx. 5. If it is supposed that our author is actually the Apostle's speaking companion here, the phenomenon has much that is striking. For it is too unnatural that any one, writing from personal recollection, should so tacitly introduce, withdraw, and re-introduce himself, without intimating, even by a single word, that he became connected with the acting personages, or how; and that he again separated from them. The circumstance in question is much more easily explained if we suppose that the author was not really a companion of Paul, but that he only wishes to give himself out as such by the use of the first person, and that he employs the first person just in the parts indicated, and not elsewhere, because he found it before him in a record which included only these parts.[2] The paragraphs subsequent to xvi. 18, in which the "we" is wanting, may in this case have been treated by the author only as free amplifications of the memorandum he found before him, in which, however, he did not wish expressly to assume the tone of an eye-witness, as they were added by himself. The strangest thing, however, the unannounced appearance of the first person, may in our author

[1] Against *Mayerhoff's* hypothesis that he had previously returned, comp. *Lekebusch*, 157.

[2] What *Lekebusch*, Comp. d. Apg. 132 f., observes in opposition to this, appears to me to require no refutation.

himself be paralleled by the equally sudden employment of the name of Paul, after xiii. 9. Still more striking is the resemblance in the procedure of the Διαμαρτυρία Ἰακώβου before the Clementine Homilies, which at first always speaks of the πρεσβύτεροι in the third person, and only at the end suddenly passes to the first: καὶ ταῦτα εἰπόντων αὐτῶν ἐγερθέντες προσηυξάμεθα. If this is in all probability to be explained by the author having found the Διαμαρτυρία already in existence, and having left it in the other parts in its more ancient form, yet introducing at the end the first person selected by him for the Clementine narrative, so the author of the Acts, according to the above hypothesis, would conversely have found the first person employed in a more ancient record, which he accepted in this form in order to identify himself with the older reporter. That he succeeded very well in his design is evident; for the "we" is to this day the mainstay of those who assert the author's ocular testimony.

At any rate, this explanation of the "we" deserves the preference over that which makes the first person come in here by the mere negligence of the author. Schwanbeck, pp. 188 ff., has indeed exhibited remarkable instances of similar negligence on the part of the mediæval chroniclers; he shows that the so-called Saxon annalist copies the "I," "my," "we," &c., from Dietmar of Merseburg, in the midst of the context, without an indication of the real subject-matter; and that the same case not infrequently occurs in this class of writers. But what was possible among the most thoughtless of the monkish chroniclers (with better historians this cannot be found even in the Middle Ages) need not on that account have been possible to a writer who used his materials with such freedom as our author, who arranged, sifted, metamorphosed, and in parts most likely freely invented his narratives according to a definite scheme steadily pursued; who likewise by many smaller traits, well fitted for the object and effect of the whole, testifies how carefully he worked, and how clearly conscious he was of what he did. Our preceding inquiry into the unity of the Acts already refutes this hypothesis.

If the author adopted extraneous records so unaltered that he even copied the "I" of the reporter without a purpose, the traces of the various portions of which his work was composed must necessarily have been clearly recognizable; and neither a single plan and a single tendency, nor a uniform character of language and representation, could have pervaded the whole. But the portions in which the narrator makes use of the first person, exhibit no essential divergence from the plan, tone, and style of the whole; and the language especially is so little different from that of the rest of the book, that even a partizan of the Timothy theory, such as De Wette,[1] found himself forced to admit that the sources were freely revised by the author. And if they were freely elaborated, it is the more improbable that the ἡμεῖς, which could only escape a mechanical copyist, should have passed unobserved by the author; i.e. this ἡμεῖς has not remained from negligence, but purposely; the author has appropriated it in order to designate himself as the companion of Paul. To this must be added the circumstance already noticed, that the first person, xx. 5, reappears exactly at the same place where we had lost sight of it, xvi. 17. On this remarkable coincidence, Schwanbeck can only say (p. 144) that it is accidental. But such a result of chance is highly improbable; and if to this we add the impediments to the separation of the parts with "we" from the remainder of the book, we can maintain with all certainty that the author intended to designate himself as the companion of Paul. And if the individual who here speaks in the first person is held to be any other than Luke, it involves the necessity of maintaining the same thing with regard to the author of the Acts; and to ascribe it as a whole, with Mayerhoff, to Timothy; or, with Hennell,[2] to Silas; or we must at least assume that it is meant to be assigned to one of these. Meanwhile, not only is the first hypothesis

[1] Int. to the N. T. § 115 a.

[2] Inquiry respecting the Origin of Christianity, p. 104 of the translation edited by *Strauss*.

extremely improbable, but also the second. Whether the author was actually one of these two, or whether he only wished to be considered one of them, it is not explicable why in some portions of his work he should have spoken of himself in the first person and without a name; in others, on the contrary, in the third person and with mention of the name; for he would thus have done all in his power to distinguish himself from a Silas and a Timothy, and to lead aside from the true state of the case the reader to whom he wished to make himself known by the *we*. From Timothy in particular he still more distinctly distinguishes himself by xx. 4 f.: συνείπετο δὲ αὐτῷ ἄρχι τῆς Ἀσίας . . . Γάϊος Δερβαῖος καὶ Τιμόθεος, Ἀσιανοὶ δὲ Τυχικὸς καὶ Τρόφιμος. Οὗτοι προελθόντες ἔμενον ἡμᾶς ἐν Τρωάδι. Ἡμεῖς δὲ ἐξεπλεύσαμεν, &c.; the expedient usually resorted to by the adherents of the Timothy hypothesis, i. e. of referring the οὗτοι only to Tychicus and Trophimus, being distinctly prohibited by the words. If the οὗτοι were taken with this restriction, either the names would have to be repeated, or οὗτοι οἱ δύο substituted for the mere οὗτοι.[1] Even in this case one would scarcely think of including in the ἡμεῖς Timothy, who has just been mentioned in the third person. As the words now stand, it is quite impossible. Finally, the phenomenon that the first person originally appears in xvi. 10, vanishes at Philippi in xvi. 17, and reappears at the same place in xx. 5, does not admit of explanation either on the Timothy or on the Silas hypothesis, whether they be extended to the whole book or confined to a portion of it; for Timothy as well as Silas was with Paul both before and in the interval. It is most inexplicable if the entire book should have originated from one of those men or even have been foisted upon them; for if it is already improbable that a memorandum of Silas or Timotheus should have been silent as to the period previous to xvi. 10, or the interval between xvi. 18 and xx. 4, or that the author

[1] In this it makes no difference whether the received text is followed, or whether, with *Lekebusch*, 164 f., the words ἄχρι τῆς Ἀσίας are omitted and preference given to *Lachmann's* reading, οὗτοι δέ.

should have employed it only for the journey from Troas to Philippi, and for the later one from Philippi to Rome, retaining the first person,—the improbability increases on the hypothesis that a Timothy or a Silas, or the person who put himself in their place, should by the strangest arrangement of chance have again found the thread of the personal narration exactly in the place where he had lost it several chapters before. Finally, if Silas or Timotheus were really the author of the Acts, or if either were merely given out as such from the beginning, it would still remain incomprehensible that tradition could name Luke alone as the author; and the same must apply to every other follower of Paul to whom the ἡμεῖς might be referred. Rather does everything conduce to make it appear that from the first Luke alone was named as the author of the Acts. Even the prologue of the two Lukan writings renders it very improbable that they should have appeared anonymously; for who would name to his readers the person to whom he dedicated his book, and yet keep silence respecting his own name? or if the dedication were merely counterfeit, what could be the object of the fiction except to accredit the origin of the book, which could not then be anonymous? Equally does the "we" assume that the reader knew who speaks in the first person; and where, save in the superscription, could that be made known to him? Hence in all probability these already contained the author's name. But then this name can have been none other than that of Luke. It seems unquestionable therefore that at its first appearance our book already gave itself out as a work of Luke.

It is quite another question whether it was really written by this follower of Paul. Its own evidence alone is naturally incapable of proving this; but if such testimony is held to be more reliable than any other, because it appertains to a book of the Christian religion, this very circumstance, far from raising its reliability, is more calculated to diminish it; for it lies in the nature of the thing that the pure historic sense, and with it the dread of literary forgery, should disappear in proportion as the individual is the more exclusively governed by another interest. Experience likewise shows that forgery of writings was especially frequent precisely in the domain of religious literature; and that neither the early Jewish nor the early Christian period in general, nor the writings of our canon in particular, are to be excepted from this rule. Finally, the current reproaches that in this view the "sacred" writers are made deceivers, forgers, &c., scarcely merit refutation; for there is hardly a hope of agreement with anybody who is not yet convinced that it is impossible before examination to pronounce a writer sacred; and who would fain annihilate by moral deterrents unwelcome scientific results without testing them. This is no affair of deception or forgery, but simply a question whether for the currency of his book the author of the Acts pursued a course in which, as can be proved by a number of the most striking examples, he would not at that time and in that society be hindered by the scruples *we* should feel; and which was at that period frequently followed by those whose morality we have no reason to doubt.[1]

Ecclesiastical tradition also is not of the kind to assure us

[1] See more on this in *Baur*, d. Kritiker u. d. Fanatiker, 64 ff., in the Tübingen Theol. Journal, 1846, 304 ff., and in *Köstlin's* remarkable treatise, the Pseudonymous Literature of the Primitive Church, ed. 1851, 149 ff. Further evidence might easily be adduced. Thus, for example, to say nothing of the Alexandrian Jews, we have from the Pythagorean school, so closely connected with Ebionitism and Alexandrian theology, titles and fragments of more than sixty nominally ancient Pythagorean writings, which were almost all supposititious; and such forgeries were deemed so little offensive that, for instance, *Jamblichus*, V. Pyth. 158, 198, expressly extols, as a proof of unselfish piety in the ancient Pythagoreans, that renouncing all personal glory, they ascribed their writings to Pythagoras. In later times also, men of the most undoubted earnestness in moral and religious sentiment have considered as permissible literary deceptions which, strictly speaking, might also be included in the category of forgeries. Thus, in the year 1534, even the scrupulous Farel published a pseudonymous report of his disputation with Fürbity, which in the preface gives itself out as the work of a Catholic notary at Ghent; and, to accredit this imposture, eulogizes Furbity, whom he despised (*Kirchhofer*, W. Farel, I. 182). Respecting the Waldenses, those harbingers of the Reformation, the latest researches have revealed that, to prove the original accordance of their doctrine with that of the Protestants, they permitted themselves manifold transformations and counterfeiting of documents.

with any certainty of the Lukan origin of the Acts. The first testimony in its favour is a full century later than the presumptive date of its composition; its mere existence cannot be proved till about the year 170, and that of the third Gospel cannot be followed up further than Justin and Marcion. Now even if we should assume that both the Gospel and Acts were already in circulation under the name of Luke, there still remains between the death of the Apostle Paul and the first evidence of their existence a period of about seventy years; and it is very likely that at least half, but perhaps also far more than half, of this period is later than the death of Luke and of most of Paul's companions. Hereby we get space enough for the composition and promulgation of pseudo-Lukan writings; and even if these should have been composed only about the year 120, their first use would in all probability be as far removed from the time of their composition as the employment of the pseudo-Ignatian Epistles by the so-called Polycarp from their promulgation; or the quotation of the Clementine Recognitions in Origen from the last revision of that writing. It is, however, by no means necessary that a spurious book should not be used till many years after its origin. To obtain general belief, such a book must, as a rule, be accepted as genuine from the first; and in that case why should it not also be used as genuine?

If we are thus referred to internal criteria for a decision as to the author of the Acts, it becomes a question, Does this book contain things which afford either the negative evidence that it was not composed by Luke, or the positive evidence that it was composed by some one else? In one case, as in the other, we should be obliged to refuse credit to its own testimony; but if, on the contrary, nothing of that kind exists in it, we should have every reason to believe its own declaration and the tradition of the Church. Now of Luke we know no particulars: the only data to which we can trust are what the Acts itself supplies, i.e. that he was supposed to be a companion of Paul. The above question may therefore be narrowed thus: Can our book be derived from a companion of Paul, and especially from one who during the period treated in xvi. 10—18, xx. 4—xxviii. 16, was in closest fellowship with him; or, on the contrary, does it contain traces of being the work of a later period and another author?

The nature of the historical narrative under consideration justifies us in returning a negative answer to the first of these questions. It is indeed not to be expected that a companion of the Apostle should be fully informed as to all the incidents recorded in the Acts. What preceded his alliance with Paul might in a great measure remain unknown to him; and of subsequent occurrences he might have obtained only partial and uncertain information, if he was not personally present; and if he had not from the first the intention of writing a work such as the one before us, he might have neglected to fill up these gaps by supplementary inquiries from Paul and other eye-witnesses. But, nevertheless, this excuse is far from sufficient to account for the historical inaccuracies of our narrative. Any one who had come with Paul to Philippi, and was present at the incident which occasioned his arrest (xvi. 17), could not possibly be so ill informed about the further development of the affair as he must have been if he wrote vers. 22 f., 26—39, in good faith; any one who during the three years between the Apostle's departure from Philippi and his arrival at Rome was in his closest proximity, must have been more than unreliable to record the miracles of the 28th chapter (vers. 7 to 10) and the Roman incidents (xxviii. 17 ff.) in this manner; he must have known that Paul *did not* speak or act and *cannot* have spoken or acted as xxi. 20 ff., xxiii. 6 ff., make him speak and act; he must also have known enough of the discourses of the 22nd and 26th chapters (to pass over the Ephesian speech) not to have made his Apostle speak of his conversion and his sojourn at Jerusalem in a manner so contradictory and unhistorical. Above all, such a person must have been sufficiently acquainted with Paul's principles and conduct to regard as quite incredible the demeanour towards him which our book ascribes to the Jews and Jewish Christians. Sundry other things we can scarcely credit of one of Paul's companions. A man of that period must have been too accurately informed about speaking in tongues (which assuredly was not confined to the Corinthian community) to regard it as the gift of speaking in foreign languages; and he must likewise have been aware, of what at that time was surely known generally, that it was not Peter, but Paul, who first asserted and carried into execution as a recognized principle the right of Gentile conversion. Thus if the book should be derived from a companion of Paul, its unhistorical contents could only be explained for the most part by an intentional fiction.

Now it cannot be positively asserted that a fiction of this kind would have been impossible to one of Paul's companions. We ourselves conjecture in many parts of the Acts an alteration of history in favour of a particular tendency; why, it may be asked, should this have been less possible to a contemporary of the Apostle than to another? In any case, the author of the Acts, apart from his book, is to us an unknown quantity; if in it we find an intentional invention of history, it seems to make no essential difference whether we place its author a few decades sooner or later. It is not, however, the same if one of Paul's comrades alters what he himself experienced for the sake of an unhistorical object; or whether a later person takes the same liberty with material derived from tradition. What we ourselves see and hear impresses itself upon us incomparably more firmly and distinctly than what has merely been related to us by others; of the latter, as a rule, we usually receive only a very vague—of the former, a minutely detailed picture, fixed in the memory with the force of actual vision and the liveliness of personal experience; and although the features of this picture may partially fade subsequently, and require to be refreshed by the imagination, it will still dwell far more profoundly in the recollection than what is merely transmitted to us by a third person. With regard to occurrences which he personally experienced or which he observed in closest proximity, the author of our book, if he recorded them unfaithfully, must have had a much fuller consciousness of the alteration of facts than with respect to those at which he was not present; that which was merely transmitted might far more readily appear to him as fluid material which he considered himself empowered to transform according to dogmatic points of view, and render it the mere vehicle of his ideas, the medium of practical religious objects; for in the Church of that period tradition was generally regarded, not from a purely historical, but from a religious and dogmatical point of view; and if some, by unconscious fabrication of myths, introduced their dogmatic prejudices into the history of the past, others might easily go a step further, and do the same pragmatically for a purpose; without thinking, however, that they were thereby falsifying history; for they were rather narrating it exactly as appeared to them most consonánt to the interests of Christianity and therefore of truth also. This confusion of ideal with historic truth, of dogmatic desires with fact, was not equally easy in the case of what had been personally experienced, for here the greater force of individual recollection necessarily reminded the author more distinctly of the contradiction between his representation and the reality. Now, by all analogy it is more probable that the New Testament writers in their alteration of history, even when pursuing a definite object, did not act with a full consciousness of their proceeding; that they had no clear, conscious design of contravening the real state of the fact; but, void of critical sense and of historical interest, they estimated the value and truth of an historical representation only by its dogmatic character and its religious effect, treating the material transmitted rather in the manner and with the freedom of an artist, though they were very imperfectly aware of the contradiction to actual history into which they stumbled, precisely from a deficiency of the historical sense.[1] As such a transformation of history must have been much more possible to a person standing afar off than to an eye-witness, it is from this side incomparably more likely that our author was a later personage than that he was a companion of the Apostle Paul.

All this naturally applies in a still greater degree if, instead of Luke, Timothy or Silas is to be made the author of the Acts, since they were in more prolonged and confidential intercourse with Paul than he was. If it is improbable that Luke should have written many things which our book communicates, it is still more improbable that the unhistorical accounts of the journey, xi. 27 ff., of the apostolic council, of the incident at Philippi, should have originated with Silas, or the incredible communication respecting the circumcision of Timothy with himself, not to mention other points which suggest themselves to every one.

Positive indications of the later origin of the Lukan writings are, however, not lacking. The prologue of the Gospel already assumes the existence of an extensive Gospel literature. We are, indeed, too little acquainted with the detailed history of this literature to define with accuracy the date at which a multiplicity of Gospel writings came into existence; still it is not likely that this spread of Gospel histories should belong to a period so early as the apostolic age; first, because a general need of written Gospels would arise only with the gradual extinction of the generation of those immediate disciples

[1] It must, indeed, appear incredible to us that such a self-deception can be possible; but the history of religion and theology in ancient and modern times affords innumerable instances of similar conduct towards material historically transmitted. We need not even take the evidence contained in the history of Mysticism and Gnosticism; neither need we refer to the assertions of older orthodoxy respecting the contents of the Bible, or to interpretations of Scripture in the New Testament and by the Fathers, evident as it is that he who violates the obvious literal sense of Scripture for the sake of a dogmatic interest would not scruple for the same reason to violate tradition in general. Examples are to be found still nearer. Does it require more for a Luke or a John to overlook the difference of their representations from actual history, than when in our own critical age philosophizing orthodoxy has overlooked the contradiction of the theses of Schelling, Hegel, and Schleiermacher, with the maxims of the New Testament?

of Jesus from whose oral tradition instruction was first derived; and, secondly, because the multiplicity of Gospels, with their essentially dogmatic significance, presupposes a multiplicity of dogmatic tendencies, such as could scarcely have been developed so early as the apostolic age, an age divided at first by the simple antagonism of Jewish Christianity and Paulinism. Even Luke himself does not describe his predecessors as the immediate disciples of Jesus, but as those who drew from the tradition delivered by these disciples: "Many have taken in hand to set forth the Gospel history as it was delivered to us by those who were eye-witnesses;" this surely implies that the many narrators were not themselves eye-witnesses. But if many of the post-apostolic generation preceded Luke as authors, we must put himself either in the second, or at the most at the end of the first, generation after the Apostles. We are still more distinctly referred to this later period by Luke's treatment of the eschatological speeches of Jesus. It is true that in these very speeches it has been attempted to find incontrovertible proof that the authors of the first and third Gospels did not write later than the end of the apostolic age.[1] For as, according to Luke xxi. 32, ix. 27, Matt. xxiv. 34, xvi. 28, the coming of Christ was to take place before the end of a generation, these passages and the Gospels concerned must have been written before the result had refuted the prophecy, viz. in the first thirty or forty years after the death of Christ. Baur,[2] however, has convincingly demonstrated that it is by no means necessary to limit γενεὰ, before which the coming was to commence, to a period of thirty or forty years; that this expression also designates the period of human life in its longest duration, a Roman seculum, or a period of from one hundred to one hundred and twenty years; that the passages Luke ix. 27 and Matt. xvi. 28,

[1] The Saxon Anonymus, in his often mentioned letter to *Baur*.

[2] Tübingen Theol. Journal, 1849, 316 ff., to which *Hilgenfeld*, die Evang. Justin's u. s. w., p. 367, and *my* small treatise in the Tübingen Theol. Journal, 1852, 299 f., add some further evidence.

point to this signification by the words τινὲς τῶν ὧδε ἑστώτων; that also at a later date, down to Trajan and Hadrian, the γενεὰ of the contemporaries of Jesus was regarded as not quite extinct; and even though the prophecy, Matt. xxiv. 34, may originally have intended an earlier commencement of the *Parusia*, still nothing hindered an Evangelist writing later from taking it in the widest extent possible. The same scholar has also justly remarked, that the very form of these eschatological speeches in Luke, compared with that in Matthew, places the expectation of a speedy visible return of Christ unmistakably in the background. That the visible *Parusia* itself was foreign to Luke, I should indeed be sorry to say, on account of xxi. 27; but so much the more striking is Luke's procedure towards all the sayings which concern the *proximity* of the Parusia. While in Matt. xvi. 28, it is prophesied that some of those present shall not die, ἕως ἂν ἴδωσι τὸν υἱὸν τοῦ ἀνθρώπου ἐρχόμενον ἐν τῇ βασιλείᾳ αὐτοῦ, in place of this it is vaguely said in Luke ix. 27, ἕως ἂν ἴδωσι τὴν βασιλείαν τοῦ θεοῦ; while Matt. xxvi. 64 makes Jesus declare, ἀπάρτι ὄψεσθε τὸν υἱὸν τοῦ ἀνθρώπου καθήμενον ἐκ δεξιῶν τῆς δυνάμεως καὶ ἐρχόμενον ἐπὶ τῶν νεφελῶν τοῦ οὐρανοῦ, in Luke xxii. 69 he says merely, ἀπὸ τοῦ νῦν ἔσται ὁ υἱ. τ. ἀ. καθήμενος ἐκ δεξιῶν τῆς δυνάμεως τοῦ θεοῦ; on the immediately impending return on the clouds he is silent; very significant, finally, is the metamorphosis in the twenty-first chapter of Luke of the speeches recorded in Matt. xxiv. The very theme of the discussion is given by Luke otherwise than by his predecessor; when Jesus has announced the impending destruction of the temple, the Apostles ask in Matt. xxiv. 3, πότε ταῦτα ἔσται καὶ τί τὸ σημεῖον τῆς σῆς παρουσίας καὶ τῆς συντελείας τοῦ αἰῶνος; Luke v. 7, instead of this second question respecting the Parusia, makes them merely repeat the first in other words, τί τὸ σημεῖον, ὅταν μέλλῃ ταῦτα γίνεσθαι. Accordingly, the answer of Jesus, which in Matthew combines the destruction of Jerusalem and the Parusia as two closely connected events, refers in Luke primarily to the destruction of Jerusalem alone; and while he more distinctly describes this as that which occurred in the year 70, on the other hand he makes the Parusia appear only in the more remote future. In Matthew the prophecy develops itself thus: as a prognostic of the Parusia (ἀρχὴ ὠδίνων, ver. 8), wars and famines, pestilences and earthquakes, and at the same time (τότε, ver. 9) violent persecutions of the Christians, are to be expected, false prophets are to appear, and the gospel is to be preached in all the world, καὶ τότε ἥξει τὸ τέλος (ver. 14). This final catastrophe itself begins with the desecration of the Temple prophesied by Daniel; when that takes place, every one is to flee (ver. 21), for there shall be tribulation such as was not since the beginning of the world, nor ever shall be, a tribulation in which all mankind (πᾶσα σὰρξ) should be destroyed, if its duration were not shortened for the sake of the Christians. But immediately after (εὐθέως μετὰ τὴν θλῖψιν τῶν ἡμερῶν ἐκείνων, ver. 29), the sun and moon shall be darkened, stars shall fall from heaven, and the Messiah shall appear in the clouds. According to Luke's representation, the Christian persecutions (ver. 12), the wars and pestilences, &c., are to occur first; the time of the latter event is not more minutely specified, but, as it seems, is to be further postponed than in Matthew, from the omission of the words, Matt. xxiv. 8 (ταῦτα ἀρχὴ ὠδίνων), and from the interruption of the connection between verses 9 and 10 (where Luke leaves out the γὰρ of Matthew, and inserts in its place τότε ἔλεγεν αὐτοῖς); whereas in Matt. xxiv. 15, the Parusia, as a part of the τέλος, ver. 14, immediately follows the desecration of the Temple; Luke, v. 20, rejecting the words τότε ἥξει τὸ τέλος, merely says, ὅταν δὲ ἴδητε κυκλουμένην ὑπὸ στρατοπέδων τὴν Ἱερουσαλὴμ, τότε γνῶτε, ὅτι ἤγγικεν ἡ ἐρήμωσις αὐτῆς; hereupon follows the injunction to fly, and the description of the time of tribulation as in Matthew; but while the latter had represented the tribulation as universal, it is by Luke referred especially to the Jews,[1] and what

[1] Ver. 23, ἔσται γὰρ ἀνάγκη μεγάλη ἐπὶ τῆς γῆς καὶ ὀργὴ τῷ λαῷ τούτῳ.

immediately ensues is, verse 24, merely the destruction of Jerusalem; after this (instead of the εὐθέως, Matt. xxiv. 28), a considerable time is to elapse until the period of pagan sovereignty has expired (ἄχρι πληρωθῶσι καιροὶ ἐθνῶν, ver. 24), and then, only at an epoch not more minutely specified, the Parusia is to commence, ver. 25 ff. But, that we must not imagine this time too near, the Evangelist has already announced in ver. 8; where, to Matthew's warning against false Messiahs, he also adds a warning against a speedy expectation of the end of the world (πολλοὶ ἐλεύσονται . . . . . . λέγοντες, ὅτι ἐγώ εἰμι καὶ ὁ καιρὸς ἤγγικε). With the same object, he has likewise (xix. 11 ff.) made use of the parable of the talents earlier, when (ver. 11) he ascribes to it the express purpose of refuting the idea of an immediate appearance of the heavenly kingdom, and for this end points out that the ἄνθρωπος εὐγενὴς had gone into a far country.[1] Similarly he makes Jesus, Acts i. 6 f., forestall the notion that the Messianic kingdom was to be expected so soon, by an exhortation to patience. According to all this, he can only have taken the γενεὰ, before the expiration of which all was to be accomplished, in the widest extent of the word, even if he did not at last neutralize this expression by some of those interpretations by which it was subsequently rendered innocuous. At any rate, the precautions are unmistakable which he takes to remove the Parusia of Christ further than Matthew, to separate it from the judicial punishment of Jerusalem, and to make it commence only a considerable time after that event. This presupposes that he did not write till a period from which the destruction of Jerusalem was already somewhat remote, and the necessity could no longer be denied of imagining the end of the world to be separated from it by many years; for this is, in other cases also, the constant course of these eschatological expectations, that their goal is never removed further than to the immediate future, and that it was not till late that the idea of a protracted

[1] See *Baur*, Untersuch. ueber d. Ev. pp. 408 f.

historical development of Christianity upon earth became habitual. Now if it is unmistakable even in Matthew that his apprehension of the eschatological speeches cannot be ascribed to a period either before or immediately after the destruction of Jerusalem, but only to a time when the city had been for a period in the hands of the Romans (for otherwise he would probably have connected the Parusia with the destruction itself, and not with the state of desolation, the βδέλυγμα τῆς ἐρημώσεως, ver. 15), Luke must have written his Gospel still later, when a longer time (καιροὶ, xxi. 24) had elapsed after the fall of the Temple. Therefore, if we do not make the single periods too short, we must go as far the beginning of the second century, or perhaps one or two decades further, for the origin of the Gospel.[1]

In the Acts itself there are two features which chiefly point to a later date for the composition of this book. First, it seems to presuppose the formation of a tradition which cannot belong either to the apostolic age or to the one immediately subsequent; and, secondly, its whole tendency renders probable a more protracted development of the antagonisms which it strives to reconcile. The first of these features is exhibited by the parallel between Paul and the original Apostles. We have already seen that this parallel is not founded on historical fact, but can only be explained by an intentional similarity in the portraiture of the two sides. Herein, indeed, in part of the narratives, the greatest originality is on the Pauline side; the stories of persecutions, iii.—v., probably arose merely from the desire of giving the many sufferings of Paul their counterpart in the primitive Apostles; and in the history of the latter, the narrative of the twelfth chapter is the only persecution transmitted to the author by tradition. Similarly, we may recognize in the conversion of Cornelius only an imitation of the Pauline mission to the Gentiles. Conversely, the Petrine appear to have been the

[1] What *Lekebusch*, p. 423, observes in opposition to this I may leave unanswered.

actual models of the Pauline miracles, for, in the first place, these stories of miracles rather point to the soil of Jewish Christianity, with its craving for wonders; secondly, their Jewish-Christian origin is testified by the accordance with the Petrine Gospel of Mark, in the healing of Tabitha, even if only one of the sources should have been employed; and in the story of Simon Magus, by its connection with the legend of Simon in Justin and the Clementine writings. Neither, judging by his whole tendency, could our author have any interest in inventing Petrine miracles; a superabundance of miraculous works on the part of Paul would rather have been welcome to him as conducive to the glorification of his Apostle; hence, if he records a considerable number of such miracles, there is a presumptive probability that they were presented to him by a Petrine tradition. But this tradition can scarcely have been of early origin. In this respect, let us consider the legend of Simon and the story of the Feast of Pentecost. Out of the actual tongue-speaking occurring in the apostolic age, a speaking in foreign tongues could be derived only at a time when not merely present contemplation, but also living recollection, of such a charism had passed away; or at least when the apostolic age was sufficiently remote to attribute to it a form of the phenomenon essentially different from that of a later period; and this the more, as our author does not make this tongue-speaking appear only at the outpouring of the Spirit at the Feast of Pentecost, but likewise at the conversion of Cornelius and the baptism of the disciples of John. Hence he must have regarded speaking in foreign tongues[1] as the normal form of the charism in the apostolic age. This idea could surely not arise till many years after the end of that period. It is the same with the legend of Simon. We are certainly very ill informed as to the age and origin of this legend; but so much is at any rate extremely probable, that it did not first arise from the passage

[1] That he can only suppose this by the later tongue-speaking has already been observed.

in the Acts, whose literary history alone forces this assumption upon us. Even if the last reviser of the Clementine Recognitions employed our book, this is yet not probable of the anti-Pauline author of the Homilies, and still less of the originator or originators of those writings which form the basis of the Homilies as well as of the Recognitions. But that the figure of Simon Magus was not wanting to them is beyond doubt. In Justin's account also there is not a single feature which would point to the Acts as its authority; and in the Acts itself we could only explain the acceptance of the story of Simon if the author found it pre-existing in Jewish-Christian tradition. Finally, if our earlier conjecture respecting the origin and signification of this legend has any foundation, we must suppose that it was already diffused among the Ebionites generally, and perhaps also contained in documents, when our author was induced to take them into account. But such development of a legend always requires a considerable time; and as its origin is not credible much earlier than towards the end of the apostolic age, this landmark takes us with all probability to the second century for the composition of the Acts.

The whole tendency of our book also refers it to a later stage of ecclesiastical development. Such a premeditated attempt to mediate between the parties in the Church was scarcely possible until after they had measured themselves with each other for some time, had worked out the points in dispute to a clear consciousness, and had begun to recognize the importance of those they held in common. This at least is the general course of these party negociations. At first the antagonism of tendencies is most strongly emphasized, the points of accordance are placed in the background; and when the antagonisms are gradually blunted, only with the lapse of time, common objects and postulates appear more distinctly, conciliatory definitions are sought, and proposals of peace and concessions made by both sides. So we must also picture to ourselves the course of the remarkable party conflict in the primitive Christian Church; nor are we entirely destitute of vouchers for the correctness of this idea. How harshly are the parties opposed to each other at the beginning, notwithstanding the convention at Jerusalem! How little as yet is there any question of mutual concessions, when, on one side, Paul without restriction rejects the whole principle of Jewish Christianity, as well as the enduring validity of the Law, and denies to all who still adhere to Law and circumcision any share in the Christian kingdom of the Messiah (Gal. iii. 10, v. 2 ff.); when, on the other side, the party of James refuse to recognize the uncircumcised as fellow-believers (Gal. ii. 11 ff.); when the same party, as we see from the Epistles to the Corinthians, would not allow the Apostle of the Gentiles to rank as an Apostle at all; when the Apostle John in the Revelation (ii. 3) describes the Pauline custom of eating sacrificial meat and the transgression of the Mosaic marriage laws (the πορνεία) as a doctrine of devils, under the most odious names! No Christianity in Judaism is the counter-sign on one side; no Christianity out of Judaism on the other; and although this latter principle is moderated in the Revelation, nay, even in the compact at Jerusalem (Gal. ii. 9), so far that the fact of Gentile conversion is acknowledged (Rev. vii. 9 ff.); converted Gentiles must nevertheless be all the more bound to the customs of the wider proselytism (abstinence from sacrificial flesh and from πορνεία), and the Jewish-Christians alone are recognized as the actual stock of the Christian theocracy (Rev. vii. 1 ff., xiv. 1). We find a somewhat greater approximation of the two parties already in the Epistle to the Hebrews and the Epistle of James,[1] but their opposition nevertheless still appears distinctly in the foreground; and while in the Acts a peaceable co-existence is suggested to the parties, even there each makes the attempt to exclude the other, notwithstanding a partial acquiescence in their ideas.[2] It is the same with the

[1] See *Schwegler*, Nach-apost. Zeit. ii. 315 ff., i. 444 f.

[2] At any rate, it cannot be supposed that on the destruction of Jerusalem the Jewish Christians had abandoned their nationality to take the side of the Gentile Christians (*Lechbusch*, p. 167), that from that time forth the greater number of them should have renounced the observances of the Law and circumcision, as it is still

so-called Epistle of Barnabas in its relation to Jewish Christianity. Now it cannot be positively asserted that a conciliatory writing like the Acts must necessarily be later than that which upholds a party standpoint more rigidly; but if in the Acts we find not only a general attempt to mediate between the parties, but at the same time perceive that a main point of conflict in earlier times, the dispute about faith and works, is passed over with scarcely an allusion, and everything reduced to the practical question of the enduring validity of the Mosaic Law and the admissibility of Gentile conversion, it is probable that this book belongs to a period in which the importance of the dogmatic antagonism between Paulinists and Judaists had already fallen into the background. And by the earnestness with which the contrast between faith and works is still discussed in the Epistle to the Hebrews and the Epistle of James, this seems to have taken place, not *before*, but probably only some time *after*, the commencement of the second century.

Several smaller features seem to be derived from the same period. I have already shown that the short and vague description of the Ephesian heresiarchs, xx. 29 f., coincides with the descriptions elsewhere of the heretics of the second century. Attention has already been drawn in another place [1] to the fact that Stephen's expectation, vii. 59, of being with Christ immediately after his death points to the ideas of the second century, according to which it was supposed to be a martyr's prerogative to spend the time before the resurrection, not in the lower, but in the upper Paradise; in other cases, at least, our author makes even the righteous enter only into the lower Paradise in Hades, Luke xvi. 22 ff. Several features, however, deserve special

often assumed without any historical proof. In this case, how could strict Judaism in A.D. 150 have the importance which is exhibited in the Clementine writings and in Justin? how could the polemics of the Epistle of Barnabas and the Epistle to Diognetus have been still possible, to say nothing of other points which are to be found in *Schwegler's* Post-Ap. Age, and in *Baur's* Christianity of the First Three Centuries, pp. 77 ff.?

[1] Tübingen Theol. Journal, 1847, 402 ff.

attention as indicating the commencement of an hierarchical constitution. Among these is the expression, i. 17, employed respecting the traitor Judas, ἔλαχε τὸν κλῆρον τῆς διακονίας ταύτης, i. e. in case this designation of the apostolic office takes into consideration the idea of the spiritual office as an ecclesiastical institution; and that this is really the case is the more probable, as in ver. 20 the apostolic office is also designated ἐπισκοπή; for from the passage, Ps. cix. 8 (τὴν ἐπισκοπὴν αὐτοῦ λάβοι ἕτερος), it is here proved that a successor to the betrayer must be chosen. Yet the apostolic office is not an ἐπισκοπή merely in a general sense, inasmuch as the leadership of the Christian community falls on the Apostles; but more definitely, so far as it is considered the prototype of the episcopal office in the Church, and essentially identical with it. From this standpoint also the narrative, viii. 14, seems to be constructed, according to which the Samaritans baptized by Philip received the Holy Ghost only by the laying on of hands by the Apostles; for although the custom that bishops alone can bestow confirmation on the baptized, cannot be traced with certainty prior to the time of Cyprian, it is nevertheless quite credible that in Jewish-Christian tradition, to which by several tokens the thing belongs, it was already connected with the episcopal tendencies which came into existence at a very early period. If, at least, in the διαμαρτυρία Ἰακώβου (ii. 3, 5), and in the Epistle of Peter to James before the Clementine Homilies (two documents, the great antiquity of which Hilgenfeld has justly recognized),[1] the episcopal constitution is taken for granted, and James is treated as the first bishop, and if the same thing was also, according to Hegesippus (b. Eus. K. G. iv. 22, 2), an Ebionite tradition, it cannot be at all strange to find in the same circle a narrative which, as here, demonstrates the superiority of the episcopal dignity by its apostolic prototype. With less probability, the apostolic council (xv.) may be regarded as an imitation of the synodical institution, for the antiquity of synods

[1] Clement. Recog. and Homil. pp. 26 ff. Theol. Jahrb. 1854, 490 ff.

cannot be traced so far up; and, moreover, this so-called apostolic council is not an assembly of heads of churches, but an assembly of the church of Jerusalem; on the other hand, the commanding position which is here attributed to the Jerusalemites, as opposed to Paul and the Gentile Christians, especially in ver. 28, expresses the idea of an apostolic college and its authority, which is obviously unhistorical, and cannot belong to a very early period.[1] That, moreover, the visible endeavour of the Acts to rebut the political charges against Christianity presupposes conditions of the time of Trajan or the following age, has been acutely observed by Schwegler.[2]

Now if all these tokens render it probable that our book did not come into existence before the beginning, and perhaps scarcely before the second decade, of the second century, there are, on the other side, several reasons which forbid us to put the date of its composition too far down. The Acts points, by its whole tendency, to a time when ecclesiastical development still turned on the antagonism of Paulinism and Judaism, which had not yet been forced into the background by any wide-spread conflict; to the time which preceded the agitation roused by Gnosticism. Although Gnosticism itself is in one aspect extreme Paulinism, and in so far the transactions of the Gnostic period are a continuation of the earlier dispute between Pauline and Jewish Christianity, the original character of Paulinism is, nevertheless, so essentially altered, that from the time of its more general influence in the Church different points of dispute from the earlier ones appear in the foreground, and the old controversy about the validity of the Mosaic Law gets an essentially

[1] *Lekebusch*, indeed, p. 425, considers it, just on account of this passage, quite "glaring" (eklatant) that the Acts cannot be a production of the second century, for otherwise this share in the decisions would not have been conceded to the Church; but the self-government of the communities was until the middle of the second century far greater than is usually supposed; even the Ignatian Epistles only require that it should be restricted in favour of the episcopal power; they do not yet assume this restriction as a fact. The Acts seem to originate with the same Church as these Epistles.

[2] Nach-ap. Zeit. ii. 119; comp. pp. 14 ff.

new phase by the Gnostic distinction between the God of the Jews and the Supreme God. Of this phase of the party conflict the Acts does not yet contain any distinct trace. Even the legend of Simon, in its later form the most decided reflex of the dispute with Gnosticism, is not yet here; the verdict on Simon (viii. 10), that he is ἡ δύναμις θεοῦ ἡ μεγάλη, does not compel us to go beyond the idea of a divine emanation, after the manner of angels, or to distinguish the God, whose organ the sorcerer is supposed to be, from the God of the Jews. The doctrine of divine powers was, however, widely spread since the time of Philo, and might have found admittance into Samaritan theology as early as the first century; from divine powers also Cerinthus derived the creation of the world and the delivery of the Law, yet without meaning to overstep the limits of Judaism; and, like other Ebionites, he made the highest of these divine powers descend at the baptism of Jesus. We should be obliged to seek the same idea of the Messiah in the statement about Simon, if, with Ritschl,[1] we were to suppose that Simon was a Samaritan pseudo-Messiah; but even were he no historical person, but merely the mythical representative of a particular opinion, there is nothing in the announcements of the Acts that would refer us for this to the more highly developed Gnosticism, which he certainly is made to represent in Justin and the Clementine writings.[2] Much rather, if a further manifestation is still to be regarded in the formation of the tradition presented in the Acts outside Paul and Paulinism, against which it was originally directed; might those precursors of Gnosis who had not yet advanced as far as the later distinction of the highest

[1] Ensteh. d. altkath. Kirche, 161 f.

[2] Even the description, Rec. i. 72 (referring, according to *Hilgenfeld*, Clem. Recog. and Hom. pp. 105 f., and *Ritschl*, pp. 158 f., to the Basilidian Gnosticism), is distinguished from that of the Acts by the very feature which constitutes peculiar Gnosticism. Simon here asserts, *se esse virtutem summam excelsi Dei, qui sit supra conditorem mundi.* As to the rest, one might ask, after our earlier discussions, whether the (otherwise unimportant) difference of this passage from the other representations of Simon in the Recognitions and Homilies is not to be traced merely to the use of the Acts?

God from the Creator of the world, be the very phenomenon in question. A second passage, too, which in itself might apply to the Gnostics, xx. 30, sounds much too general to make such reference necessary; and therefore our book is altogether without any definite notice of actual Gnosticism. Hence, although at the date at which the Acts was written Gnosticism may perhaps have already begun its career, it is improbable that it had as yet arrived at any great importance in that part of the Church from which our book proceeds; and as we know that it had already done so at Rome, the probable birthplace of the Acts, before the year 140, we cannot well go further than A.D. 130 for the composition of the Acts.

This is also evident from another side. In Acts xv. the Jewish Christians demand the unconditional adoption of Judaism by the Gentile Christians; while, on the contrary, itself gives the decision that they only required of the Gentile Christians the observance of the proselyte laws, whereas the Jewish Christians were continuously bound to the Law and to circumcision. If this representation, according to all we have seen, is derived, not from the history of apostolic times, but from the circumstances and requirements of the time in which our book originates, it follows that at that period not only must the claims of the Jewish-Christian party as a whole, but the importance of the party itself must have been so great that they had some prospect of succeeding with their claims, and a Paulinist had reason to believe that the recognition of an independent Gentile Christianity could not be purchased by smaller concessions than those suggested in our book. But these conditions we find altered, not only in and after the middle of the second century, when, as it is known, the Clementine writings themselves renounce the circumcision of Gentile Christians, but even at the time when Justin wrote his Dialogue with Trypho they had ceased to exist in this manner. In chapter xlvii. of that work, it is asked whether he can be saved who believes in Christ, yet still adheres to the Law? To this Justin replies, that such a Jewish Christian may be saved, inasmuch as he does not presume to enforce Law and circumcision on Gentile Christians, and deny salvation to those who do not observe them; although it is nevertheless a proof of narrow-mindedness (τὸ ἀσθενὲς τῆς γνώμης) to wish to observe, as a Christian, the commands which Moses gave to the people because of their hardness of heart. On the other hand, those were also to be rejected who broke off all communion with Jewish Christians. But as regards the Gentile Christians who, in the sense of the strict Jewish Christians, acquiesced in the acceptance of Judaism, they *might perhaps* be saved (σωθήσεσθαι ἴσως ὑπολαμβάνω). It is impossible to mistake the fact that the position of the parties is here different from what it is in the Acts. The claim of circumcision upon the Gentile Christians appears already in Justin to be confined to a decided minority in the Church; the strict exclusive Jewish Christianity which raised this claim is on the point of being separated from the Church as heretical; for Justin says, not only that he rejects this opinion, but he wishes salvation to be deemed dependent on the recognition of the uncircumcised Gentile Christians, and consequently he does not allow this exclusive Jewish Christianity to be reckoned as real Christianity. Even the more moderate Jewish Christianity, which limits itself to the observance of the Law, the very object demanded by the Acts in the resolutions of its council, can no longer in the time of Justin have embraced the majority in the Church, or at least in the Roman church (to which both these books belong); when even this Father, so nearly akin to Ebionitism, treats it merely as a form of bigotry to be tolerated within the Church. It is evident that, as compared with the Acts, the liberation of Christianity from Judaism had made an important step in advance. The same Jewish Christianity which the Acts assumes to be predominant, we see in Justin reduced to a minority, now scarcely able to maintain itself in the Church; that to which the Acts aspires as the most that can be obtained by the opposite side, already begins its retreat into the attitude of a party merely tolerated.[1] If this was the state of parties in A.D. 150, when the Justinian Dialogue was written, a book proceeding on the historical premisses of the Acts must have been written considerably earlier; and if it was in all probability Gnosticism which primarily decided the victory over strict Judaism, silenced the objections of the Judaists to an independent Gentile Christianity by its dangerous onslaught, and caused their alliance with their former opponents,—the datum compels us to place the composition of the Acts earlier than the conflict of the Roman church with Gnosticism; so that on this side also, about the year 130 results as the ultimate date beyond which we cannot transfer it. Much rather, if we consider how great is the difference between the state of the parties assumed in the Acts and that of Justin's time, is it probable that it was written some years before the last date, somewhat betwixt 110 and 125 A.D.

The date of its composition might be more precisely defined if we possessed more exact information about several other writings in the New Testament. As the third Gospel was, according to all appearance, used by the second and fourth, the limits between which its composition must fall might be fixed, and hence also approximately the age of the Acts, did we but know

[1] I am so far unable to agree in *Ritschl's* opinion (Tübingen Theol. Journal, 1847, 298) when he attempts to prove that the position of the parties was quite the same in Justin and in the Acts; I must rather consider *Schwegler* quite right in saying (Nach-ap. Zeit. ii. 118) that Justin already admits what the Acts seeks. Nay, I must extend the difference still further than *Schwegler*. When *Ritschl* elsewhere endeavours to show that the Acts altogether presupposes a tolerably advanced intermixture of the Pauline and Jewish-Christian parties, this assertion must be essentially limited on the basis of our book itself. The reconciliation of the parties must indeed have already commenced, if a book such as the Acts could have any effect, or indeed if its existence were possible; but it cannot have advanced to the point aimed at by the author, otherwise he would not have been obliged to labour for this object at the cost of so many expedients. In truth, with regard to the laws for proselytes imposed on the Gentile Christians in Acts xv., *Ritschl* (pp. 301 f.) is obliged to adopt the supposition that the author found this verdict already in existence on the side of the Jewish Christians, and employed the datum without comprehending it, which surely no one will think credible in such a turning-point of the whole book.

from what period the above-named books are derived. But this is no more certain with them than with the two books of Luke; we must, therefore, renounce the hope of gaining anything here for the present investigation. For the same reason we forbear to point out that relation of the Gospel of Luke to the rest. Besides the Epistle to the Hebrews and the Epistle of James, to which we have already alluded, and the genuine Pauline Epistles, which do not come into consideration here, the Acts itself, in its whole tendency, comes into contact especially with the first Epistle of Peter and the last two chapters of the Epistle to the Romans.[1] But the date of *their* origin also is not a whit more certain than that of the Acts; and their relations to the latter would thus enable us to infer only a relative date, which would be of little use. It may therefore be observed only incidentally that the first Epistle of Peter does not appear to me, according to Schwegler's theory, older, but younger than our book; for, in the first place, considering its compilatory character, the passages in which it coincides with the Epistle to the Ephesians and the Epistle of James are to be explained by its having made use of these Epistles, and not the converse; secondly, it takes for granted, ver. 13, the legend of Peter's presence at Rome, which the Acts would surely have noticed, one way or the other, had the author found it already in existence.

According to all these indications, we shall assign the origin of the Acts with most probability to the second or third decade of the second century. The absence of any indication capable of guiding us naturally renders it impossible to state the name of the author; but neither will any one who clearly comprehends the task, the conditions, and the limits of an investigation of this nature, require such a discovery either in this or in any kindred case.[2] On the other hand, it seems possible to fix with

[1] See *Schwegler*, Nach-ap. Zeit. ii. 2 ff.; *Baur*, Paul. 398 ff.; Tübingen Theol. Journal, viii. 493 ff. More on this later.

[2] As *Schwanbeck* does, pp. 125, 151, and likewise the Saxon Anonymus, p. 24 of his letter to *Baur*.

comparative certainty the locality in which it was written. As, for writings like ours, in addition to their general destination for the collective Christian Church, special local occasions may be conjectured; it is probable, *a priori*, that the birthplace of such a book will betray itself by its reference to a particular community or national church. Now there are altogether four places which appear in the Acts with special importance; in the accounts of the primitive community, Jerusalem; in the history of Paul and Gentile Christianity, Antioch, Ephesus, and Rome; whereas Corinth, notwithstanding its importance in the cause of Christianity, is treated with striking brevity. When dealing with the origin of our book, Jerusalem cannot be thought of, not merely because this city soon loses its independent importance in our account, but far more because the Greek language could proceed from Jerusalem as little as the Pauline contents. Antioch also, although for a time the principal seat of Gentile Christianity and of the Gentile mission, appears on the whole too much a point of transition to allow us to believe our book to be specially designed for the church there. It is the first station on the way of the Apostle who conquered the Roman Empire for Christianity, but it is not his goal; and even if among the sources of the Acts one should have come from Antioch, nothing indicates that the whole of it was calculated for Antioch or for any part of the Syrian church. The case seems to be the same with Ephesus. But as the theory that the Lukan writings originated in Asia Minor, and in Ephesus in particular, has recently found an ingenious advocate in Köstlin,[1] we must enter more minutely on this possibility.

Köstlin appeals in behalf of his theory first to tradition, inasmuch as the composition of the Gospel was universally ascribed to the east of the Roman Empire,[2] and the earliest traces of its existence lead to Asia Minor. However, no ancient writer names Asia Minor in particular as the place in which the Gospel

[1] Ursprung u. Comp. d. synopt. Ev. 294 ff.

[2] Evidences in *Credner*, Int. 151, 128; *De Wette's* Int. to the N. T. 190 f.

originated; but Oriental manuscripts and translations name Alexandria: Gregory of Nazianzus, Jerome and Isidore, Achaia. But what avails the testimony of writers of whom it may be assumed that they did not set out with historical knowledge, but with local wishes or learned conjectures; some with the conjecture that the book which, as was supposed, was first mentioned from Corinth (Rom. ii. 16; comp. xvi. 1), was also composed there; others with the hypothetical identity of Luke with the Alexandrian author of the Epistle to the Hebrews, or with the ambitious efforts of Alexandrian theologians to claim for their church the Pauline as well as the Petrine Gospel.[1] It would be of far greater importance if it could be really demonstrated that Luke's Gospel was first used in Asia Minor. We are absolutely ignorant whether Marcion possessed it already in his own country, or first in Rome; whether its elaboration by Marcion occurred sooner or later than its employment by Justin; still less can we assert that it was only after the middle of the second century that, owing to the heretics and Marcion in particular, it was employed in the Church.[2] Moreover, that the fourth Gospel (apparently a product of the church of Asia Minor) made use of our Luke proves the less, as we not only find it used previously by Justin at Rome, but soon after by the Clementine Homilies, and earlier still to an unlimited extent by the author of the canonical Gospel of Mark. Just as well as these could use Luke's Gospel if it came from Asia Minor; or still more easily could the author of the fourth Gospel use it in Asia Minor if it came from Rome. Finally, when Köstlin adduces on his side the multifarious accordance of the Lukan writings with the Epistles to the Ephesians and Colossians, the evidential force of this argument is counteracted by the fact that they may be shown to contain at least as many points of contact with other writings of which Asia Minor is not the home. Köstlin himself (299 ff.) shows

[1] See, respecting the supposed composition of Mark's Gospel at Alexandria, *Credner*, Int. 116.

[2] *Köstlin*, 298.

how nearly allied is the language of the Epistle to the Hebrews to that of Luke; and we must also admit that this affinity is great enough to account for the conjecture of Clement of Alexandria that the style of the Epistle proceeds from Luke; little as it really suffices *to establish* the conjecture, and perverse as it must appear when Clement's hypothesis is warmed up again in these times.[1] The same observation with regard to the Pastoral Epistles led Schott[2] to the conjecture that these works were written by Luke; and although the conclusion was certainly hasty, yet it is impossible to deny the existence of relations between the two, such as to counterbalance those between Luke and the Epistles to the Ephesians and Colossians. With respect to their store of words, they are more nearly allied to the writings of Luke, and especially to the Acts, than are the latter;[3] and in their contents they come into contact with them in some passages in a manner so striking, and so clearly exhibit the standpoint and aims of a later period, that there is every probability of the author's actual acquaintance with the works of Luke, which thereby gain a comparatively ancient testimony in their favour. As Paul in the Acts avows that he endeavours to serve the God of his fathers with a pure conscience, so in the second

[1] *Ebrard*, Exposition of the Epistle to the Hebrews, pp. 426 ff. *Lange*, Ap. Zeit. i. 185. *Köstlin* has excellently refuted both, Tübingen Theol. Journal, 1854, 425.

[2] Isagoge, 324; comp. Tübingen Theol. Journal, 1843, 542.

[3] The Pastoral Epistles contain the following words, which among the books of the New Testament appear only in those of Luke: *ἄνοια, ἀντιλαμβάνεσθαι, ἀχάριστος, βυθίζειν, δρόμος, δυνάστης, ἐκχέειν* (*τὸ πνεῦμα*), *ἐξαρτίζειν, ἐπέχειν, ἐπιμελεῖσθαι, ἐπιπλεῖον, ἐπισκοπὴ*, in the sense of the office of bishop (in another sense also, 1 Pet. ii. 15, v. 6), *ἐπιφαίνειν, εὐεργεσία, εὐσεβεῖν, ζωγρεῖν, ζωογονεῖν, ἱματισμὸς, κακοῦργος, νομοδιδάσκαλος, νοσφίζεσθαι, παγὶς, παιδεύειν, πειθαρχεῖν, περίεργος, περιποιεῖσθαι, πρεσβυτέριον, προδότης, προπετὴς, πυκνὸς, σωματικὸς, σωφροσύνη, φιλανθρωπία, φιλάργυρος*; besides them and the Lukan writings may be found *ἀπωθεῖν* only in Rom.; *ἐφιστάναι*, 1 Thess.; *ἡσυχία*, 2 Thess.; *εὐαγγελιστὴς*, Eph.; *πρεσβύτης*, Philem.; *ἐπίθεσις* (*χειρῶν*), *μαρτυρεῖσθαι*, having a good character, *μεταλαμβάνειν, περιέρχεσθαι, χάριν ἔχειν, δί ἣν αἰτίαν*, Heb.; *βρέφος* and *λυτροῦν*, 1 Pet.; *βλάσφημος* and *εὐσέβεια*, 2 Pet.; *λείπειν*, James; *νομικὸς* in Matt., *παρακολουθεῖν* in Mark, *κατηγορία* in John. The Epistles to the Ephesians and Colossians, not much greater in extent, contain only twelve words of the first, thirteen of the second class. See the Concordance and the Comparison in the Tübingen Theol. Journal, 1843, 509 ff., 505 ff.

Epistle to Timothy does he testify the same thing in similar words;[1] as in Acts iii. 17, xiii. 27, the fury of the Jews is excused by their ignorance (*κατὰ ἄγνοιαν ἐπράξατε*, iii. 17), so in 1 Tim. i. 13, Paul's zeal for persecution (*ἠλεήθην ὅτι ἀγνοῶν ἐποίησα*); as there it is repeatedly intimated that every event occurs at the time appointed by God[2] (i. 7, iii. 19 f., xx. 26), so here also (1 Tim. ii. 6, vi. 15; Tit. i. 3); as there (viii. 14 ff., xix. 6) the gifts of the Spirit are communicated by apostolic imposition of hands, so does Paul (2 Tim. i. 6) remind his disciple that he owes the charism of the Spirit to his imposition of hands. 2 Tim. iii. 11 likewise takes express notice of the persecutions of the Apostle at Antioch, Iconium, and Lystra, recounted in Acts xiii.; as in the speech at Ephesus, Acts xx. 23, it is said, *τὸ πνεῦμα διαμαρτύρεταί μοι, λέγον*, so in 1 Tim. iv. 1 we read, *τὸ πνεῦμα ῥητῶς λέγει*, &c.; and the same speech (ver. 24, *τελειῶσαι τὸν δρόμον μου καὶ τὴν διακονίαν*) seems to have been in the author's mind when he wrote 2 Tim. iv. 5, 7, *τὴν διακονίαν σου πληροφόρησον, ἐγὼ γὰρ ἤδη σπένδομαι . . . τὸν δρόμον τετέλεκα.* That 1 Tim. v. 18 takes Luke x. 7 perhaps into consideration, has already been remarked. These points of contact seem to me at any rate to prove more than those adduced by Köstlin, pp. 295 f., as evidence of a close connection of the writings of Luke with the Epistles to the Ephesians and Colossians. The first Epistle of Peter also, the Roman origin of which we must assert, with Schwegler,[3] as decidedly as its spuriousness, occupies a position at least as near to the Acts as the Epistles to the Ephesians and Colossians. Its peculiar stock of words shows its affinity with that of the Acts and the Gospel of Luke;[4] and its

[1] Acts xxiv. 14, 16: *λατρεύω τῷ πατρῴῳ θεῷ . . . ἐν τούτῳ δὲ αὐτὸς ἀσκῶ ἀπρόσκοπον συνείδησιν ἔχειν πρὸς τὸν θεόν*, &c.; 2 Tim. i. 3: *τῷ θεῷ, ᾧ λατρεύω ἀπὸ προγόνων ἐν καθαρᾷ συνειδήσει.* The *συνείδησις* is also in 1 Tim. i. 5, 19, iii. 9, Titus i. 15.

[2] *Καιροὶ*, a favourite plural in Luke and in the Pastoral Letters; see *Schmidt's ταμιεῖον*, s. v.

[3] Nach-ap. Zeit. ii. 2 ff.

[4] As appears from the review in the Tübingen Theol. Journal, 1843, 522 f., and in *Schulze*, d. schriftl. Character des Johannes, pp. 39 ff.

contents also come into contact with them not unfrequently. As Paul (Acts xvii. 30) designates the heathen age χρόνους τῆς ἀγνοίας, Peter (i. 14) speaks of the previous ἄγνοια of his readers; as the former in Acts (xvii. 23) says of the unknown God of the Athenian altar, ὃν ἀγνοοῦντες εὐσεβεῖτε, so the latter, i. 8, even of the Christian God, ὃν οὐκ εἰδότες ἀγαπᾶτε; as the Acts, xiv. 2, contrasts the πιστεύειν with the ἀπειθεῖν, so the Epistle, ii. 7, iv. 17; as the former, iv. 11 (in imitation of Paul, Rom. ix. 33), applies the passage of Ps. cxviii. 22 to the unbelief of the Jews, so the latter, ii. 7; as Paul endeavours, Acts xxiv. 16, to have συνείδησις ἀπρόσκοπος, so Peter, 1 Pet. iii. 16, comp. ver. 21, enjoins the Christians to preserve their συνείδησις ἀγαθή; as the former, Acts xx. 28, says to the Ephesian elders, προσέχετε ἑαυτοῖς καὶ παντὶ τῷ ποιμνίῳ, ἐν ᾧ ὑμᾶς τὸ πνεῦμα τὸ ἅγιον ἔθετο ἐπισκόπους, ποιμαίνειν τὴν ἐκκλησίαν τοῦ κυρίου, so does Peter write, v. 2, to the elders, ποιμάνατε τὸ ἐν ὑμῖν ποίμνιον τοῦ θεοῦ . . . τύποι γινόμενοι τοῦ ποιμνίου. The κλῆροι likewise, 1 Pet. v. 3, recall the κλῆρος of the apostolic office, Acts i. 17, 25; and the whole development of the episcopal constitution which the Acts, xx. 17, 28, takes for granted, appears to be the same as in 1 Pet. v. 1 f., comp. ii. 25.

The result is, that the writings whose origin is probably attributable to Asia Minor, are no more nearly allied with the Lukan books than those composed at Rome or Alexandria. Equally little is the comparative purity of their Greek an argument for their being the productions of countries where Greek alone was spoken.[1] For they scarcely possess this advantage to a higher degree than the writings of Justin and the Clementine Homilies, of which the Roman origin is established; and it is difficult to see why good Greek could not be written at Rome. Probably only a minority of the Roman Christians at that time were of Roman extraction; and even if our book was written at Rome, its author may nevertheless have belonged to the East by birth and education. The same supposition would also explain the fact that the author seems, as Köstlin observes, pp. 294 f.,

[1] As *Köstlin* believes, 294.

to be so well informed respecting the political relations of Asia Minor and Achaia, and that he treats the Apostle's sojourn at Ephesus with a preference which certainly contrasts remarkably with the cursory mention of his Corinthian ministry, that he has so many particulars to relate from Ephesus, that Paul, according to him, leaves his last legacy to the Gentile Christian communities in the hands of the Ephesian elders, and pays especial attention in it to the future prospects of the Ephesian church. The nature of his authorities might, however, have occasioned the more detailed treatment of the Ephesian events; and the valedictory speech, at any rate, found an appropriate position where Paul oversteps the limits of his former sphere of labour, never again to touch it.

The reasons adduced must not therefore determine us to attribute the origin of our book to Asia Minor. Much rather does everything conduce to testify its Roman parentage. A book which, with such obvious purpose, is laid out to influence the Roman community, which considers the foundation of this community to be the peculiar and divinely-ordained goal of the Pauline ministry, making Paul, only at Rome, break off definitively with Judaism and appear in the full vocation of Apostle to the Gentiles, which ignores even the pre-existence of the Roman community merely to make Paul its actual founder—such a book was scarcely written elsewhere than in the place for which it was primarily intended, i.e. at Rome. That it records nothing more of the Apostle's sojourn there[1] can prove nothing to the contrary. For its whole scheme excludes a minute account: in Paul's arrival and unrestricted ministry at Rome its object was attained, and the author might be the less disposed to enter on its further course, as he would have been obliged to record the Apostle's end, which he wished to pass over, perhaps from the same motive as he does a great part of his other sufferings. If the conclusion of our book is nevertheless at first sight somewhat strange, it is still more difficult of explanation on every other

[1] *Köstlin*, 294.

supposition than on the hypothesis that it was originally designed for Roman readers. For them, the foundation of the Roman community by the Apostle of the Gentiles was a more satisfactory termination of the narrative; whereas every one with whom this local interest did not come into play must have inquired after the subsequent fate of the Apostle. Precisely at Rome the conditions for the origin of a work like the Acts existed in a special degree. How strong even at an early period were the Judaistic party and the prejudice against Paul, we may ascertain from the Epistle to the Romans, which was intended to allay this very prejudice; and that the same circumstances still continued after the Apostle's death, we see from all that is known to us of the state of the Roman church till after the middle of the second century. If the Judaistic element was at that time powerful enough, in spite of all history, to exalt Peter by a legend universally believed to be the joint founder, and afterwards even *the first* founder and bishop of the Roman church; if from the soil of this church during the course of the second century the luxuriant pseudo-Clementine literature was produced; if the Roman theologian Justin entirely ignores the great Apostle of the Romans; if the author of the appendix to the Epistle to the Romans anxiously excuses Paul for the boldness of his writing to the Romans, and denies any claim on his part to doctrinal authority among the Romans; if the Pauline author of the first Epistle of Peter is only able to shield the doctrine of his Apostle under the name of Peter at Rome (ver. 13); if the Ebionite Hegesippus (in Eus. iv. 22, 3) bears testimony to the church of his time of its orthodoxy in the Jewish Christian sense (ὡς ὁ νόμος κηρύττει καὶ οἱ προφῆται καὶ ὁ κύριος),—the aversion to Paul and Pauline Christianity must have been so deeply rooted at Rome till far into the second century that a Paulinist, anxious for a reconciliation of party antagonisms, might well be induced to write a book like the Acts. To this must be added that the first traces of the employment of the Lukan writings point to Rome: Justin and the Clementine

Homilies, Mark's Gospel and the Pastoral Epistles; Polycarp's letter also seems to have been written here, in which a passage from the Acts is definitely used for the first time; of Marcion alone we do not know whether he first compiled his Gospel at Rome, or earlier. Although from this alone, owing to the deficiency of our knowledge of the earlier promulgation of the New Testament books, we could not conclusively infer the Roman origin of the Acts, yet the testimony of internal reasons is confirmed by this accordance of the historical traces of its existence.

Hence we regard our book as the work of a Paulinist of the Roman church, most probably composed between the years 110 and 125, or perhaps 130, after Christ. But of course it does not at all follow that its entire contents were derived from this period. We have therefore still to inquire how far more ancient sources make this probable.

Third Division.

THE SOURCES OF THE ACTS.

The hypothesis that the author of the Acts made use of more ancient writings or essays is suggested by the prologue of the Gospel, and it has also so much support in the internal constitution of the book, that we cannot be surprised that it has been universally approved by the moderns. All the more widely are opinions divided as soon as these sources are to be stated in detail, and the manner of their employment defined. Conjecture has played freely with reference to both; and from the theory of single scattered notes to that of connected books, from the hypothesis of an entirely free employment to that of a verbal transcript of the sources, scarcely a possibility exists which has not been defended by one critic or another. In what follows we shall attempt to test the arguments on which a decision depends, without, however, being able to enter on all the individual opinions hitherto entertained.

If the older ideas of the constant eye-witness of Luke or the indirectly apostolic origin of the Acts have been abandoned, there will, in the first instance, be an inclination to attribute to different sources the larger masses into which the book at first sight divides itself. In this manner Riehm[1] first endeavoured to carry out the hypothesis that the second part of our book, from xiii., rests essentially on ocular testimony and verbal information, and only with regard to the speeches not heard by Luke, and the letters in xv. and xxiii., on written authorities; whereas the first twelve chapters are almost entirely founded on single small essays collected by the author. Still more sharply does Gförer's[2] kindred opinion distinguish between the two parts. According to this critic, the first twelve chapters are a collection of chiefly unhistorical legends arranged by a zealous Petrinist, and adopted, essentially unaltered, by the author of the Acts; only the speech of Stephen is a verbally, or nearly verbally, genuine document; the last sixteen chapters, on the contrary, are a pure historical record really derived from Luke, the companion of Paul; the link between the two was but incompletely patched by the compiler of the Acts writing about the year 90 A.D. Schwanbeck also (pp. 34 ff.), in the first instance, wishes to discriminate between two parts of the Acts, which he derives from different sources, only that he extends the first to the beginning of the fifteenth chapter; but in the end this hypothesis is so much modified that it goes beyond the standpoint of Riehm and Gförer. It is still more vaguely approached by De Wette[3] with the observation that in the second part, in addition to the records of eye-

[1] De fontibus Act. Apost. Utr. 1821; comp. especially pp. 106 ff., 189 ff. *Schwanbeck* gives a good and detailed extract from this book, pp. 81 ff.

[2] Die heil. Sage, I. 383—452, especially pp. 417, 421 ff., II. 244 ff.

[3] Int. to the New Testament, § 115 c.

witnesses, further traces of the employment of various authorities are to be found; whereas, on the other hand, the first part has its characteristics, from which may be inferred some sources peculiar to itself. Credner,[1] after the example of Eichhorn,[2] contends for the essential independence of the Acts upon all written sources, and is unable to find any important difference in this respect between the first and second parts.

We must subscribe unconditionally to the latter observation. The first twelve or fourteen chapters of our book are not so profoundly different from the rest, either in contents or in language, as to oblige us to assume the employment of essentially dissimilar authorities for the former more than for the latter. If Gförer abandons the first part as legendary only to maintain the second as purely historical, the last assertion suffers such restrictions from the results of our earlier inquiry that the distinction threatens to disappear entirely; not even in the account of the journey, xvi. 10 ff., have we pure history, still less in other portions, such as the narratives of the apostolic council, the incidents at Philippi, and the conduct of Paul at Jerusalem. Hence, although the last half of the book may contain more real history than the first, this is not equally the case in all its parts, and one cannot, without further distinction, contrast a first and a second part of the Acts, as legend and history. Nor is it possible to demonstrate the linguistic difference of the two parts, on which alone Schwanbeck supports his hypothesis. Schwanbeck's assertion that the first fourteen chapters have the colouring of the Gospel both in language and style, whereas it disappears after the fifteenth chapter,—this assertion, in its sweeping generality, is decidedly incorrect. Schwanbeck (pp. 36 f.), refers for its corroboration to a number of words which occur only in the Gospel and the first part, while in the second they are either wanting entirely or are used less frequently. But even if he had cited many more, as he incontestably might have done, it would still

[1] Int. to the N. T. p. 107.

[2] Int. to the N. T. II. 30 ff.

have proved nothing. Among those words only which occur but once in the Acts, I have counted a hundred and seventy-four which exist in the Gospel also. Of these, little more than half (ninety-three) appear in the first fourteen chapters; but even if a long list were made of them, it proves nothing whatever, because a nearly equal number of other words are opposed to them, which are common to the Gospel and the second half of the Acts; and others which are wanting in the Gospel, occur equally in the two parts of the Acts. The case is the same with those expressions which have greater weight by reason of their more frequent occurrence. It may certainly seem strange that, for instance, οὐρανὸς exists in the Gospel and the first half of the Acts together (actually only i.—xi.) sixty times, in the second half of the Acts only twice; ὅσος, Gospel ten times, Acts ii.—xv. seventeen times, and henceforth no more; ἐξιστάναι and ἐξίστασθαι, Gospel three times, Acts ii.—xii. eight times, then no more; also ἔκστασις, three times in the first part, in the second only xxii. 17, &c.; but we must nevertheless have great scruples in concluding much from this, when we see that with other words and idioms the converse position exists. Thus ἐργασία, in the Gospel once, in the last fourteen chapters of the Acts four times; στάσις, there twice, here five times; ἀκριβῶς, testified as Lukan by the prologue of the Gospel, in these chapters, which also alone have ἀκριβὴς and ἀκρίβεια five times; ἀξιοῦν, Gospel once, second half of Acts twice; διασώζειν, there once, here five times; the impersonal δοκεῖ, there twice, here five times; in the first fourteen chapters these words are entirely wanting. Ἄξιος, frequent in the Evangelist (eight times), exists in the Acts, which has it seven times, only after the thirteenth chapter; ἔθος, in the Gospel three times, in the second part of the Acts six times, stands only once in the first; likewise ἐπιλαμβάνεσθαι, which occurs five times in the Gospel, six times in the second part of the Acts; μένειν appears in the Gospel seven times, Acts, second part, twelve times; πράσσειν, Gospel six times, Acts, second part, eleven times; the first part of the Acts has each of these words twice only. The πνεῦμα δαιμονίου, Luke iv. 33, corresponds with the πνεῦμα πύθωνος, Acts xvi. 17; the τίς ἐστιν οὗτος ὅς, Luke v. 21, vii. 49, with the τίς ἐστιν ὅς, Acts xix. 35, xxiii. 19; the exclamation αἶρε, besides Luke xxiii. 18, stands also in Acts xxi. 36, xxii. 22; μὴ φοβοῦ, without any accusative object, several times in Luke, in Acts xviii. 9, xxvii. 24; λατρεύειν νύκτα καὶ ἡμέραν, besides Luke ii. 37, only in Acts xxvi. 7; αὐτῇ τῇ ὥρα, in the Gospel frequently, Acts only xvi. 18, xxii. 13; τῇ ἐχομένῃ, besides Luke xiii. 33, only in Acts xx. 15, xxi. 26. Still further evidence may be found in our previous disquisitions on the language of the Acts. In the same manner, the other parallelisms between Luke and the Acts apportion themselves pretty evenly in all parts of the latter. If to this we add, that the similarity of the language in the two parts is incomparably greater than the dissimilarity, and that both coincide (even in deviations from the Gospel) in very striking peculiarities, such as the use of τε and ὁμοθυμαδὸν, there will probably be little left of their supposed difference of style but the mere general fact, acknowledged for instance even by Credner (Int. p. 282), that the language in the first part has a somewhat more Hebraistic colouring than in the second. Neither does an examination of the contents lead us further. The accumulated apparitions of angels in the first part (v. 19, viii. 26, x. 3, xii. 7, 23) constitute the sole important difference; for the second part knows of only one, of which moreover it is not quite certain whether it should not be regarded as a mere dream-vision. Even this feature also is reducible to the Hebraistic character of the description, for the interposition of an angel in a higher revelation is peculiar to later Judaism in particular; as is shown already in the Revelation of John and the other Apocalyptic literature. Whether this Hebraistic tone of the first part positively indicates the use of special Hebraistic sources is very doubtful. It is also possible that the author of our book possessed sufficient powers of imitation to approach the Hebraistic mode of thought and expression more nearly in narratives relating to Jewish soil, or that they were generally familiar to him from the gospel-tradition of Jewish Christianity, and fall into the background in the later portions of his work only because he employed special authorities for these. The first two chapters of Luke's Gospel have likewise a remarkable amount of Hebraism in language, in mode of representation, and in thought; in them also angels play a large part (see i. 11, 26, ii. 9); yet the uniform linguistic character of these chapters, so strikingly harmonizing with the like peculiarities of Luke, renders it highly probable that they are derived, as they lie before us, from the author of the Gospel, although he may have had a more ancient tradition before him. How the case may be in this respect with the first part of the Acts cannot be ascertained by an *a priori* assumption, but only by an examination of details. In this, however, we have no right, without more ado, to mass the first twelve or fourteen chapters into a "first part" of the Acts. For how do we know beforehand that these chapters in particular belong to one category with regard to their origin? Perplexity is occasioned in this respect even by the difference in the position of the thirteenth and fourteenth chapters, which some reckon in the first and others in the second part; other portions also of the so-called first part differ considerably from the rest. Besides Stephen's speech, of which this is generally admitted, we must here reckon especially the story of Cornelius, a passage occupying a perfectly independent position, and not Judaizing but Paulinist in its tendency; and the account of Paul's conversion, to which it is impossible to ascribe any other source than the almost verbally similar narratives in the twenty-second and twenty-sixth chapters. To proceed historically it is not sufficient to distinguish the leading portions of our book according to their character and sources; but with respect to each individual narrative, inquiry must be made as to its presumptive origin.

Now it is from this very point that Schleiermacher's[1] inves-

[1] Int. to the N. T. p. 314 ff.

tigations on the Acts proceed. As this critic considers the Gospel of Luke and the Gospels in general to have originated in a collection of scattered essays, he regards the Acts also from the same point of view. While he follows up in it the traces of dissimilar narratives, and points out the superfluous repetitions, the discrepancies in sundry details, the fragmentary commencement of various paragraphs, the purposelessness of individual features, the severance of what should be associated, the apparent absence of literary unity and of a settled plan, he arrives at the conclusion that it is compiled from separate narratives, which are supposed to be taken partly from the public documents of individual churches, such as Jerusalem and Antioch, partly from the records of travels by some of Paul's companions, and to have been collected by a later person somewhere about the year 90 A.D. As far as we can ascertain from his lectures, Schleiermacher did not enter on any further inquiry respecting these authorities; or seek to establish the limits at which each begins and ends; or to discover the places or persons to which they belong.

This deficiency Schwanbeck endeavours to remedy. The result of his book on the Sources of the Acts is essentially this: the second part, beginning at xv. 1, is derived from a memorandum by Silas which the compiler of the whole accepted, with some omissions indeed, but otherwise quite verbally; in xv. 3—13 alone, a passage from other sources, the lives of Barnabas and Paul, is intercalated, and some few gaps in the excerpta are filled up with small connecting formulæ. The compiler of the whole made a similar use of a second principal source, a biography of Barnabas, to which Schwanbeck attributes iv. 36 f., ix. 1—30, xi. 19—30, besides xii. 25, xiii. 1—xiv. 28, xv. 2—4. In the speech of Stephen, vi. 8—vii. 59, and viii. 2, he recognizes a third intercalation from an independent source. The rest of the book, i.—vi. 7 (with the exception of iv. 36 f.), viii. (except ver. 2), ix. 11—13, 18, is supposed to be derived from a biography of Peter, the closer examination of which, however, Schwanbeck had reserved for the second part of his book, which had not appeared when, in the year 1848, he first became involved in the work of a publicist, and was afterwards called away by an untimely death.

It is impossible to follow this tissue of hypotheses in all its complexity; meanwhile, the examination of a few decisive points will suffice to test its value. First, as concerns the supposed memorandum of Silas, it has already been shown above that the author of the travels, xvi. 10 ff., is given out by our book itself as the author of the whole; that this author, to judge by the purport of his narratives, could not possibly be Silas; that those portions of the second part in which Silas was undeniably with Paul, by no means bear an historical character;[1] that even the author, by the "we," discriminates most clearly between himself and the companions of Paul designated in the third person and by name. The supposed biography of Barnabas is negatived by the circumstance previously indicated, which Schwanbeck very insufficiently attempts to set aside, p. 242, that the three narratives of Paul's conversion, ascribed by him to two different sources, must have flowed from the same pen, and that the unhistorical account, ix. 26 ff., is most closely connected with the object of our book; likewise by the story of the journey of Paul and Barnabas, xi. 27 ff., which, according to our previous demonstration, can be explained only by the pragmatism of the Acts, and not by an independent legend, still less by actual history. The same thing is rendered equally apparent by the dependent position, also pointed out, which is occupied by the Pauline speech of xiii. to those of the first part; by the relation of the healing of the lame man, xiv. 8 ff., to the Petrine miracle, iii. 2 ff.; and by the commencement of the name Paul, xv. 9, which was shown above to be entirely in the manner of the author (Luke vi. 14). Whether

[1] To convince oneself of the weakness of *Schwanbeck's* criticism, it need only be seen how credulously he, pp. 172 ff., accepts the story of the apostolic council, and in what a forced manner he (pp. 176 f.) gives a natural interpretation to the prison scene at Philippi.

the narrative of Stephen implies a special documental authority will be examined later. All that we have learnt from our earlier inquiries as to the tendency of the narratives, iii.—v., x. f., militates against a biography of Peter as the authority for i.—vi. 7, viii., ix. 31—xi. 18. In order to believe our book to be such a rough conglomeration of different elements as Schleiermacher and Schwanbeck suppose, we must forget all our previous conclusions with regard to its unity of language and matter. Hence, if we too should inquire into the probable sources of its narratives, the question could not be intended to examine into the documents or portions of documents which the author merely put together without revision.

If, from the critical standpoint, the above-named scholars conjectured an essentially unaltered adoption in the Acts of more ancient documents, the same thing has been done by others in the interest of the older opinion, by which the author is supposed to derive the speeches and letters communicated in our book from authentic notes and transcripts. This assertion is founded by Riehm [1] on the argument that Peter's speeches characteristically accord both with the Epistles of this Apostle and also with each other in purport and language; similarly, those of Paul reciprocally and with the Pauline Epistles; even the little speech of James with the Epistle bearing his name. Ebrard has recently attempted to prove the same thing,[2] and he considers it a main argument for the unqualified credibility of the Acts. It will, however, be the less necessary for us to dwell further on the examination of this assertion, as Mayerhoff [3] has exhaustively refuted it with respect to the Petrine speeches, and De Wette [4] has pointed out so many errors in Ebrard's supposed proofs, that after the subtraction of these there remain no evidential data whatever; and as, on the other hand, Eich-

[1] De font. Act. Apost. 126 ff.

[2] Kritik. der evang. Gesch. § 124.

[3] Einl. in die petrin. Schriften, 220 ff.

[4] Int. to the N. T. § 115, note 2. *Ebrard's* rejoinder in the new edition of his work is not worthy of notice.

horn[1] has supplied positive proof, on incontrovertible grounds, of the later origin of the speeches contained in the Acts. In fact, one need only inquire, with a critically unfettered mind, whether a Peter could really have said what is attributed to him in our book, i. 18 ff., xi. 5—17, xv. 7 ff.; whether a Paul could have uttered the words in xxii. 6—21, xxvi. 12—18, xx. 23, 25, a James those in xiv. 15, a Gamaliel those in v. 36; whether the striking resemblance between the speeches of a Peter, a Stephen, and a Paul, the striking absence of the Pauline peculiarities of doctrine and language in the Pauline speeches, can be accounted for on the hypothesis of their authenticity; and the answer cannot be doubtful for a moment. The real foundation for Riehm and Ebrard's assertion is merely this, that *within* the character of thought and language common to the whole of the Acts, some subordinate and special points of contact may be found between the speeches of Peter, on one hand, and those of Paul on the other; that the first especially are of a more decidedly Hebraistic type than the latter, and are chiefly concerned with similar thoughts about the Messiahship of Jesus, his rejection by the Jewish authorities, his attestation by the resurrection, the need of repentance and conversion. This, however, is completely accounted for as follows: that the same author makes the same person speak under essentially the same circumstances; and, should a further explanation be required, it will be sufficient to suppose that the author unintentionally remembered the earlier Petrine speeches while writing the later ones; or else that from an artistic feeling he formed them both alike. But the apologists of the Acts ought not to appeal to the Petrine Epistles, for the first of them is certainly spurious; and even if in language and doctrine some echoes of the Acts (not of its Petrine speeches alone) may be found in the Epistle, this can only render it probable that it was not far removed from the Acts in the time and place of composition. So little is to be gained on this side

[1] Int. to the N. T. pp. 36 ff.

for the authenticity of the speeches transmitted by our book, that they rather furnish one of the most triumphant proofs of the free composition of the Acts by a single author. It will be shown forthwith that the two letters in xv. and xxiii. only lead us to the same conclusion.

It is certainly not intended in all this to deny the possibility that the author employed written authorities; only the nature of these authorities must be again examined, and in all probability their verbal adoption be given up beforehand. It is true that it is precisely in the language of the individual paragraphs that the different documental authorities are supposed to be recognized; a more accurate examination may, however, convince us how insecure this evidence is. Since the grammatical peculiarities and the phraseology remain essentially alike throughout the whole of our book, the evidence must chiefly rest on the stock of words. But great as is the variety in this respect offered by the individual paragraphs, they nevertheless afford no safe landmarks for the decision of our problem. I have compared 794 words which occur in the Acts only once, or but seldom in the same context. Of these 794 words, 174 may be proved by their use in the Gospel of Luke to be the property of our author, and can therefore furnish no evidence of the employment of sources. The remaining 620 are apportioned among the separate paragraphs as follows:

No.	Passage	Verses		Words
1.	Ch. i. contains of them in	26	verses	13
2.	ii.	47	,,	18
3.	iii.—v.	105	,,	48
4.	vi., vii.	75	,,	48
5.	viii. 4—40	37	,,	13
6.	viii. 1—3; ix. 1—30	33	,,	13
7.	ix. 31—42	12	,,	1
8.	ix. 43—xi. 18	67	,,	29
9.	xi. 19—30, xii. 25	13	,,	3
10.	xii. 1—24	24	,,	16
11.	xiii., xiv.	80	,,	41
12.	xv. 1—35	35	,,	12
13.	xv. 35—xvi. 8	14	,,	3
14.	xvi. 9—xviii.; xx. 4—16; xxi. 1—17; xxvii. 1—xxviii. 16	in 100	verses	134
15.	xvi. 19—40	22	,,	18
16.	xvii.	34	,,	34
17.	xviii. 1—xix. 20	48	,,	28
18.	xix. 21—xx. 3	23	,,	19
19.	xx. 17—38	22	,,	11
20.	xxi. 18—xxiii. 10	63	,,	37
21.	xxiii. 11—xxiv. 27	52	,,	34
22.	xxv., xxvi.	59	,,	38
23.	xxviii. 17—31	15	,,	9

Thus in every 100 verses occur, on an average, 61·6 of these words, in particular in each paragraph:

No. 1	50	No. 13	21·4
,, 2	38·3	,, 14	134
,, 3	45·7	,, 15	81·8
,, 4	64	,, 16	100
,, 5	37·8	,, 17	58·3
,, 6	39·3	,, 18	82·6
,, 7	8·3	,, 19	50
,, 8	43·3	,, 20	58·7
,, 9	23	,, 21	65·4
,, 10	66·6	,, 22	64·4
,, 11	51·2	,, 23	60
,, 12	34·3		

The individual paragraphs are certainly very unequal in this respect, but no fixed limits can be shown by which we can discriminate between those dependent on more ancient authorities, and those freely written by our author; for the numerical ratio fluctuates with imperceptible transitions from the lowest to the highest, and the paragraphs in which the greatest number of peculiar words is combined with other signs of greater dependence on authorities, such as No. 14, are opposed by others in which these other signs are wanting, although they contain comparatively many peculiar words, such as Nos. 15 and 16. This is very natural, as a new subject produced new expressions also. Hence in the present case such indication can have only a subordinate value, as might be expected, considering the stylistic unity of our book. Similarly, little can be proved by the connection, or want of connection, of individual paragraphs with those preceding and following, because on one hand a fixed plan pervades the whole; on the other, the abruptness of a narrative may be owing, not only to the use of a fresh source, but quite as likely to omissions in the material derived from it, or from the intervention of free fiction in the midst of the traditional material. The surest index is still the purport and tendency of the individual paragraphs. The more conspicuously a speech or a story represents our author's peculiar standpoint and serves the peculiar object of his book, and the slighter the probability of its historically faithful transmission, so much the more is there to recommend the hypothesis that it proceeds from our author himself; the less it can be explained from these points of view, the more are we obliged to fall back on extraneous sources. But neither in this way is a certain result always to be attained, for it is also possible that the author metamorphosed traditional material from his own standpoint, and employed it for his own object; hence the results so obtained must always be very uncertain in detail.

If on this basis we next examine the paragraphs containing the history of the church at Jerusalem, there are certainly many things which lead us to the hypothesis of documental authorities; but at the same time there are so many traces of the author's own literary handiwork, that we must at least suppose a very free use of these authorities. In the history of the ascension, one might indeed account for the deviations from the account in the Gospel, and especially for the transfer of the ascension to the fortieth day after the resurrection, by the influence of a new source; but it is also possible that the author himself made these alterations in order to put the ascension nearer the Feast of Pentecost. In that case he would have inserted the number forty, as on the other assumption tradition must have done, after the analogy of the Old Testament stories of Moses and Elijah, and the history of the temptation in the Gospel. The further details at all events belong to him alone; for the utterances in ver. 4, and still more vers. 6—8, are too deeply involved in the pragmatism of our book, and too dependent on those of the Gospel (xxiv. 47), to admit of their having originally existed without this connection; the expression ὀπτάνεσθαι, ver. 3, and the description of the angel, ver. 10 (comp. Gospel xxiv. 4), are also specifically Lukan, and vers. 4 f. refer distinctly to Luke iii. 16, xxiv. 49. It is the same with the story of the apostolic election, i. 12—26. That the knowledge of this fact reached the author by means of tradition is in general perfectly credible; and if he was himself so remote from the apostolic age as we must suppose, the tradition was probably a written one, i. e. he found in some more ancient book the statement that Matthias was chosen Apostle in the place of Judas; and perhaps further details respecting the mode of election. The connecting verses, 12—14, prove themselves, as has been already shown by their coincidence with Luke xxiv. 52 f., and almost more decidedly by the list of Apostles (comp. Luke vi. 14 ff.), to be the author's addition. In Peter's speech, vers. 18 f. have already struck us as historically incredible; and although the first of these verses might in itself belong to older tradition, yet the inappropriate illustration of verse 19 will scarcely suit it. As, moreover, the ideas of a later period seem to echo in the κλῆρος, vers. 17, 25, and in the ἐπισκοπὴ, ver. 20, as ver. 22 has a striking parallel in xiii. 31, the speeches of our book in general are among the elements of which the free composition by the author is most suspected, and we must at any rate place Peter's words to his account. On the other hand, the original story may have known of the employment of lots in the election; and if this story was from the first connected with the account of the event of Pentecost, it may probably also have transferred the apostolic election to Jerusalem. For the story of Pentecost we must at all events suppose an older tradition. It is apparent, even from the first Epistle to the Corinthians, that it was the Jewish-Christian party who regarded the gift of tongues as the specific appearance of the Spirit. Paul at least did not attribute this importance to it, although the thing itself was familiar to him. Even our book itself seems to assume the tongue-speaking as already given in Jewish-Christian tradition, as least if our conjectures (in which Schneckenburger preceded us, pp. 332 f.) as to the tendency of the narrative, xix. 1 ff., be correct; for if our author found it necessary to set a Pauline by the side of the Jerusalemite tongue-speaking, he must probably have found the latter before him in tradition. But in every way the record which makes the primitive church shine with highest brilliancy seems to indicate a Jewish-Christian origin. Still it is a question whether the *entire* contents of the narrative belong to this older tradition. If the miracle of speech really has the universalistic significance which we recognized in it above, that points to our author rather than to his Jewish-Christian source. The latter probably knew only of the outpouring of the Spirit and its announcement by the new spiritual language, and the Acts, by the amplification of vers. 6—11, first transformed this language into the languages of all nations, and therewith the tongue-speaking of the apostolic times into the miracle of foreign languages. A trace of it may be found in the fact that in Peter's speech, vers. 14 ff., no mention is made of this miracle, which would have been the most obvious refutation of the opponents' accusation. Yet we are not on this account entitled to assume that the speech was taken quite unaltered by our author, even should it actually rest on an older record. It has been inferred from ver. 24 that it was originally Aramaic, since it was not natural to speak of being loosed from the pains of death or being held by them; instead of the pains, must originally have stood *the bonds* of death, and this alteration must have been introduced by an incorrect translation of חֶבְלֵי מָוֶת.[1] Meanwhile this combination of words might also occur to a person who knew the passage, Ps. xviii. 5 f., only in the translation of the LXX.; for in the words, *περιέσχον με ὠδῖνες θανάτου . . . ὠδῖνες ᾅδου περιεκύκλωσάν με, προέφθασάν με παγίδες θανάτου*, it already contains the same rather incongruous combination of ideas, and when this text was once applied to the death and resurrection of Jesus, the mode of expression in Peter's speech would result easily enough. Hence, undeniable as it is that this expression is founded on an incorrect translation of חֶבְלֵי מָוֶת, it only presupposes the translation of the Psalm by the LXX., and not an Aramaic original of our speech.[2] In other respects

[1] *Bleek*, Stud. und Krit. 1836, 4, 1038, and many others after him.

[2] Still less does this follow from the phrase, ver. 33, *τῇ δεξιᾷ τοῦ Θεοῦ ὑψωθεὶς*, of which *Bleek* (elsewhere) believes that it is here and v. 31 to be understood of an exaltation *to* the right hand of God; and that *τῇ δεξ.*, by a false translation of Ps. cx. 1,

this speech so strongly resembles the other Petrine speeches in the Acts, the language is so much in the style of our author,[1] the construction in parts (vers. 22, 23, 29, 33) so Grecian, that we cannot look on its verbal translation from the Aramaic as probable. The Christological enunciations, ver. 22, as has been already shown, harmonize perfectly with the Christology of our author; and the declaration, ver. 39, prepares the subsequent promulgation of the Gospel to the Gentiles in a manner that adapts itself entirely to the pragmatism of our book. Under these circumstances we shall at any rate be obliged to admit that our author may have considerably revised the record which he possibly had before him. Still more decidedly may the concluding formula, vers. 12—17, be ascribed to the author of the whole, on account of the similar description, iv. 32 ff., and the Lukan mode of expression (twice repeated *προσκαρτερεῖν*, twice *καθ' ἡμέραν*, once *ἐπὶ τὸ αὐτὸ*, once *ὁμοθυμαδὸν*, once *καθότι*, once *ἐν ἀγγαλλιάσει*, as in Luke i. 44, once corresponding to the Lukan *ὑπάρχοντα*, iv. 32, *ὑπάρξεις*); and even if the supposition of a general community of goods corresponds too closely with the Essene-Ebionite ideal not to oblige us to conjecture that it was known to the Ebionite tradition respecting the primitive community, yet the further colouring of this trait seems due to later description. The more remote authorities, however, in one case as in the other, must be sought in Neo-Pythagoreanism, that parent of

לִימִינִי, stands instead of *πρὸς τὴν δεξιάν*. Such misapprehension of the much-used passage in the Psalms, which even Luke xx. 12 and the Acts forthwith quote correctly, is incredible; rather if *τῇ δεξ.* is not the dative of place, *τῇ δεξ.* here stands = *τῇ χειρί*. Ver. 34 shows that the author has the Psalm in the Greek translation before his eyes.

[1] Comp. the expressions, *διὰ χειρὸς* (al. *ῶν*), ver. 23, elsewhere only in vii. 25, xi. 30, xv. 23 (*διὰ τῶν χειρῶν*, besides Acts v. 12, xiv. 3, xix. 11; also in Mark vi. 21); *ἄχρι τῆς ἡμέρας ταύτης*, ver. 29, elsewhere only in Acts xxvi. 22, xxiii. 1: *καρπὸς τῆς ὀσφύος*, ver. 30, comp. *καρπὸς τῆς κοιλίας*, Luke i. 42; *τῇ δεξιᾷ τοῦ θεοῦ ὑψωθεὶς*, ver. 33, comp. v. 31; *ἐπαγγελία τοῦ πνεύματος*, ver. 33 (Pauline, see Gal. iii. 11), comp. i. 4, Luke xxiv. 49; also the words *γνωστὸς*, ver. 14, *μνῆμα* (not *εἶον*), ver. 29, *ἀσφαλῶς*, ver. 36, which in the New Testament occur chiefly in Luke; the *ἀσμένως*, ver. 41, is to be found besides only in Acts xxi. 17, also combined with *δέχεσθαι*.

Essenism, which, moreover, itself, after the precedent of the Platonic state, expanded into a myth the old Pythagorean maxim, *κοινὰ τὰ τῶν φίλων*; for it is in this society that a complete community of goods is first asserted as an historical fact, and this is done too in a precisely similar manner to that in the Acts. As a common possession of all property is here presupposed for the Christian community, so the later Pythagoreans presuppose it for the primitive community of Pythagoreans, the Pythagorean association at Croton; and even the expressions and individual traits of the description are so similar in the two cases, that it is impossible to resist the idea that one is dependent on the other,[1] which in our case must naturally be the Acts, as the more modern.

The narratives of iii.—v. are so sharply separated in their beginning and end from those around them, that they seem to form a small whole by themselves, and thus the conjecture is suggested that they might be derived from a special source. In support of this hypothesis it is usual to quote, after Bleek,[2] that

[1] Thus it is said in *Jamblich*, v. Pyth. 168, *κοινὰ γὰρ πᾶσι πάντα καὶ ταῦτα ἦν, ἴδιον δὲ οὐδεὶς οὐδὲν ἐκέκτητο*, and also 79, *τὰ μὲν ἑκάστου ὑπάρχοντα, τουτέστιν αἱ οὐσίαι, ἐκοινοῦντο*, comp. Acts iv. 32, *οὐδὲ εἷς τι τῶν ὑπαρχόντων αὐτῷ ἔλεγεν ἴδιον εἶναι ἀλλ' ἦν αὐτοῖς ἅπαντα κοινά*, and in *Diog. Laert.* viii. 10, *καὶ αὐτοῦ οἱ μαθηταὶ κατετίθεντο τὰς οὐσίας εἰς ἕν*, comp. Acts iv. 35, *ἐτίθουν παρὰ τοὺς πόδας τῶν ἀποστόλων*; and as in Acts ii. 42 ff. the first mention of the community of goods is connected with the statement (ver. 41) that after Peter's first address three thousand people were converted to Christianity in one day, so *Nikomachus ap. Porph.* v. Pyth. 20, relates that by his first address in Italy, Pythagoras forthwith gained two thousand disciples, who did not part again, but lived together in communism (*ὁμακοΐόν τι παμμέγεθες ἱδρυσαμένους . . . . καὶ τὰς οὐσίας κοινὰς ἔθεντο*, comp. Acts ii. 44, *πάντες δὲ οἱ πιστεύοντες ἦσαν ἐπὶ τὸ αὐτὸ καὶ εἶχον ἅπαντα κοινά*). Although the oldest of these writers, Nikomachus, is somewhat more modern than our book, they probably here as elsewhere all drew on more ancient records; and even independently of this, we may well be permitted to assume that, respecting the much debated communism of the Pythagoreans, certain expressions were current which may involuntarily have haunted the mind of our author. Conversely, Pseudo-Origen, Philos. p. 9, seems to have been dominated by the remembrance of the Acts (ii. 45, iv. 34, 37) when he relates of Pythagoras, *ἔθος δὲ τοῦτο ἦν παρ' αὐτῷ, ἐπειδὰν προσίῃ τις μαθητευσόμενος, πιπράσκειν τὰ ὑπάρχοντα καὶ τὸ ἀργύριον κατατιθέναι ἐσφραγισμένον παρὰ τῷ Πυθαγόρᾳ*. At any rate, this evidence testifies how nearly the representation of our book is allied to the later Pythagorean ideas, and where we must seek for the final authority for this historically improbable description.

[2] P. 1041.

the expression παῖς θεοῦ occurs only in iii. iv., but here five times (iii. 16, 26, iv. 27, 30 of Jesus, iv. 25 of David), and the phrase διὰ στόματος, besides i. 16, only in iii. 18, 21, iv. 25. Παῖς θεοῦ, however, exists elsewhere in Luke, who alone among all the New Testament writers has this expression, i. e. in Luke i. 54, 69, and the apposition ἅγιος παῖς, iv. 27, 30, has also its nearest parallel in Lukan passages (Luke iv. 34, Acts ii. 27, xiii. 35); διὰ στόματος is likewise a peculiarly Lukan expression, which we find again in Luke i. 70, Acts xv. 7, but elsewhere only in a quotation in Matt. iv. 4; for the frequent use of στόμα, comp. also Acts xxii. 14, viii. 35, x. 34, xviii. 14, Luke i. 64, for the use of the preposition the phrase διὰ χειρός. These marks, therefore, much rather favour the Lukan origin of the narratives in question. In other respects also the language of the chapters is entirely that of our author: compare the expressions ἐπὶ τὸ αὐτὸ, iii. 1, iv. 26; ἐκ κοιλίας μητρὸς αὐτοῦ, iii. 2; ἀτενίζειν, iii. 4; ὑπάρχειν, iii. 6, 12; χαρίζεσθαι, iii. 14 (comp. xxv. 11, 16, xxvii. 24); ἄχρι, iii. 21; καθεξῆς, iii. 24; στρατηγὸς τοῦ ἱεροῦ, iv. 1; ἑσπέρα, iv. 3; ἐπιβάλλειν τὰς χεῖρας, iv. 3, v. 18; πλησθῆναι πνεύματος ἁγίου, iv. 8, 31; πλησθῆναι ζήλου, v. 17; γνωστὸς, iv. 10, 16; ἐνώπιον, iv. 10, 19; σωτηρία, iv. 12; ἀπειλῇ ἀπειλεῖσθαι, iv. 17; παραγγελίᾳ παραγγέλλειν, v. 28; αἴρειν φωνὴν, iv. 24; ὁμοθυμαδὸν, iv. 24, v. 12; τανῦν, iv. 29, v. 38; ἐπ' ἀληθείας, iv. 27; μετὰ παῤῥησίας, iv. 29, 31; comp. ii. 29, xxviii. 31 (elsewhere only Heb. iv. 16; the other books always have ἐν π. or παῤῥησίᾳ alone), τὰ ὑπάρχοντα αὐτῷ, iv. 32; comp. Luke viii. 3 (elsewhere always τὰ ὑπ. αὐτοῦ, but the word is particularly frequent in the Gospel of Luke); καθότι, iv. 35; παρὰ τοὺς πόδας, iv. 35, 37, v. 2, 10; comp. vii. 58, xxii. 3, also x. 25, Luke vii. 38, viii. 35, 41, x. 39, xvii. 16 (elsewhere only in Matt. xv. 30); τί ὅτι, v. 4, 9, comp. Luke ii. 49, viii. 25; φόβος ἐγένετο, v. 5, 11; διὰ τῶν χειρῶν, v. 12; μεγαλύνειν, v. 13; ἄγγελος κυρίου, v. 19; τί ἂν γένοιτο, v. 24; δεῖ, v. 29; κρεμάσαντες ἐπὶ ξύλου, v. 30; comp. x. 39, xiii. 29, λέγειν εἶναί τινα ἑαυτὸν, v. 36, the frequent τε, πᾶς, ἅπας, the constructions with the infinitive, iii. 2, 12, 18, iv. 2, 30, the τὸ πῶς, iv. 21, the ἐγένετο δὲ, iv. 5, v. 7, the descriptive participles, iii. 4, 7, v. 5, 6, 10, 17, 20, 21, 22, 25, 26, 27, 34, the anterior position of δοῦναι, v. 31, the combination of δύναμις and χάρις, iv. 33; the mode of expression in iv. 1, comp. with Luke xx. 1. The contents also of this portion clearly reveal our author: in iv. 27, reference is made to a fact related only in Luke's Gospel, and not unconnected with his peculiar tendency; in v. 17, 34 ff., we find the same unhistorical representation of the relations of the Jewish parties towards Christianity, as in xxiii. 6 ff.; in iv. 6, v. 36, historical errors, which have their nearest point of comparison in those of Luke's Gospel; iv. 32 ff., v. 15, the same verbally similar description in part as in ii. 42 ff.; v. 15, a similar magical representation of miraculous power in the Apostles as in xix. 12, Luke vi. 19, viii. 46; in iii. 26, the destination of the Gospel for the Gentiles is indicated in a genuinely Lukan manner simultaneously with the prerogative conceded to the Jews by Luke; in iv. 11 ff., the passage of the 118th Psalm is used just as in Rom. ix. 33; iv. 12, has a completely Pauline reading respecting salvation in Christ. Finally, if there is any basis for our earlier investigations, according to which the whole story of the Apostle's two-fold imprisonment is unhistorical, and arose merely from an imitation of the tradition communicated in xii., we shall have no further scruple in pronouncing our three chapters to be the free composition of the author, and in tracing to this also the want of a closer connection of iii. 1 with the preceding part, not to the use of a fresh authority. Moreover, in these chapters, v. 1—11, 17 ff., stand equally detached. This does not exclude the possibility that single features may have reached the author by means of written tradition, which may be especially the case with the story of Ananias and Sapphira, and the statement which, after the preceding assertion of a *general* community of goods, is strangely enough made (iv. 36) to the honour of Barnabas. Here also we must ascribe the further details to our author, and not suppose any traditional authority at all for the main body of the three chapters, except the record on which our 12th chapter is founded.

It is otherwise with the said 12th chapter. The narrative of James's execution bears an entirely historical impress; the account of the death of Herod Agrippa sounds indeed legendary enough; but that it reached our author by tradition we are obliged to suppose, as a kindred story is to be found in Josephus, which, however, differs too widely from ours to be regarded as its source. The imprisonment and liberation of Peter also are scarcely inventions of our author's, for in itself they look far more like a legend than a product of literary reflection; and, moreover, we must presuppose a tradition of this sort in order to comprehend the origin of the two narratives in the 3rd and 5th chapters. In particular, the feature which is so striking in ch. v., that the liberation of the captive Apostle by an angel is completely useless, is most readily explained by the hypothesis that the author found before him the liberation by an angel. However, in this case also we must ascribe the account to the author of the whole, as the style and language in no way differ from that of the remainder of the book, but rather in many traits bear the writer's characteristics: compare the expressions *ἐπιβάλλειν τὰς χεῖρας*, ver. 1; *ἡμέραι τῶν ἀζύμων*, ver. 3; *τίθεσθαι εἰς φυλακὴν*, ver. 4; *δέειν ἁλύσεσι δυσὶ*, ver. 6; *ὅραμα*, ver. 9; *ἐκ χειρὸς*, ver. 11; *κατασείσας τῇ χειρὶ*, ver. 17; *ὁμοθυμαδὸν*, ver. 20; to ver. 7, Luke i. 9 bears a strong resemblance in expression; with ver. 11 (*νῦν οἶδα ἀληθῶς*), comp. x. 34 with the *μαίνῃ*, ver. 14, xxvi. 24 with ver. 24, vi. 7, xix. 20.

Of the remaining portions belonging to the history of the primitive community (disregarding for the present vi. f.), we may with probability trace the narratives, viii. 4—40, ix. 31—42, to older and, indeed, to Jewish-Christian sources; for the legend of Simon, viii. 9 ff., is of decidedly Jewish-Christian origin; and the same is also indicated by the effect which is ascribed in viii. 14 to the apostolic imposition of hands, as our author had no motive for inventing a trait of this kind in honour of the Apostles of Palestine. This is the more likely, as the story of Tabitha, ix. 37, corresponds with the account in Mark's Gospel, or its more ancient authority, respecting Jairus's daughter;[1] whereas our author, if regarded as the original inventor of this story, would have been more likely to bring it near the form given to it in his own Gospel. To this must be added the more general reason, that the endeavour of our book to render the Pauline miracles equal to the Petrine, implies the pre-existence of legendary Petrine miracles. But in this case also we have no occasion to attribute to our author any slavish dependence on his authorities; and as, moreover, the language of the paragraphs in question is entirely his own, we may trace back to him many material points—such, for instance, as the definite form of the speeches.

Compared with our earlier results, we must concede a disproportionately large share in the story of Cornelius (x. 1—11, 18) to the spontaneous action of the author. It has been already shown that this story really admits of explanation only from the design of justifying the Pauline mission to the Gentiles by the example of Peter, the acquiescence of the primitive community, and the authority of undoubted revelations acknowledged also by the Jewish-Christian side. This of itself prohibits the supposition that it is derived from the Petrine legend or literature. But neither can it belong to Pauline legend; firstly, because design such as must be ascribed to the story is foreign to legend in general; secondly, because the further details of the story, this artistic web of double interconnected visions, shows that calculating reflection was at work; nor is it likely that any one else should have reduced it to this form with literary skill, for its whole tendency makes it appear only as a particular in our author's plan; the language is his throughout, and its development is in all parts so like the narrative of the 9th chapter, of Paul's conversion, that we must suppose it to be

[1] *Baur*, Paul. 192.

copied from it. It has been already observed that the Lukan narrative of the centurion of Capernaum seems to have influenced the description of Cornelius. Hence, even if some tradition should have given rise to our narrative, scarcely more can have been derived from it than the notification that Peter won over to Christianity a centurion named Cornelius, who in that case must probably have been not a Gentile, but a proselyte. But, on the whole, it almost seems likelier that the story had not even thus much traditional foundation, but that it is pure fiction.

If the same source supplied all the traditional material which we have hitherto recognized as the probable foundation of the accounts of the primitive community in our book, we should conjecture with the greatest probability that it was a Petrine writing; such at least is suggested by the narratives, xii., viii. 4—25, ix. 32 ff.; and the account of the event of Pentecost, in which Peter plays the principal part, would easily lend itself to this hypothesis; on the other hand, the incident between Philip and the Ethiopian, viii. 26, could be only casually mentioned in a writing of that description, though there is nothing to hinder us from deriving this story from another source. What manner of Petrine book it may have been that our author used as his groundwork, it is naturally impossible to discover with certainty: the conjecture[1] that it was the Κήρυγμα Πέτρου is decidedly wrong in so far as concerns that K. Π., the fragments of which Credner collected and commented upon in his Beiträge, I. 351 ff. The latter was perhaps even more modern than the Acts. One might rather think of the older work of the same name, which probably formed the original of the later writing, and likewise the most ancient stratum of the pseudo-Clementine literature, and from which much has passed over into the latter.[2] But this also, so far as we can ascertain its contents from our Clementine

[1] On which *Credner*, Einl. I. 282, and *Riehm*, de font. Act. Ap. 176 ff., should be compared.

[2] See *Hilgenfeld*, Clem. Recog. and Hom. pp. 41, 45 ff.

writings, does not seem well suited for the groundwork of our narrative. For although it appears from Recog. i. 22, 40 ff., that this writing also touched upon the history of the Apostles, the extract in the Recognitions mentions scarcely anything of that which is related in the first part of the Acts. Hence, if no further data should be found, we shall be compelled to leave the question unanswered.

There still remains of the pre-Pauline history chapters vi. and vii., in which are related the installation of the seven deacons and the execution of Stephen. Of this portion it has been almost generally supposed in recent times that either the whole, or from vi. 8 forwards, is derived from a source of its own; especially in the speech, vii., it is believed that positive traces of such a peculiar composition may be found. And it cannot be denied that the speech is distinguished by its peculiar arrangement, as well as the fineness of its details. But who can prove that it might not be the work of our author? Paul's speech at Athens is also very peculiar, and yet it is unlikely that it is derived from any other than the author of the Acts: our whole work is carried out with great subtlety, and is rich in references which, often unmeaning at the first glance, are nevertheless closely connected with the purpose of the whole; and thus just the most characteristic part of Stephen's address is well fitted to be the composition of our author. The style and language of the speech, and of the whole section to which it belongs, are, even by Schwanbeck's admission (p. 250), not different from those of the previous and subsequent portions; much rather in this respect everything leads us to recognize our author. The number of the words which occur only in this part is not out of proportion to that of other parts; and equally little does the construction or phraseology betray striking peculiarities. On the other hand, we here find much that has no parallel except in Luke. Immediately, in vi. 8 (to limit our proof to this portion of the whole), if the combination of χάρις and δύναμις is, as has been already shown, in Luke's peculiar manner, so is σοφία and χάρις, vii. 10; συζητεῖν, vi. 9, besides Mark, stands only in the two books of Luke; ἰσχύειν, vi. 10, is likewise a favourite in both (compare especially xxv. 7), also ῥῆμα, vi. 11, 13, particularly combined with λαλεῖν; with vi. 12 compare iv. 1, xix. 29, xxiii. 27; παύεσθαι, vi., among the historical books of the New Testament exists in Luke alone; ἔθη, vi. 14, ἀτενίζειν, vi. 15, vii. 55, are some of his favourite words; the question, vii. 1, recalls Acts xvii. 11, Luke xxii. 67; the address, vii. 2, besides the many passages having ἄνδρες ἀδελφοὶ, reminds us especially of xxii. 1; ἡγούμενος, vii. 10, besides three passages in the Epistle to the Hebrews and a quotation in Matthew, stands only in Luke xxii. 26, xiv. 12, xv. 22, in the same meaning; γῆ Αἰγύπτου, &c., vii. 4, 29, 36, 40, is Lukan; so are ἐξαποστέλλειν, ver. 12, μνῆμα, ver. 16, αὐξάνειν καὶ πληθύνεσθαι, ver. 17 (compare vi. 7, xii. 24), ἄχρις οὗ, ver. 18, ζωογονεῖν, ver. 19; δυνατὸς ἐν λόγοις καὶ ἔργοις, ver. 22 (Luke xxiv. 19, compare Acts xviii. 24), τεσσαρακονταετὴς χρόνος, ver. 23 (compare xiii. 18), ἀνέβη ἐπὶ τὴν καρδίαν, ver. 23 (Luke xxiv. 38), also the use of καρδία, ver. 39, 54; διὰ χειρὸς, ver. 25, ἐν χειρὶ, ver. 35, σωτηρία, ver. 35, τῇ ἐπιούσῃ, ver. 26, ἔντρομος γενόμενος, ver. 32 (compare xvi. 29, and the more frequent ἔμφοβον γίγνεσθαι), εὐφραίνεσθαι ἐν, ver. 41 (εὐφρ. frequent in Luke; the construction as in χαίρειν ἐν, Luke x. 20), χάριν εὑρίσκειν, ver. 46 (Luke i. 30), ὁ ὕψιστος, ver. 48, οὐκ ἐν χειροποιήτοις κατοικεῖ, ver. 48 (xvii. 24), διαπρίεσθαι, ver. 54 (v. 33), ὑπάρχειν, ver. 55; ἑστὼς ἐκ δεξιῶν, ver. 25 (Luke i. 11), ὁμοθυμαδόν, ver. 57, φωνῇ μεγάλῃ, ver. 57, 60 (viii. 7, xiv. 10, xvi. 28, xxvi. 24, Luke i. 42, viii. 28, xix. 37, xxiii. 46, iv. 33, also, as here combined with κράζειν), νεανίας, ver. 58, θεὶς τὰ γόνατα, ver. 60 (ix. 40, xx. 36, xxi. 5, Luke xxii. 41). It has already been shown that the trial as well as the last words of Stephen strikingly resemble the trial and last words of Jesus as given by Luke; and the affinity of our speech with those of Paul at Antioch and Athens was likewise demonstrated; all of which is most readily accounted for by unity of authorship. All these tokens make Stephen's speech, and the historical narrative connected with it as it lies before us, appear only as the work of our author. Schwanbeck's objections to this view (see Schwanbeck, pp. 250 f.) have not much weight, and are already refuted by the results of our inquiry.[1] This certainly does not exclude the possibility that our author may have employed a special treatise, or some pre-existing notes upon the death of Stephen; and in an account of this sort words might already have been put into Stephen's mouth which resembled our speech in fundamental ideas; for well as this speech suits the tendency of our book, some one else may also have worked in the same direction, or a really historical record about the martyr may have offered our author a peg on which to hang his discourse. The fact of his execution obliges us to assume that Stephen came into sharper collision with predominant Judaism than the Apostles of Palestine; and that this collision was connected precisely with a controversy against the service of the Temple is the more credible, since even within the limits of Judaism and Jewish Christianity, Essenism and Ebionitism regarded the sacrificial system as a defilement of true religion.[2] Still, the Stephen of our book goes far beyond Essenian principles; for while the Essenes, though rejecting sacrifice, put great value on the Temple, Stephen is reproached (vi. 14) because he prophesied the destruction of the Temple and the abrogation of the Mosaic Law; and he himself, vii. 48 ff., alludes to the building of a Temple in general as an error. Thus the precedent of

[1] *Schwanbeck* appeals, 1st, to the completeness of our narrative, but it has already been shown how little follows from this; and, 2nd, to the preponderance of the oratorical over the historical element in it, whereas the reverse is the case in all other portions of the book; but in the parts ii. 1—41, xiii. 13—52, xvii. 16—34, xx. 17—38, and others, the rhetorical element decidedly preponderates. Finally, when *Schwanbeck* finds an important difference between our speech and the characteristics of the rest of the book, this assertion, according to the evidence above, must be so limited that no further inference can be drawn from it.

[2] See Jos. Ant. xviii. 1, 5; Clem. Rec. i. 37 ff.; and also *Hilgenfeld*, Clem. Recog. pp. 58 ff., who also quotes the passage from the Epistle of the Hebrews in Epiph. xxx. 16, *ἦλθον καταλῦσαι τὰς θυσίας, καὶ ἐὰν μὴ παύσησθε τοῦ θύειν, οὐ παύσεται ἀφ' ὑμῶν ἡ ὀργή.*

the Essenes would not account for his principles; and the question arises whether, so far as they are here represented, they do not point back to the presupposition of Paulinism. At all events, their further details must belong to our author. For to have taken from an older authority the fine details running through the whole speech, he must have adhered so closely to this authority, that the entire accordance of our speech with the style and expression of the rest of our book would be inexplicable. Hence, while we must leave it undecided how far the theme of his work was supplied to the author by a more ancient record, we can attribute the work in its present form to him alone.

Of the Pauline parts, the sections in which the narrator makes use of the first person (xvi. 10—18, xx. 4—18, xxi. 1—17, xxvii. 1—xxviii. 16, perhaps also 19, 21, 22, and the first three verses of xxi.,[1] with the exception of the opening words, favour the conjecture that they are derived from an older authority. On this supposition alone can it be explained how the author came to speak so just in these parts. If he wished to give himself out for one of Paul's companions, as we have found probable, it would have been most natural to put the first person in one consecutive part, in the whole history of the period during which he wished to have been with Paul. But the first person not only disappears in xvi., with the arrest of the Apostle and his departure from Philippi, but again, in xx. 16, it is exchanged for the third, although the writer, according to xxvii. 1, appears Paul's comrade in imprisonment. The most natural explanation of this phenomenon is the hypothesis that it was only in the parts designated that the author of our book had a record in the first person before him, but that he could not make up his mind to continue the first person in those portions which he added from other authorities or from his own resources. If he had not

[1] That these verses also partially belong to the record of the eye-witness, whom we must, perhaps, imagine at Philippi, is probable, owing to the "Macedonian standpoint," on which *Schneckenburger*, p. 43, and *Lekebusch*, pp. 184 ff., should be compared.

had the intention of passing for one of Paul's companions, it cannot be doubted that he could only have derived the first person from a written authority. But many points of detail also favour our opinion. The exactness with which Paul's journey and the occurrences pending its duration are described in the parts indicated (xvi. 11, xx. 5 f., 13—15. xxi. 1—8, xxvii., xxviii. 11 ff.), cannot be explained by the object of our book, and recurs nowhere else in the same manner; and although picturesqueness of narrative is not foreign to our author, even where he obviously colours freely, it is vain to seek for passages comparable with xxvii. 14 ff., 27 ff., 37 ff. The language also of the parts in question has much that is peculiar. That of all portions in our book it contains the greatest number of words which do not recur again, would certainly in itself prove little, for a great proportion of these words are nautical terms,[1] for the employment of which the purport of the Acts offered no other occasion. The acquaintance of the reporter also with the parts of the ship, the manipulations of the sailors, the phenomena of a wreck, and the nomenclature of these things, is not a decisive token, though it deserves observation. On the other hand, our paragraphs contain some very peculiar constructions and idioms. Among these are, xxiv. 3, ἀναφανέντες τὴν Κύπρον; xxvii. 14, ἔβαλε κατ' αὐτῆς ἄνεμος; xxvii. 28, βραχὺ δὲ διαστήσαντες καί βολίσαντες; xxvii. 40, ἐπάραντες τὸν ἀρτέμονα τῇ πνεούσῃ; just the same use of κατέχειν in κατεῖχον εἰς τὸν αἰγιαλόν; xxvii. 10, ὅτι with the infinitive following; xxvii. 34, πρὸς τῆς ὑμετέρας σωτηρίας; of single words observe the thrice repeated πόλις, xxvii. 7, 8, 16, which with Luke is elsewhere found only in Acts xiv. 18; the twice repeated χρῆσθαι, xxvii. 3, 17, otherwise unknown to the Lukan writings; the three-fold τῇ ἐπιούσῃ, xvi. 11, xx. 15, xxi. 18, for which is elsewhere substituted (vii. 26, xxiii. 11) τῇ ἐπιούσῃ ἡμέρᾳ or νυκτὶ. In general, the preference of these paragraphs for participial constructions is worthy of notice. But with these peculiarities the language of the passages shows much that bears

[1] See the abstract in *Baumgarten's* Comm. ii. b, 389.

the stamp of the general Lukan type. Observe the expressions, τῇ ἡμέρᾳ τῶν σαββάτων, xvi. 13, — τῶν ἀζύμων, xx. 6, — τῆς πεντηκοστῆς, xxi. 16, and with this xiii. 14, ii. 1, Luke iv. 16, xiii. 14, 16, xiv. 5, xxii. 7; διανοίγειν, xvi. 14, compare Luke xxiv. 45, 32, and others; πνεῦμα πύθωνος, xvi. 16, compare Luke iv. 33; ἐργασία, do.; ἄχρις, xx. 6, and ἄχρις οὗ, xxvii. 33; ἱκανὸς, xx. 8, 11, xxvii. 7, 9, τῇ ἐχομένῃ, xx. 15; τῇ ἑξῆς, xxi. 1; θέντες τὰ γόνατα, xxi. 5; the infinitive with the article, xx. 7, xxvii. 1, 4, 7; the periphrasing σταθεὶς; xxvii. 21, δεῖ, xxvii. 21, xxiv. 26; ταννῦν, xxvii. 22; μὴ φοβοῦ, xxvii. 24 (xviii. 9, Luke i. 13, 30, ii. 10, v. 10, viii. 50, xii. 7, 32), χαρίζεσθαι (τινὰ τινὶ), xxvii. 24, elsewhere only in iii. 14, xxv. 11, 16 (χαρ. is in general a special favourite with Luke); ἐγένετο, with infinitive, xxvii. 44; οὐ τὴν τυχοῦσαν, xxviii. 2, compare xix. 11; μηδὲν ἄτοπον, xxviii. 6, compare xxv. 5, Luke xxiii. 41; ὑπάρχειν, xxvii. 12, 21, 34, xxviii. 7; συνέχεσθαι, xxviii. 8, compare xviii. 5, Luke viii. 37, and especially Luke iv. 38 (elsewhere only in Matt. iv. 24); τὰ περὶ ἡμῶν, xxviii. 15; finally, in the whole section the frequent use of τέ. But it is still more important that the contents of the parts in question contain some things which we cannot well trace to an eye-witness. Although the expulsion of the demon at Philippi, xvi. 16, may admit of a natural explanation, this incident becomes questionable by its connection with the imprisonment and liberation of Paul and Silas; likewise in the incident with Eutychus, xx. 9 ff., the description in the tenth verse, which too much resembles the restorations from the dead in the Old Testament, seems to be of later origin; in the same chapter, verse 16 is open to strong suspicions of an unhistorical pragmatism; the little episode, xxvii. 21—26, which could be omitted without interruption of the context, looks very like a *vaticinium ex eventu* in behalf of a tendency; and likewise, verse 31, the words, which are in suspicious affinity with Luke xxii. 18, ουδενὸς γὰρ ὑμῶν θρὶξ ἐκ τῆς κεφαλῆς πεσεῖται; finally, the miracles at Melita (xxviii. 8—10) far outstrip the bounds of credibility; and even if the adventure with the viper is possible, the saying of the aborigines, verse 6, is very improbable.[1] These features testify that the record of Paul's fellow-traveller in our book has not remained without additions and revision. Moreover, it is actually the parts quoted in which the Lukan peculiarities of language are most distinctly perceptible. On the other hand, it cannot be supposed that this record contained nothing more than what the Acts makes known to us out of it; but what that may have been, and what was the general nature of the treatise in question, cannot now be discovered. Luke, however, may be regarded as its most probable author; at least, it is most easily to be conceived how the author of the whole book came to put this particular name at the head of it.[2]

Next to the sections above discussed, the missionary journey has most appearance of having originally formed an independent whole. Especially does the beginning of this part, which relates

[1] The share of the author of the whole would be still greater if, in the interest of the Silas- or Timothy-theory, it is assumed that others besides the "we passages" are derived from the memoranda of a companion of Paul. In this case, the brevity of the records, xvi. 6, xviii. 23, xx. 2 f., the absence of historical truth in the statements, xviii. 18, xix. 11 f., would be doubly striking. This theory, however, requires no further refutation.

[2] When the opinion given above is opposed (*Lekebusch*, p. 81, 384 f.) by the argument that the unity of the Acts, and especially the continuous form of its language, prohibits the separation of the author of the travels from the author of the whole book, this has already been answered in the text. We do not suppose, indeed, that the author incorporated the travels-account unaltered, but that he revised, altered, abbreviated, and amplified it—in a word, that he used it as freely as any other documental authority. The above argument could therefore affect us only if it were generally impossible to produce a uniform historical account, notwithstanding the employment and partial repetition of older records. When *Lekebusch* further inquires why the author, if he dealt so freely with his authority, did not reduce the remaining material to the form of a record by an eye-witness, he might as well ask why Virgil did not make Æneas relate the whole of the Æneid, or Plato put all his Socratian dialogues into the mouth of Socrates. He did not do it, just because he did not wish to be regarded as an eye-witness of the whole history, or as a companion to Paul in all his journeys, but only as *that* follower of Paul whose treatise he employed—i.e. as Luke. To carry out the part which he had selected, he could introduce his own additions in the first person only where they encroached on the context of the Lukan record. But as he placed the name of Luke at the head of his book, and used the first person only where Luke was with Paul, this will be most naturally explained by the employment of a memorandum attributed to Luke.

anew, as something quite unknown, that Saul and Barnabas were at Antioch, not look at all as though it were originally derived from the same person who, in xi. 22 ff., relates the settlement of these two in Antioch, and has only just (xii. 25) mentioned their return from Jerusalem to this city. Hence one might be disposed, with Bleek, to assume an independent treatise as the source of our record; or at least to conjecture that its contents were derived from a different source from xi. 22 ff., wherever the latter notice may have come from. On the other hand, however, it must not be overlooked that this source must at any rate have been expanded and revised with the greatest freedom by the author of the Acts. In addition to the language of the paragraph being entirely his, as one easily sees, there is much in the individual narratives that enables us to recognize his handiwork. In the account of the punishment of Elymas in xiii. 9, the πλησθεὶς πνεύματος ἁγίου, ἀτενίσας εἰς αὐτὸν—in ver. 11, the περιάγων ἐζήτει χειραγωγοὺς, comp. with ix. 8, point to our author. The manner in which the name of Paul is introduced in ver. 9, we already found to be analogous to the introduction of the name of Peter in the Gospel; that it comes from the author of the whole book is shown by the perfect regularity with which the Apostle is previously named Saul, and subsequently only Paul. Of the speech, xiii. 16 ff., it was likewise proved above that it bears resemblance to the speeches of Stephen and Peter, which would not admit of explanation if they were written independently of it, and that it must therefore originate with the general author; moreover, compare with ver. 16, xii. 17, xix. 33, xxi. 40; with ver. 25, xx. 24; and Luke iii. 16, with ver. 27, xv. 21, Luke xxiv. 25 ff. It has also been previously shown that the declaration in xiii. 46, and the corresponding continued practice of the two messengers, appertain exclusively to the pragmatism of our author; we have likewise demonstrated the dependence of the story of the healing of the lame man at Lystra on iii. 2 ff., and the analogy of the scene in xiv. 11, especially the saying in ver. 15, with x. 25 f. Verse 16 ff. recalls xvii. 24, 27, 30. The observations in xiii. 2, 4, xiv. 26, seem to belong to the author of the Acts, who had a special interest in very strongly emphasizing the higher command to enter on the first mission to the Gentiles. Under these circumstances, the authority from which our author derived his materials, unless he used it very incompletely, must have been almost too scanty for an independent treatise, and one would rather conjecture that it must have been separate notes, perhaps taken from a more comprehensive work, from which he spun out the record before us.

This conjecture is still more obvious with regard to the three accounts of Paul's conversion. These accounts are related to one another by so thorough, and in a great measure verbal, affinity, that it is quite impossible to trace them to different sources. One and the same authority, however, could scarcely have contained all three, else it must have been a complete biography of the Apostle, or some work of similar extent to ours; but even then one must inquire what could have occasioned the three-fold repetition of the same story and the variations of the three accounts. In our book both may be explained, as to the main point at least, by its object; any other book could not have the same interest in recording three times the call of the Apostle of the Gentiles, and in intervening traits such as those communicated in ix. 26 ff., xxii. 17 ff., xxvi. 20, which, unhistorical as they are, are intelligible only from the general tendency of the Acts. These very peculiarities prohibit the hypothesis that the author derived one of his accounts, perhaps that of the 9th chapter, from an older authority, and he framed the others in imitation of it; for if in so doing he adhered to his source with sufficient fidelity to follow it, in a great measure verbally in both repetitions, the important variations of fact are the less comprehensible; but *each* of the three accounts contains unhistorical elements, which can only be explained by the object of our book: the first and second, by the assertion that immediately after his conversion Paul went to Jerusalem to the Apostles; the first and third, by the statement respecting Paul's ministry in Jerusalem and Judæa; the second, by the story of Christ's appearance in the Temple. To this must be added, that the language in all three accounts alike is that of Luke; that xxii. 20, distinctly looks back to vii. 58, viii. 1; that the whole arrangement of the intersecting visions in the 9th chapter, as already observed, has a striking affinity with the story in the 10th.[1] Thus in all the three accounts we are able to recognize the pen of our author alone, and it becomes a question whether, beyond the Pauline Epistles (Gal. i. 13 ff.,[2] 2 Cor. xi. 32) and the generalities offered by ecclesiastical tradition of Paul's conversation, he had any further authority for his description; or at least whether this source contained more than the main features that Paul was healed of his blindness by Christ's appearance at Damascus and baptized by Ananias.

We are also inclined to consider the Epistle to the Galatians as the sole authority for the so-called apostolic council, xv. 1—35. It has been already shown that this account, so far as it differs from the representation in the Epistle to the Galatians, should be regarded as unhistorical, and as the product of the peculiar pragmatism which dominates our book; that the speeches of Peter and James can belong to no one but our author; that the supposed resolutions of the assembly at Jerusalem were never made; that consequently the apostolic missive, vers. 28, 29, cannot have been issued; that this missive betrays but too plainly the style of our author by a construction closely adhering to the prologue of Luke's Gospel. It is scarcely necessary to add, that the language of the whole paragraph is throughout that of the rest of the book. What does it prove against such decisive tokens when, in behalf of the authenticity of the speech in ver. 13 ff., the name of *Συμεὼν* is adduced,[3] which our

[1] Comp. also in detail ix. 11 and x. 5 f.

[2] A reminiscence of the expression, Gal. i. 14, *περισσοτέρως ζηλωτὴς ὑπάρχων τῶν πατρικῶν μου παραδόσεων*, is apparently contained in Acts xxvi. 11, *περισσῶς τε ἐμμαινόμενος αὐτοῖς.*

[3] *Bleek*, pp. 1036 f.

author, quite as well as the writer of the second Epistle of Peter (i. 1), may purposely have inserted to produce an archaic Jewish appearance;[1] and for the composition of the missive by James, the Greek salutation with χαίρειν, ver. 23, and the precedence of the name of Barnabas, ver. 25, both of which have been already discussed? Even the words, in which the letter stands alone among Lukan writings, ἀνασκευάζειν, διατηρεῖν, εὖ πράττειν, ἐπάναγκες, ἔῤῥωσθε, can prove the less, as they may be met by other Lukan expressions, likewise rare in the New Testament, ἔδοξε, ὁμοθυμαδὸν, μηδὲν πλέον (only besides in Luke iii. 13). Finally, when Ritschl,[2] abandoning the remaining contents of the 15th chapter, and especially the speeches included in it, endeavours to rescue as authentic the apostolic decree, or at least its essence, vers. 28 f., it has already been shown above how little it avails, after the loss of everything else, to maintain these last positions. Here therefore we can only return to the opinion, that in all probability, except the passage in the Epistle to the Galatians, the author had before him no other older record of the transactions at Jerusalem.

For those portions which treat of Paul's second missionary journey, as well as for the earlier notices of the church at Antioch (xi. 19 ff.), we should be inclined to assume more ancient authorities. But here again, not only does the language testify an independent revision by the author of the whole, but the contents exhibit evident traces of his agency. To him alone can appertain the report of the circumcision of Timothy, xvi. 1 ff.; for even granting that tradition represented this Paulinist as being circumcised, and that he actually was so, Paul, according to his own principles, cannot have circumcised him. To this also belongs the statement in xvi. 4, which stands or falls with

[1] How little this sort of mimicry is foreign to him is shown also by the Συμεών, Luke ii. 25, and the Σίμων ὃς ἐπικαλεῖται Πέτρος, which is inserted in Acts x. 5, xviii. 32, xi. 13, only because it is supposed that Peter is still quite unknown to Cornelius.

[2] Entstch. der altkath. Kirche, p. 121.

the historical existence of the apostolic resolutions. The narrative of the incidents at Philippi, xvi. 19 ff., has already shown itself to be far too unhistorical, and at the same time too similar in its composition to those of the 5th and 12th chapters, to be attributed to any other than our author, who may, perhaps, have spun them merely out of a general notice like that of 1 Thess. ii. 2; possibly, however, he may have had before him a somewhat more detailed narrative. To him likewise undoubtedly belongs, with the other speeches of the Acts, the speech at Athens and the whole scene before the Areopagus; for this historically improbable transaction has no other object than to furnish an occasion for the speech; and the latter, according to our previous observations, by its contents and arrangement, can be traced only to our author. The language, too, betrays his style in the formulæ, *παρωξύνετο τὸ πνεῦμα αὐτοῦ ἐν αὐτῷ*, ver. 16 (comp. Luke xxiv. 32); *τί ἂν θέλοι*, vers. 18, 20 (comp. ii. 12, Luke i. 62); in periphrasis with the participles *ἐπιλαβόμενοι*, ver. 19, and *σταθεὶς ἐν μέσῳ*, ver. 22; in the *τανῦν*, ver. 30. Hence, even if our chapter, and especially the speech, is distinguished by a comparatively large number of words peculiar to itself,[1] we shall have to explain this phenomenon merely by the remark that here, where he makes Paul speak to a purely heathen and even philosophical audience, the author is less cramped than usual by Jewish-Christian ideas and expressions. How much of the further records as far as xx. 1 our author found before him, how much he added himself, can scarcely be determined with accuracy. In general, we shall probably be right in attributing the outline of the Pauline journeys, and all in which no particular tendency is betrayed, to older authorities, the nature of which, however, can scarcely be discovered; on the other hand, it is very probable that some portions originated solely with our author, although he may perhaps have found points of attachment for them in the legends or

[1] Chap. xvii. has thirty-four words which are only found here in Luke, but twenty-six of them alone appear in nineteen verses, 16—34.

documents he employed. Among these is the much discussed and continuous trait that Paul always preaches first to the Jews, and only when they reject him, to the Gentiles; probably also the account of the Jewish accusation, xviii. 13; perhaps also the vision, xviii. 9, as neither is without a pragmatic tendency; more decidedly, after our previous inferences, must we reckon among them the journey and the shaving of the head, xviii. 18—23, and the characteristic representation of John's disciples, xviii. 25, xix. 1 f.; although the remaining statements respecting Apollos seem to be historical, and the story of John's disciples may likewise be connected with an older tradition;[1] likewise the story of the Apostle's wonder-working handkerchiefs, xix. 12, which incurs great suspicion of being imitated from the corresponding story of Peter, v. 15; furthermore, vers. 19, 21, the statement that Paul made the positive resolution to go to Jerusalem; also the lively description of the Ephesian insurrection probably proceeds primarily from our author, whose manner it suits, although it offers scarcely any stumbling-block to criticism; at least one can hardly regard as traditional the speeches of vers. 25 ff. and 35 ff., which contain no peculiarity of expression. The linguistic character of all these portions does not differ from that of the remainder of the book.

In ch. xx., the observation in ver. 16 at once leads us to recognize the pragmatism of the author. We have already found it probable that to him belongs the Ephesian speech, vers. 18 ff.; not only is the language entirely that of our author,[2] but also

[1] Which may have arisen from an actual recollection of an historical incident, but perhaps also from dogmatic motives. At least there is something striking in the number twelve of the baptized, xix. 7, which so remarkably corresponds to that of the Apostles of Palestine. Or might the story, as an ultra-Pauline counterpiece to the Ebionite legend of Simon, have referred originally to the primitive Apostles, so that its meaning would have been to tell the Ebionites that their Apostles themselves were first led by the Pauline *πνεῦμα* beyond the Jewish narrowness of the Baptist and his disciples?

[2] Comp. the expressions, *γίνεσθαι μετά τινος*, ver. 18 (vii. 38, comp. Luke ii. 14, otherwise only in 1 Cor. xvi. 10); *δημοσίᾳ*, ver. 20; *διαμαρτύρεσθαι*, vers. 21, 23, 24; *καὶ νῦν*, vers. 22, 25, comp. iii. 17, x. 5, xiii. 11, xxii. 16; *ταν ῦν*, ver. 32; *τελειοῦν τὸν δρόμον*, comp. xiii. 25; *διέρχεσθαι*, ver. 25; *νύκτα καὶ ἡμέραν*, ver. 31 (xxvi. 7,

its whole standpoint and tendency; and as we know too that he freely puts his own thoughts in the mouth of his hero, we shall the less doubt that he has done so here also. From our author alone can be derived the narrative, xxi. 18—26, which is somewhat superficially attached to the preceding record of an eye-witness by the *σὺν ἡμῖν*, ver 18; as this narrative, utterly unhistorical, can be explained only by the standpoint of our book, and of ch. xv. in particular. We should doubt whether any traditional occasion was given for it. Of the Jerusalemite and Cæsarean portions, the two discourses of chs. xxii. and xxvi. have been already proved to be the free composition of the author; how it stands with neighbouring stories (xxi. 27—40, xxii. 22—29, xxv. 13 ff., xxvi. 24 ff.), we know not exactly, but it is probable that they are founded on a tradition, perhaps on a shorter notice in the memorandum of the travelling companion, previously and subsequently employed, and which can scarcely have been entirely silent respecting this period. Yet traits such as xxii. 28 f., xxv. 14 ff., 25, xxvi. 31 f., and the whole tone and language of the portion in question, show that our author amplified the traditional material with perfect freedom. The case may be similar with the trial, xxiv. 1—23, and with the ensuing discussion, xxiv. 24 ff. The preceding narrative (xxiii. 11—35) certainly contains too little historical motive for us to believe it to be invented by the author; but as little can it be supposed that he had authentic information of all the separate conversations, such as that between Lysias and the two centurions, vers. 23 f., or possessed a transcript of the letter of Lysias, vers. 26 ff.; a purpose may, moreover, be suspected in this letter; and the announcement of ver. 11, with its close connection with the subsequent rescue from death, seems almost too well suited to the pragmatism of our book not to be its own production after

Luke. ii. 37, also in Mark iv. 27, but in another sense); *παύεσθαι*, ver. 31; *παρατίθεσθαι*, ver. 32; *ὑποδεικνύναι*, ver. 33; *ἀντιλαμβάνεσθαι*, &c.; and in the narrative verses, *μετακαλεῖσθαι*, ver. 17; *ἱκανὸς*, ver. 37; *θεὶς τὰ γόνατα προσηύξατο*, ver. 36, comp. vii. 60, ix. 40, xxi. 5, Luke xxii. 41.

all. In the narrative, xxv. 1, the repetition of the motive employed in xxiii. 15 already raised our suspicions; and it must remain undecided whether the author did not himself evolve this trait. More positively may the transaction before the Sanhedrim, xxii. 30—xxiii., be put to his account, as the great historical improbabilities under which this record labours can find their explanation in his standpoint and interest alone. The position here assigned to the Pharisees and Sadducees towards Christianity is the same that we already found in chs. iv. and v.; and the part of Paul as a pious Jew corresponds entirely to the unhistorical representation of his relation towards Judaism which pervades the whole book. Only vers. 2—5, with the apologetic terms of their conclusion, seem to take into account some story hostile to Paul of contemptuous conduct towards the high-priest. For similar reasons we must also pronounce the final scene at Rome, xxviii. 17 ff., to be a free fiction of the author. Historically regarded, not only are the details of this scene, but also the whole, improbable in the extreme; the more suitably it is adapted as the key-stone of the whole book to all that we have heard of Paul's conduct from the time of his first appearance, the more effectually does it serve to display the object in which our book culminates, how Paul by the will and dispensation of God, rejected by his fellow-countrymen, came to Rome as the Apostle of the Gentiles. The author of such a narrative could only be the author of our book.

This investigation of the origin and the sources of the Acts serves to confirm the results previously obtained respecting its object and its credibility. The more doubtful it makes the purely historical character of the book, the more distinctly does its ecclesiastical significance become apparent, and herewith the circumstances of a period respecting which there is so great a deficiency of other certain intelligence. If we sacrifice much of a presumably historical record of the apostolic age, we obtain in its place direct and authentic information concerning the state of the Church at the beginning of the second century. It is a question whether this acquisition does not counterbalance the loss; and whether a smaller but certain possession is not of more value than a greater one which, contested on all sides, is perhaps in reality only to a very small degree our free property. Even if it were not so, the consideration ought not for a moment to hinder the historical critic from the performance of his duty.

